FAMILIES OF A NEW WORLD

FAMILIES OF A NEW WORLD

Gender, Politics, and State Development in a Global Context

edited by

LYNNE HANEY
LISA POLLARD

ROUTLEDGE
NEW YORK AND LONDON

Published in 2003 by
Routledge
29 West 35th Street
New York, New York 10001
www.routledge-ny.com

Published in Great Britain by
Routledge
11 New Fetter Lane
London EC4P 4EE
www.routledge.co.uk

Copyright ©2003 by Taylor & Francis Books, Inc.

Routledge is an imprint of the Taylor & Francis Group.
Printed in the United States of America on acid-free paper.

All rights reserved. No part of this book may be reprinted or reproduced or utilized in any form or by any electronic, mechanical, or other means, now known or hereafter invented, including photocopying and recording, or in any information storage or retrieval system, without permission in writing from the publishers.

10 9 8 7 6 5 4 3 2 1

Library of Congress Cataloging-in-Publication Data

   Families of a new world : gender, politics, and state development in a global context / edited by Lynne Haney and Lisa Pollard.
      p. cm.
   Includes bibliographical references and index.
     ISBN 0-415-93446-X (hardback)—ISBN 0-415-93447-8 (pbk.)
    1. Family—History. 2. Family policy—Cross-cultural studies. I. Haney, Lynne A. (Lynne Allison), 1967– II. Pollard, Lisa.
   HQ515 .F345 2002
   306.85'09—dc21

                                                                     20022014651

Published in 2003 by
Routledge
29 West 35th Street
New York, New York 10001
www.routledge-ny.com

Published in Great Britain by
Routledge
11 New Fetter Lane
London EC4P 4EE
www.routledge.co.uk

Copyright ©2003 by Taylor & Francis Books, Inc.

Routledge is an imprint of the Taylor & Francis Group.
Printed in the United States of America on acid-free paper.

All rights reserved. No part of this book may be reprinted or reproduced or utilized in any form or by any electronic, mechanical, or other means, now known or hereafter invented, including photocopying and recording, or in any information storage or retrieval system, without permission in writing from the publishers.

10 9 8 7 6 5 4 3 2 1

Library of Congress Cataloging-in-Publication Data

   Families of a new world : gender, politics, and state development in a global context / edited by Lynne Haney and Lisa Pollard.
      p. cm.
   Includes bibliographical references and index.
     ISBN 0-415-93446-X (hardback)—ISBN 0-415-93447-8 (pbk.)
   1. Family—History. 2. Family policy—Cross-cultural studies. I. Haney, Lynne A. (Lynne Allison), 1967-   II. Pollard, Lisa.
   HQ515 .F345 2002
   306.85'09—dc21

                                                                                           2002014651

CONTENTS

Acknowledgments   vii

1 Introduction
In a Family Way:
Theorizing State and Familial Relations   1
    Lynne Haney and Lisa Pollard

Part One

FAMILIALISM AS STATE IMAGINING

2 The Promise of Things to Come:
The Image of the Modern Family in State-Building,
Colonial Occupation, and Revolution in Egypt, 1805–1922   17
    Lisa Pollard

3 Familiar Territory:
Prostitution, Empires, and the Question of U.S.
Imperialism in Puerto Rico, 1849–1916   40
    Laura Briggs

4 Imagining the "New Jewish Family":
Gender and Nation in Early Zionism   64
    Alison Rose

Part Two

FAMILIALISM AS STATE BUILDING

5 "Rooted in the Soil":
Family Ideals, Land Reclamation, and Irrigation
Resettlement as Welfare in the United States, 1897–1933   85
    Laura Lovett

6	The State and the Widow: Pension Debates in Inter-War Years Australia Joy Damousi	99
7	Forging Families: Gender, Reform, and the Popular Front State in Chile Karin Alejandra Rosemblatt	119
8	Colonial Africa: Transforming Families for Their Own Benefit (and Ours) Cynthia Brantley	139

Part Three

FAMILIALISM AS STATE REFORM

9	Welfare Reform with a Familial Face: Reconstituting State and Domestic Relations in Post-Socialist Eastern Europe Lynne Haney	159
10	"They Say, 'Oh God, I Don't Want to Live Like *Her*!'": The Marginalization of Mothering in German Post-Socialism Elizabeth C. Rudd	179
11	Reinstating the Family: Gender and the State-Formed Foundations of China's Flexible Labor Force Eileen M. Otis	196
12	Markets Not States?: The Weakness of State Social Provision for Breadwinning Men in the United States Ann Shola Orloff	217

Notes	245
Contributors	295
Index	297

ACKNOWLEDGMENTS

This volume had its genesis in the activities of a dissertation-writing group at the University of California, Berkeley from 1995–1997. The group consisted of sociologists and historians working on research in which images of ideal womanhood and motherhood accompanied state building and/or state reform. With financial support from the UC Berkeley Townsend Center for the Humanities, we embarked on a collaborative project to explore how and whether the prevailing construct of maternalism could be applied to our case studies. From this exploration emerged the concept of familialism, which seemed like a promising way to capture the social processes operating in the diverse historical and national contexts of our work. Because we began to conceptualize familialism in our discussions with other participants in the group, we wish to acknowledge their contribution to this collection. The work of several of them appears in the volume.

We developed and expanded on the framework of state familialism after presenting it at a series of conferences—including those of the American Historical Association, Middle East Studies Association of America, the Social Science History Association, the European Social Science History Association, and the Berkshires Conference on Women's History. We thank all of those who read, listened, and responded to our ideas. Throughout the process of conceptual and empirical expansion, two scholars were of particular importance to us. Sonya Michel offered encouragement and inspiration at several critical junctures—challenging us to work through the complexities of familialism and convincing us of its importance. She also provided valuable suggestions on the introduction, the structure of the collection, and the content of the individual chapters. Julia Adams provided critical feedback on the collection's conceptual framework. With keen theoretical insight, she pushed us to think more broadly about the dialogues we were engaged in and to contemplate the project's larger relevance.

We received valuable assistance from our "home" institutions—New York University and the University of North Carolina at Wilmington. We are particularly grateful for their financial support, in the form of travel grants, research funds, and administrative assistance. In addition, many of our friends and colleagues offered much-needed help and encouragement. Ruth Horowitz, Katherine Fleming, and Kathleen Berkeley, in particular, gave good advice and answered difficult questions; Miranda March provided excellent editorial assistance. We also want to thank the staff and editors at Routledge, particularly Ilene Kalish, for their assistance, support, and patience.

Finally, we are enormously grateful to our families, literal and extended, for their encouragement, tolerance, and humor. The Glasser-Goldfarb clan, Lisa Musacchia, the Peritz family, András Tapolcai, and Misi made life easier, and certainly more pleasurable, as *Families of a New World* took final shape.

Introduction

IN A FAMILY WAY

Theorizing State and Familial Relations

LYNNE HANEY and LISA POLLARD

In classical liberal theory, the family is conceived of as a realm unto itself, distinct from civil society and immured from incursions by the state. This theoretical separation does not, however, hold up very well under historical scrutiny. The simultaneous development of modern states and the bourgeois family in the West, and the attempted imposition of a Western family model throughout the colonial world, not only challenge the notion that states and families occupied "separate spheres" but call for further inquiry into the nature of their relationship during the period of nation- and empire-building that spanned the eighteenth through the twentieth centuries.

The essays gathered here show that heightened scrutiny of familial behavior seems to be the counterpart, or byproduct, of the practices of states of all sorts and at different stages of development. States have attempted to mobilize families and deploy familial images for a variety of political ends. Sometimes the family has been deployed as a metaphor for imagining the state; at other times, the family has been used in more concrete terms as a model for state-building. At still other times, the family has been used to move state policies in new directions or as a vehicle for state goals. This collection contributes to the development of a comparative framework for analyzing such diverse state developments and thinking about the links among state-building, political movements, social policy, and families. We begin our efforts to map these phenomena by gathering them under the term "familialism."

Beyond Maternalism

Our approach builds to a great extent on recent feminist scholarship on state formation and development.[1] Overall, this research has focused on the origins and evolution of Western welfare states, with the construct of "maternalism" playing a central role in many accounts.[2] Since its formulation in the early 1990s, the construct has taken on several different meanings. Most often, it has been used to describe female reformers active in the early stages of welfare state development. By exalting women's capacity to care, these reformers claimed positions for themselves in political life and in newly emerging welfare bureaucracies.[3] Individually and collectively, maternalist women entered economic and political arenas previously monopolized by men. In doing so, they sought to interpret and administer the needs of women and children through new welfare institutions and policies.

Feminist analyses of maternalist women have been careful to locate them in particular national and historical contexts. Social and political changes in early twentieth-century France, Britain, Germany, and the United States accorded women new public opportunities. The expansion of welfare bureaucracies, the rise of new caretaking professions, increased access to higher education, and the growth of the social sciences all underlay the activism of maternalist women. Lest we glorify these women's activism, feminist historians remind us of the tradeoffs involved in their politics: maternalist women gained political power by conceding an essentialized principle of gender difference; they achieved professional status by shortening the leash that tied other women to home; and they secured new protections and provisions by emphasizing women's dependency on men or the state.[4]

In addition to describing a form of activism, the term maternalism is also used to identify discursive and ideological movements that specifically targeted women as mothers. Here the emphasis shifts from the political agency gained by some women to the lack of agency experienced by others. Maternalism is not necessarily linked to particular political groupings or forms of activism but instead refers to a political vision based on women's roles as caregivers and nurturers—a vision that can be articulated by both women and men. It is a worldview, a way of envisioning the social order, that extolls the virtues of domesticity and infuses social institutions with "womanly" virtues. When embedded in welfare systems, it connotes the state's sponsorship of and reliance on reformed motherhood. As Seth Koven and Sonya Michel have argued, maternalism frequently merged with discourses of citizenship, class, gender, and the nation.[5] To some extent, analyses of maternalism have also been located in specific national and historical contexts—traced to turn-of-the-century political culture, religious movements, and class and racial anxieties in the West.[6] Yet some analysts also use this construct to interpret contemporary welfare politics, arguing that it has become a fixture in Western welfare policies and institutions. As Ann Orloff points out, it was not until the 1996 Personal Responsibility and Work Opportunity Reconciliation Act that the U.S. welfare system bid "farewell" to maternalism.[7]

These conceptions of maternalism fostered innovative studies of the welfare state, allowing scholars to expose the gendered underpinnings of state welfare systems. Indeed, the maternalist framework clearly influenced many of the case studies in this volume. From the nineteenth-century Middle East to early twentieth-century Latin America to late twentieth-century Eastern Europe, a number of the authors found that state regulation was accompanied by discourses that could be loosely termed maternalist. But many of the cases we have identified as "familialist" call for an expanded or even an entirely new approach. For example, some of them center on areas and time periods in which there was no welfare state to speak of, such as societies under colonial occupation, or at moments when the state itself was being imagined, envisioned, and contested. In such contexts, the state was hardly in a position to offer welfare benefits to mothers, and mothers were hardly able to use the welfare system to gain political or professional authority.

Other cases strain the notion that modern states usually develop a distinctive "welfare apparatus." In state socialist and communist regimes, responsibilities usually associated with the welfare state were fulfilled in other social institutions, such as the extended family, the workplace, and the centralized economic plan. Thus, authors discovered that state socialist regimes often positioned themselves in ways that mirrored welfare state projects, but did not always replicate them. To get at these positionings—and the ways they rest on idealized notions of families—it is necessary to shift from a narrow focus on the modern welfare state (often rooted in maternalism) to one that encompasses multiple state forms and regimes and a variety of founding ideologies and motivations.

Working with this wider lens, our contributors show that state intervention into family life did not always occur exclusively, or even primarily, through mothers. Many of the policies, laws, and public campaigns discussed here redefined a wide array of domestic roles and responsibilities. In particular, several of the chapters examine the ways states refashioned notions of male familial responsibility, reinterpreting debates from the perspective of the paternal. For instance, while most research on widows' and mothers' pensions stresses their implications for maternal ideologies and practices, Ann Orloff points out that these policies also transmitted powerful messages about the male breadwinner, while Joy Damousi, examining interwar Australia, and Karin Rosemblatt, analyzing Chile under the popular front, document instances of state policies that either focused on or had important implications for male roles.

Nineteenth-century colonial regimes also pursued a familial agenda that went beyond the regulation of motherhood. Laura Briggs shows in her chapter, for example, that while the colonial state in Puerto Rico initiated crusades that targeted prostitution, these campaigns also included plans to reform desire and cathexis through reordering domesticity, confining sexuality to the heterosexual family, and censuring non-traditional conjugal relations. Similarly, in India, Western colonial "experts" set out to undermine local customs like widow burning and child marriage. While these actions certainly impinged on maternal behavior, they extended beyond it to regulate relations among spouses, parents, and extended kin.[8] The same can be said of the early socialist regimes in Eastern Europe. Although these regimes initiated several campaigns to resocialize mothers, they were often accompanied by attempts to reform the nuclear family itself, along with the prevailing domestic division of labor.[9] Thus, although women frequently appear to be the conduits or targets of state intervention, these studies demonstrate that broader familial relations are also transformed—whether deliberately or inadvertently—when state actors and policies champion and regulate motherhood.

Family reform was (and is) not always primarily about the family. Scholars taking a broader view, including most of the authors in this volume, have found that the family, whether literal or figurative, was often merely a convenient vehicle for other agendas. Political or economic reform frequently reorganized relations within and among familial bodies like the nuclear or extended family, the village, and larger political structures. Such reorganization is perhaps clearest in colonial regimes. In nineteenth-century Egypt, Lisa Pollard explains in her chapter, British colonial policies set out to reform masculinity as a way of positing a new contract between the nation-state and its citizens. Decades later, political debates in post–World War II Britain deployed familial imagery to cast the nation as an affective community and to re-inscribe Britain's relationship to the empire.[10] In these cases, it was not the nuclear family per se that underwent reconstruction, but the nation as an affective, family-like entity. There is a host of contemporary examples of the state's reorganization of familial bodies for non-familial purposes. For instance, Eileen Otis' chapter shows how recent labor policies in China created a "floating" population of female migrant workers—a population that used state policies to reconfigure their relationship to their natal families and traditional marriage systems. These women's experience with rural to urban migration, albeit temporary, often led to new ties with their natal families and a rejection of patrilocal marriage.

Thus, the chapters in this collection, along with the existing literature, expand the maternalist paradigm in three ways: they encompass multiple state forms, not only Western welfare states; they reveal how state regulation can redefine an array of familial roles and responsibilities, not only those associated with mothers; and they explicate the resulting reorganizations in different familial structures, not only in nuclear families. To capture these shifts, we deploy the term familialism—a terminological change that turned out to imply much more than we anticipated.

Beyond the Western Welfare State

The construct of familialism has several meanings. As with maternalism, scholars often use it to connote a particular type of state regime. Usually associated with patrimonialism, familial states merged family lineage and political authority; they were regimes in which actual familial norms and principles constituted the political structure and elite. Hence, just as maternalism referred to a particular kind of activism, familialism referenced a specific state form based on lineal networks and patterns. Much of the scholarship on familial states is geographically and historically specific. In Africa and Asia, for example, the familial has been used to analyze political regimes in which patriarchal family structures and forms predominate. It has also been used in these regions to explore the political dynamics resulting from the absence of state regulation—that is, traditional, familial social forms are said to prevail when modern state control is lacking.[11] In Western Europe, familial states are associated with the patrimonial regimes of the eighteenth century. For instance, in one of the most influential formulations of the familial state, Julia Adams explicates the links between familial practices and state building in the early modern Netherlands.[12] She uncovers how the reproduction of the Dutch patrimonial elite was familialized—based on the practices of marriage, inheritance, and patriarchal authority. Political claims were justified through references to heredity and lineage. Political office and rights were distributed according to family ties and position as opposed to a rational-legal logic or simple patronage. And family feuds, tensions, and conflicts constituted state politics—structuring the rise and eventual decline of Dutch patrimonialism. Although Adams' analysis is limited to the specificities of the Dutch case, she presents the familial state as an "ideal type"—and calls for its elaboration in other, non-European states and regimes.

To a large extent, *Families of a New World* heeds Adams' call by exploring the familial principles, patterns, and norms underlying state development in both Western and non-Western contexts. In doing so, the chapters also make a conceptual contribution to formulations of familialism. First, as in the research on maternalism, this collection uses familialism to compare discourses and movements across time and space. Following larger moves in state theory, we appropriate familialism to tap into the "state/culture" nexus—that is, to illuminate how social discourses about families shape, and are shaped by, state development.[13] Our case studies analyze the ways in which power relations are imagined, secured, and reformed through techniques of rule based on the familial.[14] They refer to familialism as sets of symbols, narratives, and metaphors that center on ideal relations within and among familial bodies. Familialism has also appeared as a classifying category—a way of separating the West from the non-West, the "civilized" from the "barbaric," and the modern from the backward. In some cases, familialism emanates from state structures in an attempt to engage, reform, or redirect the popular imagination; in others, from the popular imagination to produce a response to state structures.

Once familialism is conceptualized as a discursive and ideological frame, it can be extricated from its grounding in particular regimes and historical eras to do important comparative work. *Families of a New World* does not trace the transition from a family-based state to a nation-state in a specific locale; rather, it reveals familialism at work in different geographic and historical contexts. Our chapters analyze non-Western regions under colonial occupation and socialist states. They also interrogate states undergoing profound regime changes and state reform programs designed to extend or modify their domains of rule. Using a common frame, familialism enables us to transcend disciplinary, regional, and historical boundaries. At the same time, it serves as a way of bridging the many streams of work on states and families.

Transhistorical comparison indicates that while familial states characterized the transition from the pre-modern to the modern eras, familialism also appeared throughout the nineteenth and twentieth centuries. Familialism was central to the age of imperialism, over the course of which the trope of the family often served as a vehicle for shaping the relationship between the West and the territories under its control.[15] The marital and domestic habits of non-Westerners were frequently held up by colonial officials who then used them to draw conclusions about local politics and the ability of local populations to govern themselves.[16] The realpolitik of Western foreign policy was undergirded by the *moralpolitik* of local families; the behavior of these families became a justification for Western intervention. Westerners claimed to be appalled by such customs as the seclusion of women in the Islamic world; *sati* (widow burning), and regulations against widow remarriage in India; child marriage in India; and the clitoridectomy in sub-Saharan Africa.[17] Jeremiads against such practices and laws limiting or prohibiting them served to divide "modern" and "moral" Westerners from members of non-Western societies. It was seemingly easy for Europeans to justify colonial rule over a "backward" and "immoral" populace, when local populations were engaged in such appalling domestic traditions. Easier yet was locking them out of governmental positions because of their family politics: effeminate Indian men, for example, who could not protect their wives and daughters from the funereal pyre were deemed inadequate to the task of governing their own country.[18]

Like the nineteenth-century intelligentsia who championed debates over household practices to separate themselves from the British and exert the control they had lost in the public arena, colonial citizens in Africa and the Middle East used familial and domestic rituals to shape platforms of resistance.[19] Nationalists often defended those practices criticized by colonial powers, labeling them as "deeply ingrained" customs and as central to the "national" history.[20] Familial imagery thus underlay efforts by both colonizer and colonized to define the state and its responsibilities. Both groups appropriated marital, sexual, and domestic issues as a mode of self-definition, modernization, and the delineation of tradition, and resistance often crystallized around them.[21]

In other cases, familialism surfaced as a strategy for ushering in new state forms and policies, serving as a tool for integrating citizens into state agendas and programs. For example, early state socialist regimes in Eastern Europe often distinguished themselves from their capitalist predecessors through campaigns to redefine familial behavior. These states are known for their deployments of kinship-familial metaphors.[22] In socialist rhetoric, society became a family—or, in Katherine Verdery's terms, a classic *"zadruga"*—composed of individual nuclear families embedded in a broader familial organization headed by the father-state.[23] As a family head, the state made the key allocative and redistributive decisions, thus positioning the populace as recipients of state kindness and benevolence.

In this familial arrangement, both women and men were situated as dependent children, reliant on state support and subjected to state regulation. Through its role as family head, the socialist state is said to have emasculated Eastern European men and undercut their familial authority. In fact, some have analyzed the relationship between the father-state and its female children as almost incestuous, citing the state's ideological commitment to gender equality and state policies enabling women to combine work and motherhood as evidence of this "affair."[24] To be sure, studies of concrete state institutions reveal that state actors frequently allied themselves with women in their domestic battles—scolding uncooperative husbands, protecting women from abusive spouses, and disciplining men to become better partners.[25] As both a metaphor and an institutional agenda, then, familialism facilitated the building of the socialist state.

Just as the transition to state socialism embodied familialism, so too has the contemporary transition from communism to capitalism. As Susan Gal and Gail Kligman argue, two narratives of the family underlie the postsocialist transition.[26] The first, which can loosely be termed "re-traditionalization," was closely allied with the political opposition under state socialism. Much like nineteenth-century intellectuals in the Middle East who championed the family as a way of recovering the power they lost in colonial public life, East European intellectuals heralded the "traditional" family as a mode of political resistance. They advanced a vision of the family that clearly demarcated the private and the public and ended up valorizing hierarchical familial relations.[27] This vision persisted as former dissidents entered the post-socialist state—often becoming indistinguishable from the familial imagery adhered to by the Christian nationalists. In this narrative, the family remains a haven in a heartless world, a site of refuge amidst chaos and unpredictability. Thus, an idealized and romanticized "bourgeois" family form served as a model and a metaphor for transition.[28]

This narrative coexists with another familial discourse in which family form is closely linked to state form. Instead of isolating the two, the discourse presents a relationship between state and family that is characterized by a historically specific division of labor whereby social duties and functions are divided up according to the state's needs.[29] In contemporary Eastern Europe, this narrative has been used to justify a re-shuffling of social responsibilities. As state subsidies for childrearing are withdrawn, carework is restored to its "proper" place in the home; as maternity leave policies and child allowances are cut, domestic work is re-privatized in "appropriate" families; and as women lose employment guarantees, they are returning to their "rightful" roles as nurturers in the domicile.[30] Because this form of familialism justifies the reassignment of reproduction to individual households, the state has used it as a rationale for abdicating its previously paternal obligations.

Clearly, familialism not only operates in colonial and state socialist regimes; Western states have also sponsored programs that, while claiming to target individuals, served to shape and structure families to serve their interests. Examining Australia during the first half of the twentieth century, Joy Damousi shows how the right of widows to collect money from the state became a vehicle for ordering and controlling familial behavior. While it would be impossible to argue that the well-being of widows was of no concern to the state agencies in whose care they were placed, the ways in which state funding privileged widows with children illustrates the extent to which Australian politicians were intent upon keeping the family intact. Likewise, Laura Lovett finds evidence that in the United States during the Progressive Era, state projects designed to help industrial workers by allocating land in rural areas in fact encouraged the proliferation of the nuclear family by providing economic and moral models for family members. In both cases, proto-welfare programs aided individuals while also cementing their place within a family.

Imagining, Building, and Reforming Familialism

Though by no means an exhaustive inquiry into familialism, *Families of a New World* maps many instances of the intersection of state campaigns, policies, and evocations of family life. In these instances, familialist strategies appear as a reflection of the state, an extension of state politics, and the result of state endeavors. The collection is organized to reflect these versions of familialism—familialism as state imagination, as state building, and as state reform.

The chapters in Part One illustrate moments in history when families served as sites for debates about ideal forms of statehood. In these essays, family forms and metaphors become a way of imagining the state. By the same token, familial ideologies offer platforms for contesting or reinscribing political relationships, alliances, and structures. All three of the authors in this section show how familialism emerged as a means of demarcation, separating new forms of government from old, new economic relationships from traditional ones, and modern norms from conventional behavior.

Opening the volume, Lisa Pollard's essay on turn-of-the-twentieth-century Egypt illustrates how critiques of elite and royal households became central to British colonial policy. The British linked Egyptian practices such as polygamy and the seclusion of women to the production of unsound motherhood in order to legitimize the occupation of Egypt and construct a pseudo-colonial state (1882–1922) in which Egyptians were restricted from participation in politics. The vague, open-ended nature of the protectorate state and the power of colonial officials to appoint and dismiss Egyptian officials at will reflected the belief that something was wrong with the Egyptians, particularly among the ruling classes—something that had to be fixed before they could govern themselves. While the British did very little to "fix" those things, Egyptian nationalists attended to the arenas the British found "wanting." As in other colonies, the intelligentsia appropriated the marital and domestic relationships that horrified the British and engaged in heated debates about them. In the press, the schoolroom, and, later, political parties, the relationship between the future of the nation and the transformation of the household became a topic through which otherwise frustrated and disenfranchised nationalists could address their future as a nation. British and Egyptian discourses about the state and family included arguments about women and their rights as individuals and mothers, but debates about marriage and motherhood had more to do with political exigencies than with the needs and aspirations of actual women.

Laura Briggs' essay on late nineteenth-century Puerto Rico reveals a similar logic at work in the U.S. colonial project. Here the notion of "failed nuclear families" became a justification for imperialist intervention. The construction of a modern Puerto Rico—in which the United States would take an active role after 1898—was premised on placing all citizens in nuclear families and restricting sexuality to such familial structures. Briggs argues that prostitution reform, control of venereal disease, and general "family regulation" served as leitmotifs for United States "doing good" abroad, suggesting that the transformation of Puerto Rican sexuality and, along with it, family life, cloaked U.S. imperialism in beneficent clothing. Briggs contends that, contrary to arguments about the "accidental" nature of U.S. intervention in Puerto Rico—that is, the targeting of Puerto Rican prostitutes and the spread of contagious diseases justified their intervention—the United States actually emulated a set of colonial practices already established by powers such as Great Britain and France. As in other colonial discourses, women and their sexual behavior were overtly targeted in U.S. claims about the good they could do in Puerto Rico. At the same time, it was also the failure of the Puerto Rican state to control and regulate sexuality and of Puerto Rican men to protect women from vice that justified the U.S. reforming mission. As in Egypt, while American men and women alike claimed to speak for Puerto Rican women and their maternal and conjugal rights, those rights had less to do with granting women political agency than with legitimating colonial rule.

A third inquiry into the relationship between idealized familial behavior and the shape and function of the nation-state moves the volume to fin-de-siècle Vienna. Here, Alison Rose discusses the transformation of East European Jewish families and its connection to the establishment of a Jewish homeland in Palestine. Through an examination of the writings (both fiction and non-fiction) of Theodor Herzl (1860-1904) and other leading Zionist figures, Rose shows that their vision of the as-yet-unembodied Jewish state encompassed a new family form. This family would replace those that allegedly weakened the Jewish community in *galut* (diaspora) by failing to produce Jews who could solve the problems of Jewish marginalization and persecution in Christian Europe or regenerate diaspora culture. According to Herzl and his contemporaries, both traditional and assimilated, bourgeois Jewish families were inherently problematic to the process of building a state for Jews. On the one hand, *shtetl* families produced physically weak men who could not "stand up" to Christian men and strong-willed women who further emasculated their husbands. Assimilated families socialized women who neither tended to the religious needs of their families nor championed the Jewish community through support of the Zionist movement. The new Jewish woman, who would take her place at the center of this "new family," was left relatively undefined in Zionist writings, but it was clear that she would be assigned the role of teaching her children to live within the new Jewish state. While Herzl did not intend to grant political agency to this woman, her existence was central to a state-building project.[31]

In the Egyptian and Puerto Rican cases, metropolitan family forms were upheld as a model for colonial populations, while in the case of East European Jews, the ideal family did not exist in the metropole but had to be created. In all three cases, critics blamed flawed families for political failures and envisioned a reformed family as key to an ideal political regime.

The chapters in Part Two explore the relationships between states and families as states work to shape families and their behavior. Here actual families are harnessed to move state projects in particular directions. These essays show how familialism serves as a foundation upon which state programs and institutions are erected; they focus less on the familial as an imaginary and more on the familialism underlying specific state policies, debates, and campaigns—that is, as a technique of state power. The authors in this section demonstrate that while state agencies certainly took an interest in the transformation of the personal and economic condition of their citizenries, state-sponsored programs also did much to shape and structure the behavior of the individual *qua* family member. They also suggest that states may have found it more practical or efficient to shape individual behavior through the family.

Cynthia Brantley's chapter on British Nyasaland in the 1930s and 1940s provides a transition from the familial as part of a colonial imaginary to the familial as a mode of colonial state-building. The chapter reveals how colonial fantasies about African tribes and tribal customs were used to implement agricultural programs. In an attempt to augment the production of cash crops and improve the nutrition of local tribes, the British forced the production of certain crops, revamped the agricultural division of labor, and changed rights to land tenure, at the expense of traditional growing patterns.

To do so, colonial officials relied on anthropologists' work on the region to inform them about the suitability of the tribes to the new tasks at hand. As a result of misinformation about tribal structures, the British pursued a disastrous set of policies that provoked massive male out-migration for waged work and actually slowed agricultural production. Thus British policy not only restructured the Nyasaland economy but transformed familial roles and gender relations within local tribes. In the end, Brantley argues that, for the British colonial state in Nyasaland, "family" had one definition: a man in charge of his wife and children. Such notions vastly disrupted the matrilineal family structures and authority relations that had ensured the provision of food and adequate nutrition to local tribes for decades.

In Laura Lovett's chapter on the Progressive-Era United States, the American government literally built the living space—"homes on the land"—in which it sought to shape the behavior of rural families. Lovett argues that the Reclamation Act of 1902, while preceding the establishment of the welfare state, provided a kind of social insurance by offering families a rural alternative to strict dependence on industrial wages, thus providing some protection from fluctuations in the economy; under its terms, the federal government would sell reclaimed land to homesteaders, who would then repopulate the West. Lovett illustrates how land reclamation advocates articulated the benefits of their plan by offering a vision of what settler households could become: "producer" families with access to gardens, orchards, and areas for livestock. These families would ultimately be more self-sufficient than industrial ones because they would not depend solely on male breadwinners, leaving women in non-wage-earning domestic roles. Instead, the labor of *all* family members—paid and unpaid, male and female—would be mobilized in order to "decommodify" male workers, freeing them from total dependency on the market. While the producer family ideal did feature women as mothers and homemakers, Lovett argues that it introduced a significant variation to the male breadwinner family model by calling for women's productive labor in the garden as well as the community center.

Examining the granting of widows' pensions in the inter-war years in Australia, Joy Damousi argues that the state was centrally preoccupied with preserving the nuclear family. In order to prevent further fragmentation of the family unit, the state made it possible for widows with children to remain in the home. By assuming the economic role of the deceased breadwinner, the state reinforced the ideal of domestic roles for women. At the same time, however, the state took active measures to ensure that widows' sons and daughters became wage-earners in the hope that they would ultimately relieve the state of its economic responsibility. The professionalization of social work in Australia in the 1930s further concretized the relationship between the state and family and reinforced the self-sufficient nuclear family ideal even in the absence of men. While neither widows nor their children fully cooperated with the state, legislation from the inter-war years exposes the state's ideals of family life and attempts to regulate it.

In Chile, Karin Rosemblatt illustrates the relationship between state-led social change and the family through an examination of policies implemented by the popular front coalition government from 1938 to 1948. During the popular front's tenure, medical and social security agencies saw to the "proper constitution" of Chilean families, citing familial behavior as the cause of the nation's past difficulties and, concomitantly, as the source of its future success. Through education, material incentives, and legislation, state agencies attempted to break men of bad habits such as drinking, gambling, and extramarital sex. Popular Front officials defined suitable male deportment as monogamous and productive. Men who learned to make home life a priority would become hardworking laborers and good citizens. While women were clearly given a role in Chile's domestic-economic transformation—they were to provide unrestricted attention to domestic matters so as to make home life attractive to men—the onus of Chile's transition rested largely on men. Breaking men of bad habits would start a chain of events that would produce a generation of more productive Chilean citizens. Rosemblatt argues that by the early 1950s, Chileans had come to accept and practice state-promoted models of proper home life.

While the first two groups of essays in this collection examine how familialism was used to facilitate state-building, the final section documents the reverse, showing how the familial may be deployed to assist states' reform of—and often retreat from—social life. These final essays analyze what may loosely be termed "reprivatization," a process through which states are reconfigured to bring about a shift in their own roles and obligations. In many of these instances, the state draws on familial models and metaphors to abdicate its social responsibilities. This occurred noticeably in the restructuring of the formerly communist states of Eastern Europe. In other instances, familialism is used to secure a state refocusing—that is, a shift in the targets and modes of state regulation. Interestingly, all the essays in this section focus on the contemporary period, from post-socialist Eastern Europe to late-communist China to the post-AFDC (Aid to Families with Dependent Children) United States.

The first essays in this section examine state restructuring after the collapse of state socialism in the former Soviet bloc. Lynne Haney's chapter examines the post-socialist world of welfare to reveal how the collapse of state socialism in Eastern Europe led to massive reforms in state policy. She compares policy debates and welfare practices in the Czech Republic and Hungary to reveal how these states embarked on divergent reform paths. She also suggests that these paths were related to different constellations of global and local forces—political actors that led Hungary on a path toward a liberal welfare state and the Czech Republic toward a social-democratic model. Despite these differences, Haney illuminates how, in both cases, state restructuring was justified through narratives of the family, which made East European welfare reform synonymous with familial reform. In Hungary, reform was presented as the victory of the imagined family over the collectivist state and ultimately as a way to reprivatize the family. While similar in content, Czech familial narratives were deployed to justify the state's continued engagement in domestic life. Through this comparison, Haney argues that familialism is a malleable discourse. Far from determining the direction of state reform, it can be appropriated by political actors in competing and conflicting ways.

Elizabeth Rudd's chapter moves to the economic realm to explore the implications of privatization and the rise of capitalist markets on familial relations in the former East Germany. Rudd explicates the shifting role of the state in economic and social life. Unification has been marked by the end of full employment guarantees, the rise of a gender ideology that makes motherhood incompatible with wage labor, and the withdrawal of policies designed to help women combine work and motherhood. Rudd reveals that these shifts resulted in the redrawing of the boundaries of work and family. This redrawing then led to a devaluation of familial work and the marginalization of motherhood. Through an analysis of the life histories of three women, Rudd charts how families are coping with this restructuring. As women confronted the new costs associated with motherhood and new forms of discrimination against working mothers, their strategies of combining work and family changed. In this way, Rudd's research unearths the interweaving of economic and state policy and the ways in which they rearranged the arenas of work and family—thus making it more difficult for Germans to bridge these social realms.

Eileen Otis extends this focus on the dynamics of economic reform to contemporary China, analyzing Chinese state residential policies for their effects on female labor and familial relations. By reforming the Household Regulation System, which restricted the rural population from migrating to the city, the Chinese state created a new female workforce effectively confined to low-wage urban labor markets. Forbidden to remain in urban centers and denied urban citizenship, these women "floated" among social spaces, thus constituting the flexible workforce necessary for state and economic reform. Otis reveals that pre-existing institutions, such as the family, aided these reforms by providing an economic buffer to support a flexible female workforce. At the same time, Otis claims that state policies also reconfigured familial institutions and loyalties. Spurred by state policies, urban migration had complex and even contradictory effects on women's familial relations. It strengthened their ties to their natal families, while weakening their connection to the patrilocal marriage system. In the end, Otis argues, state migration policies had a paradoxical effect: they reinforced the patriarchal family structure while creating the conditions for its disruption.

After traveling across time and space, our case studies end with an analysis of the politics of welfare reform in the United States. Ann Orloff's chapter makes a strong case for moving beyond a narrow focus on women and maternalism in the study of welfare development. She documents the profound implications of American social policy for the position of men and their paternal responsibilities, providing a broad historical overview of the ways in which the "male breadwinner" ideology underlay the development of the welfare state. By examining paternity regulation, child support enforcement, and the Personal Responsibility and Work Opportunity Reconciliation Act (PRWORA), Orloff argues that the contemporary U.S. policy regime has become geared toward disciplining men and (re)socializing them into "breadwinnerhood."

Part One

FAMILIALISM AS STATE IMAGINING

2

THE PROMISE OF THINGS TO COME

The Image of the Modern Family in State-Building,
Colonial Occupation, and Revolution in Egypt, 1805–1922

LISA POLLARD

By the mid nineteenth century, a class of Egyptians (the *effendiyya*) trained to serve the state had come to see monogamy and nuclear families as the sine qua non of successful state rule. The *effendiyya*'s view of the relationship between family structure and politics resulted from the transition that took place in late eighteenth- and early nineteenth-century Egypt from confederation-based politics to a nation-state. In order to implement reform and modernization programs, the founder of the nation-state, Mohammad `Ali (r. 1805–1848), and his descendants created—and then relied upon—a body of state servants whose education made the connection between monogamy and modernity explicit. When, in the 1880s, Great Britain extended its de facto colonial rule into Egypt, the ideals of this new governing class collided with a British discourse about them and their family life. In that discourse, the open-ended tenure of the British occupation and its accompanying isolation of the Egyptian ruling classes from politics were attributed to the wretched domestic practices of the Egyptian ruling elite. Relying too often on travel literature and fantasy, the British claimed in 1882 that they were forced to take Egypt on as a "veiled" protectorate because, in part, the familial and sexual habits of the Egyptian ruling elite had produced a ruling class of Egyptians incapable of governing themselves. Egypt's financial and political crises were couched in personal critiques as the British argued that they would have to stay in Egypt until the body familial—as well as the body politic—had been reformed. Despite the existence of a generation of Egyptians who viewed the relationship between monogamy, the nuclear family, and the nation-state in a manner quite similar to Victorian Britons, and despite the efforts of the Egyptian state to inculcate "modern" domestic behavior in its citizens, the British were convinced that Egyptians needed to be thoroughly reformed before they could be trusted with self-rule.

During the 1919 Revolution, in which Egyptians rebelled against British colonial rule, the *effendiyya* presented images of modern families to the British as evidence that such reform had been completed—a step that should have resulted in an end to the occupation. The political culture of the Revolution was steeped in highly domestic imagery, signaling the extent to which domestic and familial reform shaped the relationship between the British and the Egyptians. The *effendiyya* exalted for themselves behavior that can readily be referred to as "maternal," attaching great political significance to acts such as caring for the nation's children and for its poor, sick, and homeless. Even the British, who were eager to dismiss the Revolution as driven by Bolshevism, Turkism, and pan-Islam,[1] not sincere desires for independence on the part of Egyptians, noted that:

> There were endless general expressions of admiration for the noble hospitality of the Egyptian people, and for its wonderful success in proving its political solidarity by demonstrations.... Attention was diverted mainly to such matters as the necessity of more interest on the part of Egyptians in trade, the uses of trade unionism, and the necessity of charity on the part of the rich toward the poor.[2]

Debates and iconography from the Revolution suggest that men who wished to govern in post-Revolutionary Egypt, or those who supported the men who sought leadership in independent Egypt, claimed to live in monogamous, reformed households. Revolutionary iconography also suggests that preoccupation with the nation's children and dedication to improving domestic life connoted a real concern for the nation's progress and its welfare. Both to contest British arguments about them, and to demonstrate to one another that they were capable of replacing colonial rule with a viable political order, *effendi* nationalists touted a vision of an independent Egypt in which their families heralded the future national family, and in which the shaping of the national family would be given pride of place. Familialism, in the 1919 Egyptian Revolution, was both a commitment by the *effendiyya* and the revolutionary leadership to a certain kind of behavior, and a suspended promise that such behavior would later be shaped and supported by an as yet unformed nation-state.

Hard Facts or Colonial Fantasies:
The Family Politics of the Egyptian Ruling Elite

The British occupation of Egypt and the official commencement of Anglo-Egyptian rule began in the early summer of 1882. Reacting, allegedly, to the wave of anti-foreign sentiment that characterized Egypt's political climate in the early 1880s and to an outbreak rioting that had taken place in the harbor city of Alexandria earlier that year, the English fleet anchored off Egypt's northern coast in order to land troops, quell the riots, and restore order. Between June and September 1882, a number of battles took place between the British, who had both territorial and economic interests in maintaining order in Egypt, and Egyptians who wished to put an end to foreign influence in their political and economic affairs. The Egyptians rising up against the British rallied under the slogan "Egypt for the Egyptians" in support of an army officer named Ahmed `Urabi (1840–1911), who claimed that Egypt's Khedive, Tawfiq (r. 1869–1892), was corrupt, autocratic, and a lackey to the British. By September 13, 1882, the British forces had succeeded in defeating `Urabi and his followers, and the British colonial experience in Egypt began. While the invasion was, on the surface, designed only to put down the rebellion, restore order, and bolster the power of Tawfiq, the British would not leave Egypt until 1952.

Whether they were for against the idea of empire, most Britons agreed that continued access to the Suez Canal, as well as repayment of loans, were adequate reasons for invading Egypt in 1882 and thereby quelling the alleged anarchy that accompanied the `Urabi uprisings.[3] Once the occupation had become a fait accompli, however, there was little accord over what to do with Egypt.[4] The Gladstone government was reluctant to keep the country; officials on the ground were reluctant to predict how long it would take to secure it. What resulted was a kind of "policy of no policy," through which a plan for either remaining in Egypt or leaving would later be legitimated.

Gladstone's determination to leave Egypt and his ministers' reluctance to confirm the possibility of a quick withdrawal resulted in numerous investigations by British officials into Egyptian institutions. To be sure, Egypt had been studied by European government officials before: the Goschen and Cave missions of the 1870s were designed, for example, to size up the shape of Egypt's government and economy, and articulate what kind of "recovery" might be expected of it. Their investigations were responsible for the shaping of the Casse de la Dette Publique that was set up to monitor the Egyptian government until it began to pay back its loans successfully.

What was different about the investigations that accompanied the occupation, however, was often the domains that they targeted. As officials such as Lord Dufferin (1866–1918), British Ambassador to the Sublime Porte at Istanbul and Her Majesty's Envoy Extraordinaire to Egypt, and Foreign Secretary Lord Granville (1818–1891) began to penetrate the more hidden realms of Egypt, they claimed to "discover" things that threw into doubt Gladstone's policy of a quick invasion followed by a quicker withdrawal. Said Granville in a dispatch to Gladstone written shortly after the occupation: "Indeed, from the first moment when we began to look round in the country which we had rescued from anarchy, it was clearly seen to be wanting in all the conditions of independent life...."[5]

Gladstone was primarily concerned with gathering information about the potential reform of Egypt's military and its political institutions. Granville and Dufferin were thus charged with sizing up the political and military arenas, a task that proved difficult given the paucity of information that the Gladstone government possessed. Dufferin responded after only ten days in

Egypt, stating that the establishment of liberal governing institutions would be "more or less a leap in the dark." He attributed the Egyptians' unreadiness for self-governing institutions to the tyranny of the khedives and the childishness of the Egyptian people.[6]

Dufferin did not provide ample instances in which Egyptian political institutions had actually failed to function. Rather, Dufferin's rhetoric reveals his uneasy stance as a kind of "tourist," relying on hearsay and stories about Egyptian heritage rather than actual encounters with Egyptian elites.[7] Indeed, discourse about territory and economics gave way in official dispatches to debates about how the Egyptians should be understood. In dispatches that often read more like nineteenth-century travel literature than "official" debates about finances and territories, the ability of the Egyptian nation to govern itself was attached to descriptions of institutions which, on the surface, seem to have little to do with the ability of the Egyptian ministry and body politic to function. Evelyn Baring (later Lord Cromer), Egypt's first British consul general, openly admitted that much of what he "knew" about Isma`il had been gleaned from travel literature.[8]

Isma`il Pasha (r. 1863–1879), under whose administration the financial crisis that led to the occupation began, was most frequently targeted in this discourse. Despite the fact that Isma`il was out of power when the occupation took place, it was the characteristics of his rule and his behavior that seemed to be conflated with the inability of the Egyptian government to govern. Isma`il occupied a curious place in the minds of the Europeans who thought that they knew and understood him. To some Europeans, he had been a praiseworthy ruler. He had, in fact, created a modern military, laid 1,000 miles of railroad track, dug 50,000 miles of irrigation canals, and established hundreds of primary and secondary schools throughout Egypt. The Cairene upper classes spent their leisure time in well-landscaped parks and gardens, in museums and galleries, at the zoo, or visiting one of the world's finest opera houses. Such accomplishments led many Europeans to consider Egypt a marvelous instance of progress.

Other Britons, however, claimed that such programs were in fact undermined by Isma`il's "perverted" ambition, stating that while he had been successful in transforming Egypt, his policies were in fact "erroneous" because of the "sensual self-indulgence" that undergirded his private life.[9] Lord Milner, who was sent by Her Majesty's Government to oversee the implementation of some sort of protectorate state, claimed that Isma`il's disordered finances were the result of his morals as well as his economic principles.[10]

Stories circulated not only about Isma`il's immorality, but about the disreputable origins of Tawfiq.

> Tewfik [sic] is supposed to have owed his exalted station to an accident. Isma'il on one occasion visited a lavoratory in the Palace and found there one of

the minor slaves of the Harem—known as Kandilji—whose duty it was to look after the lighting of the Harem apartments. The girl attracted His Highness's notice and in due course Tewfik saw the light of day. As he was Ismail's eldest son, his mother became Birinji Kadin (the first lady) and Tewfik was heir to the throne.[11]

The sexual politics of Isma`il's mother also figured prominently in the British project of characterizing and knowing Egypt. Stories circulated about the voracious and disturbing sexual habits of Isma`il's mother, Khosayr Hanem, in which she drove through Cairo looking for young lovers, only to have them executed when she was through with them.[12] Whether these rumors were true or not, their circulation cemented the relationship between the private life of Egyptian elites and their political aptitude. As Victorian templates for connubial as well as parental behavior were assigned to the Egyptian body politic, the domestic habits of the khedives and their wives were not merely the object of British fascination or scorn. Rather, they became elevated to the position of an official yardstick by which the British measured and understood Egyptians and their politics. One Briton in fact concluded that Isma`il's achievements were considerable for a "prince born and bred in the harem."[13]

Such discourse rendered the domestic habits of the khedive and his family symbolic of the Egyptian body politic and its ability to govern itself. Isma`il's sexual practices appear to have given life to a whole host of economic ills that would have to be reformed in order for Egypt to regain its independence.

"Table Talk"—or the Home Economics of Nationhood

In the last decades of the nineteenth century and in the decades leading up to the Revolution, the household and its activities became common topics of discussion and debate in Egypt. The home and its inhabitants served as tropes through which national characteristics were described in the Egyptian press. And in the Egyptian schoolroom, lessons on domestic behavior gave the state greater control of an increasing number of its middle- and upper-class citizens. For the *effendi* nationalists who worked within the school system, such lessons were instrumental in creating and instilling loyalty in Egyptian schoolchildren. In both the press and the schoolroom, the *effendiyya* used the family to contest British claims about upper-class Egyptian domestic behavior, and to shape a set of bourgeois, nationalist characteristics.

Beginning under Isma`il's reign, the Egyptian school system came increasingly under state control. Isma`il attempted to bring greater numbers of Egyptian youth (male and female) into the state's orbit by controlling the curriculum. By the time of the British occupation, the syllabus of instruction was, at least in theory, uniform everywhere (it included such topics as writing, arithmetic, grammar, history, geography, a modern language, and the principles of politeness, or morals), and all teachers were required to have a certificate granted by local notables or a delegate from the ministry of public education.[14]

After the British occupation of Egypt, the national educational system became the site of hotly contested debates between the British who dominated the system, and Egyptian effendi nationalists, many of whom worked within the state bureaucracy. The British attempted to limit the Egyptians' education in order to keep Egypt a predominantly agricultural region, and in order to avoid a repeat of the mutiny that had taken place against them in India in 1857.[15] For nationalists, however, education was a means of cultivating loyalty, efficiency, and productivity in Egyptians, and of assuring that they would be capable of serving an independent state. As their struggle against the British intensified, the educational system also became an arena in which "the nation," its history, and its future were articulated and contested.

It was in the shaping of Egyptian schoolchildren's manners and habits that Egyptian nationalists connected private behavior with the success or failure of the nation to govern itself. Textbooks of all sorts carried recipes for personal conduct, which often couched powerful lessons in history and politics. Just as often, they connected personal behavior to the project of strengthening the Egyptian body politic. The public school curriculum in the years following the occupation reveals an increased preoccupation with the private life of Egyptian schoolchildren. In 1885, for example, the public, primary-school curriculum covered a course called *durus al-ashya'*, or "object lessons," which included such topics as proper dress, keeping one's clothes clean, the use of soap, the house and all its rooms, and how best to build a house.[16] It also included *adab* (morals) and *tarbiyya* (upbringing), which consisted of lessons in basic manners, how to keep the body clean and healthy, behavior for both private and public life, the best clothes to wear, and the best manners for eating.

In 1906, adab and tarbiyya were separated from "object lessons" and made part of a new class called *tahdhib* (self-edification).[17] By 1901, this class was listed as having as its purpose the production of "the best of human behavior for interactions at home and outside the home; care of the body; proper clothing; manners for eating; correct times for eating," and the cultivation of the things that the person had to do in private "such that the order of the public sphere (*al-hi'a al-`amumiyya*) would be preserved." By 1907, a course called *al-tarbiyya al-qawmiyya* (state upbringing) had come into existence. The course was taught in the elementary, primary, and secondary schools, which by 1916 were teaching 10,421 girls and 27,337 boys.[18] By the 1920s, the course was called "national upbringing and morals" (*al tarbiyya al-wataniyya wal-akhlaq*).[19]

The private politics of habits and manners were building blocks of programs that taught nationalism and productivity.[20] Cleanliness and personal hygiene as well as habits and mannerisms deemed proper for the modern era were central to textbooks on subjects ranging from reading to *adab*. Arabic readers, for example, couched cultural critiques in lessons on the Arabic alphabet and grammar.

The domicile figured centrally in such textbooks. A reader first printed in 1905 titled *Reading and Pronunciation*, for example, after presenting the Arabic alphabet, listed several hundred simple words, which included "wood, bricks, carpenters, engineers, and plumbers."[21] It then repeated those words in the context of basic lessons, asking questions such as, "What do proper homes need?" and "How do we build proper houses?" The answer was that the kinds of homes that would produce sound, modern Egyptians required "order, cleanliness, and ventilation." Huts, tents, or dark or crowded quarters were listed as belonging to "another world," a pre-modern world that had to be done away with so that a new era of modernity could be ushered in.

Students were also taught that their private habits had a bearing on the good of the nation. A text written for a "state upbringing" course ca. 1910 taught students that their love of the nation as small children depended on learning manners "such that you can, later on, be capable of serving your nation. The behavior of ignorant people is vile and is by no means the kind of behavior that will serve the nation."[22] Textbooks on morals published in the decades leading up to the Revolution make clear that the development of the behavior that would lead to a strong and independent nation was an extremely personal task. Children learned that love for the nation began at home with cultivation of love for the family:

> The Nation consists of a group of families. And if the families that make up the nation are enlightened, refined, rich, strong, then so too will the nation be all of those things. And if those families are possessing of fallen morals, if they are poor, if they are uneducated, then the nation, like those families, will be corrupt, poor and backwards.[23]

Early twentieth-century textbooks were highly prescriptive about what kinds of family relations were proper and fitting to the national struggle. First, children were instructed that the proper home consisted of a father, mother, and their obedient children. Polygamy was very clearly discouraged, as was the habit of having extended family share the domicile. Thus, the family was redefined to fit the models of Victorian domesticity; Arabic readers often contained lessons with titles such as "a man and his wife," "a mother and her son," "a father and his daughter," in which very precise definitions for household relationships were laid out. Parents were enjoined to care for the nation by cultivating an understanding of these relationships in their children:

> The care of children and the overseeing of their tarbiyya in the home is the biggest of parental responsibilities. It is what supports the social order. Failure to meet up with these responsibilities is the biggest crime that one can commit because it is, ultimately, a crime against the nation.[24]

Thus the process of liberating Egypt was cast as a family affair. Children learned that their every action, from cleaning and dressing to interacting with their relatives, had a higher meaning. Shaped in the domestic realm and then transported into the world outside their homes, their habits and morals served as the foundation upon which modern, independent Egypt would later be built.

This equation between domestic behavior and the success of the nation appeared in the Egyptian press as well. From the early 1870s onward, the printing press and the political journal were active arenas in which the *effendiyya* articulated their political aspirations. In the mid-nineteenth century, the *effendiyya* lacked a political forum in which to organize themselves or to articulate their demands. Hence, Egypt's new elites funneled their energies into societies and formed cultural and literary salons, as well as political "clubs." While the goals of such organizations were not always clear, they did include "mutual networks" against European hegemony, the corruption of the royal family, and absolute rule. The press took up the slack created by the lack of an organized political arena. Isma'il's willingness to allow private Egyptians to fund and print their own newspapers, coupled with substantial increases in the number of literate Egyptians, led to an astonishing boom in the late 1870s in the number of privately-printed books, Egyptian newspapers, and Egyptians who could read them. (Between the early 1860s and 1881, the press went from a readership of zero to tens of thousands.)[25] Such growth in the press allowed for the possibility of a widespread, articulate national political consciousness.

Throughout the 1890s and into the first decade of the twentieth century, the politics of the occupation, the paucity of administrative opportunities for Egyptians, and the lack of organized political parties caused "the Egypt question" to continue to be the outstanding issue of the day. The task of defining "Egypt," its aspirations, its history, its citizenry, and the "nationalist" riposte to the occupation shaped journalism throughout that decade. While the political platforms, like the intellectual orientations, of each of these papers differed, what seemed to unite them was their attention to defining what it meant to be a proper, middle-class Egyptian ca. 1900. The 200,000 readers who bought weekly and monthly newspapers in 1900 were exposed to an endless stream of essays and editorials on such topics as politics, economics, history, Western and Islamic civilization. Inherent to essay writing in the 1890s and the early 1900s was a struggle to define the Egyptian condition.

Throughout the 1890s, "Egyptian-ness" was most frequently evoked and articulated through debates and discussions that, at least on the surface, had little to do with the high politics of the British, the khedives, and constitutional reform. As the male- and female-authored press grew throughout the 1890s, the link between domestic activities and the success of the public realm became a more common one. "Politics" and the "political press" came not only to include discussions about the home, but also to depend on them for the clearest articulations of what it meant to be a nationalist.

Newspaper columns dedicated to topics pertaining to the home were often the grounds on which such definition saw its clearest articulation.

Political journals were full of articles on women and "questions" about reforming women and their position in Egyptian society; often, periodicals dedicated to "politics" and "science" also included columns called *tadbir al-manzil* (home economics), in which subjects that superficially pertained to women actually couched greater discussions and debates. Definitions of Egypt as a nation, narrations of Egyptian history, and articulations of bourgeois nationalist culture all coalesced in columns on home economics.

Syrian immigrant Jurji Zeidan's monthly journal *al-Hilal* (The Crescent), for example, carried a semi-regular column called "*hadith al-ma'ida*," or "table talk." According to the editors, the column was included in the journal to give "healthy advice on food and drink and other household needs." By early September 1900 it also included advice on the family and its health. "We call it table talk in order to indicate that it includes the kinds of things that should be talked about, in terms of food, and, at the same time, humorous and useful topics of discussion."[26] The table was thus positioned as a place where health was addressed; at the same time, food, eating, and table manners shaped discussions that were considered useful to Egyptian families.

Abdullah Nadim (1845–1896), who was exiled for his role in the `Urabi rebellion and only brought back to Egypt in 1892, also included the discussion of household topics in his monthly journal *al-Ustadh* (The Professor). (*Al-Ustadh* was best known for carrying satirical attacks on Lord Cromer and his politics, so much so that Cromer demanded Nadim's expulsion from Egypt.) The journal did not have a regular home economics column, but topics and debates involving the domestic realm were as frequent in it as articles on politics. Seemingly political articles also dipped into the domestic realm, and household issues were often used as a means of discussing nationalism, politics, and national "progress." Articles such as "National Life," from August 1892, and "Why They Progressed and We Did Not, Even Through We Were All Created Equal" from November of that same year, both attached "progress" and "nationalism" to the ability of governments to centralize and enforce education. Government reorganization in Egypt, it was argued, had strengthened the family not only because it had improved Egypt's material landscape, but because it had provided the education through which new templates for behavior were established.[27]

Marital practices and the habits of couples inside and outside of the home were common topics of discussion in the early nationalist press. Proper ages for marriages, the pros and cons of arranged marriages, choosing the "right" spouse, all found their way into the press. Rashid Rida's (1865–1935) *al-Manar* (The Lighthouse), which is commonly associated with Islamic reform and conservative politics, often ran articles on the home, on questions pertaining to families, and on "Egyptian" behavior. In one such article, Rida claimed that if reformers really wanted to create a sense of Egyptian identity, they had to start by reforming Egyptian home life. He argued that the biggest problem affecting home life was the marital practices of a new generation of Egyptian men, who were refusing to marry women who were not well educated. The education of women who would influence their husbands and children at home was, according to Rida, the first step in the struggle to create a national, Egyptian lifestyle.[28]

Al-Muqtataf, a journal edited by Faris Nimr and Yaqub Saruf, Syrian émigrés to Egypt, was billed as a "Scientific, Industrial, and Agricultural Magazine." The journal ran a regular column on *"tadbir al-manzil,"* which was intended to

> explicate and illustrate topics of general importance to members of the household knowledge about the upbringing of children, the planning of meals, clothing, living quarters, decoration and things to that effect. This knowledge will benefit each member of the family.[29]

An article on cleanliness carried by *al-Muqtataf* in the spring of 1895 illustrates the many uses of home economics. The author of "The Secrets of Cleanliness" asked why it was that Egyptian clothes and bodies got so dirty, and what could be done about it. He began by discussing Egypt's "cleaner" past saying: "If a high priest from the Pharaonic era . . . saw what the Nile has become, he would cry. . . . He would prefer to go back to living in the land of the dead."[30] The author did not claim to know why Egypt and the Egyptians had become "dirty"; he was certain, however, that modernity was characterized by cleanliness. Teaching Egyptians the "secrets of cleanliness" would both connect them with the great history of their ancestors and bring them into a new age. His approach to Egypt's problem was quite specific:

> What is true about Egypt is that clothes get dirty easily because of the dust in the wind that sticks to them, as well as the dirt that the body excretes. . . . The human body excretes twenty-three ounces of sweat every twenty-four hours. When it dries, it doesn't go away; rather more than an ounce of it sticks to our skin. . . . It won't wash out unless you mix an alkaline solution with the water in which you wash the clothes.[31]

Tabdir al-manzil played a number of roles in the male-authored press. It prescribed the direct application of science to the home, making the domicile a place where knowledge and scientific activity were not overlooked. The author's insistence upon "Egyptian dirt" created a common culture of Egyptian-ness, presenting a problem with which all Egyptians were bound to struggle. Finally, the scientific combating of dirt within the household allowed Egyptians not only to become modern, but to reconcile themselves with the greatness of their ancient past. The home was thus a site where modernity and history were championed.

The creation of Egyptian-ness through domestic practices was also a prominent feature of the women's press in the 1890s.[32] The first Egyptian women's magazine, *Jaridat al-Fatah* (The Young Woman), edited by Hind al-

Nawal, was announced as a "Scientific, Historical, Literary, and Satirical Newspaper." The newspaper carried a *tadbir al-manzil* column as well as articles on health, economics, and *tarbiyya*. Like the male-authored press, it contained articles that consistently blurred the boundaries between public and private, domestic and political. In its fourth issue, for example, the journal ran "The Politics of the Home," in which the relationship between the home and the public realm was clearly delineated. The author claimed that *tadbir al-manzil* was one of the most important issues of the age because it was crucial to relations both inside the home and in the public sphere: "The house that is well-mannered and well-furnished enables its [male] owner to learn and take charge of the rights and responsibilities he has to the members of his household, and those outside his household."[33]

Alexandra Avierno's *Anis al-Jalis* (The Intimate Companion) did not have a regular column on *tadbir al-manzil*, but did frequently include columns called *al-hayah al-manziliyya* (domestic life); *sh'un al manzil* (domestic affairs); *al-hayah al-zoujiyya* (married life); *mamlaka fil beit* (the house a kingdom); and *tarbiyyat al-atfal* (children's upbringing). Prescriptive literature on such topics as breastfeeding (modern, middle-class women were encouraged not to use wet nurses),[34] household products, and nutrition, in *Anis al-Jalis* and other periodicals, reminded women that the attitudes and behaviors cultivated within the home would be reflected in the endeavors of their sons and husbands in the public realm.

Thus in the decades leading up to the Revolution, the home and its activities served as an arena where a bourgeois nationalist lifestyle was defined and in which lifestyles that did not support the process of modernizing Egypt were subjected to critique. At the same time, the household and its affairs came to symbolize politics and political struggles. In both the classroom and the press, Egyptians were reminded that their bourgeois, modern behavior had political ramifications. While women often appeared to be central to these discussions, women and men alike were enjoined to participate in home economics.

The Family Politics of the 1919 Revolution

During the 1919 Revolution, the effendi nationalists who supported Sa`ad Zaghlul as their national leader mobilized—to great effect—the domestic imagery of secular, bourgeois nationalism. Zaghlul was not an elected official; rather, he was an ad hoc leader who presented himself first to the British as a liaison between them and the Egyptian nation and, later on, as the leader of that nation. The Egyptian Revolution broke out in March of 1919 when Zaghlul was exiled by the British. (Zaghlul had first caught the ire of the British in November, 1918, when he and a group of Egyptian nationalists calling themselves the Wafd [the Delegates] requested permission to represent Egypt at the post–World War I peace conferences in France). By April 1919, Zaghlul's exile had led to an outbreak by riots, boycotts, and demonstrations all over Egypt, and the British thus changed their minds and allowed Zaghlul to travel to France.

Once he had succeeded in being appointed Egypt's negotiator, Zaghlul had to gain the support of the Egyptian masses whose social and economic background he did not necessarily share, and whose interests he did not always represent. In other words, Zaghlul had to create himself as head of the Egyptian nation. To do so, he arranged in absentia for the creation of the Wafd's Central Committee, the membership of which consisted largely of the *effendi* graduates of Egypt's public schools, and called upon the Committee to establish public support for him and for his party. To do so, the Central Committee organized and led demonstrations, created and distributed leaflets and brochures, and mounted press campaigns against the British and in favor of the Wafd.[35] British intelligence reported that a large portion of the agitation against them was entrusted to the *effendi* class, and correctly labeled the *effendiyya* Zaghlul's propaganda machine.[36]

The use of domestic imagery and debate by *effendi* members of the Wafd's committees had two main functions during the Revolution. The first was to display to the British that the order of things had changed in Egypt. The domestic relations that had defined the khedives in the late nineteenth century did not apply to them; readiness for independence was signaled through images of reformed domestic and familial behavior. At the same time, domestic imagery helped cement the relationship between Wafd leadership and the masses by connecting them through a nationalist lineage.

The relationship between party politics and domestic reform was not new to the Revolution, but rather had its roots in the establishment of political parties in Egypt under the tenure of Cromer's successors, Sir Eldon Gorst (1907–1911) and Lord Kitchner (1911–1913). As a means of addressing some of the political and economic grievances held by the Egyptians against the British administration, both men allowed more Egyptians access to higher-ranking positions within the administration. They also allowed for the formation of political parties, lifting Egyptian politics out of the printed realm to which it had been confined. On the eve of World War I there were three major parties in Egypt: the Constitutional Reform Party (*hizb al-islah al-dusturi*), the People's Party (*hizb al-ummah*) and the National Party (*al-hizb al-watani*). Each seems to have been concerned both with liberating Egypt and with reforming the domestic practices of its citizens. In the decade leading up to the Revolution, *tadbir al-manzil* was thus not simply an abstract means of discussing nationalism. Rather, it appears to have been central to the process through which political aspirations and platforms became concrete.

Ahmad Loutfi al-Sayyid (1872–1963), for example, symbolic head of the People's Party and editor of its newspaper *al-Jarida* (The Paper), called for the reform and reorganization of the family as a first step toward constitutional government in speeches given to members of the party on various occasions.[37] His platform for the eventual establishment of a constitutional regime in Egypt was the creation of a system of public education that would "rid the nation of its childlike ways," and teach Egyptians sound familial relationships.[38] Egypt's political and economic situation, he claimed, would not be remedied without the total transformation of the Egyptians' most personal relationships, the reform of which would be his party's charge.

The minutes taken from a National Party Congress in Brussels in 1910 likewise indicate that the household had become central to shaping party platforms. Debates over the building of hospitals and schools and the education of women took up as much floor time at the conference as did the discussion of politics. Discussions of Egypt's readiness for self-rule were sandwiched between lengthier and more heated debates over infant mortality, motherhood and education, and disinfecting Egypt's homes.[39]

During the Revolution, slogans, chants, and iconography delivered the message that the family politics of middle- and upper class Egyptians had been reformed. Central to the pageantry of the Revolution was a display of those family politics to the outside world. (In the words of one Egyptian, for example, "We want the whole world ... to know even our most intimate secrets."[40]) Revolutionary slogans, images, cartoons, and literature reveal that at the heart of the struggle to liberate Egypt lay an attempt to demonstrate to the British and the other European powers that the political order of Isma'il and his ministers no longer existed. Just as the British used the inadvertently displayed family politics of the khedival order to form the politics of the protectorate, the Egyptians displayed domesticity and concern for the nation as a family in order to proclaim themselves ready for self-rule.

The sexual practices of the khedives, for example, formed a common motif in revolutionary discourse. The following circular, intercepted by the British, is reminiscent of previous attacks on Khedive Isma'il:

> How beautiful is the child of an adulteress, who slept with a he mule or a wild donkey. He was born five months after the marriage, while the mule is generally born after eight months. We are going to deliver ourselves from the rule of a wicked king in the future. Kings do their work skillfully, but Fuad is being "used" (like a woman) in his grand palace. ... Hell, where is thy torture for the husband, the wife and the child of a harlot?[41]

King Fuad, placed on the throne by the British at the start of World War I, was thought by many nationalists to be a puppet ruler and, therefore, an illegitimate candidate for the throne.

Sound motherhood, by contrast, called revolutionaries into battle for the nation:

> Verily your mother Egypt, who nourished you with her good production, suckled you with the water of her Nile, let you enjoy her breeze, opened for you her wide breast ... calls you with a voice chosen with tears and a breast

Fig. 2.1.

full of burning sighs and communicates spiritually with the nobility of your souls.⁴²

Indeed, central to the behavior that would lead to the Protectorate's demise were maternalism and domesticity. Effendi nationalists often used images of mothers and domestic activities to embody the ideals of the new order. A political cartoon (figure 2.1), taken from an illustrated periodical printed in the early spring of 1920, is reminiscent of discussions about "table talk" and home economics that cemented the relationship between domestic reform and modern, political culture. Printed in a popular magazine—one of the very few contemporary illustrated magazines in Egypt at the time of the Revolution—the cartoon is a clear indication of the extent to which domestic activities and national liberation formed part of a similar agenda. The waiter represents England, the diner is Egypt. He asks her, "What will you have, my lady?" She responds: "A platter of independence and, along with it, a dish of freedom." Here, international diplomacy is forged in a modern dining room.⁴³

While this image depicts a woman dining in a public place, it evokes the discussions about "table talk" and household behavior that were so common to the turn-of-the-century press and schoolroom. This woman is sitting upright, and dining at a table, an image that contrasted directly with those produced in the West in the nineteenth and early twentieth centuries, in which Egyptian women were portrayed as endlessly lounging and reclin-

Fig. 2.2.

ing. In such depictions, women engaged in far less "functional" activities than this caricature suggests—gossiping, smoking, sexual intrigue—and were passive, voiceless, and without will.

At this dining-room table *cum* conference table of international politics, however, it is a well-refined, well-postured, well-mannered woman who does Egypt's bidding. Egypt clearly knows the protocol involved in dining in the league of modern nation-states. This is not the image of a clumsy, backward, colonized entity seeking entrance into the league of refined, modern nation-states: This woman, while obviously not European, asks for what she wants with all the ease of a Western counterpart; she is literate and confident. While her attire suggests the maintenance of a certain degree of "non-Western-ness," it also reveals that Egypt is modern, and has a taste for the latest fashions. Her arms are bare, her shoes fashionable.

Modern Egyptian motherhood was a common motif for claiming Egypt's potential as an independent nation. In this cartoon (figure 2.2), "Mother Egypt" (dressed in somewhat traditional attire) is seated on the back of the Sphinx (often used in the Revolutionary press to symbolize the nascent Egyptian nation). She is breast-feeding the infant "Bank Misr," which was founded in 1920 by a group of Egyptian landowners and industrialists as a means of funding an independent Egyptian economic policy. It was intended to be a purely "Egyptian" bank. The cartoon's caption reads:

> This picture represents the newborn Bank Misr and the foreign banks in Egypt. Bank Misr is represented as a newborn baby being breast-fed the milk of his mother. And who is his mother? None other than the Egyptian Nation, the

beloved, splendid Egyptian Nation sitting on its oldest and most famous manifestation—the Sphinx. While mother Egypt attends to breast-feeding her newborn—about whom she is overjoyed—the child's older brothers sidle up to take a look. Their eyes are full of jealousy and rage, but they cheer each other on by saying: Will the baby live? Will the baby live? We say: Yes the baby will live if he continues to nurse from the breast of his mother![44]

Because Egypt is depicted as a breast-feeding mother, it can be argued that its financial solvency would be ensured when its citizens, its children, and its institutions were thoroughly nurtured in the blessings of motherhood. Modern motherhood (mother Egypt's shoes suggest that she is "modern") would instill in Egyptians the morals and virtues, the absence of which had allegedly led Isma'il into the grips of colonialism. The sins of Isma'il were thus purged through maternal, domestic activities.

The role of modern motherhood in bringing Egypt to independence was also the subject of advertisements designed to sell the products with which perfect motherhood would be achieved. This ad for "Lactogol" baby formula (figure 2.3) was published in the summer of 1919. Its subjects appear to be straight out of one of the demonstrations and are depicted marching and carrying placards. (The most common depictions of women in the demonstrations, then as now, are women marching with placards.)

Rather than reading "Freedom and Total Independence," as did many of the placards carried by women in the demonstrations, the advertisement says: "Nationalist Mothers: Your most sacred duty is to raise healthy sons for the Nation. So feed them Lactogol."[45]

The deleterious results of the failure to reform Egyptian family politics are forecast in the following caricature (figure 2.4), published in January 1920 while the Milner Mission was in Egypt. Lord Milner was sent to Egypt in December 1919 to investigate the causes of the Revolution and to advise the British government on the best course of action. His recommendation, albeit hesitant, was that Egypt needed to be independent.

Here, Lord Milner is Egypt's "nanny." The caption reads: "He withholds from Egypt the milk that it needs to survive; instead, Milner gives Egypt a rattle—a toy—to distract it and keep it quiet. Egypt, of course, responds by screaming louder." Baby Egypt's bottle reads: "complete independence," and the rattle reads "personal freedom," a reference to the concessions the British were willing to grant the Egyptians without, in fact, granting them independence.

Milner is lampooned not only as a woman, but as a "bad mother." He pretends to take care of Egypt, while giving it nothing but distractions. The caricature seems to suggest that unreformed motherhood—a return to the days before modern domestic sciences were learned and debated by bourgeois Egyptians—brought Egyptians continued occupation. The caricature might

Fig. 2.3.

Fig. 2.4.

also be a warning against too much Europeanization: was the use of European-style nannies and other western customs getting Egypt anything more than false promises of independence?[46]

In addition to portraying Egypt as a nation, the *effendi* nationalists whose job it was to guarantee support for the Wafd, created images of the Wafd as the natural head of a united Egyptian nation. Here the rhetoric about the new fathers and the new families that was central to the school lessons and the national press in the decades leading up to the revolution manifested itself in concrete images. Depictions of Wafd leadership appeared in the press as giving birth to the Egyptian nation and nurturing it to maturity. The ability of the Wafd to lead the nation was frequently evoked through its relationship to mother Egypt, and to activities associated with maternalism and domesticity.

During the Revolution, it was not uncommon for nationalists to use journals and magazines to illustrate "good" or "sound" nationalism by telling stories about the domestic lives and activities of men who were labeled "exemplary nationalists." Often, such activities were more akin to maternalism than has previously been reckoned with by historians. Politicians, doctors, members of wealthy landowning families—bourgeois nationalists—were all depicted in the context of their public and private lives in order to highlight, for the reader, the kinds of activities, sentiments, and virtues that had come to form the culture of modern nationalism. Among the stories told about such men were anecdotes about their upbringing, their domestic habits, and familial affairs. In such stories, written as short biographies, male nationalists were enjoined to behave in the public realm in the same way that mothers were asked to behave inside the home. Sound nationalists were consistently depicted as "rearing" the nation's children, and as embodying the virtues that were required of the "good mothers" who stayed at home.

Mohammad Tawfiq Nasim (1875–1936), for example, twice head of the new Egyptian Ministry and an early Wafd member, was hailed for leading the nation in its struggle against the British, and therefore fit to lead the nation to full and proper independence. Nasim was also celebrated for the relationship he enjoyed with his wife and children, and for "enjoying the pleasures" of domestic life.[47] Similarly, Adly Yeghen (1864–1933), liaison between the Milner Mission in Egypt and the Egyptians who negotiated with the British in London, was congratulated both for his political efforts and his domestic relationships. Egyptian confidence in him at the time of the negotiations between the British and Sa'ad Zaghlul was rooted not only in his education, his experience, and his ability in the political realm but in his domestic affairs, past and present. Nationalist Dr. Abd al-'Aziz Nazmi was included in such reviews as the result of his role as founder of various philanthropic organizations, including an orphanage for children called the Freedom Orphanage (*malga'a al-huriyya*). The editors of *al-Lata'if al-Musawwara* and other journals, such as *al-Ahram*, characterized as "truly nationalist" all of the doctor's charitable activities, which included the establishment of a society for the protection of children, a society for the feeding of the poor, a school for nurses, a society against the spread of prostitution and against the continuation of white slavery. At the same time, Nazmi was given credit by the press as actively creating a nationalist Egyptian youth through his activities in charitable organizations.[48] The domicile in which he nurtured the aspirant nation, extended to include the nation's poor.

The maternal aspect of revolutionary culture was immortalized by the poet Hafith Bey Ibrahim (called "the Poet of the Nile"). Ibrahim's poems were carried in most magazines and newspapers during the Revolutionary period. His paean to Nazmi's orphanage, also entitled *"Malga' al-Huriyya,"* equated nationalism with raising the nation's children. Like the orphanage's founder, Ibrahim called on his fellow nationalists to insure the nation's success by caring for its children.

> You men who are earnest about nationalism: The time has come to insure the future of those who will inherit the nation. Build orphanages, factories, irrigation canals, and agricultural syndicates. Who knows—perhaps those whom you help will turn out to be a full moon to light the way; they might turn out to be another Sa'ad (Zaghlul); they might turn out to be another (Mohammad) Abduh; they might become another poet like Shauqi or they might turn out to be a brave knight.... How many souls of great men rest within the bodies of orphaned children?[49]

The founding and funding of the Freedom Orphanage held pride of place in the press during the months of the first revolutionary uprisings. In April and May of 1919 the press was full of announcements of public meetings of the orphanage's governing board, and advertisements for local theatrical performances, the proceeds of which were donated to the orphanage.[50] The project was often pitched as a means of reclaiming Egypt's lost youth from the Europeans who were busy building schools, hospitals, and orphanages to take care of Egypt's disadvantaged. Philanthropy was certainly not new to Egypt. Christian and Muslim beneficent organizations proliferated in Egypt from the last third of the nineteenth century. Women's groups played a predominant role in philanthropy, especially that directed towards women and children, in the decades leading to the Revolution.[51] Despite the fact that Freedom Orphanage's activities were not unique, its establishment during the Revolution seemed to capture the imagination and the enthusiasm of the Cairene public.

Al-Ahram waged a large campaign for money to build the orphanage. Beginning on April 9, 1919, with a "call to action" from Nazmi, the paper listed almost daily the names of Egyptians who were contributing to the campaign, and the amount of money that they had pledged. By mid-summer of

Fig. 2.5.

1919 the orphanage opened its doors to children who had apparently been picked up by the police. On July 5th, 1919, *al-Ahram* reported that the orphanage housed 69 boys and 22 girls. On that day, members of most of Cairo's major newspapers toured the orphanage and it was generally reported that it was producing "productive" men and women.[52] The portraits of the children and the orphanage printed in *al-Lata'if al-Musawwara* showed the children to be clean and well dressed, orderly and obedient. Those images were contrasted with pictures of children who had not benefited from the nationalists' care—filthy, ragged, and miserable.

Another cartoon (figure 2.5) which appeared in the *al-Lata'if al-Musawwara* during the campaign depicts Egyptians as a family of men and women, rich and poor, Muslim, Jewish, and Christian (*al-ummah al-misriyya min gamiat al-tawa'if*), gathered around a figure which, we are told, represents humanity and the Freedom Orphanage itself. On the left stands an Egyptian woman, surrounded by her male compatriates, holding a placard that reads "The Egyptian Nation" (*al-ummah al-misriyya*). These are the Egyptians who have participated in the collection of funds for the orphanage. At their feet are a group of clean, healthy, well-dressed children—"children of the rich"—presumably the product of modern households and a proper upbringing. Next to them, however, is a group of naked, scrawny, faceless children all of whom plead for the nation's assistance. Unlike those children who stand with the men and women of the nation, these children have no faces and are indistinguishable from one another.[53]

In the center of the cartoon another female image is portrayed, representing the orphanage itself, to which the nation looks for guidance. A mother figure, she holds a small baby, she is clothed in the garb of a Greco-Roman warrior, of the kind often used in French revolutionary iconography to represent the ideals of constitutional government,[54] and she wears a sash that refers to her as "humanity" (*insaniyya*). It is to her that the men and women of Egypt look; it is from her that the faceless poor seek assistance. At her feet, a clean, well-dressed child hands her a sack of money to support the orphanage. She thanks him in the name of the faceless, voiceless poor.

In his interaction with her, in his participation in the fundraising, the young boy acquires face, voice, and citizenship. He represents *al-Lata'if al-Musawwara* itself, which had dedicated the proceeds of a special issue to the campaign to raise money for the orphanage; the sack of money represents that contribution. The boy *qua* magazine is juxtaposed with that of a group of members of the traditional Egyptian elite who represent other periodicals. They are inactive, dejected; they look at mother Egypt but do not interact with her. The child states that he has taken action rather than settling for words, as his contemporaries did; the proof lay in the bag of money that he alone offered. The other papers attempt to defend themselves. *Al-Ahram* for example, says, "I announced the campaign, I drummed up support, I made a lot of noise, and advertised the names of those who participated. Doesn't that count?" As depicted here, the old order neither cooperates fully with mother Egypt nor participates in the creation of her citizenry. Clearly, "New Egypt" is given voice and citizenship through its role in nurturing children, in playing a maternal role in the national household. Egypt is a new creation, distinct from the old regime, characterized by new virtues, in particular, those of maternalism, charity, and concern for the poor.

Conclusion

The iconography of the 1919 Revolution suggests that the acts of giving birth to and nurturing a family were not at all restricted to women. The household and its activities, central to which was a kind of maternalism practiced by both sexes, was the arena where new sexual and social relationships were created, political acumen was demonstrated, and a new secular, Egyptian bourgeois culture was defined. As in other British colonies, to be a good "mother" meant, for men as well as women, to refute a whole host of colonialist claims about the weaknesses of the political and social order.[55] Displaying sound "maternal" behavior in order to shape the national family also symbolized the Egyptians' readiness for independence.

In Egypt, as in India, sub-Saharan Africa, and elsewhere, the family under British colonial occupation served as a symbol for those things about Egypt that were not Western, Christian, or modern—as the British defined them. The shape of the family was made synonymous with the ability of the nation to govern itself. The condition of the familial realm was used as a yardstick by which Egyptian backwardness (or, by contrast, progress) was measured, and by which further colonial tutelage was legitimated. Egyptian nationalists later took on British definitions for quite different ends—using the familial metaphor as a means of critiquing problems inherent to their own political system, of defining themselves as modern, and, finally, of demonstrating to the West that they were ready for independence.

At the same time, the family was used as the arena through which nationalist discourse could be translated into concrete practice. The turn-of-the-century press and the classroom both "taught" bourgeois Egyptians how to behave like denizens of a modern nation-state. "Table talk" was no longer just a metaphor: to know how to behave at a modern table brought entitlement to the cultural capital of modernity, and power to negotiate with the British.

Central to this familial discourse and practice was the image of the mother. The prevalence of maternal imagery in the decades leading up to the Revolution has led scholars to believe that the discourse of domesticity in turn-of-the-century Egypt was about women—women using the home and the family to define and empower themselves, and men using women and images of them to define modern Egypt as they might have it. Like the Western women examined by scholars in Seth Koven and Sonya Michel's edited volume, *Mothers of a New World*,[56] Egyptian women championed "maternalist" activities, from authoring prescriptive literature about modern domestic practices to engaging in philanthropic projects aimed at improving the lot of mothers and children. At the same time, however, Egyptian men also appropriated concern with the domestic realm in order to trumpet their own agendas. Because the independent Egyptian nation-state that was proclaimed in 1922 did not offer women an active role in governing, it is tempting to conclude that men's concern with domesticity stemmed from a determination to limit women to the home and thereby create a political arena in which only men would participate.

There are other differences between Egyptian political culture and that of the maternalist cases of the West. For one, the British colonial and nascent Egyptian states' critiques of and reform programs for "mothers" were linked to the denigration or exaltation of political and economic arenas that had nothing to do with the actual care and maintenance of mothers and children. Additionally, concern with domestic, maternal activities in Egypt—both real and metaphorical—was promoted by a variety of political actors, not just women endeavoring to gain political power. Home life was not just the lot of women; to be masculine in Egypt under British occupation meant to be "feminine"—to know "table talk" as well as women were expected to know it, and to provide for the nation's children.

The effect of such family politics upon Egyptian culture is still potent. In Mohammed Fadel's recent film, *Nasser 56*, for example, the relationship between the bourgeois, nuclear family and the ability of the Egyptian state is made evident.[57] Gamal Abdul Nasser, on the eve of his decision to nationalize the Suez Canal, is frequently depicted caring for his wife and children at moments of enormous political import. He dismisses meetings so as to be present at his children's birthday parties; he hurries from cabinet meetings in order to attend to his children's request that they be allowed to leave the oppressive heat of Cairo for a summer vacation in Alexandria. He discusses politics with them at the dining-room table and while brushing his teeth. Although his wife appears to be a knowledgeable homemaker, it is Nasser whose behavior within the context of his family is linked to the ability of the nation to govern itself. It is the nation that ultimately triumphs, but it is the family, headed by a properly domesticated father, that assures its success.

3

FAMILIAR TERRITORY

Prostitution, Empires, and the Question of U.S. Imperialism in Puerto Rico, 1849–1916

LAURA BRIGGS

From Donna Haraway to Ann Stoler to Gayatri Spivak, the problem of imperialism increasingly occupies center stage for U.S. feminist theory. In Haraway's *Primate Visions*, we have perhaps the most ambitious historical account in recent scholarship of U.S. imperialism, one, she argues, whose traces can be found in primatology's accounts of nuclear families. From Teddy Roosevelt hunting in the Belgian Congo to the eugenicists of New York's Museum of Natural History organizing slain gorillas into taxidermied family groups; from the post-War U.N. Declaration of Universal Human Rights to stories of the cooperative family groups of Oldivai Gorge's prehistory and the gentle ¡Kung San bushmen; from Mobil Oil's ads featuring Jane Goodall's tender hand-holding with a chimpanzee as a symbol of interracial and international cooperation to apes in space, Haraway shows how science, race, family, and imperialism have mutually constituted each other. Likewise, for the nineteenth century, Ann Stoler argues that the bourgeois domesticity we are accustomed to consider "metropolitan" or even "Victorian" was in fact produced in the colonies, a domesticity that defined what was truly "English" (or Dutch, French, Belgian, Spanish, or German) about the increasingly creolized English (etc.). Notions of domesticity, she suggests, solved colonial problems of race mixture, class, and status through regulation of marriage and sex and the (re)production of a kind of family in which culture could be reliably transmitted.[1] In Spivak, we find the disturbing suggestion that idioms of rights—particularly women's rights—and the defense of the subaltern have done and continue to do important work for imperialism, from the British and *sati* ("white men are fighting with brown men over brown women's bodies") to U.N. women's rights non-governmental organizations that, she says, contribute to the spread and intensification of capitalism by working to make loans and other forms of capital available to women and hence contributing to the monetarization of everything.[2]

This chapter offers an argument for thinking about ideologies of family, sexuality, and reproduction as animating U.S. imperialist and racial projects, specifically those related to Puerto Rico and Puerto Ricans. Taking up the proposition that Haraway, Spivak, and Stoler could be said collectively to have offered, I suggest that discourses of domesticity and science, reproduction, and sexuality enabled U.S. colonialism. In particular, I am interested in the ways that the notion of the failed nuclear families of Puerto Ricans—or, put positively, the work of "modernizing" Puerto Rican families, sexuality, and reproduction—has provided a legitimating argument for U.S. colonialism, beginning with prostitution reform and VD control and continuing through the twentieth century from eugenics to overpopulation to the "culture of poverty."

These imperialist projects were, I argue, consistently yoked to one of the two great modernist narratives—women's rights or scientific progress—often both. I do not mean to suggest that these arguments were or are cynical; quite the opposite, they were deadly earnest and acutely felt. My question is simpler: what kind of intervention did they authorize? What political and cultural work did it do to write melodramatic press accounts in the thirties of starving children in Puerto Rico in need of milk and medical care that only the United States could or would provide? In the sixties, of overpopulation causing poverty and poor women tied to large families? U.S. imperialism has never identified itself as imperialism, only as "doing good." If we mean to understand it, we have to look beyond the sentimental logic in which that imperialism cloaks itself, in which failing to act (intervene) is to sanction violence against women and children, and look instead to the violence of colonialism.

This chapter examines prostitution policy and its continuities from "other" empires to U.S. imperialism. I argue that the United States participated in a colonial discourse that at once was biomedical and familial: the imperative to register prostitutes, subject them to medical exams, and treat their disease if found sick. The paradigmatic codification of this policy was the British Contagious Diseases (CD) Acts. While historians of England and the United States have characterized the CD Acts as essentially designed to address problems in England's port cities and garrison towns, I will show that they were essentially a colonial matter, characteristic not only of Britain but of all empires, including that of the United States. The CD Acts began earlier, were repealed later, and were more extensively enforced in the colonies than the metropoles.[3] I am interested in showing that U.S. colonialism emerged neither by accident, *ad hoc* in response to uncontrollable circumstance, nor in isolation from other colonialisms, as many diplomatic historians have suggested, but rather inserted itself into an already established set of colonialist practices, specifically prostitution registration. The CD Acts and their analogues served to "organize" disorderly women, often limiting their mobility in segregated districts, enrolling them as imperial citizens through the essentially bureaucratic process of registration, sometimes restricting their clients by race (specifying the nationalities of men they would serve, be it soldier or laborer). Syphilis (only irregularly distinguished from gonorrhea) was no mere inconvenience, but a frightening disease that sometimes seemed to go away of its own accord, caused horrifying disfigurement, madness, and death. Modern methods of registration, gynecological examination, public health, statistics-keeping, organization and orchestration of populations could keep it at bay.

Tropical medicine was deployed in the service of protecting armies and colonial populations from venereal disease. Where histories of prostitution and venereal disease policy make science causal in one way or another, I argue that on the contrary, the science of venereal disease was inserted into the colonial organization of armies, labor forces, and the various forms of sanctioned domesticity. Indeed, its scientific questions and conclusions were illegible *without* the colonial context. Segregation and quarantine methods of containing the threat of syphilis spread first throughout the British Empire, then through other empires as well. It was also adopted as U.S. policy wherever the U.S. military was sent. The French and German imperial apparatus developed additional tools as well. Drawing on the emerging field of tropical medicine emerging in British India, German researchers sought and found the "tropical parasite" that caused syphilis and initiated research on arsenical compounds for treatment of the disease, research that concluded with the development of salvarsan, a reasonably potent medicinal. The development of salvarsan, in turn, justified the continued incarceration of prostitutes.

Where registration certified and sanitized a variety of sexual and domestic arrangements, the opposition it generated—a liberal repeal movement—argued for putting everyone into nuclear families. Modernity required "modern" families; prostitutes, soldiers, and unmarried laborers failed to constitute nuclear families. Liberalism of a variety of stripes—metropolitan, missionary, and creole nationalist—envisioned an end to state-sanctioned vice, seduced women, lecherous men, and other (archaic) forms of corruption in favor of state repression of prostitution, healthy bodies, and racially homogeneous nuclear families. The movement against the CD Acts, strong in the "metropole" and weak in the colonies, turned after 1900 to advocate incarceration of prostitutes as a women's rights measure. This chapter traces the history of colonial regulation of prostitution from 1840 to 1917, the year of the U.S. entrance into World War I, beginning with British India and concluding with a detailed examination of policies in Puerto Rico.

The Contagious Diseases Acts as Imperial System

Prostitution was a subject of obsessive interest for colonial powers and is a fascinating topic for scholars as well. Prostitution is a tremendously flexible symbol, a revealing facet of social organization, and an often difficult way of life. As Gail Hershatter suggests, it provides an excellent entrée into the ways colonialism reorganized sociality and culture "on the ground,"[4] at considerably closer range than the often abstract narratives of economy or diplomacy take us. It is simultaneously a form of labor, and hence a strategy of economic accumulation and a site of repressive state intervention, and a question and symbol of sexual transgression, always fraught with danger, immorality, and contagion.[5] As feminists have noted, prostitution is also an important site of cultural negotiation over power and the social organization of gender in the domestic, sexual, and reproductive spheres. As Ruth Rosen puts it, prostitution illuminates

> a society's organization of class and gender: the power arrangements between men and women's economic and social status; the prevailing sexual ideology; ... the ways in which female erotic and procreative sexuality are channeled into specific institutional arrangements; and the cross-class alliances and antagonisms between reformers and prostitutes.[6]

It is this multivocality of prostitution—simultaneously a kind of reform movement, a kind of medical and public health research and supervision, a military problem, a potent symbol, and a way of life and means of earning a living that makes it so interesting to understand in the colonial context. Prostitution, as Cynthia Enloe points out, is always one of the key questions for an army about garrisoning troops outside of "domestic" borders, and one of the first and always extensive negotiations with the receiving society. It has been a rich source of metaphors about the situation of colonized nations, and as an actual (non-metaphoric) relationship, it has been a site of complex negotiation of forms of colonial labor and domesticity.[7]

Colonial prostitution and its regulation was the subject of considerable debate in the nineteenth century, specifically around the British Contagious Diseases Acts. From 1864 to 1886, the CD Acts required that prostitutes working in and near areas where soldiers were stationed in Britain be registered, "inspected" internally for signs of syphilis at regular intervals, and confined to a "lock" hospital if found ill. That policy, or another like it, was also enacted in England's colonies, generally for a longer period of time and often far more extensively. Indeed, a policy of required medical inspection and lock hospitals existed in some form in British India from the end of the eighteenth century, predating the enactment of the English policy by a half-century.[8] The registration and inspection policy did not begin with the British—its origin was Paris, and French colonies enacted it as well—but the relentless march of the British imperium assured that its international spread would be associated with the English legislation. The prostitution policy embodied in the CD Acts was certainly regarded as an India measure by reformers in the United States. A Rockefeller Foundation official, writing in 1916 of the history of opposition to the CD Acts, claimed that the Acts "enforced a medical examination of prostitutes for the protection of the troops against venereal disease both at home and in India."[9]

The enactment of the first of the English CD Acts in 1864 also corresponded roughly to the bloody 1857–59 Indian uprising and the arrival of more than 55,000 troops in the subcontinent to protect European life and property, where they remained for the rest of the century. The measures were legislated at a moment when British policy was particularly concerned that only the strength of its army secured its imperial holdings. Religious objections to the state's sanctioning of "vice" could be overridden in the paranoia of the post-Mutiny period; syphilis and other venereal diseases were simply another thing that "threatened the army from without," in historian David Arnold's phrase.[10]

The management of the relationship between Indian prostitutes and British soldiers was part of a broader British organization of domesticity in the colony.[11] The apparent taken-for-grantedness of soldiers' "need" for prostitutes need not have been so. No one ever breathed a word of suggestion that the vast numbers of unmarried women missionaries who encircled the globe were in need of paid sexual service to maintain their health. Hydraulic models of spermatic pressure notwithstanding, the soldiers' requirement for prostitutes had to be produced and culturally managed as part of an ideology about working-class masculinity. Furthermore, it was not universally true that what was being sold was merely sexual; it could equally be domestic. The Indian Medical Board, in seeking ways to curtail venereal infection among the troops, recommended in 1810 that

> inducements might be held out to the men to attach themselves individually to individual Native women, [since] it [is] well known, how much more efficient those Corps are, which have Native women attached to them, than those are which have not been so provided.... The soldiers so attached, if they have been at all cautious in their choice, are not only kept free from the venereal infection, but have more attention paid to providing and dressing of their victuals and to other comforts conducive to health than can be given in this climate by European women, who in general are not equal to the exertions necessary.[12]

In other words, British officials were concerned not simply with soldiers' purported "need" for heterosexual outlets, but the improved efficiency of the Army when "Native" women did the reproductive work of caring for the cleanliness, feeding, and comfort of soldiers.

After the Mutiny, the British regarded the question of soldiers sharing domesticity with Indian women—though not commercial sex—quite differently. Concubinage was sharply condemned as suspect and disloyal. Indian prostitutes were no longer regarded as engaged in one practice along a continuum of potential practices with soldiers; they were increasingly described as belonging to a separate "caste." Indeed, the Contagious Diseases and Cantonments Acts passed in India after the Mutiny differed from the English CD

Acts in one important respect: they required prostitutes to register with authorities, then volunteer for routine medical exams for signs of venereal disease; under the English Acts, a police officer had to swear before a magistrate that a woman was a "common prostitute" in order for her to be subject to such measures. In other words, English women were treated as involved in a criminal *act*, where Indian women were understood as belonging to a class, of *being* (ontologically and essentially) prostitutes. Moreover, prostitutes for "English use" were not supposed to engage in sex with Indian men; in this sense, too, they were constituted as belonging to a particular kind of class, one that was monitored not only for disease, but for maintaining some peculiar kind of racial purity.[13]

Other measures, too, reconstituted the kinds of domesticity Englishmen could find. Officers were urged to bring their (English) wives to India in order to prevent them taking up with local women. The prevalence of Burmese concubines and wives among English government officials there created something of a scandal in India, and the effort to keep the upper classes in line occupied considerable energy. In the military, the terms of enlisted men were also greatly reduced. With the introduction of the "short service" system, working-class recruits were no longer expected to serve for life, but first for twenty-one years, then for six years. Celibacy was no longer thought impossible, though recourse to prostitutes was more commonly anticipated; at any rate, the questions of marriage and concubinage were no longer expected to arise. For those of us trained to see questions of sexuality and domesticity as essentially trivial, it is worth noting that the entire imperial British military was organized around it.[14]

Each of these iterations of policy regarding domestic arrangements and prostitution represented a different configuration of class, race, and family. If the nineteenth century was the moment of multiple efforts to consolidate an English bourgeois domesticity organized around the nuclear family, these were articulations of it.[15] In the early part of the century, not everyone had to be in a nuclear family. Lower-class enlisted soldiers were not expected to marry, but to devote themselves life-long to the business of serving the empire, much as many of their counterparts in domestic service anticipated belonging life-long to the family they served, not their own. In India, soldiers could be "expected" to take up with Indian prostitutes. Their relationships might or might not produce a kind of partial domesticity; if it did, it was presumed to be good for the empire. The haphazard and contested early life of registration represented an effort to make these liaisons safe, not so much for soldiers per se, but for the army as a whole; to the extent that prostitutes were made imperial citizens through registration, they were also being rendered safe. In the post-Mutiny period, however, domesticity was policed differently. Upper-class officers were supposed to form white nuclear families. The interesting—and shocking—difference between Burma and India represented a kind of shift in ideologies about and for the upper classes; in Burma, they could not necessarily be relied upon to regulate themselves and form exclusively white nuclear families; many in the upper classes were quite convinced, and prepared to argue for, the suitability of Burmese women as concubines and even wives. Meanwhile, lower-class English enlisted men, too, were transformed into potential heads of nuclear families through the short-service system; after their soldiering years, they were expected to settle down and form families. In this sense, they became more like factory laborers. Hence, the new, more extensive and more regularized CD Acts became less about sanctioning a kind of interracial domesticity and more about keeping soldiers safe for the day when they would become husbands and fathers of (white, English) women and children.

The CD Acts and other similar legislation spread throughout the British Empire from India. Small-scale regulation of prostitution existed in Gibraltar, Malta, Hong Kong, and Victoria, Australia, before the passing of the first English domestic Act in 1864.[16] Subsequently, registration spread rapidly through British Asia, including Singapore (1870), Malaya (1864), then later in Egypt and the Sudan (1898).[17] CD Acts were also passed in Queensland (1868) and Tasmania (1879).[18] Registration spread more slowly in Africa. According to Megan Vaughan, British officials in Africa were reticent about intervening in the sexual lives of women. In Uganda and Southern Rhodesia, the British military preferred to devolve that responsibility onto local, tribal power structures. Thus, there were not CD Acts as such but, in British eastern and southern Africa, a series of acts were designed to strengthen local elite men's control over prostitution, adultery, morality, etc. There were two exceptions to this generalization. In the decade before the First World War, mandatory medical inspection was introduced in response to an apparent epidemic of syphilis among the Baganda in the Uganda protectorate (an epidemic that by the mid-1920s seemed not to have been syphilis at all, but yaws).[19] The more significant exception was the Cape Colony, where a CD Act was passed in 1868 under pressure from the War Office, which claimed that British troops were being "more than decimated" by venereal disease. The other source of pressure was that of military physicians, often recently arrived from India.[20] The legislation was, at first, short-lived; a reform movement, led by Cape liberals and ministers opposed to the apparent state sanction of vice, got the legislation repealed in 1872. A few years later, a movement began to reintroduce the acts in order to protect the colonist, as concerned and a second act was passed in 1885. A few years later, the first lock hospital was erected in Cape Town.

Registration also spread quickly through other colonies and metropoles. In the three decades after the passage of the CD Acts in England, similar measures were introduced in a multitude of places, including Java, Sumatra, Argentina, Cuba, Guatemala, Brazil, and elsewhere in Latin America, Japan, Russia, and German Africa.[21] It was already the rule in the French Caribbean and Africa. Thus, in the space of a handful of years in the nineteenth century, registration and medical inspection of prostitutes went from being an anomalous policy in places colonized by the French and some localities in India, to being the rule throughout the areas of European governance and imperial Japan. Hence, prostitution policy provides a good window into the ways that imperialism is not a series of isolated incidents belonging to divergent geographies, but an international system, composed by imperial powers in communication with each other, constituted in part by ideologies and policies associated with domesticity.

Of course, the registration of prostitutes intervened in divergent situations in these places. In areas like Malaya, Singapore, and Sumatra, registration had less to do with protecting imperial armies from venereal disease than worrying about migrant, colonial male labor forces from China, Japan, and elsewhere. These male laborers, like the English soldiers of the early nineteenth century, were not expected to form families, but rather to engage in whatever kinds of sex and domesticity prostitutes were prepared to offer. Elsewhere, as in twentieth century India and South Africa, the issue was also about protecting the white nuclear families of the colonists. The mode of transmission was vague; when concerned citizens in the Cape Colony complained that "respectable families have become infected through their nurses and washerwomen,"[22] it is unclear whether they were referring to casual contact or wet nursing, rape, and seduction. As the nineteenth century progressed, however, it became imaginable for laborers to have families; as Lenore Manderson puts it for the Malay states, "at the point at which the ... colonial government decided that the cost of continued immigration of laborers was greater than the cost of public health interventions within the colony, the child was discovered."[23] In the discourse of maternal health and venereal disease circulated internationally by physicians—about which more will be said below—the interests of mothers were characterized as endangered by prostitutes, because syphilis and gonorrhea could be carried to the conjugal bed by soldiers and laborers, affecting maternal fertility and child health. Hence, the CD Acts and their analogues became a strategy for protecting the (internally racially homogeneous) families of both colonists and colonial laborers. Concerns about interracial sex (and reproduction) clearly were also at play in the impulse toward registration in different localities; one cross-cutting issue was the international migration of European Jews because of a combination of economics and pogroms. Reports of Jewish prostitutes engaging in "interracial" sex (variously defined) surfaced from India to South Africa to Argentina to the United States.[24] In Singapore, as in India, prostitutes were registered and distinguished based on the nationality of the men they served, and were understood to be more or less responsive to the legislation; Japanese women were "clean," but Chinese women were "dirty," "backward," and had to be forced to undergo medical treatment.[25]

The Problem of U.S. Imperialism

It is customary to think of the events of 1898 in Puerto Rico, Cuba, and the Philippines as principally military in nature, and to suggest that the year itself marked the first insertion of the United States into the community of imperial powers. Neither is particularly true. The United States had long since begun territorial expansion, and the military invasions of 1898 brought trailing after them substantial social and cultural changes (to say nothing of enduring civil war in the Philippines and to a lesser extent in Cuba). Whether the character of these changes involved "the advantages and blessings of enlightened civilization," as the invading General Miles promised the Puerto Rican people within days of his arrival, was certainly a matter of perspective. The phrase itself, however, was neither idle nor cynical. North Americans were utterly committed to this version of what they offered the "Latin races," whom they sought to convert in matters of government, culture, health, and most substantially, I will argue, in their organization of family, sexuality, and reproduction. This moralist-idealist version of colonialism was particularly important in Puerto Rico, where the absence of armed resistance to the North American invasion confirmed for the United States the essential benevolence of its mission, and indeed, increasingly was used as a counter-example to the prolonged Cuban and Filipino bloodshed.[26]

Before asking what manner of change 1898 represented for those areas newly occupied by U.S. troops, however, it is important to clarify what 1898 meant for the United States, or more precisely, what it did not. Historians have produced an extensive literature of what might be termed the "accident" theory of U.S. imperialism, in which the sinking of the battleship *Maine* in Havana harbor inflamed public opinion and forced President William McKinley's hand, causing the Spanish-American War (or, more accurately, the Spanish-Cuban-Filipino-American War). Having thus been dragged unwittingly and virtually unwillingly into a role as an imperial power, the United States enacted a desultory version of the part (with the exception of Teddy Roosevelt, who with hopeless but charming boyishness, carried it off with enthusiasm). After World War I, the upright and ministerial Woodrow Wilson took us out of the whole sordid affair with his sober righteousness, and at the Versailles Conference, tried to get Europe to follow. Failing that, the nation retreated again to its customary isolationism. Absent from this version is all that came before 1898—the ongoing continental war culminating in the Mexican-American War, the subsequent U.S. incursions in Mexico, repeated landing of troops in Nicaragua, Argentina, Uruguay, Cuba, China, Angola, and Hawaii, the efforts beginning in the mid-nineteenth century to capture a territory in the Caribbean for a naval base (Haiti, the Dominican Republic, and Cuba were all considered), the 1896 Republican platform calling for the annexation of Hawaii and the building of an isthmian canal.[27]

In 1889, the United States participated in a Berlin Conference, in which Germany, England, and the United States agreed to divide the islands of Samoa among them.[28] Also absent is the continued expansion after this period of U.S. political, economic, and military influence of the sort characterized most vehemently in Korea and Vietnam.

As Amy Kaplan has argued, following William Appleman Williams, the identification of 1898 to 1917 as the period of U.S. imperialism serves to segregate it from earlier and later moments, thus forming the core of an argument that the western continental expansion on the one hand and the Cold War on the other were not imperial policies.[29] Where the British proudly called their territorial acquisitions empire-building, the United States—except among some people between 1898 and 1917—has been deeply invested in presenting itself as opposed to imperialism, to the extent that even the Spanish-American War was justified as an anti-(Spanish) imperialist gesture, just as the overthrow of the Arbenz government in Guatemala in 1954 and the Allende presidency in Chile in 1973 could be described as anti-(Soviet) imperialism. To speak of "imperialism" in the U.S. political context is to refer to an illegitimate, morally reprehensible form of power over a victimized people, hence the popularity several decades ago of the "internal colonialism" model for making sense of anti-Chicano racism, or the description of African-Americans as "Third World" people.

The elusive paradox of an anti-colonialist imperial power, to use Williams' phrase, has impoverished our language and our analytic tools for understanding how to characterize U.S. expansionism and influence outside its borders. Oscar Compomanes warns that even the characterization of an anti-colonialist imperialism may be too precious, for, he argues, it takes the rhetoric of U.S. imperial "difference" or "new-ness" (including the notion of a post-1945 "neocolonialism" in which the United States is preeminent) too seriously, simply reiterating the notion of "American exceptionalism" which has authorized a great deal that is ugly in U.S. history, not least U.S. imperialism itself.[30] The rhetoric of newness refers not only to a structure of masking, but a structure of legitimation of the nation's imperial mission. We must take care, then, in referring to the discursive structure of North American imperial legitimation, not to replicate its logic, not to be seduced by its sense of itself as "new." Yet in certain respects, U.S. imperialism must be different, if only by virtue of being played out on a different continent. The current scholarly task is to tease out its continuities and discontinuities in order to develop an account of U.S. colonialism.

U.S. Imperialism, the WCTU, and Prostitution

Prostitution policy is a good example of the ways that U.S. colonialism both preceded 1898 and was tremendously indebted to the style of colonial administration of European powers. It also provides an excellent example of the widespread denial evident in the historiography that places the United States in a colonial system. Historians have argued that regulation—as opposed to prohibition—of prostitution did not exist in the United States.[31] In the words of Alan Brandt, prostitution "regulation [was], quite simply, anathema to the Progressive moral code."[32] Yet this is true only if one excludes the activities of U.S. military officials and civilian governments overseas. Regulation was *always* the policy of the U.S. military overseas.[33]

More frequently than U.S. historians usually note, troops were dispatched in the early decades of the twentieth century to secure colonial holdings or defend U.S. interests. As Howard Zinn writes, the United States

> engineered a revolution against Colombia and created the "independent" state of Panama in order to build and control the Canal. It sent five thousand marines to Nicaragua in 1926 to counter a revolution, and kept a force there for seven years. It intervened in the Dominican Republic for the fourth time in 1916 and kept troops there for eight years. It intervened for the second time in Haiti in 1915 and kept troops there for nineteen years. Between 1900 and 1933, the United States intervened in Cuba four times, in Nicaragua twice, in Panama six times, in Guatemala once, in Honduras seven times.[34]

Wherever it went to combat "foreign" threats, the U.S. military instituted prostitution regulation. Cuba, Haiti, Nicaragua, Santo Domingo, the Panama Canal Zone, Hawaii, and the Philippines all had some policy of reglementation from the moment of U.S. occupation, and this continued throughout the pre–World War I period.[35] In Santo Domingo at the turn of the century, U.S. colonial authorities restricted prostitution to certain neighborhoods.[36] U.S. troops occupied the city of Vera Cruz, Mexico, in 1914, and the army and the Red Cross undertook enforcement of a segregated district and medical inspection there. A writer for the social work journal *The Survey* took pains to emphasize the superiority of U.S. oversight of the system. Where Mexican officials were all male, lax in finding clandestine prostitutes, and susceptible to bribery, the U.S. military was more efficient, and the Red Cross more sensitive to the possible embarrassment or even abuse when only men were conducting the examination. "Upon the occupation of Vera Cruz by the American forces, an army physician was placed in charge of each civil hospital in Vera Cruz, and female nurses were assigned to assist in rounding up all prostitutes and in making the examinations."[37] In 1916, a popular magazine in the United States described the difficulties faced by U.S. troops encamped on the Mexican border in pursuit of Pancho Villa: "intemperance and immorality" were the two things that endangered troop strength. It added, "Although all may be quiet along the Rio Grande, as long as our regulars and militia are stationed there, yet they remain liable to the physical and moral perils that in camp life act as the enemy within the gates."[38] A surgeon described the implementation of the policy in the Pershing expedition in Mexico in 1916: "The prostitutes were surrounded by a barbed-wire fence, every woman was examined, and only those found uninfected were retained for duty."[39] Where U.S. troops went, they set up systems for controlling prostitution and venereal disease, generally medical inspection, segregation, and regulation of prostitutes—in short, measures similar to the British CD Acts. Likewise, towns in Texas, Arizona, and Florida where troops were garrisoned to fight "foreign" threats also implemented reglementation policies, as did briefly occupied cities like Vera Cruz.[40]

After 1898, the United States clearly had colonies, and in these areas, too, the military instituted registration. In Cuba, the U.S. military government briefly repealed (1898) then reinstated (1899) prostitution regulation.[41] Early in the twentieth century, the Canal Zone was a site of extensive U.S. government management of a trans-Caribbean migrant labor force; by way of analogy with the British Empire, it was rather more like Singapore and Malaya, for example, than like India. The Canal Commission frequently paid the passage for West Indian laborers to come to the Zone, a practice that got them in trouble when it was discovered that some of the laborers were women. In 1906, the *New York Independent* and the *New York Evening Post* ran articles accusing the Commission of importing prostitutes from Martinique; they responded, in a congressional inquiry, essentially that they were simply providing domestic servants and sometimes women who entered into "common law" marriages.[42] According to a later (1923) report by a military physician stationed there, after the canal was completed,

> The system of the segregated district was adopted. All prostitutes were to be forced to live in the section set aside for them; medical examination of the women was to be performed weekly; and men were to be examined prior to being permitted to enter the district. Chemical prophylaxis was to be compulsory for every man leaving the district, and police guards were to be so placed that only one entrance and one exit were available.... The objections, both moral and sentimental, in the States to a segregated district were recognized, but it was thought impossible to avoid such a district unless the military police could prevent prostitution.[43]

In the Philippines, the American military established a "tolerance" zone, or segregated district, for prostitution in 1901, ostensibly as a venereal disease control measure.[44] From 1900–02, the military also issued medical certificates to prostitutes, though the Women's Christian Temperance Union (WCTU) kept up a continuous and very public campaign against it. Ostensibly, they won; Col. Clarence Edwards of the Insular Affairs Division at the War Department agreed to stop issuing cards. In fact, as both Edwards and the WCTU knew, inspection continued, though without benefit of certificates.[45] (Indeed, in 1989, prostitutes near the Subic Bay naval base were still subject to registration and medical inspection, and base-related prostitution was among the reasons cited by the Philippine government for refusing to renew the lease for the base. But that is to get ahead of the story.)

Like other colonial powers, the United States managed domesticity in its colonies and wherever the military went in a variety of ways. In places like Vera Cruz or on the Mexican border in 1916 (there were troops stretched from Brownsville, Texas, to Nogales, Arizona), the military policy was to permit soldiers to engage in brief sexual liaisons with prostitutes, to the exclusion of allowing rape, concubinage, or marriage among the troops. At camps within the borders of Mexico, General Pershing organized prostitution inside the bounds of the military camp. Reformers from the YWCA complained vigorously about the military situation on the border, on the grounds of both vice and race; while brothels were as segregated as the military—often with black, white, and Mexican prostitutes occupying different neighborhoods—soldiers went where they liked. In defense of the border prostitution, however, military officials insisted that soldiers could not be permitted to deflower Mexican daughters or even take up with them; one officer argued, "If prostitution were not provided, these men would disobey orders, go to Mexican villages and get mixed up with the women and thereby possibly bring on war."[46] In the Canal Zone, in contrast, the U.S. government was in the business of organizing (racially homogeneous) nuclear families among the laborers; white workers were allowed to bring their wives, and the Canal Commission paid the passage of at least one group of West Indian women who served variously as laundresses, lovers, and prostitutes for the West Indian laborers. Finally, in colonies like Puerto Rico, the Philippines, and Cuba that already had a significant creole Spanish elite, the United States military simply endorsed the existing Spanish policy of protecting the families of *gente decente* (respectable people) from rowdy women, unsanitary prostitution, and the danger of contagion through "quarantine" in segregated neighborhoods, weekly or biweekly pelvic exams, and mandatory medical treatment.

The Anti-Regulation Movement and Debates over Prostitution

The CD Acts and their various colonial successors generated an international movement for repeal. It was organized under the leadership first of Josephine Butler and her English Ladies National Association (LNA), then subsequently, the American WCTU and Butler's Salvation Army. Alongside and in tandem with the women's movement for repeal there were also other kinds of (mostly male) reform groups: Protestant clergy groups, a physician movement, and after the turn of the century, their joint organizations under the medico-religious name of "social hygiene." For Butler, the WCTU, and the clergymen, the movement was a social and missionary Protestantism, with a good dose of women's rights language thrown in. In the twentieth century, it took on the mantle of science, modernity, and the state without altogether abandoning the languages of either Protestantism or women's rights. It emerged in the mid-nineteenth century as the successor to the international anti-slavery movement, and used a similar language; prostitution was "sexual slavery" or "white slavery," and the goal of the movement was "abolition." While Butler was the earliest and most visible leader of the cause of repeal in England, her movement faltered in India; while Butler was committed to repeal there, English women were divided on the issue. It was the U.S. organization, the WCTU, that most prominently carried the fight for repeal into the twentieth century. Unlike the LNA, the WCTU had already begun the work of establishing chapters throughout the world to advocate an end to "demon rum," and hence was better positioned to wage the locality-by-locality struggle to end "legalized vice," which continued until World War II. After the failure of the LNA to effect repeal in India, in part because the organization shrank drastically after the success of repeal in England in 1887, Butler turned to another temperance organization, the (largely male) Salvation Army to continue the struggle, though being smaller and expanding more slowly than the WCTU, it was forced to play second fiddle to that organization.

The history of Butler's English repeal movement is well known. As Judith Walkowitz brilliantly chronicles in *Prostitution and Victorian Society*, Victorian ladies formed a cross-class alliance with prostitutes in English port cities and garrison towns over the horror of the internal exam. Protestant ladies, too, objected for proto-feminist reasons to the CD Acts: men accused of immorality were winked at, while women suspected of the same act were detained, arrested, and subject to a humiliating medical examination. Forming the *Ladies National Association* (LNA) in tandem with the (male) National Association, women's activism proved difficult for Parliament to parry, in spite of, or perhaps because of, the fact that women lacked the vote, for it made women's political activity so much more unexpected. Where proponents of the CD Acts focused on immoral women as the cause of vice, the LNA looked to seduction and pimps, turning the problem into one of innocent women and predatory men. The English movement generated international support, sparking similar movements throughout the world, notably in the United States. In 1887, the LNA succeeded in forcing Parliament to repeal the Acts.[47]

Butler attempted to refocus the LNA on repeal in British and other colonies, and effectively kept the organization together for another thirty years around the issue of colonial repeal, although on a considerably smaller scale. The organizations' overseas networks, however, grew stronger and remained enthusiastic about continuing the repeal fight. Moreover, it seemed important to many in other European colonies that the British imperial struggle be won, as it had a direct effect on events in other colonized places. For example, in 1888, one of Josephine Butler's Dutch correspondents wrote about the social evil in the Netherlands East Indies. There, she wrote, the military considered

> introducing the Anglo-Indian system of having separate tents inhabited by the licensed women in the camps. At present at a fixed hour in the evening the doors of the Barracks are opened in order to admit a certain number of these poor victims.... The fact stated here shows that the bad example set by the English government in India is infecting Java, and no doubt other Colonies of other nations.... If you should succeed in your next great attack upon India, it will be an immense lever for us.[48]

While the U.S. center of the movement, the WCTU, is mostly remembered as a temperance group, a considerable portion of its energies went to the cause of "purity," or anti-prostitution. In 1890, half their publications were about purity; this attention increased after the turn of the century. The organization also extended its international reach, forming the World's WCTU in 1883. Colonial prostitution was a contentious issue within the organization. Two North American women, Elizabeth Wheeler Andrew and Dr. Katherine Bushnell, traveled the world for the WCTU, organizing against the regulation of prostitution. They sharply criticized an 1893 *Union Signal* editorial advocating the acquisition of Hawaii, and suggesting that North Americans could do for the progress of Hawaii what the British had done for India; Andrews argued impassionedly that the British authority in India was undermined by its support of vice. Together, they published a book, *The Queen's Daughters in India*, that condemned British registration and "inspection" of Indian prostitutes, and subsequently traveled to South Africa and elsewhere to organize a WCTU chapter to oppose the CD Acts. Meanwhile, enterprising women journalists wrote stories of women's unwilling bondage to exploitive men in Hawaii, India, Hong Kong, and the Philippines for the *Union Signal*.[49]

The repeal movement in South Africa was typical of the sort developed by the WWCTU. Development of the temperance movement in South Africa was the biggest factor in organizing opposition to these new acts. With the establishment of the Huguenot Seminary in 1874, staffed partly by American missionaries with close ties to Mount Holyoke College in Massachusetts, the temperance and purity movements developed a center. At their instigation, Mrs. Mary Leavitt of the WCTU visited the Cape in May 1889, and seminary students and their teachers organized a South African WCTU. Also the Salvation Army arrived in 1883 and a local branch of the YMCA in 1865; both were involved in social purity work. The WCTU started a rescue home in Cape Town, and in 1891, passed a resolution stating that, "As a Union, our hearts burn within us at the indignity done to women through the Contagious Diseases Act, and we pledge ourselves to use our influence to bring about its repeal." In August 1891, Elizabeth Wheeler Andrew and Dr. Katherine Bushnell visited the Cape as part of the tour initially commissioned to study the CD Acts in India. In 1901, the Cape Attorney-General argued for repression rather than regulation of prostitution, telling the House of Assembly that,

> There are certain houses in Cape Town which any Kaffir could frequent, and as long as he was able to pay the sum demanded, he could have illicit intercourse with these white European women. This was a matter of the gravest importance, for once the barriers were broken down between the European and native races in this country, there was no limit to the terrible dangers to which women would be submitted, particularly in isolated places.

In the Transvaal, Africans who had sex with white prostitutes were punished. In 1902, the Aliens Immigration Act barred the immigration of Eastern European Jews, and virtually eliminated continental prostitution at the Cape. The CD Act was repealed in 1919. As the woman suffrage movement took off, it was leading suffragists like Julia Solly and Olive Schriener who were the main opponents of the CD Acts.[50]

However, not all the leadership of the WCTU was convinced of the need for repeal in India or elsewhere in the tropics. Indeed, an irreconcilable break occurred between Josephine Butler and the WCTU precisely over the issue of the CD Acts in India, with Butler calling for colonial repeal, and the U.S. organization taking the position that domestic repeal was sufficient.[51] Despite its years of opposition to medical inspection, the National (North American) WCTU had long entertained a certain ambivalence with respect to colonial contexts. When Butler pushed the campaign against the CD Acts into India in the 1890s, she encountered resistance from her compatriot, Lady Henry Somerset of the WCTU, who publicly endorsed regulation in India. Frances Willard, the North American president of the WCTU and close friend of Lady Henry Somerset, expressed her ambivalence over the conflict. "We in America have practically no standing army; we have no 'oriental difficulties,'" wrote Willard, whereas "the British Government must deal with 'a condition and not a theory.'" Willard's remarks were taken to be supportive of Somerset, provoking a major conflict within the WWCTU and ultimately causing Butler and numerous chapter leaders in the British colonies to openly break with the WCTU in 1897. The year before, ironically, "America" did acquire its own version of "oriental difficulties" in the tropics.[52] Willard's death a year later enabled the organization to return to the issue of repeal with all its former zeal, though not before providing a window into the ambivalence within the movement about advocating rights for colonized women.

The repeal movement in the colonies did employ a language of women's rights to argue for an end to the CD Acts. The NA and the WCTU deployed a notion of sanctified womanhood, reduced from a natural dignity to state of wretchedness because of men's cruelty and lust. Indian women, argued

Butler, were "helpless, voiceless, hopeless. Their helplessness appeals to the heart ... these pitiful Indian women, girls, children, as many of them are. They have not even the small power of resistance which the western woman may have." This sort of language cropped up, too, in the WCTU's official newspaper, *The Union Signal*. While on the face of it this seems to be an essentially egalitarian argument, locating woman's rights on an international scale, it was also excessive and exaggerated. The language of sentimentality deployed in the Indian context indicated a fundamental mistrust of colonized women's ability to defend themselves. Antoinette Burton has argued that the idiom of Indian women's victimization produced a logic in which English ladies were active, assertive, capable of controlling their bodies and defending others, while Indian women were passive, dependent, and in need of being defended.[53] Sentimentality is not an innocent language; it produces the speaker as someone who is the master of her fate, while the spoken about needs her protection.

Defenders of the Acts, too, deployed a language of woman's rights. Prostitution was the bulwark of the family, they argued, protecting innocent women and girls from men's lust. Drawing on early Christian writings, some (especially Catholics) compared prostitution to a sewer, as a necessary outlet for filth that kept the rest of the city clean. In places like Singapore, where Chinese and Japanese labor migration was extensive, English defenders of the CD Acts and similar regulation argued that the acts were a progressive measure, preventing indentured servitude or other forms of forced prostitution. Within Japan, liberals defended the acts on these grounds as well. The state, they argued, could rescue women held against their will, but only if registration made governments an essential third party to the two-way contract between the pimp or brothel-owner and the woman or her family.[54] Another kind of defense of the Acts was the assertion that they protected laborers' wives and children by preventing their fathers' and husbands' acquiring VD from prostitutes.[55] In places like India and the Cape, two kinds of women's rights arguments for the Acts held sway. First, following the trajectory of tropical medicine's expansion into "native" areas, the advocates of the CD Acts argued that women were receiving treatment for their diseases which they otherwise would not get, and that the possession of a registration ticket improved a woman's ability to entice soldiers, hence her earning potential.[56] Second, as we have seen, white women and their families were endangered by nurses and domestic servants who might carry VD.

These struggles over who spoke for women, public health, and medical progress were complicated by the question of alliance with the state power of the colonizer. While on the face of it defenders allied themselves with the state and repealers did not, their relationships to the state became increasingly indistinguishable. As one historian points out, for England, "long before the

Acts were repealed, the hard core of the Antis had moved on to demanding 'social purity,' censorship, legislation against male homosexuals, and school crusades against masturbation."[57] Furthermore, advocates of repeal of the CD Acts also supported the abolition of prostitution, a fact whose importance increased in the twentieth century, when the Americans especially began to advocate widespread imprisonment of prostitutes. Explicitly built on the model of "rescue homes," wherein Protestant women attempted the work of "reclaiming" and rehabilitating the prostitutes who came to them, imprisonment in state and federal facilities also bore more than a passing resemblance to the "lock hospitals" that repealers had spent decades condemning.[58]

The alliance of the anti-regulation forces with the state became increasingly prominent in the years leading up to World War I, when the WCTU explicitly undertook work under the auspices of the U.S. government and the U.S. military. Even before then, however, the purity movement took up the banner of "social hygiene," a term associated with physicians and reformers with close ties to government and business. An international physicians' campaign for "Sanitary and Moral Prophylaxis," offered an ideology that was tremendously appealing to "purity" workers, specifically through popular education in a number of countries to focus attention on the danger that venereal disease posed to wives and children of "immoral" men. Begun by Alfred Fournier at the turn of the century in France (where Fournier's research on neo-natal syphilis provided another expression of that country's panic about "depopulation"),[59] the movement construed venereal disease as a threat to the family:

> Of syphilis it may be said that it is a most pernicious foe to the family; it is antagonistic to all that the family stands for. The function of the family is to create life, the effect of syphilis is to damage or destroy life. The function of the family is to produce children, healthy, well-formed and vigorous; the effect of syphilis is to so vitiate the process of nutrition that it results in beings blighted in their development and stamped with physical and mental inferiority.

Where Fournier largely urged attention to syphilis, an American, Prince A. Morrow, added gonorrhea, claiming that, "The influence of gonorrhea as a depopulating factor is even more marked," and that "the racial danger of gonococcus infection is especially manifest in its sterilizing influence upon the procreative capacity of both men and women." Morrow argued that

> The dangers to the health and life of the mother which come from the introduction of these diseases into marriage ... form the saddest chapter in the martyrdom of women. [I] direct your attention [also] to the racial dangers of these infections, manifest not only in the loss of potential citizens to the State, but in the production of physical and mental weaklings, the blind, the deaf mutes, the epileptic, and other degenerates who fill many of our institutions for defectives and impose an enormous cost upon the community for their support.[60]

Morrow, following Fournier, effectively argued that venereal disease was not just a "tropical" problem affecting non-white women and the colonial military, but one affecting the reproduction of all of the cherished institutions of the metropole: innocent womanhood, babies, the family, the "race," and the nation. It was a tremendously effective argument, one taken up by both Butler's groups and the WCTU. The CD Acts promulgated in India, argued a repealer echoing Fournier, "cannot leave unimpaired the sanctity or happiness of the English home."[61]

Languages of scientific progress and women's rights continued to certify the positions of both regulationists and repealers, authorizing extensive intervention into the organization of domesticity for colonizer and colonized. Whether pronouncing on the servant problem in South Africa or paying the passage for women in Martinique to provide Canal Zone laborers with sex and/or clean laundry and companionship, colonizing governments and their liberal reformers disagreed with each other over the proper form of colonial domestic arrangements, but agreed on the need for their management. In the international colonial system, there were only a handful of available positions. Prostitution and domestic policies were not organized in response to local situations, or only very generally; instead, they emerged from a handful of boilerplate models, indebted mostly to the British Empire. The United States, far from belonging to the international colonial community only through its response to a series of accidents (paradigmatically the explosion of the battleship *Maine*), was conspicuously part of a colonizing system, evident in its adoption of British and other colonial norms for the organization of prostitution.

Puerto Rico

A version of the CD Acts, the institution of a "red light" district and mandatory medical inspection, was instituted in Puerto Rico under Spanish rule in 1876. This act, echoing the activities of other colonies, ended a half-century-long period of repression. It coincided with a period of growing urbanization, particularly in San Juan (which had historically been the island's second most important city, after Ponce). Prostitution seems to have been increasing in San Juan in this period, with the migration of many unmarried male laborers, the city's growing importance as a naval port, and the migration of many impoverished and young women, presumably seeking domestic or sex work.[62] The institution of the segregated district for prostitutes also immediately followed the abolition of slavery, and was part of an extensive system of limiting the movements of freed laborers, black and white. By the 1890s, the majority of the women in San Juan were black or mixed race.

Puerto Rico and Cuba were the last outposts of the Spanish empire in the Americas, most of which had become independent nations in a string of revolutions in the first decades of the nineteenth century. At the end of that century, it seemed clear that these, too, were destined to separate themselves from Spain, with a revolution in Cuba beginning in 1895 and the stirrings of a liberal autonomist movement in Puerto Rico. However, the long delay had worked to produce one of Latin America's more conservative ruling classes in Puerto Rico. Puerto Rico shared with the Dominican Republic the distinction of being the only Spanish American colonies without a significant movement for independence from Spain. For both, their proximity to Haiti inaugurated a peculiar feature of political demography following its 1801 revolution: they became the recipients of wave after wave of conservative (monarchist) colonists, fleeing with their slaves from the republican, slave, and Indian revolts that rocked the West Indies, South America, and Spain in the first half of the century. This trend was slowed in the Dominican Republic by the Haitian occupation of 1822-44, but continued unabated in Puerto Rico. Indeed, the tendency was exacerbated with the granting in 1815 of the *Cédula de Gracias*, in which the Spanish crown attempted to "whiten" the population by offering land grants for white immigrants and their slaves, about six acres for every free white and three for every slave. Puerto Rico was thus one of the last regions in the Americas to abolish slavery, maintaining it until 1873, and even then sharply limiting the autonomy of free black and white laborers, whose movements were controlled through a *libreta* (passbook) system.[63]

There was, nevertheless, a significant Liberal Autonomist movement in Puerto Rico, one whose fortunes rose or fell according to the fate of liberals in Spain. They strongly endorsed registration as essential to a "modern" nation, enjoining a sharp geographic separation between *gente decente* and prostitutes. As the leader of the Puerto Rican liberal movement, Luis Muñoz Rivera, wrote in 1893:

> We pity the fallen woman, but we must avoid at all costs her contact with the honorable woman. Let us offer shelter and bread to the Magdalene who repents. But total rejection is the only possible response to the Magdalene who persists in dirtying herself. In this way, her contaminating spray will not reach our face, nor tarnish the purity of our society.[64]

In the liberal stronghold of Ponce, on the southern coast, the late 1890s saw a severe crackdown on prostitution. Prostitutes were required to carry a *libreta* showing their medical stamp; those who did not were thrown in jail. The police sweeps apparently picked up women who were not prostitutes; Eileen Findlay's careful reading of newspapers from the period finds numerous petitions from women demanding to be release from jail who claimed that they were married, in consensual unions, and/or gainfully employed. That these would qualify as defenses clarifies that the police action was aimed at poor, unattached, disorderly women.

The invasion by North Americans in 1898 and the institution of a military government represented losses for the Autonomist Party. In 1897, Liberal

Autonomists had managed to wring some concessions from Spain, including an autonomist charter and a seat in the Spanish legislature. The advent of American rule nullified these rights, and threw the local economy into disarray by upsetting trade relations with Europe. What the North Americans did not disrupt, nature did, as a succession of hurricanes finished off coffee agriculture, the traditional basis of both small-holders and the *hacendado* (plantation) elite of the mountainous regions, allowing Americans eventually to build a monopoly in sugar agriculture. Many members of the ruling classes returned to Spain, France, and elsewhere in Europe.

According to both U.S. officials and the public, one of the purposes of the U.S. presence was to improve public health and reduce unnecessary mortality. As one traveler's narrative had it:

> When the Americans took possession of Porto Rico it was one of the dirtiest, filthiest, and most unsanitary of countries. Lack of adequate water supply, carelessness, and an utter ignorant disregard for the simplest rules of hygiene and sanitation had made the island a menace to human health, life, and comfort.

By 1914, when this traveler's tale was published, he could confidently say:

> There is no greater monument or more lasting proof of the triumph of modern sanitation and science than the present condition of Porto Rico as compared to its past state. To-day Porto Rico is one of the cleanest, the most sanitary, and the healthiest of countries, and it is doubtful if another city in the world can compare with San Juan for cleanliness and health. There is every reason for a reasonably careful person to live free from all ills and die of old age.[65]

Public health was a constant component of different kinds of writings about Puerto Rico. Journalist Sylvester Baxter claimed that, "The island's record in sanitation has a world-wide import," emphasizing the U.S. military's work related to identifying the pathogen associated with hookworm. He suggests that in matters of public health, these "fruits of the War with Spain have a value so incalculable that in comparison all other fruits of the conflict seem insignificant." A writer for the *Nation*, arguing for continued American involvement in insular affairs, insisted that, "It cannot be emphasized too strongly that the Porto Ricans are a sick people."[66] Despite these lofty goals, from 1898–1902, the death rate increased steadily; for the next 25 years, it remained more or less constant.[67] In other words, in the context of international gains in public health and longevity, the accelerated concentration of wealth in a few hands—mostly American—effected by the U.S. presence probably made the health circumstances of the majority of the population worse, rhetorics of science notwithstanding.

American efforts to control prostitution were certainly affected by both economic disorder and the rhetoric of public health. Despite weak efforts to abolish it, Puerto Rican and U.S. military officials maintained in force a policy that required registration at the "Special Hospital for Women" in San Juan (or elsewhere for non-residents) and mandatory medical treatment if found ill.[68] This de facto state of things was formalized in 1905, and until 1917, prostitutes were required to undergo weekly medical examinations at the Special Hospital for Women—in permanent quarters beginning in 1905—and those outside the city had to register at local police stations.[69] Just as the Spanish had, the United States endorsed a policy that attempted to segregate prostitution from respectable folk as a bureaucratic and public health solution worthy of a modern nation.

The U.S. administration also attempted to organize nuclear families among poor people in Puerto Rico. In the first of several twentieth century efforts to reduce the number of people in "consensual unions" or common law marriages—the official marriage rate was only around fifty percent in 1899—U.S. officials introduced a series of measures to encourage marriage. As the attorney general for Puerto Rico, A.C. Sharpe put it,

> Family life is the recognized basis of true civilization. American law and institutions regard the relation of the husband and wife as one of the most sacred guarantees for the perpetuity of the state. Marriage is recognized as the only lawful relation by which Providence has permitted the continuance of the human race, and the history of mankind has proved it to be one of the chief foundations of social order.

With the future of civilization, the state, and the human race dependent on marriage, U.S. colonial officials in 1899 passed laws allowing civil matrimony—without benefit of priest—and eliminating fees associated with marriage. When these did little to change the marriage rate, in 1902 the legislature passed a law allowing the full right to divorce—making Puerto Rico the first place in Latin America to permit it. What followed was not the intended acceleration of the marriage rate, but an explosion of divorce petitions—including women complaining of marital infidelity and domestic abuse. Unintentionally, colonial officials handed Puerto Rican women and feminists a potent new weapon in their struggles for equality.[70]

Missionary women, in contrast, sided with colonial officials in the effort to produce respectable families. There was an active and effective WCTU chapter in Puerto Rico, which although initially uninterested in the "purity" cause, nevertheless located themselves symbolically and metaphorically in a family tableau. The chapter was organized in response to a temperance referendum on the island, and sponsored small morality plays in their ultimately successful effort to drum up support for temperance among Puerto Rican voters. Edith Hildreth, then vice-president of the chapter, reported that at a play held at the YMCA: "Uncle Sam, the twenty-six dry states, and the District of Columbia were featured. A small native boy, in tears, took the part of Porto Rico, and in response to a question from Uncle Sam he replied, 'I want to get in on this, too!'" She added, "Great applause greeted the words of the child."[71] This image, figuring Puerto Rico as a small child (in tears, no less)—here cast in the masculine, probably a response to the rather awkward problem that despite their campaigning, women could not vote—was a motif that was to be reiterated in a later anti-prostitution campaign. Members' activism was attributed to the WCTU's "motherly instinct."[72]

Among their first acts, U.S. colonial officials worked to organize domesticity in Puerto Rico, including "sanitary" prostitution and nuclear families. There was nothing particularly unique or original about these acts; they belonged to an international organization of colonial militaries, laborers, and creole families. In Puerto Rico, we can see how domesticity was both a lever for transforming and reorganizing the colonial state and an utterly banal exercise.

Conclusion

In a review article provocatively titled "Where Is the Postcolonial History of Medicine?" Warwick Anderson argues that historians of medicine have singularly failed to see the ways that Western medicine is colonial. He argues that rather than look to European germ theory as an "origin" of one thing or another, we ought rather to see a different circuit of scientific theory and medical practice: the ways military organizations of public health in the colonies were brought home to the metropole. "During the early twentieth century," he writes,

> medical officers from the United States developed a public health program in the Philippines more structured along the lines of new practices of colonial warfare than following the contours of the latest European theory. In late-nineteenth-century colonial wars, with dispersed and mobile military forces whose goal was the reformation of the population, the occupying power was obliged to collect intelligence (which is simply the medical and military knowledge of foreign bodies) and to develop effective means of communication, standardization, and registration.

Anderson argues that germ theory (the epoch-maker of medical history) didn't *determine* anything; rather, it was deployed in the service of an overall military strategy. Finally, it was to return to the mainland in the form of repressive measures for quarantine control, often under the leadership of the same physicians who organized the Philippine campaign.[73]

I have been arguing in a parallel vein that the venereal disease control measure of prostitution registration participated in a somewhat less familiar colonial circuit, that constituted by the cultural work of organizing bourgeois domesticity. Like Anderson, I would contend that the changing science and medicine of venereal disease was as much an effect as a cause of the CD Acts and their colonial corollaries. Following Stoler, I have argued that domesticity was organized in the colonies, not the metropoles. By way of corollary, it stands to reason that the disputes over the CD Acts and the regulation of prostitution were not primarily metropolitan but colonial events. I have endeavored to show that the CD Acts' existence in the colonies preceded, followed, and exceeded their metropolitan existence; properly told, regulation in London, Paris, and St. Louis would be footnotes to an essentially colonial narrative. *Contra* the American exceptionalist account, I have argued that registration and medical examination were U.S. policy as well. Colonialism, far from being a series of disparate events, was a system, and one from which we cannot exclude the United States. The political and cultural organization of families was one of its products, and one of the things that organized it. The work of producing "modernity" in the colonies had a great deal to do with creating and organizing nuclear families.

4

IMAGINING THE "NEW JEWISH FAMILY"

Gender and Nation in Early Zionism

ALISON ROSE

In the midst of an escalating crisis of Jewish identity in fin-de-siècle Vienna, the Austrian Jewish journalist and playwright Theodor Herzl (1860–1904) founded the movement known as political Zionism.[1] After fantasizing about other far-fetched solutions to the Jewish problem, ranging from challenging anti-Semitic leaders to a duel in order to defend Jewish honor, to organizing a mass conversion of the Jews to Catholicism, Herzl ultimately settled on the Zionist notion and poured all of his energy into the creation of a Jewish political entity and the Zionist movement. While many of his contemporaries believed he had lost his sanity, and his employer, Moritz Benedikt, the Jewish editor of the Viennese daily *Die Neue Freie Presse* prohibited him from publishing any of his Zionist ideas in that paper, Herzl succeeded in rapidly expanding his circle and in creating an organized international movement with its own press and yearly congresses. Many important personalities such as Max Nordau, Martin Buber, Nathan Birnbaum, Heinrich York-Steiner, and Leon Kellner joined Herzl in his Zionist mission, central to which was the establishment of a Jewish state.

The Zionist movement of the late nineteenth century responded to the ever-increasing awareness of the potential danger of life in exile. *Galut* (exile) had been a defining characteristic of Jewish life for nearly two thousand years, from the time of the destruction of the Second Temple to the creation of the State of Israel in 1948. The term refers to the feelings of a nation uprooted from its homeland and subject to alien rule. While the term Diaspora (dispersion) refers to the situation in which many members of a nation live outside the homeland, *galut* applies only when there is no longer a political-ethnic center. Within their situation of exile, the Jews in the premodern period maintained a degree of separateness, which shielded them from external influences. With the coming of Jewish emancipation, the traditional isolation of the ghetto, the secluded residential quarter for Jews, would gradually give way to the forces of modernity. Many Jews in Eastern Europe, where modernization occurred later, continued to live relatively isolated traditional lives in the *shtetl* and small Jewish towns until the Russian Revolution. The Yiddish term for a small town, *shtetl*, describes not only a unit of dwelling but a way of living. Life in the *shtetl* revolved around the closely knit and intimate community where the home and the larger culture were intertwined. This lifestyle became the focus of both the nostalgia and the criticism of Zionists.

Over time, Zionism became factionalized. The two primary factions, political and cultural Zionism, differed both in the way they envisioned the nature of the future Jewish state as well as in their understanding of the priorities of the nascent movement. While political Zionists, such as Herzl and Max Nordau, believed that the struggle must focus on building a nation in order to put the Jews on equal standing and restore them as a strong and independent people, cultural Zionists, such as Buber, Berthold Feiwel, and the Russian Jewish writer Ahad Ha'am (Asher Ginzberg) asserted that the Jews' return to Judaism and the restoration of a Jewish culture must precede, or at the very least accompany, the establishment of a Jewish state. The political Zionists, influenced by the concerns of West or Central European Jewry, focused their attention on the dual crises of assimilation and anti-Semitism. The cultural Zionists, in contrast, were influenced by the East European perspective and prioritized the need to solve the problems of Jewish life in Eastern Europe, such as poverty and overcrowded living conditions which stifled the development of Jewish spiritual and cultural life. It was within these frameworks that the early Zionists imagined and conceived the nature of the new Jewish state and its citizens. By examining images of the new Jewish family in the pre-state Zionist period, this chapter will demonstrate how Zionists envisioned a transformation of the Jewish family and gender relationships in order to serve the foundation of the Jewish state. In doing so, I will focus on relatively unexplored terrain, examining the role of the Jewish family as constructed in the imaginations of early Zionists. Among other things, I will show that while a clear image of the "new Jew" emerged in Zionist writings, the image of the "new Jewish woman" became inextricably connected with the emergence of a "new Jewish family" and her role within it.

The Jewish family has historically been idealized as warm, supportive, and nurturing. In times of crisis, the Jewish family and home served as a refuge from a hostile world, at least in theory.[2] However, the forces of modernity threatened to change the structure of the Jewish family and this became an increasing concern for certain Jewish intellectuals. Michael Meyer describes the transformation of Jewish identity in the modern world as an emerging Jewish self-consciousness, which contrasted with the all-encompassing character of Jewish existence in the ghetto.[3] He writes, "In pre-modern times the congruity between family and society prevented Jewish identity from becoming a problem."[4] Meyer describes how the process of modernization, from a Jewish perspective, threatened to break this continuity by exposing Jews to non-Jewish ideas, causing a conflict with the forces of tradition. Chae Ran Freeze has recently demonstrated that the Jewish family of Eastern Europe, which served as a basic institution for social bonding and cultural transmission, resisted the challenges of modernity, but "it was hardly immune to change and inevitably reflected the broader transformations in nineteenth century society."[5]

In this connection, nineteenth-century Jews—social scientists, communal and religious leaders, and Zionists alike—raised concerns about the negative impact of modernity, specifically certain social issues such as the decrease in Jewish fertility, intermarriage, prostitution and vice, and divorce, on the future of the Jewish family. According to Mitchell B. Hart, "Zionist demographers took the statistics on declining birth rates and rising intermarriage and conversion rates as the surest indicators of the crisis modernity presented to the Jewish people."[6] In a sense, Zionism proposed a dual solution to these concrete and quantifiable problems. On the one hand, the Jewish homeland or nation would replace the traditional Jewish home as a sanctuary from the dangers of modernity. The Jewish citizens of the new Jewish state would in a sense be transformed into one big *mishpochah* (extended family), and the homeland in itself would constitute one large and safe refuge from a hostile world. On the other hand, the new Jewish state would address social problems, such as intermarriage and declining fertility rates, and insure the Jewish future.

In addition to the growing concern with demographic trends resulting from forces of modernity, Viennese Zionists mounted a critique of assimilated Western Jewry as morally and physically degenerate.[7] Jewish Emancipation and its antecedents were predicated on the notion that by giving up their traditional isolation and autonomy and becoming modern citizens of the state, Jews would earn equal rights. This implicitly assumed that by assimilating, or relegating Jewish identity to a purely religious and individual realm, problems such as Jew-hatred would disappear. With the rise of modern anti-Semitism in Western Europe and the continuation of anti-Jewish violence in Eastern Europe, Jews in various segments of the community began to argue that assimilation had failed to bring about its intended result. Zionists argued that in leaving the ghetto, the Jews had abandoned their traditions but had not succeeded in actually joining the general society. Through long periods of isolation they had become degenerate, both physically and morally. After being subjected to years of confinement, emancipated Jews were exposed to the pressures of city life, where it was thought they became more prone to mental disturbances and weakness of the nerves. The term assimilation, defined by social scientists as a structural and measurable phenomenon, became a polemical tool burdened with negative connotations yet lacking a clear meaning. Zionists used it to describe non-Zionists and vice versa. Zionists incorporated aspects of the socialist view, found in Karl Marx's essay "On the Jewish Question," which criticized the materialism of German Jews.[8] The materialism of the bourgeois Jews in turn prevented them from integrating successfully and led to their negative traits, causing the rise of anti-Semitism. Hugo Bergmann (1883–1975), a leading figure in the Prague Zionist student organization "Bar Kochba," epitomizes the intensity of these criticisms:

> These gifted Jews are champions of atheism and materialism, subversives and demagogues, present wherever people wish to be hyper-modern, i.e. to destroy values that have endured for centuries. Jews—even women—are marching at the head of the agitation directed against marriage and the family, and share, as leaders and led, in all the perversities of present-day urban society.[9]

In short, the typical Zionist stance held that whether they remained in the ghetto or tried to integrate into European society, the Jews would remain degenerate until they removed themselves from European society and returned to their homeland. The only viable solution to the Jewish crisis, therefore, lay in the Zionist movement.

Women and Gender in the Zionist Movement

Research has begun to focus upon the roles played by women and the discourse of gender in the Zionist movement.[10] David Biale writes, "Zionism promised an erotic revolution for the Jews: the creation of a virile New Hebrew Man as well as rejection of the inequality of women in traditional Judaism in favor of full equality between the sexes in all spheres of life."[11] In practice, however, the notion of a virile New Hebrew Man inhibited the realization of an egalitarian society. According to Michael Berkowitz, Zionism was "a predominantly and self-consciously male affair."[12] Despite Zionism's proclaimed openness toward women, they remained marginal in the movement. "In part the luster of Zionism derived from its claim to have created an equitable order between Jewish men and women. It is no surprise that this myth does not hold up to scrutiny, regarding the movement in Europe or the yishuv." The Zionist movement concentrated on distancing itself from perceived traditional gender relationships of the East European *shtetl*, in which the physically weak (yet at the same time privileged, due to his access to Jewish learning) Jewish man was dominated by his strong-willed and worldly wife. In contrast, Zionism criticized the bourgeois Jewish woman for not working for the Zionist movement, as well as failing to attend to the Jewish religious and cultural needs of the family. In this sense, Zionists idealized the domestic attributes of the traditional Jewish woman.

The transformation of the Jewish family in the Zionist imagination should be understood in the context of the Zionist discourse of gender and stereotypes of Jewish gender roles. In responding to a longstanding stereotype of the femininity of the Diaspora Jewish male, which had so deeply entered into

Jewish self-consciousness of the period (evidenced in the writings of Otto Weininger in particular, as well as many others), Herzl and his contemporaries saw in Jewish nationalism a redemption of sorts.[13] In achieving nationhood through the political establishment of a Jewish state, the Jews would also transform their nature and refine their masculinity through engagement in the productive physical work of nation building. Klaus Hödl argues that in attempting to modernize the traditional relationship between the sexes in Judaism, Viennese Zionists defined the role of the woman primarily as educator of the family.[14] "The 'Eshet Hayil' (Woman of Valor) of the *shtetl* world, namely the hardworking, dynamic woman of traditional Jewish society, became the housewife, who was entirely dependent on her husband. The earlier 'masculine' type of East European Jewish woman was detached from the ideal of the 'lady,' that is, she was 'feminized' through the attribution of new qualities."[15] Zionists criticized the physically weak male Jew, arguing for the need to restructure gender relationships, and to modernize institutions such as traditional marriages arranged on the basis of material concerns rather than true compatibility and love. Nevertheless, they still tended to romanticize the traditional Jewish women as fulfilling their roles as guardians of Jewish tradition and maintaining the integrity of Jewish family life.[16]

The "gendered politics" of European and, more precisely, German nationalism also shaped the way Jewish nationalism incorporated gender. In his pioneering study of the relationship between nationalism and respectability, or the need to control sexuality, George Mosse pointed out that modern nationalism and respectability emerged at roughly the same time, and formed a mutually beneficial alliance.[17] This alliance served to strengthen the distinction between the sexes by asserting it as a bourgeois ideal. "Woman was the embodiment of respectability; even as defender and protector of her people she was assimilated to her traditional role as woman and mother, the custodian of tradition, who kept nostalgia alive in the active world of men."[18] More recently, describing the emergence and interaction of ideologies of national identity and gender identity among middle-class German-speaking Austrians during the 1880s, Pieter Judson demonstrates that assigning sex identity to national categories like patriotism co-opted the support of women. At the same time, nationalism aimed to unite divergent groups that otherwise might have erupted into conflict, such as social classes and sexes. For these reasons, ideologies about gender emerged alongside ideologies of nationalism.[19] Zionism, like other nationalist ideologies, drew upon a discourse combining the language of nation and gender. It has been suggested that this language was spoken as a matter of course from a masculine voice. As Margalit Shilo remarks, "the Zionist revolution, like other national movements, centered on masculinity.... The Zionist movement encouraged male solidarity as a central constituent in the building of the nation. Zionism and masculinity were practically synonymous."[20]

Political Zionism and the New Jewish Family

This background influenced the way male Zionists envisioned (or failed to envision) the role of women in the future state. Max Nordau (1849–1923) popularized the notion of "Judaism with muscles," suggesting that the Jews needed to become physically and sexually healthy by returning to nature, sports, and physical work.[21] However, his image of the new Jewish woman remained ambiguous. At first he opposed the movement for women's emancipation; later, he felt that emancipation would make little difference because he believed women would not be able to overcome their family-centered nature. According to Nordau, women were needed to temper the harshness of life by serving as mothers and homemakers.[22]

Nordau had expressed his views of bourgeois marriage in his early work, before he became sensitized to his Jewish identity and attracted to the Zionist movement. In *Die conventionellen Lügen der Kulturmenschheit* (The Conventional Lies of Our Civilization) (1883), he mounted a criticism of the bourgeois conceptions of marriage and sexuality.

> Marriage is the only kind of union between man and woman countenanced by our society. But what have the lies of our corrupt civilization done to marriage? It has been diminished to a business agreement that gives as much place to love as the contract between two capitalists who form a commercial partnership. The pretext of marriage is still, as ever, the preservation of the species, but this is a pathetic lie, for the contemporary marriage has nothing to do with the mutual biological attraction of two sexual beings but with common material interests.... When a wedding is planned, everything is considered—the living room and the kitchen, the caterers and the honeymoon; only one thing is forgotten—the bedroom, in which the future of the family, the nation, the human race is created. Must not decay and ruin become the fate of nations in which the egoism of the couple triumphs in the marriage, while the child in the same is an undesirable, at best, an indifferent accident, a not easily avoidable, but thoroughly unimportant consequence?[23]

This passage not only demonstrates Nordau's Darwinian position on human sexuality, but it also has a strong resonance when read in light of the connection between family and nation and the future Zionist movement. If the bourgeois notion of marriage, which centered on meeting the material needs of the two parties rather than their sexual needs, would lead to the doom of the nation, it follows that the reorganization of marriage and family would be essential in securing the survival of a new nation. The solution could not be to dissolve the institution of marriage, because that would leave women at a disadvantage. Rather, Nordau's solution lay in requiring that any civilized society provide for the material needs of its women to alleviate the need for them to sell themselves through marriage or prostitution.[24]

Nordau repeated this message in his plays, *The Right to Love* (1893) and *Doktor Kohn* (1902).[25] Both told stories of tragic love affairs, which resulted from the limitations of society's conventions in love and marriage. In *The Right to Love*, the wife decided to leave her husband for her seducer, only to discover that the seducer had no interest in marrying her or in raising her children. She returned to her husband to live a loveless bourgeois marriage of convenience rather than a marriage based on physical attraction. *Doktor Kohn*, written after Nordau became involved in the Zionist movement, is a similar story with a Jewish theme. Dr. Kohn, a Jewish university lecturer in mathematics, refused to convert to Christianity in order to attain a professorship. A proud Zionist, he also loved and planned to marry a Christian woman, Christine. This brought about a complex set of circumstances leading to Christine's brother insulting Dr. Kohn, exclaiming, "A man of honor would not bring discord into a united family." Because Dr. Kohn felt that he had not only to defend his own honor but also that of the Jewish people, he was forced to fight a duel in which he was shot and killed. Thus, due to the social conventions of the times which determined the suitability of matches—in this case, anti-Semitism—the fate of this couple was tragic. These plays and the ideas put forward by Nordau in *Conventional Lies* demonstrate his belief in the importance of family serving and strengthening the nation. However, when Nordau spoke of the Zionist solution in his well-known address to a Zionist gymnastic club in 1903, calling for the creation of a *muskeljudentum* (Jewry of muscles), he focused exclusively on the transformation of male Jews from the persecuted and weak ghetto Jews to "deep-chested, tightly muscled, courageous men."[26]

Herzl also lacked a clear, consistent notion of the role of women in the Jewish state. Like other Zionists, when it came to women and Zionism, he stressed their passivity. His views have been attributed to a number of factors, including the influence of his cultural milieu and his personal relationships with women.[27] In much of his work, Herzl expressed the view that the means to attract women to the cause lay in their contribution to building a new Jewish family. He aimed to redirect the virtues of Jewish women for the cause and at the same time to rehabilitate their negative traits (just as with Jewish men) through their work on behalf of the Jewish state. In all his work, he regarded the upper class Jewish women, and with them the typical bourgeois families of Western and Central Europe, with great disdain. Yet he idealized the self-sacrificing, hardworking woman who devoted herself to the Zionist cause and praised the Jewish woman who left politics to men and devoted herself to family.

In an address before the Women's Zionist Association in Vienna (*Wiener zionistische Frauenverein*), Herzl declared that women had not contributed significantly to the Zionist cause.[28] He began the speech (which he described in his diary as "a rather absent-minded lecture"[29]) by suggesting that while women had contributed practically nothing to Zionism, they could potentially, through the use of successful propaganda, become everything. He also claimed that Zionism would make women into better mothers. As they became more educated, he explained, they would understand how important Zionism was for children, the citizens of the future. In *Der Judenstaat* (The Jewish State, 1896), the pamphlet in which he set out his plans for a political solution to the Jewish question, Herzl did not specifically envision a transformation in the nature of the Jewish woman as part of the creation of a new society. Rather, he suggested the creation of a new Jewish family, as a solution to the "degeneration" of Jewish life in *galut*. "Members of a new civilization marry young. This will promote general morality and ensure sturdiness in the new generation; and thus we shall have no delicate offspring of late marriages, children of fathers who spent their strength in the struggles of life."[30] This vision of the transformation of families and their contributions to building a new society became a central theme in Herzl's literature.

In 1894, shortly before coming to the Zionist solution, Herzl wrote the play *Das Neue Ghetto*. He concerned himself with the "Jewish question," negatively portraying the assimilated Jewish middle class as materialistic and superficial. The female characters, Hermine Hellmann, who marries the idealistic Jewish lawyer Dr. Jacob Samuel at the beginning of the play, and even more so her sister Charlotte Rheinberg, were particularly shallow. In the words of the stockbroker Wasserstein, "Remember, Miss Hermine will want to live in the same style as her sister, Frau Rheinberg. Fine clothes, jewelry, the theater, concerts. That means a lot of money."[31] In contrast to these pseudo high-society Jewish women, Herzl depicted the traditional Jewish family life of the ghetto (meaning Eastern Europe) sympathetically. Rabbi Friedheimer spoke defensively of the ghetto: "True, the ghetto was crowded and dirty, but the virtues of family life flourished there. The father was a patriarch. The mother ... (lays his hand lightly on that of Frau Samuel) lived only for her children, and they honored their parents."[32] The image of Jewish women in this play, which was Herzl's favorite, should not be taken out of context. He also portrayed the male Jewish characters, with the exception of Samuel, as stereotyped caricatures of the materialistic and morally bankrupt Jew. He aimed not for a sympathetic, positive portrayal of the Jews but, on the contrary, for a "self-emancipation from negative Jewish qualities."[33]

Herzl developed his vision of the ideal Jewish future in his utopian novel *Altneuland* (1902). The novel tells the story of a Viennese Jewish lawyer, Friedrich Loewenberg, who left Vienna with a misanthropic non-Jewish officer named Kingscourt. Loewenberg, heartbroken by the marriage of his beloved to another man, answered an advertisement, which led to his friendship with Kingscourt. Together they set sail for a remote island, visiting a primitive Palestine on their way. After twenty years in isolation, they return to find that a "new society" has emerged there in the meantime. Herzl painted the New Society as an ideal world without any conflicts, religious antagonism, economic troubles, or social problems. Technology also played a central role in his vision of the future state, both in *Der Judenstaat* and in *Altneuland*. Herzl envisioned a land of peace, prosperity, and progress, where Jews, Arabs, and Christians lived beside one another in complete harmony. The cultural life described in *Altneuland* bore a very strong resemblance to European culture, with the characters speaking German or their native languages rather than Hebrew. Although Herzl rejected the idea of Jewish assimilation into European society, he seemed content with the Jews taking the positive and progressive elements of Europe with them to the new state. "With pride, Herzl speaks of transferring into the renascent state the most advanced values that the Jew can bring with him from his former homes."[34]

On their return to Palestine, Loewenberg and Kingscourt find the Litwak family, whom Loewenberg had saved from starvation before he left Vienna, and their antithesis, bourgeois families such as the Loefflers. While the impoverished Litwak family underwent a complete transformation in their new habitat, living a comfortable and contented life as full participants in the New Society, the bourgeois families remained essentially unchanged. The Litwak family had immigrated from Galicia to Vienna, where they lived in dire poverty in a one-room apartment. When Loewenberg came across them twenty years later in Palestine, he found that David, once a little beggar Jewish boy, had become "grave and free, healthy and cultured, a man who could stand up for himself."[35] The baby had grown into a woman, Miriam Litwak (modeled on Herzl's sister Pauline, who died at the age of nineteen), who completely devoted herself to the New Society. David described her work as a teacher. "She isn't doing it for the salary. I should be well able to keep my sister. But she is performing the obligations, which she has because it also gives her rights. In our New Society women have equal rights with men."

> It goes without saying that they have the right to vote and use it. They worked loyally with us when we created our administration, and their enthusiasm for our great aim was a constant source of inspiration to us. After that it would have been blackest ingratitude on the part of the men to relegate them to the kitchen or the seraglio, even if called by some other name.[36]

Political equality did not detract from women's devotion to family life. "Don't imagine that our women have become worse housewives because they've been given the vote. My wife, for instance, never goes to meetings—political meetings—I mean." David explained, "While she was nursing the boy, she forgot about her inalienable rights. Before I married her, she belonged to the radical opposition—that's how I met her, as a political opponent. Now she confines her opposition to the home; but it is an entirely loyal opposition you must understand." To Loewenberg, Sarah was "an ideal of maternal and wifely happiness," and Miriam was a "delightful girl" who performed "duties no girl of the Loeffler set would have dreamed of."[37]

Sasha Eichenstamm, the daughter of the President of the New Society, never married, focusing instead on charitable activities. Through the character of Sasha, Herzl demonstrated how the New Society would be organized to provide an outlet to women who otherwise would have no useful role in society.

> She is an eminent oculist also, the head of our largest clinic. A grand woman. She has never married, but devotes all her life to the sick and the poor. She is a wonderful example of the part that spinsters and lonely women can play in a sensibly organized society. Half a century ago they were derided or felt to be a burden to their families. Today they are a blessing to others and lead happy lives. Our Welfare Department, for instance, is run exclusively by such women.[38]

Although Sasha was extremely accomplished, especially for a woman at that time, she possessed all the qualities of Herzl's ideal Jewish woman: she dressed plainly, found her happiness in helping those in need, headed the greatest eye clinic in the world, and was modest about her accomplishments. She demonstrated the notion that the New Society, or the Jewish state, would serve as a "home" by taking care of all its citizens.

In spite of the equality of the sexes, the New Society still valued traditional roles for women. Even the female Muslim character, Fatma Bey, found contentment in her seclusion. Miriam and Sarah both defended Muslim customs with respect to women, describing Fatma as "a most cultivated and charming young woman."

> "Don't imagine that Fatma feels unhappy or frustrated, though," added Sarah. "It's a very happy marriage indeed. They have charming children. But the wife does not step outside the bounds of her peaceful seclusion. That's also a form of happiness, which I certainly understand, in spite of being a member of the New Society. If my husband wished it, I shouldn't mind living like Fatma!"

Later, when the group was leaving for a tour of the country, they stopped at Reshid Bey's house to pick him up. Fatma fluttered a handkerchief from an upper-story window. Once again, Miriam commented on her contented nature, and Loewenberg declared his admiration for "a woman who remains contentedly at home."[39] While giving equal rights to women, the New Society sought to maintain the distinction between men and women. This also influenced the education of children. The best students traveled to foreign lands in organized groups in order to learn foreign languages and customs. "'The girls don't go on these trips,' said Miriam. 'It is our belief that a growing girl's place is at home with her mother, even though she must learn something to fit herself for a career and do her duty by the commonwealth.'"[40]

Women who devoted themselves to the New Society, to charitable causes, or to their families, served the New Society without sacrificing their femininity. In contrast, the bourgeois, materialistic women had absolutely no useful role. Herzl described these women just as he had in *The New Ghetto*, the only difference being that in *Altneuland* they had become outcasts. For example, the Laschner women, who were seated next to Loewenberg at the opera, were described as "two overly dressed heavily bejewelled women." Loewenberg also met Ernestine Loeffler, now Mrs. Weinberger. His idealized image of her quickly melted away.

> There she sat, down below, and at first he was subject to a strange illusion. Why, Ernestine looked exactly as she had done twenty years ago! The same delicate features, the same slender figure. But after a minute he realized that this young girl was not Ernestine, but her daughter. Mrs. Weinberger was the fat matron beside the girl, dressed too youthfully in gaudy colors, her features faded and bloated. She looked up at him, smiled invitingly and nodded delightedly when Friedrich bowed.[41]

Later, they came upon some Jews, "overdressed ladies, idling men. They sat under the palms, commenting on the passers-by, flirting, gossiping—just as they do all over the world." For some reason, this comforted Kingscourt. "Why, here they are at last, the Jewesses with the jewels! I was feeling quite nostalgic for them! I thought: my dear Adalbert, perhaps we were not in the land of the Jews at all, but the whole thing was a hoax! And now I see it's true. Here are the ostrich-feather hats, the gaudy silks, the jeweled Israelite women."

Herzl acted on his belief in the potential of Zionism to bring about a transformation and improvement in Jewish women and bourgeois Jewish families by taking practical steps to involve women in the Zionist Congresses and the Zionist movement. At a special women's caucus held in 1898, prior to the Second Congress, women were not only seated as delegates but given full voting rights. This was quite unusual for the time, when women had been granted full suffrage only in New Zealand and some states in the United States.[42] Women's equality in Zionism, Priska Gmür perceptively points out, benefited men as well as women. In a small movement with insignificant numbers, women boosted membership. In cultural Zionism, which placed value on the revival of Jewish tradition, "it was virtually impossible to bypass women in their capacity as the traditional 'guardian of the Jewish house.'"[43] In other words, by giving women rights, Zionists expected them to provide services to the movement.

This, however, opened the door for the kind of criticisms found in some of Herzl's writings and those of other Zionists. At the Second Congress, Rozia Ellmann read a proclamation stating that women must devote themselves to Zionism and stand by their husbands.[44] Gmür interprets this as follows: "The ideal female Zionist thus appears as the true companion of the man on whose side she fights for the common Jewish cause, thus for an almost familial cause, as she maternally empathizes with their suffering and selflessly feels solidarity with them—a pattern of argumentation which is encountered over and over again in the voting of other women."[45] In this context, Zionist women founded their own associations, committees, and organizations to work on limited areas such as youth education in Jewish religion and culture, watching over Zionist ideals in the family—in short, being the guardians and transmitters of Jewish culture and tradition.

Like Herzl, other Viennese Zionists criticized contemporary Jewish women for not adequately serving Zionism. For example, on December 15, 1900, Leon Kellner (1859-1928), the Shakespearean scholar who was among the first followers of Herzlian Zionism, delivered a lecture entitled "Our Women" to the Zionist Women's Association in Vienna, in which he spoke primarily about the shortcomings of bourgeois Jewish women and the historical background that was responsible for these traits.[46] According to Kellner, Jewish women's love for jewels had evolved historically. In order to describe modern Jewish women, he used an evolutionary analogy to living organisms, which developed traits that lost their use over time. Women had adopted many qualities and bad habits, which had since become superfluous, from their "oriental home." In the insecure circumstances of earlier times, Jews adapted to the disruptive lifestyle of reckoning with daily torment, settling down only to be driven away from a place. It was for this reason, he asserted, that the Jews bought their women costly jewelry; it was nothing other than a savings bank. "The preference for jewels has still to this day been maintained by the Jewish woman. Today, thank God, the premises for such an investment of capital are lacking.... Away with diamonds, the Jewish woman must learn to walk modestly."

Kellner discussed the excesses produced by the emancipation and assimilation, mentioning the names of the two most prominent salon women, Dorothea Mendelssohn and Rahel Levin. Gradually, Jews became aware that girls must be educated in more than just piano playing—in a vocation. He reproached the bourgeois Jewish mother, commenting that she had a pathological excessive love for her children, which oftentimes led her to neglect her husband. Comparing her to Glueckel of Hameln, the only known Jewish female writer of the seventeenth century, he concluded with the statement, "It is truly moving how this modest Jewish woman, who could not write and dictated her memoirs, in her entire behavior, in all of her deeds, identified with her people; the love of Israel filled her entire life."[47]

Kellner maintained that modernity did not threaten Jewish men's national self-awareness as it did Jewish women. The men were continually reminded of their solidarity with their people through the practice of religious duties. The women's role as the "guardian of the Nation" obliged them to transmit Jewish values in the family and deemed their national identity crucial to the future of their people. The report of the lecture evening concluded:

> Herr Prof. Kellner was not sparing of the Jewish woman of our time in his lecture; he sharply chastized her faults, and if one or another of the numerous audience members came to the lecture on "Our Women" with the intention of hearing her praises sung, she would have departed rather disappointedly. But all the more worthy of consideration were his words. Let the seeds sprout fruitfully, that lay in the abundance of useful stimulation and suggestions of the lecturer.[48]

Kellner's lecture emphasized Zionist women's passivity and their role as transmitters of Jewish values in the family and "guardian of the Nation." A sense of women's importance in serving the state by providing the anchor for family life permeates his generally negative indictment of bourgeois Jewish life.

Heinrich York-Steiner (1859–1935), the author of the stories "Maskir," "Talmud Kessuboth 110b," and "Der Talmudbauer" (The Talmudic Farmer, 1904), belonged to Herzl's early circle, and spoke regularly at Zionist women's organizations.[49] In "Der Talmudbauer," he told of the encounter of a young man brought up in a struggling religious family in Jerusalem and an enlightened Zionist woman in a settlement. Through his encounter with Miriam, Chaim was exposed to modern enlightened ideas and the notion that Talmudic laws found a form through nature and practical application. He "became more masculine" by working in the sun and fresh air, started to dress in modern attire, cut off his sidelocks and shaved his beard. While in other York-Steiner stories, non-Zionist female Jewish characters met with tragic ends, Miriam was intelligent and independent, tolerant and open-minded, but secure in her faith. Like the families in Herzl's *Altneuland*, the various types of Diaspora Jewish families changed in the new circumstances, forming new combinations and new types of Zionist families. Chaim and Miriam abandoned traditional norms of marriage, making their own decision to get married. To the objection that they could not be married because neither had money, Miriam answered, "We could never ask for something better, than to become an honest settler-couple on the home soil of the holy land. People will trust us and make money and land available to us."[50] An additional aspect of the Zionist movement, particularly the youth movement, influenced York-Steiner's story: the generational rebellion against traditional forms of marriage, arranged marriages, and financial considerations.

On April 6, 1901, York-Steiner led "a lively discussion" on how to educate children in Jewish religion. The discussants concluded that the Jewish woman must first educate herself in Jewish belief, in order to properly educate her children. To do so, she had to become involved in charitable religious activities. Among the ideas that came up in the course of the discussion were the establishment of homes for the poor and Jewish nursing. A report in *Die Welt* described the discussions as animated and pleasurable and concluded with the following admonition to women:

If our Jewish women pay attention to the warnings that were heard on both these evenings, if they immerse themselves in the nation, open their hearts to the poverty that shows itself at every turn; if they observe and listen, when Jewish thought lives even underneath poor clothing, then they will also acquire that education of the heart, then they will find that national awareness, that strength of character, which makes it possible for them to remain Jewish mothers in spite of the pressure of the circumstances of Jewish women.[51]

Charity would not only lead to an improvement in the character of those women who participated as donors, but it would also enable the impoverished recipients to achieve their potential as Jewish women.

Cultural Zionism and the New Jewish Family

Berthold Feiwel, born in 1875 in Pohrlitz, Moravia, became involved in the Zionist movement early on through Herzl. In his student years he founded the *Jüdische Volksstimme* with Max Aickel and Robert Stricker. Later, Feiwel became one of the leading spirits, along with Martin Buber, of the oppositionist group the "Democratic-Zionist Faction" (called "the Faction" for short), which made its debut at the fifth Zionist Congress in 1901. Although the Faction consisted of only thirty-seven delegates, its power exceeded its numbers and it sometimes dominated the entire Congress.[52] Herzl entrusted Feiwel with the editorship of *Die Welt*; when he resigned due to illness, Martin Buber took over, but also resigned after a few months. Herzl praised their work and gave them full editorial freedom to express their ideas.[53] Nevertheless, he worried that the cultural movement threatened the unity of Zionism. Because of their concern with the creation of a national culture and their belief in the need to preserve Judaism by teaching Jewish values and Hebrew language to future generations, cultural Zionists often expressed concern over the role of Jewish women and Jewish families.

In an article on the Jewish woman and family, Feiwel criticized bourgeois Jewish women. He asserted that the best women were the least spoken of and therefore Jewish women must have become thoroughly bad because anti-Semites, who once spared Jewish women in their criticism, now targeted them. He held Jewish women accountable for the rising hostility in anti-Semitic criticism of women.

> The tone in which the Jewish woman is spoken of today ever more frequently in newspapers and books, in theater and even by speakers in public gatherings, is widely distanced from the almost harmless irony of earlier times.... The reproaches that are raised against the Jewish woman are severe: She is vain and superficial, dressy, arrogant, urgent, extravagant—but this is not much: She is also a bad despotic housewife, a bad spouse and mother, the bearer of loose and sinful marriage-, family-, and society-morality. She offends morals and good taste.[54]

According to Feiwel, once anti-Semites had even candidly praised Jewish women as women, mothers, and guardians of the family; he quoted an anti-Semitic leader as saying, "I am an anti-Semite, but no hater of Jewish women." This attitude toward Jewish women used to prevail. What changed? Rather than attribute the change to the growing aggression or the changing nature of anti-Semitism, he asserted that Jewish women had changed for the worse. "The times have changed for the worse, and the Jewish woman with them."

Using Nordau's terminology, Feiwel described the current state of Western European women as "degeneration." He warned that while anti-Semites exaggerated the situation and the danger that these women posed to non-Jewish society, they could actually threaten Judaism, by working for its disintegration. "These women—if one may generalize about them—work consciously or unconsciously at the core of the Jewish family and in smaller or larger circles of their society for the dissolution of Judaism." They threatened *Nationaljudentum* more than assimilated men, because domestic assimilation was harder to control and to correct than the large-scale and public antinationalist activities of men. The Jewish woman, Feiwel warned, not only herself became de-Judaized but also transformed the Jewish family through assimilation and destroyed the personality of her husband, her sons, and most of all, her daughters.

Feiwel also argued that Jewish school alone could not give Jewish children a feeling for Judaism. The religious feeling could only come from the home. When Jewish mothers failed to teach their children to regard Judaism positively, even a good Jewish education at school would not help. His solution was to develop a Jewish consciousness in women through emotional influences. They needed to come back into touch with their "racial instincts" through religion, family, work, and contact with anti-Semitism. "Religion and family are the foundation on which to base her national consciousness.... [Also essential is] the participation of the wife in the livelihood of the husband and personal contact with anti-Semitism."

While remaining critical of the contemporary Jewish woman, Martin Buber placed slightly more emphasis on the positive, albeit romanticized, image of Jewish women of the past. Buber (1878–1965), a religious philosopher and native of Vienna, became involved in Zionism as a result of his encounter with Herzl, joining the movement in 1898. Buber came to advocate cultural over political Zionism and to believe that "the cultural renaissance of Judaism rather than anti-Semitism must be made the fountain and driving force of Zionism."[55]

Buber defined the phrase "Zion of the Jewish woman" not as something that could only take place in the future when the Jews returned to their homeland where the new Jewish woman could emerge, but as an "inner Zion of the soul." A transformation in the souls of Jewish women would bring about Zion. He particularly idealized Jewish women of the ghetto who created a culture within the family, helped in the family business to enable their husbands to pursue study and spirituality, supported their husbands, and educated their children. Afflicted with degeneration, the Jewish women of his day compared unfavorably with these ghetto women. He argued that during the ghetto period, persecution gave rise to internal strength. As persecution became more petty and perfidious, Jewish life disintegrated. Emancipation reinforced this trend by ending the isolation of ghetto life. Particularly susceptible to assimilation, women emulated the surrounding culture, paralyzing Judaism and its independent culture. This led to "degeneration" as Jewish women looked for fulfillment in luxury and ostentation and became idle and snobbish.

Buber held Jewish women responsible for the downfall of their people, but also counted on them for its future regeneration. In *galut*, he asserted, the Jewish home is the Jewish nation; hence the importance of Jewish women in the cultural rebirth of Zion. The Jewish woman needed to work alongside the man to disseminate the national idea. But because of her love and deep understanding, she could do even more than the man.[56] Buber's belief in the need for a spiritual, cultural rebirth prior to a political solution led him to emphasize the potential of Jewish women in working for Zionism. It was in the spiritual realm, after all, that women's perceived strengths could be most beneficial. He also asserted that women had greater intuition and talent than men when it came to economics. They could better understand the causes of Jewish poverty and therefore had better solutions. But their talents could only come to fruition if Jewish women educated themselves to value, foster, and develop Judaism.

Like other Zionists, Buber stressed, above all, the need for Jewish women to nurture their families. The new Jewish woman, he predicted, would not be ashamed but proud if her child looked Jewish. She would make sure that her children were physically healthy and "nip in the bud the primary affliction of modern Jews, the over-growth of the life of the nerves." It would be the job of the new Jewish woman to bring about a future generation of Jews who would have a balance of mind and body, and would be educated in Judaism as well as in humanitarian wisdom. "The Jew of the future will be a complete Jew and a complete human being at the same time."[57] Buber concluded by saying that one word, "love," summarized the Jewish woman. She had love for the grand destiny of her people, the love to help the poor and oppressed Jews, and love for the dream of a future nation. This love was necessary to bring about the Zion of the soul, the creation of a Jewish culture, which would then make possible a territorial Zion.

Conclusion

In exchange for equal rights, Zionist leaders envisioned Jewish women forming the basis of new Jewish families which would serve the nation by providing a supportive, nurturing environment for the "New Jew," creating and shaping the citizens of the future, as well as fulfilling the social, cultural, and educational needs of the new society. They emphasized the importance of the Jewish woman as housewife, mother, charity worker, and guardian of religious tradition and values. They criticized the contemporary Jewish women as materialistic, assimilated, ostentatious, and superficial, asserting that they would be brought back to Judaism through Zionist national awareness. The Zionist family would mirror neither the Jewish family of the ghetto nor the assimilated bourgeois family of Western Europe. By providing an escape from the restrictions and unhealthy conditions of ghetto life, which stifled Jews physically and sexually and gave rise to unnatural gender relationships, the Zionist movement would restore the Jewish family of the ghetto to a new level of vitality. Paradoxically, Zionists often idealized traditional Jewish women for their role as guardians of the family, and their devotion to their children and husbands.

Never delineated as specifically as the "new Jew," the "new Jewish woman" of Viennese Zionism emerges as a collection of varied, at times contradictory, images, understood primarily in her relationship to family life as the wife and mother. According to most Zionist writings, Jewish family life would be transformed in the process of creating a Jewish state. As a result, future generations of Zionists would emerge in order to ensure the future of the Jewish people. Criticism of Jewish women for their lack of Jewish feeling, their level of assimilation, and most especially for their materialism and love of luxury, entered into almost all the Zionist works on women. The Jewish woman of the contemporary European world needed to be transformed from a bejeweled, assimilated, self-centered, degenerate Jewess into a virtuous, nurturing, charitable, feminine, and nationally-minded Jewish mother. The transformation could take place in the context of a Jewish homeland. As a result, the Zionist family would then serve the Jewish society in several ways. While Herzl's declaration that women should have equality in the Zionist movement may not seem to have had a positive impact on the perception of women's roles either in the movement or in the future state, it did encourage the participation of women through the formation of women's Zionist organizations, societies, and agencies. But it also led to the marked tendency of both men and women to focus on the passivity of women in the Zionist movement and attribute it to the bourgeois Jewish women's assimilation into their world and distance from their traditions.

The general perception of gender in fin-de-siècle Vienna influenced the image of the ideal Jewish woman in Zionism. Certain stereotypes of women, such as their affinity for social work, their preference for art and culture over politics and ideas, and their innate materialism, were absorbed from Viennese modern culture and incorporated into Zionist ideology. Zionist leaders used Jewish women as scapegoats, blaming them for assimilation, for the lack of support for the Zionist movement, and for the moral deficiencies of Diaspora Jewry. In spite of the statements regarding women's equality in a future Zionist state, the images of Jewish women that pervaded their ideology as a whole idealized both traditional Jewish women and regarded the modern women's movement as antithetical to Judaism and Zionism.

Zionists found the solution to the problems facing Diaspora Jews in general and Jewish women in particular in working for Jewish national renewal. The new society would create an order in which certain "unnatural" gender characteristics of the ghetto would be rectified, while undesirable aspects of bourgeois family life would be transcended. Reversing the image of the traditional relationship between the sexes in the East European ghetto, Zionists believed that Jewish men would become more manly by working the land, while Jewish women would become more feminine. Hence, Zionists' connection to traditional Judaism was paradoxical. On the one hand, they emphasized Jewish identity and awareness as well as Jewish spirituality and culture as prerequisites for Jewish national renewal, especially for women. They criticized modern Jewish women for their apathy toward tradition and their lack of knowledge and feeling for Judaism. On the other hand, they viewed the traditional Jewish relationship of the sexes as an unnatural byproduct of Diaspora life, which needed to be corrected. Ironically, the resulting Zionist ideals of masculinity and femininity were not rooted in Jewish culture, but incorporated from European bourgeois culture. Feeling the need to assert their masculinity, in contrast to the image of the feminine Jewish male, Viennese Zionists in the end relegated Jewish women to a more passive and depoliticized role. European nationalism and respectability exerted a strong influence on the development of Zionism in nineteenth-century Vienna and its accompanying gender roles.

Never clearly delineated, the role of women in Zionism suffered from a basic contradiction between the notion that the Jewish state would resolve the issue of gender inequality by granting women an equal status in the new society and on the other hand the argument that women had a unique contribution to make to Zionism because of their female nature. Although the latter idea predominated over the former, the concept of difference never completely eclipsed that of equality. Moreover, the need for women's active involvement in the work of building the Jewish state, as well as the influence of the women's movement, continually challenged the limitation of women's roles to the domestic sphere.

A more concrete and realistic notion of the role of the family in the service of the future state only emerged in the Yishuv itself. The Zionists who settled in Palestine were frequently young, idealistic, and unmarried. For some, the Zionist Youth Movement served as a surrogate family.[58] The initial difficulties of life in the Yishuv required delaying family life and, particularly, having children. These difficulties prevented some of the idealized views of the early Zionists from being implemented until much later. For women, Zionist ideals were particularly hard to attain: The harsh realities of life in the new settlements prevented many women from settling. For those who did, childbirth proved especially difficult. Young pioneers (*Chalutzim* and *Chalutzot*) initially focused their energies on more urgent issues, leaving ideals for another day.

Part Two

FAMILIALISM AS STATE BUILDING

5

"ROOTED IN THE SOIL"

Family Ideals, Land Reclamation, and Irrigation Resettlement as Welfare in the United States, 1897–1933[1]

LAURA LOVETT

In recent years, a majority of scholars have come to assume that a certain family ideal has structured the origins and development of the early U.S. welfare state, namely one that assumes a "father/breadwinner who works for a wage and a mother/wife who provides unpaid domestic work."[2] This ideal, scholars argue, produced the popular image of men as providers and undergirded the ideology of the family wage, which asserted that industry must provide wages sufficient to support an entire family. Protective labor legislation, child labor laws, mothers' pensions, and compulsory education further reinforced this ethic, as did tenement and housing reforms, insofar as they permitted "mothers to fulfill their duties in safe, clean domestic environments."[3] As the state gained greater authority to regulate aspects of public and private life, an "industrial family ethic" ensured that a set of hierarchical power relationships based on who did the wage earning would be maintained within the family.[4] While maternalist reformers challenged some aspects of this family ethic by claiming political agency for themselves as mothers, they also reinforced the family ethic as they advocated policies ranging from mothers' pensions to the Sheppard-Towner Act.[5]

The focus on maternalist social policy in scholarship on the early U.S. welfare state has obscured the initiatives of other social actors, based on different principles.[6] In this essay, I seek to broaden the discussion of this period by drawing attention to a set of social policies based on a vision of the family that was significantly different, namely, that of the "producer family." This vision informed the campaign for what one historian has called the "first and most durable example of the modern welfare state": the Reclamation Act of 1902.[7] Under the terms of this act, the proceeds from the sale of public lands were to be expended for the "survey, examination, construction, and operation, and maintenance of irrigation works in the sixteen arid states." Revenue from the sale of thousands of acres in each state was to be spent on irrigation projects in the states where the money originated. Newly reclaimed land in each state then would be sold in small parcels to homesteaders who would repopulate the West. Advocates of nationalized land reclamation and resettlement, such as George Maxwell, William Smythe, and Elwood Mead, articulated their visions of the benefits of such irrigation projects in terms of a return to a model of the family which was not solely dependent on industrial wages. In the place of an industrial family ethic or ideal, they proposed a producer family ethic where families became more self sufficient by living in homes or communities which had large gardens, orchards, and areas for livestock.

The producer family ideal was advocated as a form of "decommodification"; that is, it freed the family from strict dependence on industrial wages and so offered some protection from fluctuations in the economy. Welfare theorists have argued both that decommodification is "a precondition for a tolerable level of individual welfare and security,"[8] and that in order to come to terms with how welfare is gendered, accounts of decommodification must consider unpaid work in addition to the relationship between paid work and welfare.[9] In this instance, focusing on reclamation and resettlement policies as family-oriented social policies allows us to see how some policy makers sought to mobilize the labor of all family members—both paid and unpaid—for the purpose of freeing male workers from complete dependency on the market. Where other historians have focused directly on the role of women as the makers and objects of social policy, I approach the gendered relationship between unpaid and paid labor in reclamation and resettlement efforts by analyzing the ideal of the family at the core of these campaigns and policies. Efforts to reclaim land, thus, reclaimed the family as the key to decommodification.

George Maxwell and the Campaign for Nationalized Irrigation

For the first third of the twentieth century, lobbyist George Maxwell campaigned tirelessly to create a new "safety valve" for the United States. Convinced that frontier expansion had acted as a check to the effects of industrialization and urbanization, Maxwell sought to create new "frontiers" by resettling urban families in "homes of the land" created by national irrigation and land reclamation efforts. Like other turn-of-the-century reformers, Maxwell believed that something had to be done to protect workers and their families from the vicissitudes of the capitalist wage system. In Maxwell's mind, returning workers to homes on the land would allow them to become more self-sufficient and less dependent on a wage-based economy. As such, Maxwell's scheme for nationalized reclamation and resettlement represents an attempt to create a form of decommodification—to allow people to live independently of the wage labor system.

The association of homemaking and nationalized reclamation was an explicit part of the strategy of reclamation's "militant evangelist."[10] Born in Sonoma, California in 1860, Maxwell began his career as a court stenographer and later became a lawyer himself, specializing in California water laws. Beginning in the 1890s, he expanded his interest in this area by launching himself as a lobbyist for national water policies. Maxwell and others rhetorically framed their campaign for nationalized reclamation legislation by appealing to the promise of the "homes on the land" that would result. Irrigation settlements and homesteads were to be as much a product of reclamation policies as the dams and canals that we now associate with efforts to bring water to the arid West. While national dams can be celebrated as technological marvels, Maxwell's vision of the society to be built on reclaimed land was profoundly nostalgic and conservative. The ideal of the home on the land and the family that inhabited it represented for him a return to an agrarian past in which the home was a site of production and women were agents of both production and reproduction.[11] This ideal of the home and family challenged the centrality of wage earning in the household economy.

In his role as lobbyist and editor of six journals, Maxwell was in a position to ensure that the case for nationalized irrigation was associated with homemaking. His strategy arose from his discouraging experience trying to protect water rights at the state level. Until the mid-1890s, irrigation had been undertaken by private canal and land companies, with some exceptions. In 1887, California passed the Wright Act, which used the New England township ideal as a model for districts that would share the costs of irrigating and elect directors to oversee the projects. Local mismanagement and other problems led to the failure of the wealthiest Western state to irrigate much of the proposed two million acres.[12] Francis G. Newlands, the senator from Nevada who was ultimately responsible for passage of the 1902 act, had encountered similar obstacles when he tried to irrigate the Truckee River Valley.[13]

Their experience, along with interstate conflicts over water rights and the addition of five new states and territories in 1889, convinced Newlands, Maxwell, and others that if irrigation and reclamation legislation were to succeed, it had to be passed at the national level as federal legislation. Maxwell himself entered the effort to nationalize irrigation in 1897 when he formed the National Irrigation Association. Aiming at the passage of a federal reclamation act, the organization set up offices across the country and provided Maxwell with an avenue for promoting national legislation.[14]

The construction of a national policy like the Reclamation Act of 1902 (also called the Newlands Act) required serious effort, since it was seen as extending far too much sectional favor to the West as well as stepping on the individualistic toes of Western pioneers. Indeed, historians have pointed to Western opposition to the bill as evidence that the ideology of individualism was too strong to allow for federal subsidies to be considered. As one often cited study of irrigation put it, "The West remained a prisoner of its belief that free enterprise alone should manage the work of irrigation."[15]

As Maxwell's irrigation campaign developed in the late 1890s, he placed increasing emphasis on the rural home as the solution to perceived problems of class warfare and the ill effects of urbanization, a formulation that was taken up by other irrigation advocates. As the National Irrigation Policy resolutions of 1901 phrased it, "rural homes are the safeguards of the nation, and the congestion of population in the great cities of the East is a growing menace to the stability of our republican institutions, and there is no longer an outlet upon the public lands in their present condition for our surplus population."[16] Both Democrats and Republicans declared the same support for reclamation in the 1900 election, with Republicans specifying that they advocated it in order "to provide free homes on the public domain."[17]

It took careful political engineering on the part of President Theodore Roosevelt to secure what has been called the country's first flirtation with socialism. He began by ordering Newlands to rework his bills, omitting controversial language describing what the government would do with reservoirs and canals in terms of "nationalized" programs. Roosevelt himself articulated his support for reclamation in terms of his vision of both the rural home and the role of national government in reform. For him, national irrigation and reclamation constituted an agrarian path toward national strength, and this, in turn, was linked to the home. In his First Annual Message in 1901, he advocated nationalized irrigation and asserted that reclaimed land "should be reserved for actual settlers." As Roosevelt put it, "The policy of National Government should be to aid irrigation . . . in such a manner as will enable people in local communities to help themselves."[18] Such statements allowed him to justify strong national government in the name of aiding the settler or homebuilder.[19] The consonance between Roosevelt's statement on irrigation and Maxwell's vision was not accidental: Maxwell had helped him write this part of his address.[20]

Although it is not clear whether Maxwell's efforts influenced Roosevelt's subsequent policies, Roosevelt did continue to support national efforts on behalf of rural families.[21] In a 1907 pamphlet entitled "The Man Who Works With His Hands," Roosevelt clearly equated the status of the nation with the status of the rural family. "If there is any one lesson taught by history," he argued, "it is that the permanent greatness of any state must ultimately depend more upon the character of its country population than upon anything else. . . . It would be a calamity," he continued, "to have our farms occupied by a lower type of people than the hard-working, self-respecting, independent, and essentially manly and womanly men and women who have hitherto constituted the most typically American, and on the whole the most valuable, element in our entire nation."[22] As he moved to nationalize his conservation policies around the same time, Roosevelt articulated his agenda for country life and the rural family in tandem with his agenda regarding conservation of natural resources. "Conservation and rural-life policies are really two sides of the same policy," he wrote, "and down at bottom this policy rests upon the fundamental law that neither man nor nation can prosper unless, in dealing with the present, thought is steadily taken for the future."[23] The rural family, like other national resources, had to be preserved and managed.

In the meantime, Maxwell and his allies continued to make the home a centerpiece of their campaign for a nationalized irrigation movement. In December 1901, the National Irrigation Association changed the name of its organ from *National Irrigation* to *The National Homemaker*, and in 1903 shortened that simply to *The Homemaker*. Each issue of the newly retitled journal carried a quote from Roosevelt: "Throughout our history the success of the homemaker has been but another name for the upbuilding of the nation." Before the passage of the 1902 Reclamation Act, the magazine had naturally focused on the need for nationalized irrigation and its widespread support; afterward, it celebrated their success and began to dwell on how national reclamation would be implemented. A new statement of the "plan of campaign" for the National Irrigation Association directed its membership to ensure that public lands be reclaimed by settlers, not speculators. To help make the case, Maxwell's rhetoric about the home became even more sentimental. For example, in a speech in 1902, Maxwell promised that the recipient of benefits from the Newlands Act, as the 1902 Reclamation Act was called, would be typified by "the man who is free from all the uncertainties of a wage-earners' employment, the man who gathers his wife and children around his own hearthstone, the man who has his home upon Mother Earth, the man who draws his living straight from Nature's granary."[24] The evocation of "Nature's granary," "Mother Earth," and the wife and children gathered around the hearthstone was more than Victorian hyperbole. Maxwell's nostalgic vision of the self-sufficient rural family was an essential component in his economic plan for resettlement and reclamation. Allowing families to draw their living from the land was a means of decommodification; it freed them from their dependence on "a wage-earner's employment."

By 1902, the stage had been set for a radical reconsideration of the role of the federal government in the lives and welfare of its people. By conducting the campaign for national water in terms of families, irrigation and reclamation activists engaged themselves in a much more far-reaching effort to engineer homes and towns as well as dams and irrigation canals. In *The Homemaker*, Maxwell had hinted that there was a growing movement to redistribute the nation's population. With the goal of allowing anyone who was willing to have the chance to own their own home on their own land, the movement began to manifest itself in school and vacant-lot garden programs, nature-study programs, and farm-training schools.

George Maxwell's Homecroft Ideal

Maxwell's advocacy of homebuilding took a specific form—that of the "Homecroft." Inspired by the rural housing built for workers by the Cadbury Company (famous for its chocolates) outside Birmingham, England, Maxwell borrowed the English term for a small garden and offered it as the logical extension of reclamation efforts. As he defined it, a Homecroft was "an individual home on the land, however small, owned and intensively cultivated by the occupant and his family." Homecrofts were intended to make families more self-sufficient, but they were not supposed to replace wage-earning entirely.[25] A Homecroft would provide a worker's family with food and extra income from the sale of homemade arts and crafts. This surplus would make the Homecroft family less vulnerable to the fluctuations of a wage-based economy. Maxwell's slogan for the Homecroft Movement captured his ideal: "Every Child in a Garden ... Every Mother in a Homecroft ... and Individual Industrial Independence for Every Worker in a Home of His Own on the Land." As such, Homecrofts were almost a material, tangible form of decommodification—a cushion against the vicissitudes of the market.

In 1902, Maxwell launched a magazine to publicize his vision of how irrigation could remake the entire country; calling it *Maxwell's Talisman*, he offered it as an amulet for curing social ills. The magic of connecting people with land in a program calling for cooperative endeavors, home ownership for workers, and children's education reforms would reinforce civic and social interactions in country and suburban villages and towns. In these new communities, according to Maxwell, "industry can be so firmly anchored that it cannot be drawn into the Commercial Maelstrom that is now steadily sucking Industry and Humanity into the Vortex of the Great Cities."[26] Where Maxwell's reclamation efforts represented an attempt to manipulate the country's land and population by redistributing both water and people, his Homecroft efforts evinced a determination to tie people to the land for the short and long terms. He would ease the population onto the land and instill in their children a love for it. Homecrofts would thus be built near factories or other places of employment and would contain special educational facilities for working with the children of laborers in public gardens.

Maxwell was careful not to identify his efforts with the "back-to-the-land" movement which, since the Civil War, had urged city workers to move to the country in an attempt to cure the ills of urbanization by simply putting workers onto the land. These included Horace Greeley's land colony in 1870, Archbishop John Ireland's attempt to have urban Catholics reproduce themselves at a higher rate by setting up five agricultural colonies in Minnesota and Nebraska in 1873, the Salvation Army's three settlements for the poor, and many others.[27] Most of these colonies were a response to the depression of 1873 and its visible effects on displaced workers. Colonies had the appeal of housing and employing urbanites while developing the unimproved lands of the West. Theories about these lands included an argument that the Great American Desert could be fundamentally changed by cultivation, since abundant rainfall in the early 1870s produced the perception that plowing actually produced rain. The region's true aridity disproved this theory and provided an example of the need for irrigation that would later be used by Maxwell and others.[28]

Instead of entirely removing the worker to the country, Maxwell urged giving him a home in the suburbs, "where he can have a garden and poultry yard, and where his children can have sunshine and fresh air without stint." The effects of this plan would become apparent since it would "have largely done away with the evils that are causing the denizens of the congested quarters of our great cities: physical degeneracy, tuberculosis, and social, moral and political dangers too numerous to be enumerated." Maxwell argued for an organic connection between the physical surroundings and the physical welfare of the people inhabiting such places. As he described his ideal, having "each family in a home and each home on a garden" would produce "health and strength by the labor of cultivating food for the family."[29]

Maxwell's perception that a connection existed between social ills and the congested quarters of crowded city neighborhoods was not idiosyncratic. From 1865 to 1910, the Parks and Playgrounds Movement used open space and trees as curative antidotes for urban life, with Boston initiating the first outer park movement under the guidance of Frederick Law Olmsted in 1893. This was the same year that the Columbian Exposition's "White City" demonstration of urban aesthetics launched nationwide what was called the City Beautiful movement with its increasingly rural-inspired aesthetics—sweeping vistas, tree-lined boulevards, parks and civic centers constructed like monumental town halls.[30]

A shift in perceptions about ideal civic beauty also brought a shift in perceptions of civic problems. Notably, what for generations had been seen as the "housing problem," localized in overcrowded tenements, became a "slum problem." Slums included the street and neighborhood along with the dwelling itself as the source of concern. Historian Carol Christensen points out that Progressive era focus on "family" as the primary site of influence meant that streets and neighborhoods had to be reformed for the sake of the children growing up in them. Tenements in the worst crowded quarters were torn down to build five million dollars' worth of small parks in New York in 1894, and large spaces were opened up near the most densely populated area in Boston in 1889. These actions addressed the characteristics associated with slums, replacing their darkness with open, grass-filled, natural spaces.[31]

Even as the City Beautiful was brought to its most crowded precincts, though, the problem was being redefined. It was not simply a need for light and nature that caused urban ills; it was congestion. Elgin Gould, a major proponent of the idea of philanthropic housing, urged that reform-minded capitalists build worker housing on city peripheries. The newly emerging transportation technology—streetcars—would allow better-paid workers to leave the tenement districts, reducing crowding in those neighborhoods.

As overcrowding came to be seen as the primary cause of urban problems, reformers turned to decentralization as the answer. The 1906 Committee on Congestion of Population in New York City urged that cities be allowed to restrict factories to suburban areas or to places where employers could assure urban officials that "due regard" for the "welfare" of workers, including "securing the proper transport facilities," was assured. Concern about congestion inspired the first National Conference on City Planning and the Problems of Congestion in 1909, financed by Henry Morgenthau. The "cure" for congestion embraced by the first decade of the twentieth century was redistributing the population from city centers to outlying areas.[32]

In the context of Progressive urban reform, Maxwell's Homecroft Movement sought to combine the connection to nature promoted by the parks movement with the decentralizing spirit of the city planning movement. Maxwell first attempted to establish a Homecroft Community in 1905 in Watertown, a suburb of Boston. He had left the Chicago headquarters of his publishing enterprise to accompany his children when they moved to Boston for college.[33] The central feature of the experiment was not the wholesale settlement of city dwellers, but a series of gardens and guildhalls. In 1905, Maxwell bought an estate in Watertown, and by 1906 he reported that the old residence on it was being used for a guildhall and shops.[34] Maxwell's plan was to "build a model demonstration and transform Watertown as it existed into what would have been, in reality, in a very practical way, an Educational Institute in the new Art and Science of living from the Land on the part of all people in an industrial Community."[35] As it came to be, the Educational Institute consisted of a gardening program which emphasized a connection to the land through nature study as well as the practical business of growing food, and the Guildhall, which emphasized the production of arts and crafts. One acre of the old estate's grounds was subdivided into gardens while the building itself housed craft and education programs. A local newspaper story on "The New Sociological Experiment at Watertown" reported that over 100 children were learning to garden and over 200 others had applied.[36] Elizabeth S. Hill was appointed the gardens director and supervised the program for children of all ages. Hill was herself an advocate for school gardens and promoted them as a means of nature study.[37] Both Maxwell and Hill were early leaders in the school garden movement, urging that each child spend some part of the day in direct contact with nature.[38]

By this time, the vegetable or "kitchen garden" was quickly becoming an anachronism in most urban and suburban homes. Such gardens had long been considered a female domain, and in all but the wealthiest homes before the turn of the century, tending the garden was an important part of household life. Even in town homes, any land behind the house was used for a kitchen garden and poultry yard along with other light agricultural pursuits, space permitting. In this way, even the urban or town home was a site of production. But with improved transportation and distribution networks as well as the rise of chain and self-service grocery stores, the home became a site of consumption rather than production.[39] With a grocery store on the corner, there was a decreasing need for storing out-of-season fruits and vegetables in root cellars or in canning jars. The rise of suburban life and the emergence of domestic science further shifted the role of middle-class women in the home from that of a domestic manager who oversaw the production of household goods to that of an educated consumer who wisely selected from the myriad of choices offered to her as "Mrs. Consumer."[40] As part of this shift, gardening books like Mabel Osgood Wright's *The Garden of the Commuter's Wife* (1901) began to urge women to convert the kitchen garden into a showcase for flowers. The home thus became a symbol of upward mobility and modernization, and the backyard became a play yard and site for display rather than a "home factory."[41]

In this context, Maxwell's call for intensely gardened home plots represented a nostalgic return to the home as site of production. At the same time, resisting the social changes that made the home a consumer showcase served to reinforce the family as a social and economic unit and assumed that women would supplement their husbands' wage income yet remain dependent. Keeping the family in contact with the land was, for Maxwell, a means of maintaining the virtue and vitality associated with Jeffersonian agrarianism.

While Maxwell would eventually establish Homecroft communities in Arizona, Minnesota, and Indiana, as well as Massachusetts, he was always in need of funding to expand his efforts. Beginning in 1907 he actively sought federal funding to help establish Homecrofts, calling for the establishment of a postal savings bank for this purpose. Although this early effort was not successful, the return of U.S. servicemen from overseas after World War I presented another opportunity to campaign for nationally subsidized Homecrofts as an alternative to soldier's pensions. As a result, Maxwell's insistence on the economic independence to be gained through Homecrofts reached its peak shortly after the war.

A tradition of granting bounty lands to veterans had begun after the American Revolution and continued through conflicts from the War of 1812 to the Mexican-American War. During the Civil War, the Homestead Act of 1862 superseded the tradition on the assumption that soldiers, like all Americans, would take the "free lands" in the West as they desired.[42] When the tradition was revived during after World War I, a series of a dozen national bills were proposed which changed the tradition of allocating land to soldiers.

Each of the bills made some provision for associating the bounty lands with reclamation. One bill made land claims part of a provision that would employ returning soldiers in the reclamation service with a right to acquire the newly reclaimed land at a reasonable fee. Other bills suggested ways to put the soldiers directly onto the land. One called for the Treasury Department to establish a National Colonization Board to develop the colonization of agricultural lands, while another called for the Department of the Interior to finance the preparation of farmlands, including reclamation and clearing, and then supply the buildings, implements, and livestock needed by the returning veterans. Similar proposals were made in almost every state, as well.[43]

On March 5, 1920, George Maxwell testified before the House Ways and Means Committee in support of the Fletcher-Smith Bill, which proposed settling returning soldiers on reclaimed land.[44] Maxwell favored the bill as an alternative to monetary bonuses or pensions for veterans. From his perspective, a cash bonus or pension was not in the soldier's best interest because they did not stabilize present jobs or buffer against falling wages. With characteristic flair, Maxwell warned of the disastrous effects that vast numbers of unemployed men could have on wages and prices as they drove the economy into a depression. Pensions, he warned, would do little to prevent what he termed a "cycle of collapse." What was needed instead was a solution that would prevent complete unemployment and minimize competition for labor. Not surprisingly, Maxwell argued that his scheme of providing small farms and Homecrofts on reclaimed land was exactly what was needed.

In this context, Maxwell presented Homecrofts as an economic alternative first and a social alternative second. In his testimony before Congress, he explained that Homecrofts provided a noncompetitive form of employment for the wage earner and unemployed alike. The food produced in Homecroft gardens and the small income from the sale of household crafts would buffer against the effects of unemployment and prevent employers from lowering wages in a competitive job market. In his words, "Give the ex-service man the increased value of a quarter-acre lot near his place of employment, ... and you have given him a larger bonus right there in the increased value of his property than it is proposed to give him in the form of a cash bonus, and you have in addition given him an anchorage on the land, which is of value to him beyond estimation in money. He has an anchorage against industrial vicissitudes that would enable him to ride out any storm." According to Maxwell, this small measure of self-sufficiency would also draw the Homecrofter out of his dependency on wages and in the long run counter the social unrest inevitably produced by increasing class division.[45] The Homecroft ideal thus entailed a revival of the family home on the land as a site of production. It was an economic plan designed to address the flaws of a wage-based economy and the type of society which it produces—designed, in other words, as a means of decommodification.

William Smythe, Elwood Mead, and the Settlement Ideal

While Maxwell's Homecroft movement was his own creation, using an ideal of the producer family to advocate for the creation of irrigation colonies had a number of advocates. Like Maxwell, William Smythe worked as a publicist for irrigation, editing *The Irrigation Age* from 1891 to 1895. Motivated in part by the depression of 1893, Smythe articulated an ideal of the irrigation community whose self-sufficiency would insulate it from an erratic economy.[46] Smythe organized a number of colonization efforts, including the "Little Landers" colonies in southern California. This utopian experiment promised settlers that with intensive cultivation a single acre would supply a living and food for a single family. Smythe sold the acres for between $350 and $550 apiece on land directly across from the Mexican border in a place he called San Ysidro in 1908. Similar projects were undertaken by Smythe near Los Angeles (in a suburb named "Los Terrenitos"—Spanish for little lands—now Tujunga), and a third colony near San Francisco called "Hayward Heath," close to present-day Hayward.[47]

Smythe represented the Little Lands colonies as a place for the "Spritual Man of the Soil." His philosophy of "a little land and a living" was spelled out in an inscription on the clubhouse wall in San Ysidro, "The Hope of the Little Lands," which proclaimed that "Individual Independence shall be achieved by millions of men and women, walking into the sunshine without Fear of Want. That in response to the loving labor of their hands, the Earth shall answer their prayer: 'Give us this day our daily bread.' That they and their children shall be Proprietors rather than Tenants, working not for Others but for Themselves."[48]

Despite his high hopes, Smythe's Little Lands colonies revealed the problems with implementing the homeacre idea. Residents required outside employment to make ends meet; they were unable to cultivate intensively if they were older or retired; and many were too poorly trained in local growing practices to make a living from the Little Landers Market in San Diego where they sold their produce. In addition, fighting, which took place directly across the border in 1911 when the International Workers of the World (IWW) encouraged a socialist insurrection against the Mexican government, discouraged growth of the colony at a crucial stage in its development. Of those who stayed, a flood in 1916 left 150 Little Landers homeless, two dead and the land ruined for farming. Hopes of rebuilding were further destroyed by the large number of younger men who joined the military to fight in Europe the next year. By 1918, Smythe's first colony was no longer viable and he left Southern California.

Elwood Mead refined Smythe's settlement model with two soldier settlement colonies in the California's Central Valley. These were meant to use irrgated land to serve the dual purpose of providing farms for servicemen returning from World War I and providing white farm workers the opportunity to become landowners.[49] Mead's irrigation colonies at Delhi and Durham in California's central valley were state-subsidized communities modeled on settlements Mead had visited in Australia.[50] Unlike Smythe's Little Lands communities, Delhi and Durham were carefully planned and heavily overseen by agricultural experts and state authorities. Potential community members were screened for suitability, with special attention to their interest and potential for success in a rural farm setting. Like Smythe, Mead was explicitly planning a community, and his colony at Durham developed a cooperative economic strategy of shared means of storage and distribution of their individual farms' produce. Like Country Life reformers, Mead also recognized the importance of the "Farmer's Wife":[51] the success of the farm depended on the training and support of farm women, he believed. If families were to stay on the land, they had to be incorporated into the economy of the household. By building communities, Mead also hoped to reduce the sense of isolation associated with rural farm life. Crucial to his vision were community centers in Delhi and Durham, which would become sites of the active social life necessary to keep families on the land.

Despite Mead's careful planning, the community at Delhi did not flourish. Moreover, the very idea of community-centered settlements was not always warmly received. Representatives of the National Grange argued that soldier settlements would increase competition with farmers. For them, the soldier settlement idea was "fundamentally un-American" and "paternalistic, socialistic, communistic, bolshevistic, or anything of that kind" to boot.[52] Private and state reclamation colony schemes continued, but it was not until the Division of Subsistence Homesteads of the Resettlement Administration became part of the New Deal's National Industrial Recovery Act in 1933 that reclamation settlements gained national support.

The Producer Family

Maxwell's image of the home and family on the land played on popular anxieties concerning the social ills created by urbanization and the economic and social turmoil caused by industrialization. The Homecroft offered an ideal of the family whose self-sufficiency insulated it from industrial life, and invoked a romanticized rural life at the heart of American agrarianism.[53] Ironically, national efforts to reform farm life under the rubric of the Country Life Movement began with a similarly romanticized view of the value of the rural family, but by the 1920s the focus had shifted from rural life to farm business. Government programs for modernizing agribusiness had a direct impact on farm women. Government policies sought to separate women's labor from the farm's productive labor and the imposition of a separate spheres ideology urged women to become consumers instead of producers.[54] While many rural women resisted the suggestion that they take a less active role as producers within the farm family, their views—and Maxwell's—were in the minority.[55]

Maxwell tempered his nostalgia for the rural life by rejecting a complete return to the land. Over the course of his advocacy for Homecrofts, Maxwell's ambitions for entire colonies on reclaimed land gave way to suburban communities, such as those in Duluth and Indianapolis, whose gardens and livestock yards could help insulate them from a fluctuating economy. Nevertheless, the ideal of the family that he advocated remained significantly different from the "industrial family ethic" associated with the U.S. welfare state.[56] By refiguring the home as a site of production essential for economic stability, Maxwell sought to restore women's roles as producers as well as consumers in an era when they were being urged to be only consumers. At the same time, Maxwell offered an alternative vision of how the state ought to intervene on behalf of the family. This view was at odds with models of state intervention on behalf of urban families and, as agribusiness was modernized, it was even at odds with the model of the rural family being advocated by the government.[57]

Maxwell's focus on the producer family precluded support for the other types of decommodifying policies being proposed and in some cases passed during this important period of welfare state development in the United States, including veterans' and mothers' pensions, soldiers' bonuses, and various forms of social insurance which were meant to compensate for fluctuations in wages or employment. In Maxwell's opinion, because such policies were based on the principle of an exclusive male breadwinner earning a family wage, they provided little or no economic stability. Instead, the ideal of the producer family led Maxwell to emphasize social policies that established funds for the purchase of homesteads, the purchase of quarter-acre lots for Homecrofts, or, in the case of returning soldiers, the direct transfer of reclaimed land. Maxwell promoted these kinds of policies as individualistic, since they put families on the land, encouraged greater self-sufficiency, and did not require additional governmental support. Contrary to the rhetoric, however, every settlement project, including the Homecrofts, required further intervention to provide agricultural training and govern the community.[58] Nevertheless, the types of social policies that Maxwell and other reclamation and resettlement activists advocated were guided and reinforced by a producer, rather than an industrial, family ethic, which sought to decommodify the male breadwinner through the labor of other family members.

Conclusion

For Maxwell, Smythe, and Mead, reclaiming the land offered a means of reclaiming the family. Like campaigns for other welfare policies, particularly mothers' pensions, the push for reclamation called for state support by claiming to uphold and preserve the family, but unlike those other policies, this one introduced a significant alteration to the ideology of the male breadwinner and family wage. The Homecroft and Settlement ideals maintained that women's responsibilities included productive labor in the garden, the orchard, and the livestock yard as well as the guildhall and community center. This labor by women was interpreted as freeing the family from total dependence on industrial wages. Thus it was crucially important for the decommodification of the male wage-earner and so for the decommodification of the entire family.

Although Maxwell, Smythe, and Mead established communities in California, Arizona, Indiana, Minnesota, Ohio, and Massachusetts, these communities are not the sole legacy of their efforts. The ideal of greater self-sufficiency was recognized and incorporated into New Deal community programs such as the Subsistence Homestead Program. Indeed one of Maxwell's last Homecroft efforts was to try to establish a homecroft community in Zanesville, Ohio, under the auspices of the Subsistence Homestead Program. Zanesville was not chosen for the program, although other Homestead communities realized the ideal of decommodification promoted by Maxwell and others. These attempts to reconfigure the American family by mobilizing the labor of wives and mothers as well as other family members reveal that the male breadwinner regime was not hegemonic during the first half of the twentieth century, and thus they challenge scholars to broaden their interpretive framework for this period.

6

THE STATE AND THE WIDOW

Pension Debates in Inter-War Years Australia

JOY DAMOUSI

> Everybody desired, when unfortunate circumstances arose, that the widowed mother should be enabled to keep her home together, to live under the roof she had when her husband was alive, and to keep her children with her.[1]

In 1925, Millicent Preston-Stanley, the first woman to be elected to the New South Wales parliament, president of the Sydney Feminist Club, and member of the Australian Federation of Women Voters,[2] vociferously defended the granting of a pension to all widows. In a heated parliamentary debate, Preston-Stanley accused the governing Australian Labour Party (ALP) of dishonesty and deception for not allowing all widows to be eligible for the pension, and for making the pension available only to those with dependent children. "During the last week," she announced,

> I have received hundreds of letters from women of every class and section, in which the writers definitely state that they supported the Labour Party at the last elections under the clear impression that widows would receive a pension, on account of the fact that they were widows.[3]

Although she supported the bill, because she was "a believer in child endowment, and [it] is a step in the right direction," she argued it was, nevertheless, insidious that the government "is not paying the same to those who have not children as to those who have."[4] She believed it was only when greater numbers of women shared the political responsibility of shaping social legislation would there be a more equitable and just effort to provide all widows with financial assistance. "I feel that had we had women in Parliament," she stressed, "it would have been done long ago."[5]

In her belief that the widows' pension should be broadened to include all widows and not simply widowed mothers of a dependent family, Preston-Stanley was a lone voice. The dominant opinion among the lawmakers was that only means-tested mothered widows should receive the pension. In

1926, when the widows' pension was introduced in New South Wales, for widows with children under the age of 14, it was the first of its kind in Australia. Widows whose husbands had died in military service were supported, but it was not until 1944 that the Commonwealth introduced a civilian widows' pension.[6] The New South Wales pension stipulated that widows who received £78 or more a year and those without children were ineligible. Widows with children were to receive a pension of £1 and 10 shillings per week for each child under fourteen.[7] This initiative was part of NSW Premier Jack Lang's wider package of reform implemented between 1925–1927, which included a 44-hour-week, workers' compensation, family endowment, and reforms to industrial arbitration.[8]

In this chapter, I pursue several arguments which emerge from the discussion about the widows' pension and charity during the inter-war years. The first is that in the relationship between the family and the state it was the survival of the family that preoccupied the state and the lawmakers, and not the plight of widows per se. The ideology that informed these discussions reflected, in Ellen Ross' words, the "fantasies of finding the perfect mother."[9] The introduction of the pension was a means to prevent further fragmentation within the family unit by allowing women to remain in the home and not become breadwinners. Its aim was to restore the stability between public and private life and reinforce the boundaries between these two spheres. But as Tamara Hareven points out, families did not always conform to such prescriptions, and they exercised considerable agency in the ways in which they "planned, initiated, or resisted change; [they] did not just respond blindly."[10]

Through a study of the records of one charity organization in Victoria—the Charity Organization Society (COS)—I tease out enduring assumptions about "the family." Established in 1887, the COS co-coordinated Melbourne's charitable relief until 1967. An analysis of the views that informed the judgments made by charity workers point to two further arguments about building families during the inter-war years. First, the expectation that sons and daughters would provide for their families has a long history, dating from the early nineteenth century. It is based on romantic fantasies about motherhood, children, and the family, which continued—albeit in a revised form—to frame the attitudes of charity workers during the inter-war years. The assumption that there was an enduring emotional bond between family members and that children were obliged to contribute to the family economy permeated the ways in which both governments and charity workers assessed the widows' cases. The resistance by children of widows to these expectations is a striking feature of this period. Another aspect of the changing relationship between the state and families during the inter-war years is that of the role of the charity worker. During the 1930s, social work became a profession in Australia. Up until then, benevolent and philanthropic organizations tended to the poor and underprivileged. In the period under discussion there was a move toward professionalization, which ushered in a shift to listening to the women and attempting to direct their behavior, rather than simply observing their economic circumstances. This new approach did not, however, modify the earlier moralism; it simply provided a new language with which to discuss the plight of the poor.

Finally, I examine the role of gossip and rumor in shaping assumptions about poor families. Drawing on recent scholarship that considers the role of silence or denial within families to "protect themselves from social stigma or condemnation by the law,"[11] this chapter discusses how silence, secrecy, and evasion were interpreted. Charity workers believed such behavior reflected deceit and deception, and they used shame both to elicit information from the widows and to exert their social and political power.

Defining Widowhood

When New South Wales Premier Jack Lang rose to speak to the issue of the widows' pension, on December 2, 1925, his government had only recently been elected into office. As Preston-Stanley reminded him, one of his chief platforms was a pension for all widows. On the eve of the election, the ALP had placed an advertisement in the *Sydney Morning Herald*, which declared:

> Pensions for widows will crown Labour's fine humanitarian record.... Labour if returned to power will at the earliest possible moment provide pensions for widows now and hereafter.[12]

Along with members on both sides of parliament, Lang fiercely promoted a glorified image of the mother and of an idealized nuclear family when discussing the necessity for granting the pensions:

> The main purpose of the bill is to keep homes together and allow the mother to keep her children with her and rear them in much the same atmosphere and under as nearly as possible the same conditions as when the bread-winner was alive.

As with many discussions about charity and welfare up to this time, it was not the politicians' intention to encourage indolence and thrift, but to ensure that when a widow was left with a large family, the pension was sufficient to avoid forcing her to become a breadwinner, but instead "to enable [her] to devote the whole of her time to her home and children." Lang stressed that the state "owes a duty to the mothers and the children of the state. The aim of the bill is to give the benefit of home life and a mother's care to the children who have been bereft of their father—the breadwinner for the home." The state would therefore provide as a breadwinner would have done.

During the inter-war years, there were many families for whom this assistance would have provided a much-needed source of income. World War I had had a devastating impact on Australian families. Although most of the

60,000 men who perished were single, many of them were chief breadwinners for their families, and even those who returned left families destitute. As Judith Allen has shown, returning men created violent and abusive relationships, and innumerable instances of desertion and alcoholism were a direct result of the war.[13] In this context of dislocation and fragmentation, the eugenics and infant welfare movements flourished to rigidly prescribe and define the attributes of "good" mothering and notions of the model family. The values of efficiency and science saturated childrearing advice manuals as mothers were expected to adhere to strict scientific instructions in rearing their children.[14] But this advice was aimed at middle and upper-class mothers in order to ensure "quality" breeding, while it was assumed that poor mothers would be oblivious to such instructions.

Social reforms had been introduced to assist the underprivileged. In the 1920s, the number of welfare recipients increased. Stephen Garton estimates that in 1912 there were 90,000 old age and invalid pensions in Australia, and by 1929 this number had risen to 200,000. In 1925, the pension was 20 shillings a week, although rents were usually above 10 shillings.[15] The poor received the assistance of friends and neighbors in time of desperation, and communities offered assistance to each other.[16] Neighbors certainly "clubbed" together to assist each other financially,[17] but this was not always the case, and, as we shall see, when charity workers visited poor households, it was the neighbors who were often the most damning and judgmental of those in need. Although there had been efforts to provide support to the poor through pensions, the inter-war years were marked by a reluctance of governments to provide adequate support.[18] Provision was informed by a belief in a circumscribed notion of the family, as the following statement made in 1923 in the NSW parliament illustrates:

> The widow, the orphan and the babe in arms are the first call upon us . . . where a mother is engaged in rearing a family of children, she is doing her duty to the State if she rears that family satisfactorily. If . . . she has to go out into the world to try to earn a livelihood that work cannot be satisfactorily carried out. The children will suffer and the State will suffer when those children grow up by reason of the fact that the work was not properly done.[19]

The premise of the Widows' Pension Bill reflected these preoccupations, as it was founded on preserving the distinction between public and private spheres. The welfare of children and thus Australia's future was at the basis of the support for the legislation. This pension was intended as a "humanitarian measure" that would

> keep the home together while the children are at such an age that they must have a mother's care and attention. . . . The State will have done its share. It will have helped them in every possible way.

The children would then be expected—if the "training in the home has been efficient and careful, and if the mother has devoted to the children that attention which I think she will devote to them"—to repay her something of this support. The bill was meant to ensure that

> widows and their families will be lifted from charitable relief and widows will be given something which will enable them to stop at home and devote the whole of their time, care, and attention to giving that which is the most valuable thing on God's earth—a mother's love for her children.

Although Preston-Stanley agreed with such sentiments, she believed it was unfair that widows without children should be overlooked. It was unjust that widows had been misled, she argued, because the electoral promise was for widows, not for widows with dependent children only. She attacked Lang for not providing for all widows:

> Thousands of women, unquestionably, voted for the Labour party believing that their widowhood, alone, would entitle them to a pension.... The mother who is a widow, and who has dependent children, has, by virtue of her motherhood a claim to a pension, but no widow, as such, has any claim to a pension under this bill.... The Government is not paying the same to those who have not children as those who have.[20]

Despite these comments, she fervently believed that,

> to ensure justice to that child it is the duty of the government to assume the responsibility of parentage. If a family loses its breadwinner, even where the family income is adequate to maintain the normal standard, the loss is of an irreparable character.... [If] the mother has to go out to earn a living, a family of dependent children may very readily become a family of neglected children.... [This is] something... the nation must at all costs avoid.[21]

Like so many of her political allies and enemies, Preston-Stanley pursued eugenicist and nationalist purposes, conflating the concerns of the child with that of the nation. The "whole world has declared that it believes the future of a nation lies in the future of the child.... [T]he problem of the nation is the problem of the child because the child is the nation in embryo."[22]

The paternalism embodied not a concern for widows but for nation-building. Widows without children had little to contribute to this project. Moreover, the expectation was that this group of widows could be self-reliant and earn a living so they should not need financial assistance from the state. The aim was to "encourage our people, including the widows, in that self-reliant spirit, that independence which will prevent them from coming to the Government for aid."[23] In this instance, financial survival was considered to be an individual and not a state responsibility. But it was erroneous to assume that widows could become "self-reliant," as employment opportunities for them were limited. Judging from the Victoria censuses of 1921 and 1933, the majority of widows were not earning wages, and most were heavily reliant on charity.[24] Both censuses indicate that over 80 percent (81.7 percent in 1921; 82.3 percent in 1933) of all widows were not engaged in paid employment, figures that reflected the national average.[25] During this period, governments were reluctant to assist women who were single and unemployed; priority was given to unemployed men, as the concept of the male breadwinner remained a powerful ideology shaping welfare policies.[26] The irony was that while childless widows were expected to be independent of state aid, the financial circumstances created by this belief made them among the most needy in the community. Thus the purpose of the pension, stressed Lang, was familial, not charitable:

> the bill is not a charity measure providing relief for destitution, but is to give a pension to a widow to enable her to keep her home together and train her children . . . as they would have been trained if the breadwinner had been alive.[27]

Such views were not distinctive to Australia at this time. As Susan Pedersen has shown in the British case, where contributory pensions for widows were introduced in 1925, the policy on widows reflected the ideology of "the family wage as espoused by organized men."[28] While there was support for widowed mothers, the widows' pension bill was in "keeping with conventional assumptions about husbands' responsibilities and wifely dependence."[29]

A preference for children rather than widows was also evident in the arguments regarding so-called Aboriginal "half-caste" children, where it was the children and not the women who were of interest to the state.[30] As Alison Holland has argued, efforts by feminists to support Aboriginal women were very much framed as assistance to children on the basis that they were the coming generation of Australians, and not to Aboriginal mothers per se.[31] Racial assumptions, which governed questions about the unsuitability of Aboriginal women as mothers, led to the ruthless removal of their children.

Although the state was prepared to assume a paternalistic role, there was a longstanding expectation that children would make some contribution to the family economy. Further discussion on this issue took place in 1929, when the Nationalist-Country Party coalition government led by Thomas Bavin was debating whether the earnings of a son should be taken into account when calculating the widow's pension. The Labour Party—now in opposition—argued that to do so would be unjust. Lang was critical of the irresponsibility of the widows' children for not providing for their mothers, but he did not believe that mothers should also be penalized:

> We are not going to interfere with the widows' pensions, but there are some sons who are utterly selfish, . . . who have left home and have

refused to contribute to the upkeep of their mothers and we propose to make them do so.... If the son does wrong in that way punish him if you will, but do not inflict punishment on his widowed mother and his orphaned brothers and sisters.[32]

The other parties, however, wished to compel sons to contribute to their widowed mothers' income, because "there does devolve upon the children the duty of recognizing their obligation to assist their widowed parent so as not to throw the whole of the burden on the State."[33] The new bill proposed to take as a widow's income 50 percent of the earnings of children living at home, instead of 25 percent "as provided at present in the Act." This, argued Minister Drummond, would "place a certain responsibility, where it rightly belongs, on the shoulders of the widow's own family."[34]

The rationale of this deduction was that "no unmarried children, who are able to contribute and should contribute to the upkeep of their widowed parent, shall be permitted to evade their just obligations." It was important to have a "premium... put on children living away from home." Drummond believed a child should be compelled to contribute to the relief of the parent. "There is a solemn obligation resting upon a parent to provide for the children, and for the children to relieve the necessity of the parent, if the circumstances arise."[35] Whilst some agreed with this provision, others felt it to be unjust, and thought it was only penalizing the widow. As one minister argued, "We recognize the responsibility but children may not. It is not the role of the State to impose this law, and by lessening the pension, only the widow will suffer. It may also be the case that the children do not provide for their widowed mothers." In the words of Minister Connell:

> Suppose a boy is a waster and spends the whole of his money, or that a girl is selfish and will not give her mother a penny.... There are very many sons and daughters who are selfish, and do not realize their obligations, so that this provision will act very harshly on the mother.[36]

One could not assume that families would be harmonious, or that children would willingly provide. A son may have "quarreled with his family; such things happen. He may be selfish, or circumstances may arise that prevent his contributing to the support of his mother."[37]

One of the other two provisions discussed in 1929 concerned assistance to widows who had no children, but who had been left penniless. It was expected that this "indulgence" would only be temporary, before she became self-supporting:

> It is intended to help a widow who may be suddenly bereft of her breadwinner and it will enable such a widow to recover from the shock and procure employment. This pension will be given for a period not exceeding six months. It is not designed as a permanent relief, but

merely a temporary assistance to enable her to tide over a difficult period, to recover from the shock, and to secure employment.[38]

The other category of widow was that of women over 50 years of age who were destitute, childless, and of "declining strength." The provision intended to "bridge the gap between the age of 50 and 60," when she would become eligible for the old-age pension.[39] This was the only provision made for widows without children to support. At the level of policy, governments reflected the paradox that while they aimed to be progressive in providing monetary support for widows, their measures had been devised on a conventional view of the idealized mother rearing her children, without the need to work for wages. The view that the family tie came with enduring responsibilities is reflected in the shift in emphasis to children supporting their widowed mothers later in life.

Similar assumptions about motherhood, the nation and single women informed the debate that took place in Victoria. A widows' pension was introduced in 1937, and it was discussed in similar terms to those in Sydney over a decade earlier. The Minister G.J. Tuckett argued that the bill indicated a further "growing sense of the responsibility of the community towards the welfare of indigent children," despite the fact that the Bill itself "relates to payments to widowed mothers."[40] The progress report of the Select Committee on Widows' Pensions and Child Endowment argued that in its inquiries, the committee "was presented with some remarkable cases of courage and recourse on the part of these women, disclosing not merely the severity of their daily struggle, but also a degree of self-sacrifice on behalf of their children which more than demonstrated the splendid fiber of Victoria's womanhood."[41] Enlisting a romantic fantasy of childhood, the committee affirmed the belief that during the formative years of childhood, "It is imperative to retain the mother's guiding influence in the home, so that the development of wholesome personalities in the community may be stimulated."

As in the earlier debates, it was the issue of children that most preoccupied the legislators. The measure would offer payments to widowed mothers and "provide for the welfare and comfort of widows who are without means of support . . . " for themselves as well as their children. The goal was to remove the accusations of neglect of the widow who could not support her children and was charged "with neglecting her children whom she loved and for whom she would lay down her life."[42]

The evidence given to the Victorian committee confirmed these arguments. John Henry, the first witness to the inquiry, testified that it was the duty of the State that "every child 'rich or poor' has the chance for 'physical, intellectual, moral and later in life industrial development.'"[43] He was opposed to mothers working and insisted that "provision should be made for imposing an obligation on unmarried children that are working to make reasonable provision for their parents."[44] Jean Daley, the secretary of the Women's Central Committee of the ALP, connected this issue to that of the nation. In her view:

> A woman who has children to rear and has lost her breadwinner ... should have an allowance from the State whereby she can carry out the natural functions of a mother, ... giving to that child the full measure of loving care which should be the heritage of all children.[45]

The future of Australia lay in providing the pension, for our desire was "'to see a healthy race of young Australians growing up instead of half stunted people." This provision would also take the pressure off the mother to find work, and it "solves the question of equal pay for equal work."[46]

Building Families

"Contempt is the mark of the oppressor."[47]

These assumptions, especially the belief that children should contribute to the family economy, were embedded in charity workers' reports. Those unwilling to support their families were deemed "ungrateful" and "selfish," and were identified as part of the reason why widows were in desperate financial straits. Resourceful, supportive, and cooperative families were considered worthy recipients of money. In many respects the ideal family was one that conformed to a nineteenth-century model, where

> instrumental bonds between family members were strong, most certainly not excluding affectionate ties, but ... taking precedence; stability of family life was pre-eminent, even where effective ties were lacking. Husbands and wives had duties to perform for each other, and children had duties to perform for parents, irrespective of the quality of the emotional ties which bound them.[48]

Where children did not offer financial support, applications made by their widowed mothers were treated with scorn. Family dynamics did not often conform to assumptions by charity workers who invariably held a static view of the family. On the contrary, working-class families were dynamic, and a "custodian of tradition and social change."[49]

Another striking feature of the families under scrutiny is the way in which it was hoped that denial would divert any shame and stigma. The role of the charity workers, it seemed, was to investigate family secrets, often through gossip and rumor within the communities. An examination of the records of the COS reveals that the subtle but powerful mechanisms of shame and contempt were used to expose these silences and secrets and strengthen the psychological power of conventional familial discourses.

Children and Their Widowed Mothers

In 1929, Mrs. Edith Hazelwood was a 52-year-old widow whose husband had died eight years previously. Her three children had "all grown up and [were] in Tasmania." The officer reported critically of the applicant that she

> impressed me as a woman who had lived a sordid life.... She appears to be a derelict who has drifted so far away from her children and aged mother . . . that it is no longer possible for her to live with them as she should be doing, not any of her three children are married. They lived with her mother.... She is clearly not worthy of free treatment, but her case is a tragic one. Drink has probably caused her downfall.[50]

Hazelwood's relations with her children were deemed to be a part of her tragedy. The secretary of COS wrote to the dental authorities that she had an "aged mother and a grown-up son and two daughters in Tasmania, but she has drifted away from them and appears to have sunk very low in the social scale through addiction to drink and association with undesirable characters." She was not deemed worthy of any assistance.[51] The COS argued strongly for the need for children to aid their mothers in such cases. In the case of Rose Hutchinson, a 54-year-old widow with three children, the charity worker believed the children "should really be helping her."[52]

Another widow, Mrs. Christina Sandberg, aged 70, requested payment for her late husband's funeral expenses. Her two sons from her first marriage had been killed in the war, and the only son from her second was married and lived in Sydney, "earning good money." Police had "wired asking him to come to his father's funeral and to assist his mother, but he has not answered." The COS inquired about the status of the woman and her husband. The comments it received reflected the type of gossip and rumor circulated in the area, which offered a clue to charity workers investigating the nature of familial relations. "Several neighbors . . . spoke very well of Applicant," it was noted, and "[they] were quite sure they did not touch drink."[53] They received confirmation from one Rev. John Landelle that the "couple bore a good reputation." He also noted the son should be assisting his mother in her moment of financial despair:

> Mrs. Sandberg has a son . . . who is earning good wages, and who has ignored communications regarding his father's death. If you have not already done so, it might be a good thing for you to write to him on his mother's behalf.[54]

Charity workers' reports frequently discussed the behavior of the children and often condemned it. Mrs. Agnes Vessey, aged 56, had eight children when her husband passed away in 1912. Although these children were all over 20 and three were single, the level of financial commitment to their mother varied, according to reports. Vessey's daughter "is a very superior girl.

She has been engaged to be married for the past months and is greatly handicapped owing to her having to put all her earnings into the house since her brother Edward's long period of unemployment.... He is a widower and had a child which has since been adopted, as her brother could not afford to keep her." It was the married children who seemed ungrateful toward their mother:

> One of her sons, Alec, aged 22, is about to be married. He should really have been assisting his mother ... and prefers to board with his fiancée's people.... Applicant's married children also appear to be very inconsiderate to their mother and never assist her in any way.[55]

In some cases, children's non-assistance was considered to be a reason for providing help for widows. Mrs. Ellen Dare, a 78-year-old widow, had six married children, whom she had struggled to raise, "all married now and none of them helps her." For this reason, the COS had "no hesitation in recommending her for free [dental] treatment."[56] In the case of Mrs. Myra Snow, a widow of 52 with six children, who was, according to the COS officer, judged a "superior type of woman and impressed me very favorably," her referee believed she was a "very nice woman and thoroughly trustworthy," and "she did not think her children had been altogether fair to her."[57] Another widow, Rosa Johnson, received a similar assessment. She was a mother of five children, four of whom were married, but "none of them does anything to help her."[58]

The testimony of neighbors and landladies—which was often based on gossip and rumor—carried considerable weight in these cases; informants were also critical of the irresponsibility apparently shown by children of widows. In 1921, in an application by Mrs. Elizabeth Blake for free dental treatment, her landlady observed that the family was in disarray, and there had been little communication between them. She noted caustically that "her sons do nothing for her, she knows nothing of their whereabouts...."[59] In investigating the case of Rose Hutchinson, the charity worker reported "first saw the landlady Mrs. Eader who stated that she did not know much of the applicant as she had only been with her a few days ... also said she thinks applicant has only the clothes she stands up in." When the applicant was found, it was noted that she was "a refined type of woman."[60] Mrs. Margaret Nicholson, aged 63, whose husband had been killed in war service in 1916, was "well spoken of by the neighbors," although they had a "bad opinion of Mrs. Nicholson's son-in-law who lived there."[61]

Relatives who could help, but did not, were also criticized. In the case of another widow, Mrs. Emily Trethewie, her landlord reported that her deceased husband's "people who live in Tasmania are well off but will do nothing for her," nor for her four children, aged between eight and thirteen years of age.[62] On further investigation, it was noted that Mrs. Trethewie prefers not to give the address ["of her late husband's people"] as she knows it would be of no avail to write to them, and they would only enjoy the thought of her pecuniary circumstances. Her solicitors have approached them before, but they flatly declined to do anything.... Her own parents are unable to do anything.... They are old and just have sufficient [for] themselves.[63]

Her burden was further compounded because her late husband "brought home two of his illegitimate children, whose mother had died, for [her] to look after which she did for some months, and when her husband died she was mentioned ... as their guardian, as she was quite unable to provide for them she did not accept the responsibility, and as her husband's father would do nothing, she had put them on the State." The one hopeful sign was that her eldest son would soon turn fourteen and so could work and earn £1 a week. The expectation was that he would provide.

When they did provide financial assistance, children were crucial in supporting families. In June 1922, Mrs. Amy Cairns gained the assistance of her "two younger sons ... when they are in work, [and] are prepared to pay 10/- [10 shillings] weekly to the hospital during their mother's illness there."[64] She was entirely dependent on her two unmarried sons, one of whom was only seventeen. In another case, a widow of 42 lost her husband after he had accidentally died while working. Left with her seven children, she had them boarded out. She managed to gain some money, and that, together with the "earnings of the two children who are working ... [would] place her permanently in a position of reasonable comfort and self-support."[65]

By the same token, when sons were injured, the impact on the family finances could be dramatic. In the case of Mrs. Ellen Greenfall, an "elder son has recently met with an accident under circumstances which entitled him to no compensation, and would be incapacitated for work for some considerable time." In an effort "to keep the home together, the younger son was augmenting his earnings by doing some office-cleaning and by selling sweets at football matches on Saturday afternoons. The worry and strain were threatening to break down his health...."[66] Jean Clyde's financial predicament deteriorated when her son "got into trouble" and was jailed. "The shock has had such an effect on me that I have had a stroke and have been laid up nearly 2 months unable to work. I am paralyzed down the left side. I have always been an active and energetic woman ... but my object in writing to you is that Dave is my only support being a widow."[67]

Other families were denigrated from the first visit by charity workers. The case of Elizabeth Bird points to how some families of widows could do no right. Mrs. Bird, aged 53, and her seven children, were not considered worthy recipients of welfare. The Children's Welfare Department "did not consider that with four sons and a daughter of working age it was necessary for the C.W. Dept. to continue the assistance.... The sons evidently do not do their duty by their mother and Mr. Thomas [from the Department] does not feel that she has been altogether straightforward with the Dept."[68] Another report, by Dora McCowan, noted,

> The Birds are a shiftless family and don't really deserve any assistance, though they may be in present need.... The mother is untruthful.... Members of the family have had good jobs offered to them and refused and they have the reputation of being a lazy lot and quite ready to sponge on anyone.[69]

This impression, based on their inability to help themselves, was further confirmed by another officer, L. Davis, who reported in December 1929 that he visited the Bird home and

> found them in a poor-looking 3-roomed cottage, in a back street.... It was poorly furnished—not much besides three beds and a couple of chairs or a table.... The house was untidy—the beds were unmade and there was no attempt to make the best of things.[70]

Mrs. Bird argued that she remained in desperate straits, despite assistance from her family:

> I am writing you a letter to ask you if you could help me in any way to get relief for my 2 little girls.... I am a widow in poor circumstances, I have 4 sons, 3 are working in New South Wales, they are not earning enough money to keep themselves [going] and me and my children pay rent.... I was wondering if the Welfare people would just let me have the children's money for ... 2 months, so that I could move to Melbourne for my girl to get work.... I was so pushed for money that I had to pawn my ring.... Well Sir my sons allow me 10/0 each, the 3 that are at work, and that is not enough to keep 5 people and pay my way and clothe and boot the children, I would not mind if the Welfare Department could let me have their money....[71]

These cases reveal a disjuncture between the intentions of the state and the responses of the family. It also points to the evolving tension between the family as a "private entity and an object of the state."[72] The assessments made by welfare officers were reflected in judgments about widows and their families.

Moral Judgments: Looking and Listening

During the 1920s, before social workers were professionalized in Australia, applicants for financial assistance were assessed on the basis of their physical appearance rather than through their testimony. Social work became professionalized in the 1930s, and while there was more emphasis on the testimony of the women in need, officials continued to judge, assess and evaluate by looking rather than listening to their clients. Public appearance was deemed to reflect moral character. In his recollections of the inter-war years, author John Kingsmill has written that

> Everyone in the street looked like everyone else, give or take the variations [of physical appearance]. The sameness was a comfort we took entirely for granted.... There were no surprises.... For most people, even a quick trip to the local shops meant consideration of the way you looked. Appearance was more than important—it was the way the world judged you.[73]

Even during the Depression, the effort to keep up appearances was important. "It was a matter of pride, good manners, good sense," Kingsmill recalled.

> You never gave up, not in public anyway. To be poor was bad enough. To actually *look* poor was a disgrace, an open admission that you were down and out. You knew, all through the Depression, that almost everyone was struggling just to stay alive, so what did it matter, really, if a woman's dress was years old and out of date as along as it was clean and neat and had been given a life, somehow, with a blouse or a hat or a decent pair of shoes? ... The effort has been made, that was the thing.[74]

Family diversity was scorned and differences were immediately noted and scrutinized. This was the case in the instance of a widow named Mrs. Nellie Stelling, aged 41, who was the mother of a son, aged 12. In July 1929, the officer observed that the

> applicant is a most peculiar woman. She looks as though she might have some dark blood. She told me that she was an American and that she had spent most of her [time] in India. Her late husband was in the Bombay Customs and retired about 3 years ago....

The home they built was "nothing more than a wooden shack and it was a most peculiar looking place."[75] The place where she lives "is very lonely and I think possible it has got on her nerves." The officer inquired at the local post office and was told she "was a peculiar tempered woman and that her late husband was a man of education and refinement."[76] Another widow was judged through the appearance of her children. A Methodist minister recommended a widow to the COS, as "her three children under fourteen are cleanly and fairly well dressed when they attend Sunday School.... She is a good mother and the children are very regular at Sunday School."[77] The charity worker who visited Mrs. Catherine Mockett, aged 68, observed that she was a superior and "honest [woman] who bears a splendid character" with an "excellent reputation."[78]

There was comment on whether women had done much to help themselves, and on the standard of their cleanliness. Nellie Stelling was dismissed thus: "Applicant seems to be a helpless sort of individual. She says she has never done any hard work."[79] Mrs. Vessey's home was said to be "very sturdy and ... appears to be tidily kept." But her neighbor told the officer that she was "thoroughly decent and respectable." The home was said to be "poorly furnished and kept in a clean and tidy way." References confirmed that the

Vessey family was "thrifty and highly respectable in every way."[80] Mrs. Hertha Rose was a widow of 32 with five children. Her home was deemed "tastefully furnished and well kept, and the three children seen this morning are refined and well cared for." She had had a "hard struggle" since the death of her husband "from some unknown disease caused by the war." One of the COS officers wrote that she was an "exceptionally splendid type of woman" who "does the best she can for her family."[81] Mrs. May Curd was "a superior and reliable woman" whose home was "tastefully furnished and well kept."[82] The home of Mrs. Jean Clyde was described as "exceedingly well kept" and she "was a superior woman ... who has a very strong and good character and is endeavoring to keep her house going while both her husband and son are unemployed."[83]

Mrs. Margaret Nicholson, whose husband was killed in war service in 1916, was a 63-year-old mother of three married daughters. After several inquiries, the applicant's daughter's house was finally located and, according to a report, it "looked neglected and dirty." Her attitude was also wanting; after she was given "warm underwear, and ... 10 shillings which was to be the first of fortnightly installments," she "expressed no appreciation and is obviously disappointed at not getting more assistance. . . . She declares that her daughters are all very good to her, but I told her that it is not quite fair of Mrs. Drew, the daughter with whom she is now living, to charge her 10 shillings weekly for one room, as the daughter's husband is employed regularly."[84] The appearance of a home of another widow came under scrutiny in the report of another COS officer. The applicant for assistance, Mrs. Isabella Jones, aged 38, with three children, had applied for an invalid pension. The officer noted how the "house is a decent looking one and the door knob and bell were well polished. The curtains and windows are very clean and the house generally, from the outside, had a well kept appearance."[85]

Not finding a house was an instant cause for suspicion, as was one applicant's failure to make eye contact with the charity worker. Alice Tomholt noted the way in which Mrs. Susan Moreland "appears to be a quite respectable but most peculiar woman who has a rather unpleasing way of evading one's eyes when she is being spoken to. It is extremely difficult to get any information from her."[86] Her apparently evasive behavior was considered highly suspicious, and it was concluded that Mrs. Moreland "cannot be depended upon to tell the truth about her affairs."[87] The fact that Edith Hazelwood would not directly address the charity worker when she interrogated her aroused similar concern. "She could not look at me while talking," noted the charity worker, "and she appears to be a derelict."[88] Such moments often result from feelings of shame, and indignity where such behavior is a "literally ... turning of the eyes away from the object toward the face, toward the self."[89] It was also a strategy used by applicants to resist communication with those interrogating them. Shame, argues psychologist Silvan Tomkins, is often expressed "both [as] an interruption and a further impediment to communication."[90]

Shame, humiliation, and indignity are further illustrated in another case. In July 1924, one of the officers who worked for COS noted the peculiar case of Elizabeth Hannah, aged 24, a widow with three children, "all school age," whose occupation was selling newspapers. In the files of the agency, this case was distinctive because the widow involved refused any assistance or help from their agency, despite lodging a request for blankets and clothing. Before calling to see Hannah, the officer spoke to the neighbors, Mr. and Mrs. Keogh. They were

> decent people who gave an exceptionally bad report of Mrs. Hannah who they described as the most foul-mouthed, and is a woman [they] have ever had the misfortune to meet. She had her children boarded back to her by the State, but the money was taken away from her some time ago, owing to her general behavior and character. Steps have been taken by several people re having the children taken from her, but as she does not drink this cannot be done.

Her children were boarded out from her, a practice which continued during this period. The "boarding out" system saw, in Victoria in 1937, 7,450 children boarded out from their mothers; 2,200 to foster mothers; 3,400 to institutions and service homes.[91] In the case of Hannah, gossip in the community contributed to adverse impressions. "The children practically live on oats," confided Mrs. Keogh, "and I saw them running in the street in a most unkempt and neglected state."[92] In her report on the applicant, the social worker confirmed Mrs. Keogh's impression of her neighbor as a woman of "poor" character, observing how the "front window was broken and it was covered only by half a blind attached to it." When approached,

> Mrs. Hannah only opened the door a couple of inches or so, and is a most peculiar looking woman who appears to be not quite sane. She resented me bothering her and stated that she was sick of people coming to her. She hasn't got much but makes enough to keep going, she stated.... Asked her why she didn't have her children boarded back. She stated that she wouldn't have the state worrying her and would rather just manage the best way she could.... She would not permit me to go into the house, and the little I could see of the narrow passage was only partially covered with the remains of the old linoleum.... She appeared the whole time to be suppressing a desire to be abusive, and is a most impossible woman to handle.... It seems terrible that such a woman should have charge of her children. I did not hear that she was cruel to them in any way.... When Mrs. Hannah first came to the house the neighbors pitied her and did all they could to help, but they were soon discouraged by her thanklessness, and nothing is done now.[93]

Mrs. Hannah's case aroused conflicting opinions, which created further suspicions. One supporter wrote to the daily *Sun* with another perspective. J.E. Bain argued that she was "a decent, sober, respectable woman." Although she was "frail and delicate, she refuses to accept charity from Government, Ladies Benevolent Societies etc., and chooses to sell a few papers in the city and barely pays her rent. They have not a stick of furniture beyond a bed in which they all sleep. They are without blankets and clothes and boots, and do not possess a saucepan in which they could warm a drop of soup given by the kindly disposed neighbors. If you could kindly spare some clothes, blankets, etc. to cover the children I would most willing make them do or repair them. . . .[94]

The secretary of the COS retaliated by writing to the paper, insisting that Mrs. Hannah "is . . . most peculiar and allows her children to run about in such a disgracefully neglected condition that we have felt impelled to ask the Society for the Prevention of Cruelty to Children to look into the case." She "refused to allow my assistant to enter her house." The secretary requested that "[u]nder the circumstances I could not recommend you to take any notice of the appeal."[95]

This is an interesting case because of the comments of the charity officer who found offense with the widow she was attempting to assist. Welfare recipients were not meant to resist in this way, nor defend their own dignity, but were expected to be grateful and accepting of what was offered to them. Those who were more obliging were more likely to receive favored treatment. COS officer Tomholt was especially impressed with Maria Bishop, aged 63, who "was acutely sensitive about having to ask for free dental treatment."[96] The assessments of the widows' home reflected the value judgments placed on widows at this time, and these were used to assess their suitability for becoming welfare recipients.[97] One inspector from the Children's Welfare Department, Ann Moylan, told the Select Committee on Widows' Pension and Child Endowment that inspecting the state of the home of recipients of child endowment was part of her job:

> We are supposed to go through her house. A mother's home is supposed to be always available, unless she tells you that her mother is occupying a certain room, or she has a boarder or lodger, in which case we do not go into that particular room. We see her beds and the general condition of her home.[98]

During the inter-war years social work underwent dramatic changes from philanthropy to professionalism. With this shift came "an emphasis on the psychology of the client,"[99] a transition to the new terminology of the expert, and a move from volunteers to trained welfare workers.[100] Different approaches were also adopted, from explaining social problems in terms of the lack of moral fiber, to "the individual's inability to adjust to their circumstances due to psychological problems."[101] Efforts were made to cooperate with traditional organizations such as the Melbourne Ladies' Benevolent Society. In the early stages of the introduction of social work as a science, Jocelyn Hyslop, a social worker who had been trained in psychology, reassured members of the society that training would "embrace both professional workers and voluntary ones," and she urged voluntary workers to "look on the students as members of a younger generation preparing to carry on the work of their predecessors, and not as nuisances or as people only to be made use of ... much benefit would be gained on both sides."[102] She did claim, however, "that the day of the voluntary worker is done."[103]

One key shift was a new strategy of listening to the clients, rather than simply providing them "handouts." In 1937, Hyslop identified the shift and described the key defining element of social workers' approach:

> Then the woman began to talk. The social worker listened for an hour—"skilled listening," Miss Hyslop called it.... She had other and bigger personal problems, but had never had a skilled listener to tell them to. It didn't take another hour for the worker to unravel the woman's real problems.[104]

The training of social workers, Hyslop believed, "lets us in behind the problem.... All charitable work is inadequate unless you get down to root causes." She concluded that it would be "fair to assume that the voluntary social worker was less inclined to listen, or even suggest that listening was an important part of their approach." The social workers had developed a method of "asking probing questions and observing character types to discover any immoral tendencies." Their aim was to "probe the attitudes and anxieties they saw behind cases of social inefficiency."[105]

Nevertheless, the new psychologism contained distinctive elements of the older moralism associated with the amateurs. Some doubted that training was necessary to develop such skills and challenged the view that volunteers lacked such abilities. In a letter to the Melbourne *Herald* in 1932, Elsie A. Baker stated the case for the volunteers, arguing that "true benevolent work can only be done efficiently by those who have the experience of years behind them." It was absurd, she argued, to believe that a "short course of study in psychology, physiology and psychiatry can fit a young inexperienced girl to cope with present day problems such as Social Relief workers are called upon to face in everyday life." Cases that "demand tact, sympathy and understanding" are not best dealt with by "inexperienced youth," nor are these traits learned through undertaking scientific courses.[106]

Child welfare policy and reform has historically been the domain of women. Social work was deemed an obvious career choice for women, and in a trend which was common across a number of Western countries, women joined the profession in increasing numbers. But the position was fraught. The tension identified by Robyn Muncy between the autonomy and limitations experienced by women in the United States, and the difficulty of reconciling values of professionalism with "female culture," were also pervasive amongst Australian women child welfare workers.[107] Although the role of the inspector also became more scientific towards the end of the 1930s, it was still perceived to be an occupation suitable to women's temperament. When asked whether the Department of Child Welfare should employ male inspectors, Ann Moylan replied,

> No, I think the work is peculiarly a woman's for the reason that you have to ask most intimate things and discuss delicate questions, and where there is an allegation of cruelty, children have to be stripped and examined. In that case I think a male inspector would be in a difficult position and the mother would naturally be embarrassed.[108]

These child welfare inspectors and trained social workers echoed the views of the politicians who had during the 1920s so emphatically introduced the widows' pension for the welfare of children. The preoccupations of this new generation also reflected the increasing intervention of government and state bodies into working-class families.[109] This was commonly conflated with a scientific concern for child welfare and improving the home environment to ensure a high standard of "mental hygiene of childhood."[110] The establishment of children's courts, kindergarten training colleges and kindergartens, which served to monitor "child hygiene," as well as the appointment of child welfare officers, point to a pervasive belief during the 1930s of the need for institutional and state intervention into the physical and psychological health of the child through the application of "expert knowledge."[111] This was invariably conflated with the discourse of the good/bad mother dichotomy that characterized child guidance literature, as "poor mothering" quickly became the focus of child guidance professionals.[112]

The COS was caught up with these changes in the nature of social work. There were lectures being advertised on social work topics run by the Victorian Council for Social Training.[113] The links with the Victorian Council for Social Training were strengthened when the Council wrote requesting that the COS agree to make available to their tutors "a supply of case-work for the students under supervision."[114] After "a lengthy and quite sympathetic discussion, the Committee resolved that at this stage, it could not determine to what extent, if at all, or in what direction, the desired cooperation might be given, but that the matter might be submitted for further consideration at a later date."[115] Despite further requests from the Council and a desire for increased cooperation, the committee sought to defer any discussion.[116] But the change was inevitable, and the COS finally succumbed to establishing formal cooperation with the Council. The other change registered in the minutes was the acknowledgement, stated in March, 1939, that "there was a tendency throughout the world to depart from the use of the word *charity* as part of the title of social agencies."[117] It was then only a matter of time before the COS assumed closer ties with the Council. Six months later, it was reported that "five members of the COS staff were attending a discussion class on the psychiatric and mental hygiene aspects of social case-work. This class was being supervised by

Dr. Anita Muhl, visiting University lecturer."[118] The "competitive tendency in the family case-work field" was noted in 1940.[119] In the same year, the social work course at the Victorian Council for Social Training was transferred to the University of Melbourne.[120] It would not be long before children's behavior within and outside the family would be explained through the language of psychology, psychiatry, and psychoanalysis, although a degree of moralism was retained in these discussions.[121]

At the level of both legislative reform and charity work, familial ideas about the responsible mother and obliging and supportive children were being enforced during the inter-war years. But mothers did not often conform to these expectations, nor did their children. Relationships within these families reveal the very fragmentation and dislocation the state wished to cement by introducing the widows' pension. Despite such efforts, these cracks were to widen and eventually threaten the very foundation of these fragile but enduring myths of family life.

7

FORGING FAMILIES

Gender, Reform, and the Popular Front State in Chile

KARIN ALEJANDRA ROSEMBLATT

In 1939 Salvador Allende, at the time Chile's Minister of Health, Social Security, and Social Assistance, published a book entitled *La realidad médico-social chilena* (Chile's Medico-Social Reality). The year before, Pedro Aguirre Cerda, a member of the centrist Radical Party, had won presidential elections as a representative of the popular front coalition of which the Socialist Allende was a part. The popular fronts, which held power from late 1938 to approximately 1948, implemented policies aimed at bettering the living conditions of poor Chileans, incorporating them into civic life, and promoting Chile's economic development. Reflecting these popular front goals, Allende's book expressed the widespread desire for state-led social change. But the Socialist Allende also believed the state should act *with* as well as *for* organized popular sectors. *La realidad médico social* emphasized the desires of the poor, their contributions to national development, and the need to recognize those contributions by ensuring their welfare. From his perspective as a physician and as minister, Allende sketched out new health, social security, and welfare policies that would promote the popular fronts' policies.[1]

Allende's book, and the popular front program more generally, sought not only to alleviate poverty and political disenfranchisement but also to reform gender and family relations. From its first page, *La realidad médico-social* pointed to the close relation between family life on the one hand and poverty and underdevelopment on the other. Allende and other popular front leaders sought to define norms of healthy family life that would stimulate the progress of the nation and ensure the well-being of the poor. They also insisted on the need for concerted state action toward those ends. The idea that the state should act in both private and public realms to articulate a national project that favored the most needy profoundly marked the period in Chilean history that began when the popular fronts first took power.

The first page of *La realidad médico-social* featured a photograph of two children sheltered in a doorway, the smaller huddled in the arms of the other. Both children seemed to be asleep. A well-dressed man was passing in front of the children with apparent indifference. The man, only his elegant shoes and the hemline of his overcoat showing, walked toward a light in the background. Taken from below, the photograph gave the impression the man was walking upwards. Below this, readers found the following text:

> Chile has the highest infant mortality in the world. For each twenty births, one child is born dead. Our neonatal deaths are equivalent to 50.5% of those born alive; for each thousand born alive, two hundred and fifty die. For each ten children born alive, one dies before reaching one month of age; one-fourth before the first year; and almost one-half before reaching nine years. Each year, four hundred thousand children do not attend any school, which represents 42% of the school-age population. We have six hundred thousand illiterate young people. 27.9% of those born alive are illegitimate children, a figure that is among the highest in the civilized world.

The unhealthy and illegitimate children to which this caption referred harked back to the two youngsters in the photograph. In contrast, the mobile male figure symbolized the advancement and progress of the Chilean nation. The man's indifferent attitude evoked the twofold abandonment of Chilean children, forsaken both by their irresponsible fathers and by the insensitive national community embodied in the state. Elsewhere in the text Allende lamented, "Our human capital has thus been seriously affected by abandonment and social insecurity," and he suggested that reducing the number of abandoned Chileans would increase social inclusion and lead to national advancement. Healthy, fit, and legitimate children were the point of departure for a more inclusive definition of who effectively belonged to the national community.[2]

For Allende, the ubiquity of "abandoned" children—these children were either poor, sick, or fatherless (and usually these elements were seen as going together)—endangered the nation's future. Since, according to Allende, illegitimacy necessarily resulted in poverty and consequent ill health, paternal abandonment and its outcome, illegitimacy, were a direct *cause* of infant mortality and morbidity. Infant and child mortality in turn stunted population growth, putting the nation in a situation of demographic inferiority. Sickly children did not contribute to the healthy and dense population that could make Chile part of the "civilized world." Consequently, improving Chileans' health, and especially that of the country's children, was a national security imperative. By reducing illegitimacy and rescuing Chile's abandoned children more generally, the concerted action of both fathers and policy makers could remedy this situation and assure the nation's forward march.[3]

Allende's concern with reducing illegitimacy was part of a larger state campaign of gender reform. Bolstered by dramatic formulations like Allende's, during the popular front period, state apparatuses, most prominently medical and social security agencies, attempted to assure the "proper constitution" of Chilean families. To that end, they tried not only to inscribe gendered norms but also to secure conduct consistent with those ideals. With increasing insistence, diverse branches of the state prompted Chilean husbands and wives to live with their legitimate offspring, leaving aside errant ways associated with the past. Linking the well-being of women and children to their economic attachment to a suitable breadwinner, state agencies supported male workers' claim to a family wage that might allow them to properly support a family.

Being a reliable provider was at the center of the definition of suitable male deportment put forward by popular front officials. Thus, crusaders enjoined men to be consistent providers who did not economically or physically abandon their wives and children. They counseled husbands not to spend leisure time away from their families and advised male breadwinners not to waste their salaries at the races or in taverns. Gambling and drinking stimulated male irresponsibility, they argued, and squandered families' scarce resources. If men acted as responsible husbands and fathers, state agents believed, they would also become hardworking laborers and collaborative citizens.

According to the definition of femininity put forward by these reformers, raising healthy and productive citizen-workers was women's most important task. Since work outside the home purportedly forced mothers to abandon their children, experts concluded that it should be avoided. Female employment further threatened familial stability because wage-earning women were on balance less economically dependent on men and could afford to be less tolerant of their male partners. Reinforcing the notion that proper family life demanded women's unrestricted attention to domestic matters, reformers taught domestic economy to women, seeking to improve their housekeeping and childrearing skills. Men, they surmised, would be more attracted to clean and well-run homes. In addition, state campaigns sought to strengthen the family by circumscribing both male and female sexuality. Reformers railed against prostitution and "promiscuity" and devoted inordinate energy to solving the "problems" of single motherhood and illegitimacy. These attempts to control sexuality consistently focused on the ways licentiousness undermined family life.

The popular fronts perceived their gender program as functional to their project of nation-state building. However, given the popular fronts' attempt to provide previously excluded social groups a place in public debates, their formulation of gender norms could not ignore the views of those popular sectors they sought to discipline and reform in order to govern effectively. The forging of state-enforced gender prescriptions therefore implied conflict and negotiation between men and women, the rich and poor, the powerful and weak, the right and left, professionals and workers, and political representatives and those they "represented." It also demanded both coercion and persuasion. The national-popular state that evolved with the popular fronts generally rejected more unilateral formulation and more repressive means of enforcing gender norms in favor of influence and bargaining, which in any case it deemed more effective. Thus the state's success in constructing a consensus around gendered norms of familial life was forcefully conditioned by both the form and content of state actions.

Given the unequal power of the diverse social actors involved in family reform, some influenced evolving gender prescriptions more forcefully than others, but no actor was inconsequential. The vast resources of the state—not only its material force but also the legitimacy it could claim as the purported agent of a national good—made the proposals it took up particularly potent. Nevertheless, the needs and desires of diverse subaltern actors and their collective and individual manifestations continually swayed state efforts. Despite conflict and disagreement, by the early 1950s, state cajoling, legislating, policing, educating, punishing, and rewarding in favor of the family had produced its effects; Chileans widely (although unevenly and eclectically) accepted and practiced its model of proper home life.[4]

Gender, Class, and National Identity in Popular Front Politics

The popular fronts produced a spectacular realignment of Chilean political life, definitively disrupting the previous hegemony of the landed aristocracy. While the economically dominant class and right-wing political elites continued to hold immense power during the years of popular-front rule, they lost their previous political ascendance. Neither the rich nor their representatives in the Conservative and Liberal parties were responsible for the revitalization of capitalist development or the democratization of public life that characterized what has been called the "compromise state" in Chile.[5]

Mobilization by working-class Chileans pressured popular front politicians into advancing policies that favored popular sectors. Most Chileans did not vote during this period, but that did not mean they lacked tools for asserting their opinions and advancing their interests. When Aguirre Cerda won the presidential election, Chileans jubilantly took to the streets to celebrate his victory and assure that he would be allowed to take office. In the coming months, labor mobilization stepped up in an attempt to capitalize on the progressive climate that prevailed. At the same time, throughout the popular-front period, the labor press lobbied for the replacement of unsympathetic state officials and more generally for increased representation of popular demands within the state. For labor and left organizations, state intervention seemed an important means of furthering popular demands.[6]

To achieve the economic and political advancement of the Chilean nation, the popular-front coalitions sought to harmonize the needs of all Chileans. State-sponsored "Chileanization" campaigns aimed to (re)invent a national identity that encouraged citizens of all social classes and political orientations to view and express their own particular demands in terms of national prerogatives. If Chileans could be coaxed into framing their social, political, and economic endeavors in terms of a national project, social cooperation would be encouraged. Diminishing conflict would make it easier to govern, build the national-popular nation-state, and smooth the path to reforms.[7]

The material and moral reforms of gender and family relations undertaken by the national-popular state were firmly linked to its project of building a national identity. By making its presence felt within the families of poor Chileans, the state sought to smooth over gender as well as class conflict. Reformers believed that if husbands and wives acted like proper men and women, conflicting interests that tended to destabilize families would be mitigated. In addition, as the state took an increasingly active role in regulating the "private" familial sphere during the popular front period, it enlarged the arena of concerns that were articulated into its quest for political ascendance. Within the working-class family, the state worked to reformulate popular gender identities, but in so doing, it also expanded the reaches of the state itself, adding to its "repertoire of rule."[8]

Negotiating with the State: Professionals, Politicians, and El Pueblo

The process of national-popular state formation and the reform of gender relations implicit in that process were stimulated and mediated by an influential contingent of state-employed professionals. These professional elites were among the chief proponents of familial reform, and day to day, they carried it out. Animated by lawyers, public health physicians, dieticians, economists, architects, sanitary nurses, and social workers, myriad branches of the state apparatus described and advocated the exemplary behavior they presumed could lead to stable families. Medical and social security agencies, especially the state's largest health and social security agency, the Caja de Seguro Obligatorio (CSO, Obligatory Insurance Fund), were the prime vehicles for this campaign, and home visits by social workers and sanitary nurses carried the crusade out of schools, hospitals, clinics, and factories and into the home itself.[9]

Expert analyses were widely cited by politicians, subalterns, and the dominant class as well as professionals—all of whom adeptly wielded facts and figures in their struggles over the control of family, community, workplace, and state. Although professionals' technocratic imperatives undoubtedly influenced the actions and orientations of the state, professional dictates were mediated by elites' own sensibilities and by the perceived racial, class, and gender interests of subaltern actors. Professional elites themselves wavered between a paternalistic imposition of "scientifically" learned truths, which were repeatedly justified in terms of the national good, and an ability to hear and represent the demands of subalterns (which were often phrased in terms of the national good as well). After 1938, however, a large contingent of elites increasingly advocated and practiced more horizontal relations with their clients. When Allende, a Socialist, put forward his platform for reform, he clearly saw himself as working with and for Chile's poor. Social workers, all of whom were female, often portrayed themselves as working-class women's allies.[10]

Poor Chileans, both men and women, never failed to realize that some professionals represented their interests better than others. State efforts to constitute and regulate subaltern family life, initiated principally by physicians and social workers in health care and social security agencies, became a site for the expression of both conflict and alliance between state professionals and subalterns. Contention and cooperation between these actors continually shifted the interrelated contents of class, racial, national, and gender identities as they were expressed in bids for familial reform.[11]

To Reward and Persuade: The Methods and Means of Family Reform

Popular front politicians understood the state's role as "essentially pedagogical," and they went about teaching and convincing Chileans of the necessity of a proper family life. While more repressive means reinforced and complemented approaches aimed at convincing and building consensus, the national-popular state decidedly preferred to reward and prompt. Its rewards were often material, and the material aid offered by the state reinforced its moralizing mission. Aguirre Cerda's most famous motto, cited as the epigraph of Allende's book, was: "To govern is to educate and give health to the people." Thus Allende and Aguirre Cerda signaled the popular fronts' project as both moral ("to educate") and material ("to give health").[12]

To further their goals, state officials availed themselves of the courts as well as material rewards and punishments dispensed by welfare agencies. Just as often, state officials relied on persuasion and dialogue. When social workers interceded in marital disagreements in order to prevent spouses from separating, they tried to convince spouses of the necessity of reconciling disputes. State legal recognition of familial bonds buttressed those efforts by legitimating, securing, and perpetuating ties of kinship. Civil laws were a constant reminder that marriage should be a lifelong commitment, social security benefits made getting married profitable, and welfare professionals assured their clients that it was the only "correct" thing to do.[13]

The legal and judicial systems, which inscribed the economic dependence of wives and children on husbands and fathers, encouraged Chileans to marry and to bear and rear children within marriage. The Chilean Civil Code mandated husbands' and fathers' legal responsibility for the economic maintenance of those dependents. (Wives were responsible for the economic maintenance of their children and invalid husbands.) It also classified children, enhancing the privileges of being born to married parents. These children, legally classified as "legitimate," had full rights to the economic support of their parents and to inheritance. "Natural" children, born outside of marriage but recognized by a parent or parents, had rights to diminished support and inheritance. "Simply illegitimate" children, who had not been recognized, had no rights at all.[14]

In contrast to welfare and social security programs, the legal system imposed parental, and especially male, obligations without the possibility of granting benefits. This circumscribed the effectiveness of legal means for enforcing the correct constitution of families. Although women and children could and did use the legal and judicial systems to enforce their economic rights, the legal system provided inadequate recourse when fathers denied their relation to children or abandoned their families. Filiation was legally difficult to prove, and if husbands or fathers ran off, the courts and police rarely tracked them down. Legislation enacted in 1935 and 1952 tried to lighten the burden of proof in legal proceedings aimed at establishing (male) parental recognition, but it still proved difficult to corner recalcitrant fathers. One social worker complained about deficiencies and asked for legal reforms, which she hoped would incite greater male responsibility. Without such reforms, male economic contributions to their kin rested mostly on their individual good will. The legal system did not reward men who acted as responsible breadwinners.[15]

Because of the difficulty of enforcing fathers' responsibility for their children through the judicial system, reformers found other methods. The "correct" legal constitution of families, as well as the fulfillment of fathers' legal responsibility for economically supporting their children, were encouraged largely by welfare professionals, especially social workers, and not in the courts. Policing gave way to chiding, as social workers employed in disparate state agencies—and their colleagues in the private sector—coaxed husbands and fathers into adequately fulfilling their roles. In fact, social workers often referred to themselves as judges.[16]

Material incentives were widely proffered to those who complied with moralizing campaigns and legalized ties of kinship. One physician went so far as to suggest that unmarried Chileans over the age of 25 should be subject to a special tax. While this radical measure did not become law, other more partial provisions had similar effects. Under the preventive medicine law passed in 1938, married workers and widow(er)s with children received 75 percent of their pay as a subsidy when absent from work because of illness; other workers received 50 percent. Family allowances, an important state-enforced material incentive aimed at promoting civil marriage and the legal recognition of children, were not mandated for blue-collar workers until 1952. However, throughout the popular-front period, popular-front politicians, as well as representatives of other political forces, lobbied for the payment of subsidies to workers for their legally recognized children, wives, and disabled husbands. Welfare professionals within and outside the state also called consistently for the payment of family wages.[17]

Of course state officials and politicians considered material benefits to be necessary regardless of their potential disciplinary effects. Admittedly, poverty and lack of resources directly impeded both men and women from fulfilling their obligations as spouses and parents. And yet the manner in which services and benefits were doled out encouraged certain ways of acting and thinking and discouraged others. Housewives who joined the state-sponsored Asociación de Dueñas de Casa (Housewives' Association), for example, may have been interested in the low-cost food items they could acquire through their membership in the organization. But as members they had to sit through domestic economy talks. Family allowances were meant to help parents provide sustenance for their children, but they also distinguished between legitimate and illegitimate children, favoring the former.[18]

The social security system in and of itself was a powerful inducement towards stable married life. From its inception in 1925, the social security agency for blue-collar workers provided spouses and children of insured workers with health care. An early reform of the law that created the CSO granted limited widows' and orphans' pensions to relatives of the insured upon their death. But to receive medical care or pensions, the CSO demanded that ties of kinship be legally sanctioned: children had to have proper birth certificates to receive benefits, illegitimate children had to be recognized by the insured to receive health care, and spousal rights depended on the existence of a civil marriage. Even if they were legally recognized, illegitimate children received orphans' pensions only if there were no legitimate progeny. State publications that informed workers and state functionaries about social security benefits were littered with explanations of which family members were eligible for what benefits—and which were not. While subalterns struggled for the extension of benefits to relatives even if those family members were not "legitimate," in the short run, the surest way to assure relatives access to those resources was to formalize legally family ties.[19]

Clients of welfare agencies had their own reasons for collaborating with professionals or heeding their advice. In many ways women and men of the popular classes found themselves indebted to social workers, who helped them steer their way through social security and welfare mazes. Since securing benefits involved complicated bureaucratic operations in which the burden of proof was always in the hands of the recipient, clients benefited from social workers' expertise. But subalterns paid a price when they visited social workers and asked them for help in their face-offs with more impersonal and tedious facets of the state. They had to put up with oftentimes intrusive home visits, social and moral "diagnoses," and the ensuing "treatment" of social ills. They also had to listen to endless exhortations to get married and stay married.

Domesticating Men

Despite reformers' aspirations and the cooperation they often elicited from their destitute clients throughout the popular front period, familial solidarity and cohesion were never fully realized. Men's loyalty to marriage and the family wavered, and women, too, had their doubts about the institution. Citizens cooperated with or challenged the state's program of familial reform depending on their assessment of the benefits and demands that prescribed roles placed on them. Certain social actors undoubtedly benefited more than others and therefore lent their support more forcefully.

Men themselves clearly provided the most substantial challenge to proper family life. Many simply did not want to settle down and become consistent providers for their wives and children. Accustomed to migrating in search of employment or adventure, workers preferred to move on when living or working conditions were unsatisfactory or wages were inadequate. Laborers' sexual and affective ties, like their employments, were often fleeting. Welfare professionals spoke frequently of this "problem." In a typical fashion one social worker commented on "our *pueblo*'s roving spirit, which leads it to search for other horizons, with neither wife nor children posing obstacles."[20]

The masculine identity promoted by the state prompted men to labor diligently and consistently so that they might become dependable providers. Prompted by employers who considered worker mobility a threat to profits, the state endeavored to discipline males, making them simultaneously stable workers and steady providers for their families. Besides, reformers argued, industrious laborers who contributed to the economic growth and helped Chile progress proved themselves worthy and loyal citizens. The CSO's health propaganda magazine for workers *Vida Sana* admonished its readers: "The desire to be a good family member, a good worker, and a good citizen gives life an unappreciable value."[21]

Despite state attempts to define masculinity in terms of family, many men continued to define their manhood largely in terms of how they related to other men. In their view, a man proved himself in bars and brothels and by showing solidarity with co-workers. Preferring autonomy to lasting work and family responsibilities, they insisted on their right to roam and to behave raucously. In contrast, state apparatuses put forward a model of masculinity that stressed abstention, permanence, and family values.[22]

The state used aggressive campaigns aimed at eradicating immoderate drinking as a venue for promoting its vision of proper male conduct. The pernicious effects of alcoholism and its purported epidemic proportions—one medical doctor noted that in Chile "the vast majority if not the totality of men are alcoholics"—justified prohibitionist measures including restrictions on the production and sale of alcohol. It also warranted the preaching of abstention. According to reformers, drunken men distastefully shouted obscenities on city sidewalks, beat their wives, picked fights, missed work, and were prone to debilitating diseases. By contrast, men who gave up drinking would become better workers, better fathers, better husbands, and better citizens.[23]

Overcoming an addiction to liquor was a sign of the self-discipline that marked virtuous manhood and furthered national development. Alcoholics, on the other hand, were retrograde "beasts." Since alcohol debilitated a man's organism, his ability to work properly as well as his civic capacities would be diminished. He might become a criminal or lose his mental capacities. A government publication reminded workers, "Don't forget that for all good citizens it is indispensable to keep one's mental lucidity and perfect control over one's nervous system at every moment."[24] Equating alcoholism with animal instinct, *Vida Sana* chided: "Who can think, then, that alcoholism makes a man more manly? On the contrary. We must proclaim this aloud. The personality turns toward evil and the instincts appear as they were among primitive men."[25]

A didactic parable published in another issue of the magazine detailed the story of Gregorio Segundo Mesa Alarcón, a young man with an inauspicious past who nevertheless became "an exemplary citizen and worker." Like many other workers, as a youngster Mesa Alarcón had learned mistaken ideas about what it meant to be a man: "The boy grew and had to feign manhood in order to conquer his work. Manhood also meant sharing with his *compañeros*, having the same distractions, not striking a sour note. And he frequented the tavern." Suggesting that drinking was not in fact a sign of manhood and that bad habits could be changed, the story detailed how this exemplary citizen "struggled with himself," and with the help of a doctor gave up drinking. Two years later he would proclaim eternal gratitude to the doctor who had helped him. His wife and children were also thankful. Mesa Alarcón had become a good citizen, worker, and husband: a true man.[26]

A man who liked to drink was not only a bad worker and citizen but also an inadequate husband and provider. In the end alcoholism led to the breakup of families. "He is a drunkard. What will become of his wife and children?" asked *Vida Sana*. Because drunk men had a propensity to beat their wives, social workers and physicians suggested, they provoked harmful conflict that divided the family. Husbands who spent their wages in bars, like those who squandered their earnings in bets, could not be good breadwinners either. According to one social worker's survey of one hundred marital disputes between blue-collar municipal workers and their wives, in 78 percent of all cases alcoholism was at the root of the disagreements. In 52 percent of these problem-ridden families, there were economic problems, and in 36 percent alcoholism aggravated financial difficulties. In the view of this social worker, when wives tried to reform their alcoholic husbands, men resisted and marital disputes ensued. To avoid these perils, she suggested the passage of legislation allowing wives to request that a judge legally prohibit their husbands from buying alcohol.[27]

The widespread popularity of anti-alcoholism campaigns made them an effective means for addressing domestic and sexual violence. Insofar as the latter problems, which were neither part of public debate nor directly addressed by state policies, could be presented as effects of alcoholism, social workers confronted and treated them. Although a stable family life was usually social workers' principal goal, in certain cases involving male violence, social workers sanctioned the breakup of families. When C. B., a 43-year-old laundress, visited the social worker at a Centro de Defensa del Niño, a child care center, the social worker immediately focused on the fact that C. B.'s partner, E. V., was an alcoholic. According to the social worker's report, the family's problems included a faulty distribution of the income, the lack of civil marriage between C. B. and E. V., the illegitimacy of the couple's children who had neither been registered in the Civil Registry nor recognized by their father, the fact that the mother was ill with cancer, and most especially E. V.'s alcoholism. The social worker did not consider the fact that E. V. had raped C. B.'s thirteen-year-old daughter, born of a previous union, as one of the family's "problems." Nonetheless, the social worker clearly considered the sexual abuse of C. B.'s daughter to be unacceptable and found employment for the young woman as a live-in servant, away from the clutches of her stepfather.[28]

The state cooperated with workers and employers to limit alcohol consumption. Capitalists found the celebration of *San Lunes* (Holy Monday) a particularly annoying custom. After a weekend of binging, laborers who were hung over often stayed home. When workers went to work still drunk, the probability of costly slip-ups increased. For employers, limiting the alcohol consumption of workers was a way to combat absenteeism and accidents at work, and they awarded bonuses to steadfast and abstemious workers. The state itself often lamented the economic losses occasioned by alcoholism, and with the approval of administrators, its officials visited mining camps and factories to teach temperance.[29]

Workers' organizations and leftist political parties thought that workers should devote themselves to intellectual pursuits and political activities instead of drinking. Diverse representatives of the working class, from union leaders to municipal counselors, embraced prohibitionism for the sake of family and community. To encourage men to give up drinking, in some localities popular organizations worked in conjunction with authorities to set up "dry zones." When the Mayor of Valdivia prohibited the sale of liquor at union events, for example, the local Socialist newspaper applauded the initiative, adding that for the measure to be truly effective, liquor sales should be banned in the area surrounding union halls as well. The newspaper also denounced the authorization of the sale of liquor on Independence Day in the otherwise dry town of Corral.[30]

In other areas—such as the wine-producing regions—prohibition was more conflictual. Moreover, as prohibitionist measures were tried out, politicians and leftist leaders began to realize that they were of limited use. Leftists suggested that perhaps measures aimed at improving laborers' living conditions might go further towards eradicating alcoholism than prohibition.[31] Shifting the emphasis of the anti-alcoholism campaigns away from punitive and restrictive measures aimed at male laborers, they championed restraint of the rich and increased recreational opportunities for the working class. According to representatives of organized, popular sectors, capitalists were the main instigators of the excessive consumption of inebriants. The rich profited from the sale of wine and spirits and aspired to subdue subalterns' rebellious spirit by keeping them drunk. Along with, or instead of, setting up dry zones, popular organizations suggested that producers and distributors of alcoholic beverages should be taxed. One physician writing in *La Crítica* proposed that those involved in the distribution of alcoholic beverages be banned from holding public office.[32]

In response to popular organizations' own analysis of how to avoid alcoholism, the state promoted attractive alternative habits. A medical social worker noted with pride that she had convinced a young worker to give up his "incipient alcoholism" and join a sports club. On a more global level, diverse state-run programs gave workers recreational options that were compatible with their responsibilities to family, nation, and work. In fact, a new agency, the Departamento de Defensa de la Raza y Aprovechamiento de las Horas Libres (Department for the Defense of the Race and the Profitable Use of Free Time), was set up by Aguirre Cerda to promote healthy diversions in which the whole family could participate.[33]

Along with a sister program developed by the CSO, the Defensa de la Raza built soccer and basketball courts and swimming pools; set up vacation areas for workers; established libraries; worked with unions and other workers' organizations to stimulate theater and music groups; and counseled Chileans, especially Chilean men, to desist from drinking and take up sports instead. The CSO and the Defensa de la Raza contributed to the creation of recreational centers such as the Hogar Pedro Aguirre Cerda (Pedro Aguirre Cerda House), located in Conchalí, and the Centro Cívico y Cultural Valparaíso (Valparaiso Civic and Cultural Center), in the port city. In these centers neighbors found game rooms, ping-pong tables, popular restaurants, or milk bars. The centers sponsored boxing, soccer, and hockey teams; housed theater groups; taught handicrafts, domestic arts, and literacy; gave talks and showed movies. Community, union, and women's groups held their meetings there. At the Centro Valparaíso, however, dances and alcohol were expressly forbidden, as were card games and dice.[34]

Although sports and theater groups had existed before the state began its recreational project, the state discredited private sports initiatives that, according to CSO publications, had been inefficient and ineffective. In fact, sports had previously been an arena of conflict between unions and bosses, who vied for the control of sports clubs which were among the best attended popular organizations. State control assured, to the contrary, that recreational practices would articulate and propagate a vision of a disciplined and collaborative sportsman-citizen. When a youth sports club was set up at the Beneficencia-run Casa de Socorro, a settlement house in the Santiago suburb of Puente Alto, the social worker in charge stressed the development of good manners as a prime benefit for members. Good manners facilitated understanding between the sexes and social classes. Although suspicious that the Defensa de la Raza might manipulate clubs for political ends, the Socialist *La Crítica* shared a belief in the personal and civic benefits of state-instigated participation in sports events and other diversions: "For modern statesmen, it is no secret that sports have a preponderant influence on good manners [*las buenas costumbres*]. A sports-loving people is a people which can be easily channeled, directed, or oriented toward a sense of solidarity and social benefit. Sport creates a morality that contributes to smoothing egotism and leveling men. And it keeps them away from the canteen." The practice of sports would not only uplift the race; it would also diminish class conflict, the newspaper suggested. Echoing the belief that sports both improved the individual and furthered understanding among citizens, the Centro Valparaíso listed among its principal objectives: "[To] stimulate a sense of human dignity and individual improvement within civic life; [to] make known the rights derived from the liberty and equality of responsibilities that a democratic regime imposes." Exercise and recreation were national imperatives, too. And proper citizens were also proper family men.[35]

The Making of Model Mothers

When social worker Gudelia Seguel Morales asserted that "maternity is woman's essential mission," she echoed larger common sense. Consistent with those beliefs, welfare professionals acting within state agencies promoted a female identity which had motherhood as its center. They routinely referred to women as "future mothers" and depicted women's desire to bear and raise children as a quasi-instinctual craving. Because experts presumed that women desired to raise their children within stable marriages, their vision of femininity intimately tied women, as mothers, to men.[36]

Many women conspired with social workers and other state agents working to constitute families and make men into reliable family members. Given the abysmally low wages women earned, their limited opportunities for employment, and the subsequent difficulties they encountered in supporting themselves and their children in the absence of a male breadwinner, women, and especially women with children, had good reason to aspire to constant marital unions. To secure their marriages or improve the terms on which they related to their husbands, their lovers, or the fathers of their children, women clients sought social workers' intervention in their familial disputes and collaborated with social workers to reform violent and economically undependable partners. They also visited social workers to obtain direct material aid from the state. But social workers were not equally useful to all women. Since social workers were interested in promoting legitimate families, when there were competing claims to a man's sustenance—economic or otherwise—social workers generally championed the claims of the breadwinner's spouse and his legitimate children over those of lovers, common-law wives, illegitimate children, or other relatives. Moreover social workers were often judgmental when dealing with women who had sex outside of marriage and chastised single mothers and other women who departed from gendered norms.[37]

Housewives and Domestic Economy

Married women who stayed at home were generally applauded by welfare professionals both within and outside the state. Still, even among married women, the state attended to supposed female deviations from its norm of femininity by teaching women how to mother, keep house, and get along with their husbands. Thus state agents betrayed a fundamental ambiguity in their treatment of women. On the one hand, they portrayed these women as essentially incapable of violating norms of femininity. On the other hand, they suggested that constant state vigilance was necessary to assure that even married women with children did not slip into impropriety.

Efforts to regulate the conduct of working-class women reinforced state efforts to constitute families by stressing that women who acted like proper housewives avoided conflict within their families. According to domestic economy teachers hired by the state-sponsored Housewives' Association, a good wife and housekeeper valued cleanliness and managed household resources with thrift. Instead of arguing with her husband over the distribution of the household budget, she would simply plan her spending more efficiently.[38] Instructors in domestic economy trained their students to save while shopping and instructed them on how to stretch their families' income by cooking nutritious, low-cost meals. Blanca Urbina Moya, a social worker at the large Caupolicán-Chiguayante textile mill, regarded the teaching of domestic economy to women as crucial to overcoming marital disputes. The wife of a worker who visited Urbina Moya wished to separate from her violent husband of six months, and she sought to enlist Urbina Moya's help to that end. Unwilling to sanction or promote the couple's separation, the social worker took measures to reconcile the couple: she gave the woman lessons in shopping and cooking low-cost stews, measures which she reckoned would alleviate economic troubles that might trigger marital disputes. Urbina Moya considered these lessons in domestic economy as crucial an intervention as her attempts to convince the man not to hit his wife. In analyzing another problem-ridden marriage, Urbina Moya again attributed the couple's bickering to the fact that "the spouse is not prepared to be a housewife" and instructed the wife in proper housekeeping.[39]

While domestic economy teachers encouraged harmonious relations between husbands and wives, they simultaneously worked to smooth over class conflict in the name of social peace in the national community. Instead of participating in food riots or protests against the high cost of living, instead of demanding pay increases for themselves or their husbands, women should use household income frugally. However, this moralizing orientation proved unattractive to many women who articulated a more class-based feminine identity by refusing to join the Asociación and organizing in more militant, autonomous consumer groups.[40]

Maternity, Poverty, and Marriage

National uplift and the demographic defense of the race depended on convincing women to adopt modern, scientific standards of hygiene and puericulture. While state ventures in health education for mothers, which proliferated with the popular front, questioned the automatic or natural ability of women to mother, they reinforced women's responsibility for children. "Let us teach working-class mothers how to raise their children, let us repeat until exhaustion the rules of hygiene," proclaimed the CSO. Sanitary nurses, teachers, social workers, and physicians planned to teach girls and women puericulture in schools and mothers' centers. The CSO social work code mandated the formation of mothers' centers in its clinics, and the largest CSO clinics in Santiago ran Mothers' Schools, as did some milk stations. Maternity continued to be the central element of the female identity promoted by the state, despite a fledgling state recognition that women did not necessarily possess the innate ability to mother properly.[41]

Pregnant women who attended mothers' center meetings sometimes resented the maternalism of helpful young social workers and sanitary nurses who, although they were often not mothers themselves, felt they could instruct women in childrearing. When a social worker tried to explain to one participant how to bathe her child properly, the mother invoked her own experience: "Since I am the mother of several children, I have enough practice." To overcome the reluctance of "future mothers," the state was forced to take measures to ensure their attendance at mothers' centers. In a rather coercive vein, the state conditioned medical benefits and material aid on membership in mothers' centers. The state also offered incentives. At the Instituto Madre y Niño (Mother and Child Institute) in Valparaíso, members received low-cost fabrics and had access to an emergency assistance fund, made up of members' own quotas.[42]

Authorities frequently pointed out that women's poverty caused child illness and death. Because unmarried women were presumably economically disadvantaged, welfare workers believed their children were in a highly precarious position. Even in those cases where women listed as single lived in free unions and the children's father helped to support them, social workers saw the lack of a legal marriage as putting the wife and children at risk of being economically abandoned. Thus they encouraged women with children to marry, and efforts to ensure children's health propped up efforts to constitute families.[43]

While more progressive professionals ignored the sexual practices of single mothers and focused instead on the rights of children, conservative experts pinpointed the dubious morality of women who had sex outside marriage and suggested that single mothers were necessarily reluctant or inadequate mothers. Even when single mothers lived with and cared for their illegitimate children, welfare professionals characterized these children as "abandoned," "*hijos de nadie*," who were prone to pathological or delinquent behavior.[44]

In the short run, however, state welfare bureaus took it upon themselves to provide unmarried mothers with important, though limited, means for their immediate survival. Diverse institutions, including the CSO, assisted single pregnant women by setting up maternal refuges that provided women who could not count on the support of their families or lovers with a "home." Social workers at diverse agencies helped these women find employment—usually industrial homework, domestic service jobs, or laundering—or helped them set up home industries. Thus the state usurped a possible masculine role, replacing masculine protection with state paternalism. Yet state programs assisted single mothers and their children without legitimating sex outside marriage by portraying single mothers as innocent victims of irresponsible men. State paternalism clearly did not liberate women or do away with gender prescription and stereotype, although it did undermine the monolithic character of the gendered familial norm that the state itself favored.[45]

Femininity, Wages, and Work

In their efforts to "protect" mothers and children, the most progressive state agents played down moral factors revolving around proper family relations and emphasized the economic difficulties that undermined Chileans' health, limited Chile's prosperity, and tore apart working-class families. In so doing, they reflected the perceptions of working-class Chileans who argued that men and women needed family wages that allowed them to support their families properly. The state, however, recognized the necessity of family wages only for men. Despite efforts to succor mothers, even those who were unmarried, it increasingly conceived of women as non-workers and therefore never consistently proposed adequate female employment as a possible solution to the perceived demographic dangers of single motherhood, working-class poverty, and ill health.[46] State agents rarely addressed women's low wages or their exclusion from the labor market, paltry legal protection for domestic servants, or the fact that women workers were often fired when pregnant or after giving birth.[47] Although social workers at maternal refuges, CSO maternal-child health clinics, milk stations, and Centro's de Defensa sometimes helped single and abandoned mothers locate employment, the inadequacy of employment possibilities for women were never the subject of concerted state policies.

State officials generally rejected paid labor for women, arguing that work and maternity were incompatible.[48] State-enforced measures that either protected working mothers or provided them with subsidies both recognized the difficult plight of working mothers and legitimated their need to work. But protective labor legislation inscribed the discriminatory notion that because women were potential mothers, they needed special protection. Forced to pay part of a woman's salary during a portion of her maternity leave (the CSO covered the other portion) and to provide nurseries for women workers' children—legislation aimed at encouraging mothers to breast feed their children required establishments employing more than 20 blue-collar women workers to provide on-site nurseries—employers perceived that contracting women implied "extra" costs.[49] While protective labor laws had been put in place before the popular fronts were constituted, no one within the state ever suggested that they should be reformed, even after 1939. Despite the fact that employers did not consistently comply with protective labor legislation and women workers were not overwhelmingly interested in its application, during the popular fronts the state insisted on the importance of these legal norms, at least rhetorically. In this fashion it reinforced the notion that a working mother was an exceptional worker who required special treatment.[50]

Many wage-earning women rejected the notion that work and maternity were incompatible. Aware of the discriminatory effects of protective labor legislation, they chose not to seek its enforcement. Maternity leaves had turned into an "tortuous obligation," commented the head of the Feminine Section of the General Work Inspection (Dirección General del Trabajo). Given the inhospitable nature of childcare facilities and the fact that untrained personnel were hired to care for the infants, women left their children at home.[51]

In discouraging female employment, state agents argued that children required the direct and constant supervision of their mothers. In a survey of 50 women workers and 50 housewives, a social worker found it relevant to ask about the respective conduct of their children. When she found that thirteen of the workers' children were "disobedient and lazy at school" or "out of control"—compared to eleven of the housewives' offspring—she offered the broad generalization that "the number of children who have good conduct is greater among the children of women who stay at home, because of greater vigilance on the mother's part."[52] In *La realidad médico-social* Allende correlated increasing infant mortality with women's increasing labor force participation, insinuating that the former caused the latter.[53] Experts considered breastfeeding one of the most crucial determinants of an infant's health. One social worker suggested that social workers should work diligently to counter "rebel mothers who do not wish to breastfeed because they work."[54]

On the other hand, the state encouraged women to take in laundry or perform other kinds of work that could be done at home. The precariousness and lack of regulation of homework, that it was hazardous and tiring, or that women often involved their children in the work seemed not to matter much, as long as women were near their young ones. "It seems that in every woman of our *pueblo* there's a potential laundress," remarked one social worker. A colleague concurred, noting that a client had "an aptitude for laundry."[55]

Work, Sexuality, and Honor

Welfare professionals not only believed that working women were inadequate caretakers for their children; they also feared that work undermined women's ability to bear children, thereby contributing to the nation's demographic decline. Heavy factory work exhausted women and produced spontaneous abortions, they cautioned. But more troubling was the fact that women workers might consciously limit the number of children they had. As one physician noted, protective labor legislation actually encouraged women workers not to bear children. Fact-collecting social workers and physicians went to great lengths to show that married women had fewer children or more abortions after beginning to work.[56]

Reformers interested in women's work outside the home sought to enforce the state's preferred familial norm. As a result, the marital status of women workers came under intense scrutiny. Experts saw both the causes and the effects of paid employment as different for married and single women. They maintained that married women needed to work only in exceptional situations. Married women workers were essentially victims, many reformers implied, forced into the labor force by their irresponsible husbands. Yet other more conservative professionals castigated women more forcefully. According to them, married women who labored outside the home left their families in a state of "moral abandonment" and the fact that they were employed actually encouraged their husbands to act irresponsibly.[57]

That fact that so many working women were single only served to deepen state disapproval of female employment.[58] Analyses only sometimes pointed out that single women needed to work in order to support themselves and/or their children. Just as often, they saw factory work as a corrupting activity that stimulated women's independence and caused them to shun marriage and bear illegitimate children. Social worker Inés Infante found it relevant to ask women workers how they felt about marriage. When 10 percent of women factory workers, as compared to 4 percent of housewives, declared themselves to be against marriage, she emphasized the differences between the two groups, rather than the fact that most women who proffered an opinion, whether married or single, favored marriage. Working women, especially women who worked in factories, were supposedly haughty and resisted stable relationships with men. According to one social worker, when women worked outside the home they "adopted an intolerant, extremely independent attitude, refusing to accept their husbands' tutelage" and they quarreled more often with their husbands. These women were portrayed as dangerously autonomous. The social worker at the Caupolicán-Chiguayante textile mill spoke disapprovingly of a female worker with a "proud and independent attitude" who had never asked the fathers of her children for economic help. Neither pride nor independence was generally sanctioned for women, although some more progressive welfare professionals tolerated independent women if the survival of their children was at stake.[59]

In their efforts to discredit paid labor for all women, reformers tied sexual honor to maternity and work, suggesting that paid labor induced promiscuity and single motherhood. To prove this association, they surveyed single women workers and found that they had more children after they began working than before. Experts also suggested that paid labor led domestic servants, as well as factory laborers, to become prostitutes. Once a woman's appetite for money was awakened, who knew what might happen? Conversely, sexual promiscuity forced women to resort to potentially detrimental paid labor, making them bad mothers. One of the major reasons illegitimate children suffered so many physical and social problems, experts said, was because their mothers worked. A good mother was an honorable woman and honorable women did not labor outside the home.[60]

The negative image of working women was not propagated to the same extent by everyone, even among professional elites. Despite the widespread portrayal of women workers as sexually licentious, inadequate as mothers, and quarrelsome as wives, social workers, in particular, could sometimes be surprisingly sympathetic toward women who disregarded certain aspects of normative definitions of gender. The fact that social workers were women did not assure that they were not patronizing or moralistic. Yet as women—and as women who themselves worked outside the home and who believed that women should not be victimized by men—they could on occasion sympathize with working-class women's efforts to work and raise their children with dignity. They might also provide these women with some material assistance. And the working-class women who welcomed surveyors or social workers into their homes or went to health clinics for pre-natal or infant health care knew that.[61]

Conclusion

Through disparate state agencies, the national-popular state carried out its plan to "constitute" stable Chilean families. To promote national unity, progress, and harmonious relations between men and women and between diverse social classes, it encouraged men and women to accept normative masculine and feminine identities. Of course the models of family life and gender identities advocated by the state were not invented either by the state itself or by the popular-front coalitions. Prevalent gendered conceptions of family drew on pre-existing discourses and reflected gender, class, and racial struggles within civil society. Yet during the popular front period, the state became an increasingly powerful actor. Besides wielding important economic resources, as it incorporated popular aspirations into its project and sought the support of subalterns, it legitimated its claim to bear a national project, to work for the common good. That gave its project a particular force. The reform of gender relations was both the basis for and the product of the popular fronts' vigorous attempt to further a national project and build the nation-state.

The moral and material reforms of family life the state attempted had an important impact on evolving gender relations within the working class, though it is difficult to say how much of an impact. Statistical information tells us that both before and after 1938 most adult Chileans were married and most children were born "legitimate." But this only a very partial picture. It tells us nothing, for example, of the vicissitudes of a given individual's life. Nor does statistical data inform us of how many Chileans had family members, close friends, or co-workers who as single mothers, unfaithful husbands, or separated wives violated central tenets of the proposed gender order. Distorted by their desires and fears, the reports of social workers and state professionals are perhaps no more reliable. And yet these reports can tell us for example that among the workers at the Sociedad Nacional de Paños in Tomé, a cloth factory, there was one woman, separated from her husband whose three children lived with their father. The husband of a "married" coworker lived hundreds of kilometers away in Santiago, and another Paños worker with five children lived in a boardinghouse but visited his wife occasionally and had sexual relations with her. A fourth employee lived with his wife and child while two other children, born of a previous relationship, resided with their mother, who had a new partner.[62] All these workers were, according to the law, "married," and most of their children were legitimate, but from the point of view of state reformers, their lives were disorderly.

It is this panorama that state officials faced with all the tools at their disposal. While even social workers recorded subaltern resistance to their meddling, the state's project was not—in fact, could not be—built solely on the perceptions and needs of the rich, of political elites, or of welfare professionals. That was the essence of the popular fronts' project for governance: listening to and rearticulating popular demands in an unequal dialogue. Given that opening, working-class men and women bargained with and against the state. Many Chileans had good reason for cooperating with elites and experts.

8

COLONIAL AFRICA

Transforming Families for Their Own Benefit (and Ours)

CYNTHIA BRANTLEY

Early in my African studies, I confronted two significant examples of how African men and women had experienced vast transformations of the structure and meaning of "family" as a result of colonial state intervention. In the process of trying to relate to new conditions brought about by colonial demands, the style, structure, authority, and gender relations of families had become modified such that the security of the old ways had vanished while the world of the new family remained uncertain.

My first example came from a woman I befriended in 1974 who was a Giriama working in a cashew nut factory in Kilifi, on Kenya's coast. She had three children, no husband, and, rare for women in the general area, a good job. She showed me her fingertips, constantly blackened and sore from tearing the cashews from their coverings, and proudly vowed that she would never marry because her husband could have rights to her wages or other resources. "He would only buy beer," she said. When I asked how she would have a place to grow food for her children, she replied, "I work my father's land, and my wages remain mine." This confounded general expectations. In pre-colonial times, she would have brought her father some bridewealth and lived alongside her husband, able to retain separately any income she generated (though most waged jobs were reserved for men). Even in 1974, fathers did not provide land for daughters to use; they saved it for their sons. The British colonial state (and the independent state which followed it) gave men new rights to wives' economic resources—resources that previously would have been kept for the women's own use. This particular woman was choosing a new form of family (herself, three children from different men, and her father)—mostly to avoid the constraints that colonial transformations of families had brought about.[1]

The second example came when I encountered a sad old man who lived next to the mission station at Ribe in Kenya. He identified as a Chonyi and had come to this area of mixed ethnicity as a young man. He had converted to Christianity, married a local Rabai woman and fathered two daughters.

His wife had died years before, and both of his daughters married and moved away long ago. He was poor and alone. He said his life was awful because he had nobody to cook for him, and he was hungry all the time. Cooking has always been the duty of African women; a man was pitied if he did not have a woman to cook for him. But because the extended family had been replaced by the nuclear family and family farming had been replaced by low wage labor, he had been stranded without the African extended family safety net. Instead of offering Christian charity, his neighbors resented him as a burden, and he felt he could not return to his non-Christian Chonyi kin in a region where he had not been for sixty years. When I lightheartedly asked him if he would like me to teach him how to cook, he looked horrified and replied, "Cooking is a woman's job!" The family, and the roles of males and females within it, had clearly become transformed by colonialism. At the same time, however, old gender expectations held strong.[2]

In contrast to examples of state intervention taking the form of welfare programs focusing on mothers, this chapter explores British colonial intervention in Africa (Nyasaland in the 1930s) as an example of states targeting males. In British colonial Africa, colonial agents presumed that males had extensive power over their families, and hence that males would be the main agents for change. "Family" for the colonial state had one definition: a man in charge of his wife and children. Such a presumption in light of the case studies examined in *Families of a New World* holds two ironies. First, unlike American maternalist policies, in which mothers formed the core of the family unit and fathers were frequently viewed as peripheral and irresponsible, in the Nyasaland colonial state, as in most of colonial Africa, African men were presumed to hold responsibility and authority over their families. African women were considered to be dependents of their fathers first, their husbands later, and ultimately their adult sons. African men's power was presumed to persist even when they were physically absent from home for years at a time as emigrant laborers. In the view of the state, women were not heads of households.

Another irony is that the main African colonial issue of the case study I will examine is diet and nutrition, a subject generally associated primarily with women. African women carry a huge responsibility for feeding their families: they are often the ones who decide what and when to plant; they are in charge of cultivating, harvesting, and storing food, managing food resources, acquiring collectible edibles, fetching firewood and water, and cooking all meals. African men readily acknowledged women's authority over and responsibility for food and could use as grounds for divorce the fact that a wife is a poor cook. Yet the state, by defining men as the farmers, undermined the existing gender roles for providing food, crops, and meals, and virtually forgot about the significance of cooking.

The larger argument here resides in the way that, despite much evidence to the contrary, the colonial state viewed the African families as patrilineal and nuclear, under the control of the husband-father. In the process of dealing with many issues (but especially in the context of feeding the family), the state expected the Africans to adjust to roles and responsibilities to fit the patrilineal mold. Evidence reveals state presumptions about and demands on transformed African families in two vital ways. First, the state elevated the nuclear family over the existing extended family—which stretched across generations and among siblings—and undermined the latter's role in providing and distributing food resources and providing meals. Second, the state had larger needs, especially those of income and labor, which drove it to manipulate local families in ways that transformed roles and responsibilities of various family members. State intervention served, particularly, to unbalance gender relations. The state not only privileged men and denigrated women, but also elevated the male role of husband-father to the detriment of those of brother, elder, chief, and son. Although state intervention in British colonial Nyasaland was partly indirect and partly deliberate, it nonetheless vastly disrupted family structure and authority.

The evidence for this chapter is derived primarily from a British colonial Nutrition Survey[3] and subsequent Nutrition Development Unit[4] on 110 families from three villages in Nyasaland between 1938 and 1943. The Nyasaland Nutrition Survey of 1938-1939 emerged from several sources. When, in the mid-1930s, the League of Nations made an effort to ameliorate nutritional problems, measure nutrients, and standardize requirements, the British colonial state had virtually no knowledge about what their colonial peoples ate, much less the nutritional value of their diets. Missionaries, doctors, labor recruiters, and colonial officers in Africa wanted to help with African health problems. From Africa, they called increasingly upon biochemists, doctors, agriculturalists, and veterinary scientists in British research institutes for assistance. The new knowledge of nutrition about vitamins and minerals provided the colonial state with improved technology—technology that they wanted to apply to Africa. Anthropologists from the International Africa Institute and the London School of Economics proposed a study that would integrate sociological and scientific knowledge to compare the diets of at least two different peoples over an entire annual agricultural cycle. Along with those institutions, the Colonial Office, the British Medical Research Council, and the colony of Nyasaland cooperated to undertake a nutritional study, which would have developmental applications. The focus of the British actions was to improve African diets by sharing colonial technological knowledge on nutrition, particularly the new knowledge of the significance of vitamins and minerals. The state's approach to the family's responsibilities (including the roles of men and women) and its willingness to intervene were crucial elements of the colonial pattern in dealing with the confusing complexities of African families.[5]

The existing diet was not as troublesome as the investigators presumed.

Despite their careful measurements, crucial errors gave erroneous impressions. The colonial goal of development projects leapfrogged beyond the analysis of the data collected. The variation of African family forms alongside the tactics that families used to respond to difficulties were judged by preconceived notions. Finally, the sociological aspects of the families and the village conditions were, for the most part, set aside in favor of the scientific calculations, which meant that the evidence was skewed toward those preconceived notions.

British Colonial Nyasaland

In the context of British colonial states in Africa, Nyasaland was a minor player. It was small, landlocked, and lacking in mineral resources. Additionally, it was minimally endowed with cash crop potential. Its most important asset was its people: Nyasaland was densely populated. Yet, the region held a significant symbolic place in terms of several critical aspects of colonial intervention in Africa. The state of Nyasaland was born of the British movement to end the Arab slave trade in East Africa. East Africa was truly an arena of "tribal warfare" in the nineteenth century, given that Swahili slave traders and warlike Ngoni immigrants who had come from Zululand captured and assimilated people at the lake and on the plateau. Nyasaland was the place where the famed missionary David Livingstone facilitated the first mission station at Magomero in 1861, under the auspices of the Universities' Mission to Central Africa (UMCA). It was the case study for Britain's efforts to end the slave trade by replacing it with "Christianity, Commerce and Civilization." Its shape and boundaries were designed by British conflicts with the Portuguese claims on the Zambezi River and Cecil Rhodes' British South Africa Company, which had the initial administrative power. The first High Commissioner, Harry Johnson, was paid by Rhodes' company, but acted contrary to Rhodes' wishes by saving much land for the Africans rather than British settlers. Missionaries arrived before any state agents, however. Livingstone's first mission station failed, but successive missions such as the Presbyterian Church at Blantyre in the south, the Free Presbyterians at Livingstonia in the north, and finally the UMCA at Nkotakota on the southwest lakeshore, remained among many permanent missions.

Missionaries were soon joined by commercial efforts for "legitimate" commerce in the form of the African Lakes Company. In 1891, Nyasaland became a British protectorate, and both the effort at pacification of the internal warfare and the ending of the slave trade were successful. Planters came to the southern Shire Highlands in the early twentieth century, seeking their fortunes in cotton, coffee (which failed), and tobacco and tea (which ultimately succeeded). All crops were worked by African labor. Taxes were imposed as early as 1901 and Nyasaland Africans were recruited as early as 1903 to work in the southern African mines. Peoples who had lived in fortified villages during the long period of the slave trade dispersed quickly to find more fertile land and to avoid taxes. This dispersal created such problems for the administration that the government required Africans to live on European estates in the south in 1903 and, in 1912, set a minimum village size of 20 homes.

The philosophy and practice of British colonialism in Africa was one of "indirect rule," whereby British officers ruled through appointed (hopefully legitimate) native authorities. In this context, the Nyasaland government used three elements of control—economic, political, and legal. The obvious one was economic in the form of labor and taxes, but they also appointed official Native Authorities or local chiefs who had authority over the people they administered within a colonial political system under British authority. Chiefs were placed in charge of local native courts which administered justice and collected fees based on "traditional" practice. By giving men the last say in legal authority, the colonial state was removing many of the rights previously held by women.

Through their Native Authorities, Africans met many needs of the colonial state. During World War I, African labor had been critical, and men had been commandeered throughout Nyasaland to carry loads. Many villages had been coerced to provide food for soldiers who were fighting in German East Africa. The worldwide Depression of the 1930s extended even into remote African villages, and family disruption was magnified by the high percentage of men who were drawn off as emigrant laborers into southern Africa.

The colonial state expected Africans to respond to its varying needs. At the same time, it was slow to accommodate family needs and to acknowledge the degree to which its own intervention contributed to problems that might later be viewed as having been caused by the Africans themselves. For instance, African agricultural practice was basically one of bush fallowing. Fields could be worked for five or so years, and then they would be left fallow for another five so the soils could regenerate. Once colonial policy forced families and villagers to remain in one place, there was no opportunity for the soil to regenerate. Consequently, yields fell. Men were in charge of clearing the fields and beginning the first planting, but women weeded, scared birds and insects, organized the harvest, and commanded the storage. Colonial agricultural agents tended to focus their attention on staple crops such as maize and cassava as they learned about local practices, ignoring the significance for the Africans' diet of legumes, sweet potatoes, pumpkins, and (especially) greens of all kinds. Though the main ingredient of a meal was a sticky porridge made from maize or cassava flour, no Africans considered that they had eaten a meal unless the porridge came with an accompanying sauce, most commonly consisting of greens and groundnuts. The sauce was most welcomed if it included fish, beef, goat, or chicken. When the state tried to provide nutritious food for Africans under their care (soldiers, students, hospital patients, prisoners, estate workers), their solution of adding occasional meat rations reflected their own sense of a proper meal, but they still failed to deal with shortages of calcium, fat, and vitamin A or to acknowledge the value of the legumes, vitamins, and minerals in the sauce accompanying African porridge in the villages.

Not only was the colonial state *not* a welfare state but its underlying principle was that Africans had to pay for their colonial administration. This had meant the introduction of a universalized cash economy that demanded funds from the population in the form of taxes. The way the tax demand was framed changed both the way that men were regarded in the society and the way in which families were understood. Men were immediately seen as the source of taxes. Each adult male had to pay his "head tax," and also had to pay for the "hut tax" on each of his wives and adult sons who resided in their own house on the husband-father's compound. The state provided two options for "men" to obtain funds for taxes: they could either produce cash crops or work for wages. In either case, the payment of taxes to fund the colonial state disrupted family life, often minimized families' options for living together, changed labor patterns, and had a direct impact on food production.

The introduction of cash crops as an option for paying taxes in Nyasaland fundamentally altered local family life. Cash crops in British Nyasaland came to be valued more highly by the colonial state than food crops, and they mostly required family labor—labor that was also needed in the seasons during which food crops were produced. In Nyasaland, as in most African societies, land was not privately owned. But the state deemed that men were the farmers, men would have primary rights to the land, and men would control cash crops. Women, of course, would still be responsible for food crops. Thus, women's responsibilities for feeding the family intensified even while their labor was being siphoned off by the men for the production of cash crops. Hence, patterns of labor, authority over labor, and control over money were altered in favor of men. Such change occurred without compensation to the women for the loss of their own labor, normally spent on food crops, or for their need to continue to produce as much of the food crop as before. If food for a family had to be obtained from cash resources, men gained greater control over spending, while women still retained responsibility for feeding the family.

Wage labor altered family life even further. If men had the option of laboring near their homes so that that they could return to their families at night, then their contributions to the family reflected the *status quo ante*, albeit in modified form. In most cases, however, men were forced to become migrant laborers, which meant that they were gone on contract for two to ten years. Some never returned from stints as migrant laborers. But even those who did had to make continuous decisions about sending funds to the family and about the timing and form of those contributions. The family, meanwhile, had to do without the male's labor on the family farm. The case of Nyasaland demonstrates how state agents envisioned and acted upon the African family as both the unit of food production and the source of tax payment and labor. Although in some African areas, women provided the bulk of the agricultural labor for food production, in this area of Nyasaland, men and women basically shared this work while performing different gendered tasks.

Three African realities confused and sometimes offended state agents in this area, and each of these realities brought to the forefront the state's conceptualizations of the African family. One was that African families did not "own" the land; all families had "use rights" so long as they were producing from it. Another was polygamy, which missionaries particularly opposed in the belief that men should be monogamous. The last arena of state confusion was a widespread set of practices based on matrilineal ideology.[6]

Matrilineage was especially baffling, because the major male role in it was that of brother and uncle, manifested by a man as guardian of his sister and her children. A male in a matrilineal context would marry, but his children would inherit from his wife's family and her brother would have final authority over her and her children. In most cases, among matrilineal communities, a husband went to reside with his wife's family and actually provided brideservice labor to his wife's parents. A mother would have fields shared by her married daughters and their husbands; after a few years, each married daughter would get her own fields. Ultimately, a husband-father's allegiance was to his own matrilineage.

It is not hard to see that such a family situation was far from a westernized nuclear family, and that the colonial state's privileging of men as husband-fathers would have an impact on all members of such families. Any man who left to work for wages could hardly provide brideservice, and should he want to grow sufficient cash crops to meet the tax requirement, he would need more authority over the land than he previously had in his wife's village. A man could only grow extra crops on land that was controlled by his own matrilineage.

The state only encouraged and facilitated nuclear families, but it could not command them into existence. Instead, it used political authority to try to solve its economic dilemmas. Just as the state valued families headed by husbands, so too did it value communities headed by a chief who had widespread authority through which they could administer. State control thus extended to the family indirectly through villages and their state-appointed headmen. State agents were more willing to presume villages as viable units of study and as cooperative units of food production than to accept the role of the extended family. (This was especially true in the case of matrilineal practices.)

Knowing the Family: The State and Its Informants

Trying to decipher the "African family" was not easy for the agents of the colonial state, especially when their combined goal was to ensure that men performed the needed labor to bring home wages to pay the taxes and that the family improved the nutritional quality of their diet. Christian missionaries in Africa had no problem defining the proper family as the monogamous nuclear family, headed by the husband-father who had real and economic control over his wife and children. Most colonial agents agreed without giving the issue much thought, for they were drawing on the only model of family that was familiar to them. Even with this interpretation, they failed to regard the importance of family stages and its impact on feeding.

For instance, when a family has young children, the woman's responsibilities for them are extensive. Women's responsibilities to their children restrict the amount of work they can do in the fields. In contrast, a family with children over the age of ten who can help with fieldwork and domestic work enjoys some relief. A family with only boys or girls has less flexibility than one with both sexes. Families with children of marriageable age will either lose them or gain spouses, and again, the sex ratio can drastically influence a family's resources. If bridewealth needs to be paid, or if bridewealth is received, a family's fortunes change. Finally, grandparents perform an important role regarding their grandchildren, whom they tend for extensive periods, but ultimately, elders need to be cared for by their adult children. Laterally, an extended family can take the pressure off of individual conjugal families as they move through certain more stressful stages. Lacking such help, isolated, individualized, nuclear families suffer.

When the colonial state in Nyasaland needed the family to provide labor and "properly" feed themselves, agents were forced to confront the reality that African families did not reflect modern Western ones. To understand what African families were like, they turned to anthropologists, who drew upon their broader understanding of culture and language to expand the definitions and clarify exactly how interventions might permeate the African family or, more important, transform it into the "ideal family."

In Nyasaland, the anthropologist Margaret Read served the state in various capacities, and her interpretations of the different family structures ultimately served the state's interest. In 1938, when the Nyasaland Nutrition Survey began its study of three rural villages,[7] Read was also asked by Nyasaland's governor to undertake a study of the impact of emigrant labor on village life.[8] She had completed her own study of the communities of Ngoni in Nyasaland under the auspices of the London School of Economics[9] and the International Institute of African Languages and Cultures. Nyasaland had a dense population in relation to other parts of Africa[10] but very few areas that were suitable for cash crops.[11] This dense population, Africans' need for wage labor to pay taxes, and southern African demand for workers contributed to an extensive emigrant labor pattern. By 1935, it was estimated that 120,000 males had emigrated from the colony to work in Southern Rhodesia and South Africa.[12] The government had completed a study to try to understand the impact of this process on the immigrants, but had yet to evaluate how the absence of these males had affected African families.¹³ Read was given this task partly because of her knowledge of the Ngoni and because she was fluent in the language (Nyanja) of the Chewa spoken by all the Africans in this region, including the immigrant Ngoni.

As I have argued elsewhere,¹⁴ Read brought with her three prejudices. She examined the peoples of this region "through Ngoni eyes," favoring their centralized, militaristic, patrilineal cultural forms. In contrast, she was less familiar with, and demonstrated less respect for, decentralized matrilineal cultural forms. Because she had studied those Ngoni in southern African cities who had maintained immigrant communities, she viewed the impact on village life from the perspective of the emigrant, more than of the village family that had been left behind.¹⁵

How did she interpret and value family? Though she recognized that each of the three villages had its own cultural family forms, she used the Nyanja word *banja* to refer to the two or three larger units in each of the villages, but in this case, she ignored the implications of matrilineal and patrilineal differences.¹⁶ In contrast, opting to focus mainly on the conjugal unit as the primary family unit, she emphasized the differences between matrilineal and patrilineal families, showing disdain toward the less permanent matrilineal conjugal unit, which lacked the protection of patrilineal brideprice, meaning that a bride's family would have to repay it in instances of divorce. Read placed primary emphasis on what she called the "elementary family" (the conjugal unit which could include more than one wife) and the "disrupted family" (referring to old widows and young mothers with husbands away).¹⁷

Her second conceptual framework for interpreting the African family, in addition to the conjugal unit, focused on changes in marriage patterns. First of all, rather than delineating marriage as a process that evolved over time—one that included many steps by various groups and was never complete until the survival of a child—she portrayed marriage more as a "moment," implying a finality that did not really exist. As she described families within matrilineal and patrilineal realms modifying residence and marriage patterns in the early colonial period, she portrayed the changes as tending toward either Ngoni patrilineal or Western forms rather than conveying the actual interaction between matrilineal and patrilineal practices. For instance, many Ngoni men married Chewa women, whose matrilineage granted them rights to the children (who went to live with their matrilineal grandparents) and to the land. Chewa never adopted bridewealth, but many Ngoni ceased this practice and, in doing so, greatly reduced the expense of a wife, even if she were Ngoni. The one matrilineal modification that became vastly transformed was that of the residence pattern, whereby husbands resided with their wife's family. Two generations earlier, that pattern had not seemed so radical, since most marriages were cross-cousin marriages. In that case, a brother's child married a sister's child, so both husband and wife lived in the village of their matrilineage. Should the husband marry a second wife, he would often marry his wife's sister. In these instances, the man and woman both remained in their matrilineage, and the man's responsibilities to his sisters and their children could easily be met. His brideservice would contribute to the food resources of his conjugal family, his matrilineage, and his guardian family, which was that of his sisters.

Margaret Read took her preference for patrilineal forms a step further in three additional arenas. One had to do with what she considered to be the "problem" of divorce. She recognized that marriage in matrilineal forms was unstable, and that divorce was relatively easy, especially since there was no bride payment to return. She noted that women often had sequential marriages but viewed these situations from the perspective of the male as husband-father, rather than as brother-uncle.[18] In so doing, she failed to understand the workings of the matrilineal extended family, whereby a grandmother and her daughters with their husbands and children under the matrilineal guardianship of her senior son successfully maintained family stability and food production under vast conditions of change.

With the same favoritism towards men—as husband-fathers, returning emigrants, and as the primary farmers—Read viewed matrilineal organization as less suitable for crop production than patrilineal conditions.[19] First of all, she favored the Ngoni agricultural approach, which she described as rational, innovative, and efficient, in contrast with the Chewa agricultural approach, which was enmeshed in superstition (particularly with the male *nyau* secret society and women's puberty rites [*chinimwali*], which stressed the connection between the fertility of the women and the fertility of the land). Secondly, she had a particular view of how the rural family should accommodate the needs of the returning emigrant. In a patrilineal village, "the husband on returning home is sure of finding a food supply in his own village, whereas his wife in her village might have grown lazy and been living off her mother."[20] Other colonial agents, however, viewed this issue from the perspective of family life. B. S. Platt, who was director of the Nutrition Survey, recognized that an emigrant's family whose wife stays with her mother might "have a less hard time during his absence than the wife and children of an absentee under the patrilocal marriage system."[21] M. G. Marwick, a British anthropologist investigating African societies in Northern Rhodesia, commenting on Zambian Cewa [Chewa] in 1952, agreed:

> In particular, since it seems that because the matrilineage remains functional under a disturbed sex ratio, Cewa society appears to be better adapted to a high labour migration rate than might be the case with a conjugally organized people.[22]

In 1938, though, this view of matrilineal success remained a difficult one for agents of the colonial state. Richard Kettlewell, agricultural officer for the Nutrition Survey, continued to stress his belief that for the African agricultural effort to be successful, progressive male farmers had to be given incentives to improve the land, which they could do only with land ownership and access to seeds, fertilizer, and markets.[23] Although he never dealt directly with the issue of labor and did not include in his formula any labor costs, his plan implied that such farmers would have access to conjugal family labor and maybe even labor from the extended family. Once he became the agricultural officer for Nyasaland in the 1950s, he initiated "Master Farmers" programs in several regions.[24] None, ultimately, was successful, and many men in matrilineal regions also fought against giving men control over the land in any form of private ownership and for retaining matrilineal practices of land use.[25]

Finally, because Read saw family and marriage transformations as changes towards patrilineal practices rather than an exchange of matrilineal and patrilineal ones, she indirectly presumed that, eventually, patrilineal practices would overtake matrilineal ones because they worked better.[26] Certainly, brideservice and a residential pattern whereby a husband lived with his wife's family were virtually impossible once men had to find off-farm labor and wives started accompanying their husbands to their places of work, but men and women from matrilineal areas have retained their support for the matrilineage's prominence in land-holding, child rearing, and brother's guardianship. At the same time, the role of husband-father has become more prominent in matrilineal areas, though divorce has not become less common.

Transforming Families for Their Own Benefit

Ultimately, the state's main need for the support of the African family was economic, both because the family was the main food production unit and because men had to find wage jobs, even if it meant emigration. Women were expected by the state to maintain the family farm, which virtually subsidized their husbands' low wages. The state's interest in nutrition turned directly to agriculture—its practice, the staple crop, and the introduction of new crops to provide vitamins and minerals—such that state agents looked to men to remedy the problems, even if they were also the emigrants. The state essentially ignored women's role in making agricultural decisions, their constant search for collectible edibles, and their vital role in cooking meals. Emigration patterns included both a push and a pull, and when the situations in these three villages are compared, one can see a different impact on families. In each village, the number of men who left, the kinds of jobs they did, and the duration of their absence was different.[27] Most of the emigrants from these particular villages remained in Nyasaland rather than going to southern Africa, but still each village had a number of *machona* (lost ones) who never returned home or sent money to their families.

My inquiry into Nyasaland under British colonial occupation focused on the three villages that had been chosen for the Nyasaland Nutrition Survey in 1938.[28] They were located in a southwest area of Lake Nyasa that was geographically and numerically dominated by matrilineal Chewa, ruled by local chiefs. A closer examination of these three villages reveals that colonial policies affected them in different ways, depending upon their specific characteristics; none, however, emerged from the process unscathed.

The three villages under examination were located on the lakeshore (at 1500 feet), on a three-thousand-foot escarpment, and on a plateau at 4500 feet.[29] The Chewa village was perched on the escarpment, where it retained a large degree of their matrilineal practices; it was isolated from any main roads and grew maize as a staple crop. One family, headed by Chikaungu, had been the first occupants of the land in the nineteenth century, and in the early twentieth century, relatives from their matrilineal grandmother arrived and were given permission to settle in their own hamlet under the leadership of a man named Biwi. Despite matrilineal connections, three things kept these two hamlets apart.[30] At some point, Biwi murdered Chikaungu's wife under mysterious circumstances; though he was expelled from the community, the rift between the two families never healed. Biwi's descendants remained, and they converted to Christianity under the nearby Dutch Reformed Church.[31]

When it was time for clearing the land and planting, families prepared fields sequentially through communal work parties, made easier by the wife's proudly-brewed beer. The Dutch Reformed Church, however, forbade fermented alcoholic beverages, requiring that communal work parties for crop production drink only unfermented beer. This meant the two hamlets could not work together, so they shared work, not with each other, but with neighboring hamlets that held their same philosophy of beer-drinking. Finally, the rift between the two hamlets became entrenched when the state formally designated them as a single village but appointed Biwi's descendant as headman and gave the taxbook to him rather than to the proper senior authority, Chikaungu. The resulting friction also interfered with marriage patterns and the reproduction of families that were the primary units of food production. This village suffered the most from seasonal hunger when awaiting the harvest after granaries became empty, since they were not producing all the food they needed for a whole year in their own plots. In response, men and women from households in need would work on fields in another village for baskets of maize that would be brought home for the family. The state had not only undermined local authority and failed to see the degree to which its own actions were contributing to disruption, but it also misunderstood the dynamics of the matrilineal family. When the anthropologist or the agricultural officer came in and made household lists in this matrilineal Chewa village, they ignored the fact that the women were the "owners of the land" and their brothers were their "guardians." Charts that listed men as husband-father heads of households belied the authority their wives had as the main focus of each household and the primary authority over the land and its fertility, and the right for all people to be there.

The escarpment Chewa village, with a total of 30 households, named 10 *machona*, and 11 households there had no husband present. Some 55 percent of the men were away from the village, most for no longer than three to four years to hoe or carry loads. During that time they sometimes came home for visits. While Read viewed this as an indication of their lack of initiative, others might see it as a preference for remaining close to their families. The constant state of underlying friction between the hamlets in this village undermined cooperative village-level food production and prevented families from producing all the food they needed for an annual cycle. Most responded by performing individualized labor somewhere outside the village in exchange for baskets of maize. Thus Margaret Read's "disrupted families" were ultimately cared for through a process of sharing among the smaller matrilineal units. These villagers complained the most about hunger, but hunger appears, ultimately, to be more a metaphor for lack of community than for a lack of food.[32]

A second village in the study was a Ngoni village called Jere, where people lived and grew maize on the plateau. They were an immigrant population, originally derived from the Zulu of South Africa. Though they had kept large herds of cattle, they now had very few, but cattle ideology remained strong. They had assimilated many neighboring peoples through intermarriage, but their Ngoni ideology continued to inform many of their practices. Chiefs had extensive authority, and men had been organized into age sets which formed military units. The village chief, Vuso Jere, had been appointed to the position of Native Authority by the state. In that capacity, he presided over thirteen nearby villages as well as the regional court, despite the fact that this was a Chewa, not an Ngoni area, which should have been under the leadership of their senior chief, Chiko.

The Ngoni were definitely patrilineal in practice and philosophy. Men gave the parents of their brides a payment of bridewealth, usually in cattle, and wives left their natal homes to come and live with their husbands. Such a residential pattern made it easier for these Ngoni men to acquire additional wives, if they had the resources. In contrast with the Chewa matrilineal village, which was dominated by a mother and her married daughters, a Ngoni village was one of a father (and perhaps his own brothers) and his married sons. Anthropological family lists here actually mirrored the reality of a husband-father head of household surrounded by the homes of his wives and adult sons.

Households were the units of food production and cooking. Even when husbands were working elsewhere, this village, with its tradition of ranked wealth and dependencies, allowed senior men to have command over junior men, women, and their labor, ensuring that each family's fields were worked. Eating did not occur in family units, but in groups divided by age and sex. Each wife cooked separately, but she often sent food to more than one eating group. Because this was an assimilated village, direct kinship could not be the only basis of extended family. Every family in the village was attached to one of two ideological "houses" formed by the chief's two senior wives, and some of the food produced remained in the "house" granaries. The few cattle in the village belonged to the two houses, which also had command of some of the wages brought back by emigrant workers. These houses had historically been critical for the migration and expansion of Ngoni villages. At the death of the village chief, the wife of the left-hand house and all of those affiliated with her would go with her eldest son to establish a new village, leaving the first village intact under the care of the right-hand house. As is the case of all Ngoni villages, Jere had close contact with their members' previous village and the new village, Ndabwi. Since Ndabwi had better land to grow maize and tobacco, food as well as profits from tobacco frequently came to Jere village.

Given that families in this village were a better fit for the Western ideal and men had prominent authority as husband-father heads of households, colonial agents presumed that they would be more receptive to "improving" their agricultural practices to obtain more vitamins and minerals. Also, given the high level of local authority in Jere, colonial agents presumed that this village would be best able to avoid seasonal hunger because the chief could command people to work. Jere village was in fact only part of a village, and despite Ndabwi's contributions, some Jere families lacked sufficient food to avoid the hungry season.

The plateau Ngoni village had 55 households and 57 percent of their men were away. They too listed ten *machona* along with five unmarried widows and ten married women with husbands away. Given that this village was larger, the loss of male labor seemed less acute, but men often married their brothers' widows, so this situation still reflected a substantial shortage of men. Men from this village were usually gone from four to five years and held jobs in the mines or in stores or worked as houseboys. These villagers had never been reliant exclusively on labor from the conjugal family. They drew upon the resources of the age sets, the "houses," and class power to enhance food production, and they benefited from food gifts and labor opportunities from their chief's village at Ndabwi. Still, the class system works both ways, and a number of families here also had to send members to work in other villages in exchange for baskets of maize.

The third village is a perfect example of how state expectations of family modifications toward nuclear families developed into reality, but it also demonstrates that the transformations were not necessarily a benefit to food quality or family stability. This village was an immigrant Yao village that grew cassava at the lakeshore; its members were in the process of modifying their earlier matrilineal practices, primarily due to their conversion to Christianity.[33] These faith-driven modifications included the growing prominence of monogamous nuclear families, a drive for education, a desire for better paying jobs, and the privileging of the role of husband-father over that of brother-uncle. Such changes came at the expense of loyalties previously given to the extended family and of the responsibilities usually tended by brothers for their sisters, particularly widowed sisters with their children gone. There was a general pattern of slow, permanent emigration from this village, primarily because men had acquired skills that could not be used in the immediate area. There were also many young girls of marriageable age who could not find Christian husbands, since the people in the surrounding area were all Muslim.

All the members of this village were descended from one matrilineal grandmother. Liwewe, the male guardian, had guided the migration to this place, but the village was divided between those who were descendants of his free wives and those of slave wives. One man held 60 percent of the wealth in the entire village, but because he was a descendant of a slave wife, his authority was minimal. Power and influence came primarily from the daughters of Liwewe's two senior free wives.[34] Though these villagers loved maize (which could not be grown here) and truly disliked cassava, the latter staple crop helped to facilitate a transformation into nuclear families. Cassava is a root crop that can be harvested over a period of several years, so the communal clearing, planting, and harvesting which facilitated maize production was not necessary here. On the other hand, cassava alone is insufficiently nutritious, so all families had to rely periodically on some source of protein (mostly fish from the lake). Fishing was the purview of men, but so much superstition prevailed surrounding fishing nets, areas, and canoes that nets were not even inherited.[35] As women were dependent upon men (husbands, sons, brothers) for this essential part of their food resources, the removal of brothers' matrilineal responsibilities for their sisters contributed to the fact that many widows or women with husbands away were frequently hungry. This village ironically had both the most wealthy and most destitute people.[36]

The lakeshore Yao village could count on cassava as a food not restricted by season, but this did not solve the food problems of all families. This village had lost the most people. They had 30 households and could name 20 *machona*. They had 25 households with no husbands, including 13 that held widows or divorcees. In addition, there were 13 girls of marriageable age who remained single, mainly because they could not find Christian husbands nearby, so they were still dependent upon their mothers. When men left this village to work, they were often gone for as long as a decade, and they gained higher salaries, mostly working as managers on estates. In 1938, this village held 51 women but only 16 men, some of whom had returned after many years of work away. Most of the men, though they were kin to several of the women in the village, could not, or chose not to, meet the responsibilities they had for their sisters and provided resources to their conjugal families instead. In an interesting twist, however, mothers, rather than fathers or brothers, took economic responsibility for their children's needs by growing labor-intensive rice, all of which they sold in the nearby town. People in this village constantly expressed general dissatisfaction with their lot, mainly because of higher goals for material goods and better jobs that were not being met. Despite a generally higher standard of living for most families, in reality, more people suffered from hunger in this village than in the other two. While the major transformation in family structure and power had benefited many individuals, some found the changes failed to mean improvement. Given this village's Christian practices and the high value members placed on education, the serious sex imbalance led Margaret Read to predict that the village would slowly disappear. This was unlikely to happen, however, given the value all Africans place on access to land through their lineage. Instead, the village became transformed in another way. By the early 1990s, Christian Chewa men from other regions moved there to marry Yao Christian wives, who retained their rights to the land. The village had only 14 families, and only half of those represented the original matrilineage. Still, the goal of education and a skilled job to follow prevailed, and the economic isolation and poverty of widows persisted.[37]

Even though the British colonial state in Nyasaland did not always use the family directly as the unit through which they would intervene for change, underlying every effort was an assumption that the family needed to accommodate to colonial needs. That meant, indirectly, that the most appropriate African family model was the one that mirrored the Western nuclear family. Clearly the nuclear patrilineal family was the accepted one in the colonial state, despite evidence that Africans moving in that direction did not necessarily profit from it. The state failed to see the benefits of the extended family while it also relied on that same extended family to take care of the "disrupted" nuclear families in their midst. The state worked against matriliny in such a way that it contributed to the loss of one whole arena of family responsibilities performed by brother-uncles. The colonial state failed to see the significance of the brother-sister dominant role and or of the mechanisms that Africans used to blend aspects of family dynamics rather than replace what they had with a colonial family model. At the same time, they failed to see the detrimental aspects of imposing their patrilineal husband-father model onto existing African family forms without question.

One characteristic of the colonial state, particularly in the late 1930s, was its agents' belief that they had the right and the power to change both the family structure and gendered power dynamics among peoples in their "paternalistic" care. As Margaret Read pointed out, this often led them to be overly optimistic about the transformations they had wrought. Despite her view that emigrant men were improving the standard of living while village women were holding back progress,[38] she challenged those state agents who regarded the women left in the villages

> more as mothers than as wives, [who] said that if a man came home regularly, bringing presents and clothes for his wife, and, in the vernacular phrase, "put a baby in the village," there could be little objection to controlled migration.[39]

Instead, she argued against this picture of village women's contentment and understood that the state was ignoring the emotional and sociological needs of families:

> "I must have a man to help me," was the constantly reiterated cry of the women whose husbands were away, and the poignant refrains of the songs they sang about their absent husbands were more on the theme of their having to live alone than of their wanting more children.[40]

African families were always complex, and colonial impositions and options brought complications along with promise. Ultimately, family was much more than its form and function; it was the place where Africans optimally lived their lives. Dramatic economic and social implications for Nyasaland followed from extensive colonial state intervention. The state altered relations among families and between families and the land. It challenged traditional sources of rights and definitions of responsibilities. It undermined kinship practices and privileges. It disrupted usual practices for producing, cooking, and distributing food. In so doing, it manipulated families for its own purposes. The result was that the colonial state unraveled the fabric of African families and villages. This was mostly done in the name of good intentions; the goal was to provide more food and greater stability. Ironically, agents of the colonial state contributed to the hunger, conflict, and disruption they were trying to end. The examples I described at the outset, of the Giriama mother struggling to support her children by working in a cashew factory, and the Chonyi man who often went hungry because he had no one to cook for him, are but two of the many thousands of lives that were affected by colonial state intervention which altered African family practices.

PART THREE

FAMILIALISM AS STATE REFORM

9

WELFARE REFORM WITH A FAMILIAL FACE

Reconstituting State and Domestic Relations in Post-Socialist Eastern Europe

LYNNE HANEY

In the last decade, the welfare state has come into scholarly focus for analysts of East Central Europe. After years of neglecting the welfare state, area specialists have begun to document the policy shifts underway in the region.[1] In tracing these shifts, scholars tend to lump the countries of Eastern Europe together as examples of a "post-socialist" welfare regime change. To some extent, this common grouping is warranted, as similar re/distributive trends have emerged across East Central Europe. With the end of full employment, East Europeans had their first experience with large-scale unemployment. With economic marketization and privatization, regional class structures became increasingly stratified and bifurcated.[2] With the disappearance of price subsidies and socialized services, poverty rates soared—especially among the working class, the Roma, and women.[3] And with the state's withdrawal of many maternity and childrearing benefits, reproduction became privatized, thus increasing women's workloads and undercutting their ability to combine work and family.[4]

Yet underlying these commonalities are critical variations in regional patterns of welfare development. Although many of their outcomes may be similar, East European re/distributive systems diverge in the role they assign to the family, the market, and the state in the provision of assistance. In the early 1990s, scholars began to reveal key structural differences in the organization of postsocialist welfare regimes. At the initial stages of the transition, Robert Deacon detected the emergence of diverse welfare regimes.[5] Drawing on Gøsta Esping-Andersen's classificatory scheme, Deacon discovered examples of all three "worlds of welfare capitalism" in the region.[6] For instance, the Czech Republic's low unemployment rate, limited means tests, and citizenship rights made it the prime example of a social-democratic welfare regime. There were many examples of corporatist regimes in the region. With their strong church, familial, and personalistic networks, the Polish and German welfare regimes had corporatist dimensions.[7] And with its heavy reliance on the market and welfare targeting, the Hungarian welfare state was classified as an example of a liberal welfare regime.[8]

While these regime analyses have contributed to our understandings of East European welfare development, their explanatory power is hindered by two key limitations. First, these analyses tend to operate at a purely descriptive level. In part, this limitation is related to Esping-Andersen's framework itself; while this scheme is useful in documenting policy arrangements and socioeconomic trends, it is less helpful in explaining why countries embark on divergent welfare trajectories and how they change over time. In the East European context, this problem is exacerbated by the tendency to examine welfare reform in a particular country and to link reform to internal political developments in the post-1989 period. There are few systematic comparisons of welfare reform across the region. And there are even fewer analyses of East European welfare that extend beyond postsocialist politics to explicate state socialist welfare legacies and/or international patterns of welfare restructuring. As a result, we are left with no clear sense of the factors that propelled East European countries onto distinct welfare reform paths.

Second, regime analyses of East European welfare tend to position the state, the labor market, and the family as mere objects of change. This tendency can also be linked to the framework underlying their scholarship: Given its descriptive focus, regime analysis views these social arenas as sites to be acted upon. The analytical goal is then to unearth how the state, the labor market, and the family are arranged in particular national contexts. Yet these social institutions are not simply the objects of change; they can also be the motors for change. While scholars have shown this to be the case with the state and the labor market, it is also true of the family. As feminist theorists remind us, familial structures and discourses can exert powerful influences on systems of redistribution. Instead of being relegated to a residual category, the family can be both a target and an agent of welfare development—shaping the form of states and labor markets, and thus the internal dynamics of welfare regimes.[9]

In this chapter, I attempt to correct for these limitations in the East European scholarship. Through an analysis of welfare reform in Hungary and the Czech Republic, I demonstrate how these states embarked on different reform paths and how familialism played into these reform projects. By juxtaposing welfare development in these two cases, I attempt to arrive at the kind of broad conceptual arguments that are largely absent from the East European scholarship on welfare—arguments about the forces underlying welfare regime change and the use of familialism for justifying this change. More specifically, my analysis works on two levels. First, I trace the global and local dynamics of welfare reform in Hungary and the Czech Republic to explain their different modes and outcomes. I then investigate the ways that narratives of the family were deployed in these two cases to frame reform decisions. At this level, the analysis will move to the discursive arena to expose how familialism was used by state actors for quite different ends in Hungary and the Czech Republic: In the former, it was used to justify the state's retreat from domestic life, while in the latter it was appropriated to justify the state's re-engagement in the family.[10] In the end, I suggest that these case studies reveal the malleability of familialism as a mode of state reform.

Routes to Reform: The Politics of Welfare Restructuring

The story of welfare reform in Hungary and the Czech Republic is replete with paradoxes. The most striking of these is a paradox of outcomes. Hungary begins the story with the largest, most comprehensive welfare system in the region. In the early 1980s, it encompassed the full employment provisions and subsidized services that were pervasive throughout the region. It also included an extensive maternalist subsystem of welfare comprising a three-year paid maternity leave grant, universal family allowances, and local childrearing assistance funds. Yet Hungary ends the story with one of the most targeted welfare systems in the region: the contemporary Hungarian welfare system includes very few universal entitlements and benefits, and programs that were once universal in nature have been subjected to means, income, or lifestyle tests. At the national level, many of these policy reforms were enacted while a socialist government was in power.

The Czech Republic, on the other hand, begins the story with a relatively small welfare system. Up until 1989, this system consisted of relatively limited family and maternity benefits and included virtually no local-level assistance programs. Yet, in the last decade, the Czech welfare system has evolved into the most comprehensive in the region—a system that actually grew to include extensive parental leave policies as well as targeted family allowances and poor-relief provisions. And much of this expansion occurred while a quite (neo)liberal government was in power.[11]

To understand this paradox in outcomes, we need to analyze the concrete processes of reform in these two countries. Welfare reform in Hungary and in the Czech Republic differed in terms of timing, sites, and targets. It also differed according to the role played by local policy legacies and global policy imperatives.

The Local and Global Politics of Retrenchment

Contrary to popular mythology, Hungarian welfare reform did not begin with the onset of the post-socialist transition in 1989. As I have argued elsewhere, critical welfare reforms were enacted throughout the state socialist period;[12] in fact, the origins of the most recent round of reform stretch back to the early 1980s.[13] In this period, members of the democratic opposition and the critical intelligentsia began to criticize the socialist welfare system openly—criticisms for which many were reprimanded through forced emigration and police harassment. Some were social scientists who reached their critique through empirical research on poverty. They discovered that the second economy had given rise to new forms of stratification, with urban families, sectors of the working class, and the Roma population beginning to slip into poverty.[14] Others formed a critique out of their concrete experiences with these impoverished groups. In the early 1980s, a group of sociologists conducting research on poverty among the Roma was pushed into action. They formed the first non-governmental poor-relief organization, SZETA (Szegényeket Támogató Alap). First and foremost, SZETA's goal was to meet the needs of the impoverished through charity work. But it also acted as a lobbying group on behalf of the poor. In addition to serving as a mediator between clients and caseworkers, members of SZETA exerted influence on local-level officials, pushing local-level policy makers and other officials to design new programs to protect the well-being of the materially deprived.

To a large extent, these activists and social scientists set their sights on local embodiments of the welfare state, perhaps because they believed they could wield more influence in local governmental structures. If this was their reasoning, they were correct: Beginning in the early 1980s, local welfare institutions began to initiate new policies and practices. Some established entirely new agencies to meet the needs of the poor called Family Support Service Centers.[15] Others created new poor-relief programs to support impoverished clients. Still others altered the focus of existing programs. For instance, since the 1970s, Hungarian welfare offices had been administering childrearing assistance benefits (RNS). Since their inception, welfare workers used these funds to supplement the income of female clients deemed "good mothers." By the early 1980s, these same funds were being used to support clients with severe material problems; through the use of income tests, the program was effectively transformed into poor relief.

As a result of these local-level changes, the Hungarian welfare state began to develop into a three-tiered system. At the national level were a series of universal entitlements and programs. These were accompanied by a maternalist policy apparatus—by according special benefits to mothers, including three years of paid maternity leave and universal family allowances, this welfare tier was highly gendered and separated women's needs as mothers. Then, at the local level, there were policies and programs aimed at the special needs of the economically vulnerable. This three-tiered system was quite consistent with the blueprints laid out by Hungarian social scientists and activists. Given their commitment to social justice, these opposition groups rarely called for the destruction of the entitlement system. Rather, they adhered to social democratic welfare models to imagine a welfare system that successfully combined universal entitlements and family benefits with targeted poor relief.

The activities of the Hungarian democratic opposition and critical intelligentsia constitute only one part of the late socialist reform story. The second part of the story begins with the entrance of another group of political actors: representatives of international agencies such as the IMF and the World Bank.[16] These actors surfaced in the early 1980s as Hungary joined the IMF in 1982—years earlier than the other countries in the region. Soon after their arrival, these agencies began to issue policy reports urging Hungarian policy makers to develop restrictive eligibility criteria and increase the use of means and income tests. These agencies cloaked their agenda in a veil of social justice; they proposed "welfare reform with a human face" and argued that restrictive eligibility criteria would actually protect the poor. On the surface, these arguments seemed to resemble those of the Hungarian opposition, but there was a key difference: the international agencies' reform model targeted national-level social entitlements in an attempt to dismantle the universal tier of the welfare state.

To some extent, these agencies reached their goal. From the late 1980s to the early 1990s, the universal arm of the Hungarian welfare state was slowly severed. Full-employment guarantees were replaced by income-tested unemployment benefits, price subsidies were revoked and replaced with poor-relief benefits, and standard-of-living guarantees metamorphosed into over twenty different social assistance programs. In the process, the Hungarian welfare system began to look more and more like the model of a liberal welfare state, with a shrinking entitlement sphere and a burgeoning poor-relief sector. Not surprisingly, from 1984 to 1994 the overall number of Hungarians receiving some kind of poor-relief increased by 1500 percent; by 1995 the number of Hungarians that applied for some form of social assistance soared to 25 percent.[17]

Interestingly, there was one tier of the Hungarian welfare state that made it through the early stages of reform relatively unscathed. Prior to 1995, few changes were made to the maternalist subsystem of welfare, despite the fact that elimination of maternity leave and family allowances had been central to international agencies' reform platforms from the outset.[18] These agencies proved unable to reform these programs, and here was where local politics proved to be of critical importance. Through the early 1990s, few political parties included welfare reform in their agendas. Before 1995, the Hungarian parliament devoted only a few sessions to discussions of social policy and most of these were limited to procedural issues and the setting of pension levels. In part, such inaction can be attributed to the political orientation of the first postsocialist government, which comprised a coalition of Christian conservatives and moderate nationalists. They made it their mission to protect the "Hungarian family." Ideologically, these parties stressed the need for women to "return" to the home, and they were unwilling to dismantle those policies that would allow women to do so.

The shield the conservative government built around maternalist programs began to crumble when a socialist government took office in 1994. Having inherited an enormous budget deficit, the socialist government confronted intensified pressure from the IMF and the World Bank to cut expenditures. In 1995, just a few days after meetings with IMF officials, the Hungarian government announced a series of welfare reforms. Named after Finance Minister Lajos Bokros, the reform plan applied income tests to the family allowance and maternity leave programs. Such swift and comprehensive welfare reform had yet to occur in other East European countries, and its effects were quite profound. Not only did it deny some women benefits they had relied on for generations, but it created a bifurcated, two-tiered welfare structure. One tier comprised the few remaining social entitlements, while the second included more than twenty poor-relief programs targeted at the materially needy.

There were long-term effects as well: the 1995 Bokros reforms moved maternalist programs out of the entitlement sphere and into the public assistance tier, thus subjecting them to the vicissitudes of party politics. For example, when the socialist government left office in 1998, the new government vowed to reinstate these programs, but they did so in altered form. Although maternity leave and family allowances were no longer income tested, applicants had to undergo investigations of their lifestyles and child-rearing practices to establish their eligibility, a requirement that made these new programs a far cry from the entitlements they once were.

In this way, Hungary's reform path led it toward a liberal welfare model.[19] Clearly, this was not what activists and social scientists envisioned when they laid the seeds for welfare reform in the 1980s. At that time, they could not have anticipated the influence that new global and local actors would eventually wield over the reform process. Nor could they sustain their commitment to a three-tiered welfare system that merged different models of entitlement and assistance. Yet in a neighboring country characterized by a quite different constellation of local and global forces, just such a welfare model had begun to take shape.

The Local Politics of Expansion

As in Hungary, contemporary welfare reform in the Czech Republic was shaped by the state socialist legacy. Yet its legacy was of a very different sort. The Czech democratic opposition and critical intelligentsia had a different relationship to the socialist state. The Czechoslovak state was known as one of the most rigid in the region. In the post-1968 period, it quashed the kind of reform movements that emerged in Hungary and Poland. As a result, the Czechoslovak opposition did not form non-governmental groups to address and ameliorate poverty. There was no Czechoslovak equivalent of SZETA. Of course, this is not to imply that the Czech opposition was weak or ineffective—the widespread support for Charter 77, a petition calling for democratic reform, testifies to the opposition's strength and organization. But although Czechoslovaks did develop informal support networks, they were not able to formalize such arrangements through charity or poor-relief agencies.

Similarly, Czechoslovak social scientists were even more constrained than their Hungarian counterparts. They were not accorded the same degree of space for studying social problems and for publishing their work. Again, this is not to imply that Czechoslovak social scientists were unaware of social problems; many of them did conduct important research on social stratification and poverty in Czechoslovakia. Yet the Czechoslovak state refused to give this research even minimal exposure; it shielded itself from the work and politics of the humanistic intelligentsia. Hence, although there were indications that poverty was growing in the 1980s, Czechoslovak social scientists were unable to enact the kind of policy and institutional reforms established in Hungary.

As a result, the Czechoslovak state retained a "societal welfare model" through the 1980s.[20] That is, its welfare system continued to target the overall structure of society and the economic organization of state socialism. Like other East European countries, Czechoslovakia had a broad system of plan-related benefits, including full-employment provisions and price subsidies. It also had enterprise-related benefits such as subsidized housing, food, clothing, child care, and vacations. Yet Czechoslovakia did not have an extensive system of social policies to distribute benefits to particular social groups, and the few it did have were quite limited in scope. For instance, the Czechoslovak maternity leave system gave mothers 28 weeks of paid leave, which paled in comparison to the three years of paid leave received by Hungarian mothers.[21] Entire areas were left unaddressed by the Czechoslovak welfare system; there were, for example, no poor-relief programs or assistance schemes geared toward the materially deprived.

Given Czechoslovakia's continued adherence to a societal welfare model, one might assume that it would be subjected to considerable pressure to restructure from international agencies like the IMF and World Bank. Yet just as the Czechoslovak state remained relatively impervious to local intellectuals, it cordoned itself off from international scrutiny. Czechoslovakia did not join the IMF until 1990, more than eight years after Hungary. Since it kept its foreign debt at a fairly manageable level, the Czechoslovak state was not forced into debt-restructuring programs as rapidly as in countries like Hungary and Poland. Thus, prior to 1989, agencies like the IMF and

World Bank made few inroads into Czechoslovak policy circles, and even after 1989, their presence remained limited. These agencies did not build the kind of welfare state industry that flourished in Hungary. They held very few conferences or training sessions in the Czech Republic or Slovakia; while these agencies produced more than twenty reports on Hungarian social policy, they published only two on the Czech Republic.[22]

In this way, Czechoslovakia entered the transition period with its socialist welfare system relatively intact and with a considerable amount of autonomy from international agencies. These two factors go a long way in explaining its resulting welfare reform path.[23] The Czech reform path was far more domestic in nature, shaped by battles among political parties, unions, and non-governmental organizations. It was also one of the most unique trajectories in the region: After the breakup of Czechoslovakia, the Czech Republic embarked on welfare reform that actually led to the expansion of many of its social programs.

Of course, like other countries in the region, the Czech state did dismantle much of the economic organization of state socialism. Yet it did so in a distinctive way. In 1990, the state abandoned its formal commitment to full employment, but the Czech unemployment rate remained the lowest in the region through the 1990s; from 1990 to 1997, it rose from 4.1 percent to only 5.2 percent. In part, this low rate is related to the Czech approach to privatization. Instead of embarking on rapid privatization—which led to "managerial capitalism" in other countries—the Czechs privatized much of their industry through a voucher system.[24] Available to all citizens, the voucher program operated in three waves to give Czechs the opportunity to invest their company shares either directly or indirectly through investment funds. The ultimate success of the voucher system is still being debated, but at least early on, the system led to relatively high rates of public ownership. In 1996, 70 percent of Czechs owned shares in industry; by 1998, this rate had dropped to 53 percent.[25]

Similarly, while the Czech government dismantled the socialist system of price subsidies, it did so gradually and provided compensation to the population. For the first four years of the transition period, Czechs received monthly cash payments to offset the effects of price increases. Given to all citizens regardless of their income, these payments amounted to roughly 5 percent of the average wage.[26] After 1993, the payments were given only to low-income groups. Thus, unlike those East European countries that embarked on a path of "shock therapy," the Czech Republic found ways to cushion the population in the initial stages of the transition to a market economy.

In addition, the Czech system of family and maternity policy actually expanded after 1990. Unlike other post-socialist governments, the Czech state introduced new family benefits.[27] First, in the early 1990s, the state created a new parental allowance that allowed parents to take paid leave for up to four years. This benefit was paid at the minimum subsistence level. Second, the Czech government established a maternal compensation policy. Although the state can no longer guarantee mothers re-employment in their same positions upon completion of leave, this policy compensates women who are forced to move into lower paying jobs after their return from pregnancy or maternity leave. Unlike Hungary, which subjected family policies to income and lifestyle tests, the Czech Republic kept these provisions as social entitlements and, in some cases, even extended their scope. Finally, since 1990 the Czech government has erected a third welfare subsystem comprising income-tested benefits targeted at the materially needy.[28] This social assistance tier includes child allowances for low-income families' childrearing expenses, social allowances for their personal needs, and housing allowances.

Hence, the Czech welfare state combined different logics of assistance and balanced three tiers of benefits. Maintaining this balance was not always easy to achieve. As opposed to Hungary, where welfare politics was shaped by external pressures, Czech welfare politics was primarily domestic in nature. As many scholars have noted, in the early stages of the transition period, the (neo)liberal Klaus government "gave" the welfare issue to its parliamentary rivals, the Social Democrats, in part because it needed support for its economic policies and in part because it was concerned about the political ramifications of deep welfare cuts.[29] So while the Klaus government "won" on macroeconomic stabilization and privatization, the Social Democrats "won" on social policy. Czech trade unions also helped to secure this victory. Unlike Hungarian trade unions, which lost much of their power in the last decade, Czech unions remained a formidable force. They adamantly opposed all attempts to target social benefits. By arguing that the administrative costs associated with income tests were higher than what the government would save, they exerted considerable influence of the reform debate.[30]

In addition, Czech social scientists were not fully on board the reform bandwagon. Many of them retained a vision of a welfare state geared toward social justice, and therefore did not help to lay the ideological groundwork for reform. Overall, Czech social scientists tended to be more ambivalent about the bifurcated, two-tiered welfare system associated with welfare capitalism. In fact, some even began to articulate a conception of democracy premised on their social and political convictions. As one Czech social scientist put it in 1995:

> The achievement of democracy and the establishment of a market economy can present contradictory goals. Disintegration of the system of social guarantees could, under certain circumstances, represent a risk for the building of a democratic system, as well as for the development of a market economy. . . .

In this connection, it is clear that progress toward a new economic order can also be accomplished anti-democratically, through authoritarian tendencies, fed from various sources, often, however, packaged in "social security" slogans.[31]

The Czech public seemed to share these sentiments. Perhaps more important, they were willing to act on them politically. For instance, in 1995 the Klaus government made its first attempt to tinker with welfare benefits by simply announcing that it was considering a welfare reform package that cut some universal programs. This sparked public demonstrations in Prague which ultimately prompted the Klaus government to revoke its reform proposal from parliamentary review.

So, to summarize the first part of the story: The Hungarian and Czech reform paths diverged in significant ways. In Hungary, the reform process began locally as a critique of actually-existing state socialism and became increasingly global as international agencies joined forces to revamp the welfare system. This revamping occurred incrementally, beginning with local-level reforms and extending to the national-level policy apparatus. The outcome was the rise of a two-tiered, bifurcated welfare system. The Czech reform process, by contrast, was initiated only after the postsocialist transition was underway; it was quite domestic in nature, shaped less by international pressure and more by Czech party politics. Under the (neo)liberal shield of the Klaus government, the Czech welfare system actually expanded and developed into a three-tiered system that merged different modes of entitlement and logics of assistance.

Justifying Reform: The Politics of Familialism

Despite their different paths, Hungarian and Czech welfare reform had profound effects on citizens. Both reform projects included the withdrawal of critical forms of state assistance, such as full-employment guarantees, price subsidies, and socialized services. In Hungary, reform went even further to target maternal benefits and to apply means-tests to other forms of state support. These reforms were enacted by newly elected governments with tenuous holds on power and administered by welfare workers employed in new institutional structures. And they were carried out on groups with well-developed opinions about their needs and the state's responsibility in meeting them.[32] Hence, these governments had to work to justify reform to the population.

In a provocative analysis of post-socialist politics, Gil Eyal, Iván Szelényi, and Eleanor Townsley argue that the new political elite developed a series of "rituals" to translate their interests and ideologies into everyday practice.[33] These include the ritual of sacrifice, through which budget cuts were presented as an exercise in civic education to avoid excess; the ritual of purification, through which citizens were cleansed of their welfare dependency and addictions to the state; and the ritual of confession, through which citizens admitted their sins of overindulgence and dependency to prepare to live virtuously. Clearly, these rituals served as tools of legitimation—as narratives of the past and future that justified the agendas of the new ruling elites.

In the welfare arena, these narratives formed a critical part of the population's resocialization; welfare reform was often portrayed as a form of sacrifice that would rid the population of their dependent ways. Yet state officials appropriated another narrative to rationalize their welfare agendas: the narrative of the ideal family. Through discourse and practices, public officials articulated powerful conceptions of what the family and the state should become. This use of images of the family is not entirely surprising; feminist scholars have shown that reproductive relations often constitute a terrain upon which new political and cultural futures are imagined.[34] In the East European context, Susan Gal and Gail Kligman have argued that postsocialist discourses of reproduction reframe the relationship between citizens and the state; they are coded arguments about state legitimacy and morality.[35] Thus, like Eyal, Szelényi, and Townsley's rituals of postsocialism, familial narratives serve to recast the role of the state in social life.

Yet they have done so in different ways across the region. In both Hungary and the Czech Republic, welfare reform was accompanied by the politics of familialism that set new boundaries around the state and the domicile. Drawing on examples of political discourse and observations in welfare institutions, I suggest that the use of familialism diverged in these countries: in Hungary, familialism became a way to shift responsibilities from the collective to individual households, while in the Czech Republic it was used to justify renewed state support.

Familialism as (Selective) Reprivatization

Images of the Hungarian family played a central role in other political regime changes—from the nineteenth-century transition to capitalism to the twentieth-century transition to state socialism.[36] Yet what is unique about the contemporary politics of familialism is the way it served as a rationale for scaling back the state. While the early socialist state drew on the family as a metaphor for state building and as a model for its ascent to power, contemporary uses of the family are quite different. First, they include a message about how the family should take on obligations once met by the state—that is, how a non-interventionist state is preferable and the family is better equipped to protect the well-being of its members. Second, they encompass a message about precisely when state intervention is warranted—that is, when families fail to meet the needs of their members and the nation as a whole.

In order to transmit these messages, Hungarian political and state officials often ended up adhering to a quite idealized vision of the family. Much of the current political discourse is infused with domestic nostalgia, presenting the family as a haven in the heartless world of state socialism and an emotional anchor in the chaos of post-socialism. While such imagery is perhaps most pervasive in the discourse of populist and nationalist politicians, they are not the only ones who valorize the family. Many members of the former democratic opposition, who now occupy key governmental positions, adhere to a similar familial ideal. It was, after all, the opposition writer György Konrád who helped to popularize the image of the private sphere as the locus of freedom, individuality, dignity, and thus political resistance.[37]

Such arguments now have a renewed political utility. Once constituted a strong site of freedom, the family is capable of taking on the new responsibilities assigned to it. In fact, it can even be argued that the family is better able to fulfill these obligations. This reasoning was implicit in many Hungarian reform policies. As unemployment rates soar, poverty rates increase, price subsidies vanish, and child care centers close, new burdens are placed on individual households—with little debate about whether families can handle these burdens. On occasion, policy makers and politicians make these assumptions explicit, thus offering a glimpse into the familial underpinnings of welfare politics.

One such moment was the political debates spawned by the 1995 Bokros reform package, which means-tested the family allowance and maternity leave programs. Justifications for the reforms were steeped in familialism. Some politicians defended the plan through reference to "liberal values," claiming that liberal polities made a clear distinction between the public and the private, or the state and the family, and set limits on the former's intrusion into the latter. Eliminating the state's role in childrearing was thus a "critical step towards liberalism."[38] Other politicians presented the reforms as a corrective to the socialist state's collectivism, which distorted "natural" family patterns and behavior. By pulling back from the private arena, the state would then allow families to restore traditional roles and responsibilities. And there would be public benefits to such a restoration: as women became full-time mothers again, unemployment would be alleviated, men would become less dependent on their wives, and fathers would regain their rightful places as heads of households.[39]

While national-level politicians articulated such messages in critical public debates, they were also central to the practices of local-level welfare institutions. In the mid-1990s, I spent nearly two years conducting ethnographic research in Budapest welfare agencies, and I found them to be training grounds in which Hungarians learned about the shifting boundaries of the state and family. As I have argued elsewhere, this resocialization involved the materialization of need, whereby all clients' problems were reduced to monetary issues.[40] Yet underlying the materialization of need was a form of familialism, whereby Hungarians were taught that certain family problems and conflicts fell outside the bounds of acceptable needs-claims. Welfare workers made explicit what politicians often kept implicit—in post-socialist Hungary, the family was to care for itself, with the least possible amount of state assistance.

Welfare workers transmitted this message to their clients in a variety of ways. Perhaps the most common was their discourse of familial turmoil and conflict. In the socialist era, welfare agencies were willing to take on all sorts of family problems, from childrearing concerns to spousal abuse to domestic power struggles.[41] Contemporary offices, in contrast, did everything they could to shift these dilemmas back onto the family.[42] Clients regularly came to these offices to complain about aloof partners, violent spouses, or rebellious children. They sought assistance with these familial problems—someone to lecture a recalcitrant husband, to curb male violence, or to scold an unruly child—but rarely received such help. Instead, they would be shuffled out of welfare offices by caseworkers who claimed such problems were of no concern to them or told to use their "personal resources" to grapple with them. For example, when one female client explained to her caseworker that her husband had thrown their television set out the window in a drunken rage, she was advised to use her own savings to buy a new television.[43] Then there was the female client who told her caseworker stories of how she feared leaving her daughters at home with her alcoholic husband; she was instructed to hire a private babysitter to assuage her fears.[44] The message transmitted in these interactions was clear: The state was no longer responsible for resolving certain familial conflicts. "This is all so crazy," a professor of social work explained to me in an interview. "We spent generations getting the state off our backs. Now my students tell me [that] their clients want more and more help. [It is] crazy. . . ."[45]

Caseworkers' classifications of their clientele echoed this message. Most of the welfare workers I interviewed and worked with "ranked" their clients' needs: those with material resources were to go it alone, while those without such resources were (possibly) eligible for (material) assistance. Over and over again, I watched as clients in the former category were excluded from all forms of state support. Welfare workers put them at the bottom of agency waiting lists, forcing them to sit for hours to see a welfare worker. When they did make it into meetings with welfare workers, these clients were routinely given referrals to non-state agencies, such as church groups, private family counselors, or non-profit psychiatric clinics. As they administered these referrals, welfare workers often made these clients feel guilty about turning to the state for help, presenting their problems as insignificant and even frivolous. "What was that woman about?" a caseworker once asked me after meeting with a middle-class client who had family problems. "Please, I have clients who can't even feed their kids. What did she want from me?" This woman's familial struggles fell outside the parameters of the state, so she was told to look elsewhere for support.[46]

Neither welfare workers nor national politicians insisted that the state should never intervene into family life. Even adherents to the most classical liberal ideology held that state intervention into the reproductive realm was warranted under some circumstances. Across the political spectrum, politicians tended to agree that state support remained necessary when families failed to fulfill their responsibilities. Yet they disagreed over how to define familial failure. On the one hand, there was the definition articulated by welfare workers. Rank-ordering of clients dictated that those with material problems deserved state assistance, so they created elaborate systems of intervention for "needy families," which included poor-relief funds, benefits-in-kind, and poverty-survival training.[47] This material definition of familial failure was advanced by many socialist and liberal politicians. The day the Bokros reforms were introduced, Socialist Prime Minister Gyula Horn appeared on television to justify the cuts, arguing that new economic divisions had surfaced in Hungary and new state policies should be targeted at the "needy." In fact, this argument surfaced repeatedly in the 1996 parliamentary debates about welfare reform; over and over again, socialist and liberal MPs claimed that state support should be restricted to the "neediest families."[48]

Although this material justification for state intervention was perhaps most pervasive in national and local state institutions, it was challenged by a competing definition of need. In her analysis of the 1996 parental leave debate, Joanna Goven unearthed another construction of the family.[49] Articulated by Christian conservatives and nationalist politicians, this vision positioned the family as the foundation of the nation—as the site within which the nation was reproduced and sustained. These political actors recognized that, when left to their own devices, families often failed at their reproductive tasks: They neither produced enough children nor socialized them properly. And this was when state intervention was necessary. Without such intervention, Hungary would commit "race suicide," as the "proper" type of citizen would become extinct.[50] Thus, like socialist and liberal politicians, nationalists argued for selective state support for family life. But for them this intervention was a way to inculcate national norms and collective values they viewed as essential to cultural and social development.

Familialism as (Selective) Resocialization

The Czech public discourse surrounding welfare was also infused with familial ideals. Moreover, the content of the Czech ideals was strikingly similar to that articulated in Hungary; it positioned the family as a protector against the perils of state socialism and postsocialism. Here, too, such imagery drew in representatives of different political ideologies, from social democrats to (neo)liberals to conservative nationalists. If Hungarians had György Konrád to popularize such familial images, the Czechs had Vaclav Havel to give them national and international currency. Havel's writings eloquently portrayed the private arena as central to Czechs' ability to "live in truth"; comprising a world of "huddled, private circles," family life gave Czechs a sense of meaning and security.[51] Contemporary writings by many Czech social scientists reproduced this vision by painting a portrait of the family as an institution of social peace, harmony, and cooperation.[52]

Despite their similarities, Czech and Hungarian narratives of the family were used for very different political ends. While familialism was deployed in Hungary to rationalize welfare retrenchment, in the Czech Republic it was appropriated to justify welfare expansion. Czech politicians and state actors rarely idealized the family in order to shift more responsibilities onto it, nor did they rank-order families to frame state intervention as a method of mending the ways of failed families. Instead, many Czech officials deployed familial arguments to secure the continuation of state assistance. Precisely because the family served as a site of refuge under socialism, it should not be neglected; precisely because it served as a social anchor in the postsocialist period, it should be supported and sustained with public funds.

To a large extent, this politics of familialism can be related to the political dynamics of Czech welfare reform debates. Not only were these debates far more domestic in nature than those in Hungary, but they were dominated by socialists and social democrats. Having "given" the welfare issue to the left, most (neo)liberal Czech politicians maintained a "cheerless silence" on welfare reform.[53] As a result, the Social Democrats set the tone of reform, which changed very little through the 1990s. In 1993 Parliamentary debates about social policy, these politicians argued that neediness should be defined in "social" terms: "The existence of social subsidy benefits available to all households is a responsibility that cannot be surrendered."[54] Later that year, in a debate about the expansion of maternity leave and family allowances, Jindrich Vodicka, the Minister of Labor and Social Affairs, echoed this reasoning: "[We will not] surrender the possibility of the state not only to formulate but also to directly pursue particular goals of social policy"—goals that included a "strong safety net" for all families.[55] Then, in 1995, the Social Democrats led the public charge against the Klaus government's proposal to target social benefits. As one of them asserted: "This [proposal] will harm families, all families.... [It is] unacceptable."[56] Or, as another put it: "This [proposal] is an attack on social solidarity. There is no social benefit [to] targeting social subsidies.... Differentiation between families is divisive and unwise."[57] Interestingly, after these proclamations, public support for the Czech Social Democratic Party rose steadily—which is perhaps an indication of the Czech population's commitment to welfare universalism.[58]

By the late 1990s, another issue took on public relevance and pushed other politicians out of their "cheerless silence." Demographic data began to reveal that Czech women had postponed childbirth into their late twenties and early thirties; as a result, the Czech birthrate plummeted to 1.2, which was below the reproduction level. Few Czech policy makers took these data lightly. Public debate shifted to figuring out how state support could resolve the "demographic crisis," and politicians from across the political spectrum began to argue for further interventions into family life. As Rebecca Nash has shown, the resulting political discourse expressed an awareness of the demands placed on Czech families, particularly on young families.[59] Many of the state officials interviewed by Nash portrayed Czech women as rational actors, opting to pursue new opportunities instead of starting families.[60] Once it was posed in cost/benefit terms, policy makers viewed state policy as a tool to increase the benefits of childrearing. As one MP noted in 1998, "We must find a way to motivate citizens to have children."[61] In 1999, the Czech government, comprising Social Democrats and (neo)liberals, increased social benefits to families. In 2001, it introduced higher birth payments and relaxed the rules restricting those on parental leave from working outside the home. These changes were also justified through reference to the state's role in protecting the well-being of the family.

While arguments like this surfaced explicitly at key political junctures, they had become embedded in the everyday discourses and practices of Czech welfare institutions. As in Hungary, Czech welfare agencies were a training ground for the resocialization of the population. Yet the training that Czechs underwent seemed to be quite different from the Hungarian retraining. In my interviews with and limited observations of Czech welfare workers, I was confronted by an ethos I had not encountered in Hungary. Over and over again, the caseworkers claimed to provide "comprehensive care" to their clients.[62] They placed a premium on remaining close to their clientele and spent a significant amount of time in the communities they served.[63] "It is important that families see me around," one caseworker explained in an interview. "So they will trust me and feel comfortable coming to me with their problems."[64] In 1996, welfare workers in Prague demanded they be given cell phones so clients could reach them at all times—even after working hours. "I want to be on-call always," another caseworker proclaimed, "so if there is a problem, I can respond immediately."[65] The head of a Prague welfare office put this ethos best when she told me: "We are like mothers. We try to be compassionate. The clients open up to us and confess—just like with their mothers."[66]

Most of the Czech welfare workers I interviewed believed that they were on a mission to support and care for Czech families. They also claimed to run their offices like a family. When I asked them to describe the organization of their offices, Czech welfare workers often represented their work in familial terms. In my interviews with workers in a Prague employment office, for instance, I was struck by the discourse used to characterize the agency's division of labor. Those who set eligibility and benefit levels were described as "rational disciplinarians." Those who conducted employment counseling were said to be "understanding," "empathetic," and "down to earth." And those who did psychological treatment and alcohol counseling were identified as the "emotional ones." One welfare worker introduced her colleague, the agency psychologist, to me in this way: "She's the nurturer. She understands the clients. She gets inside their heads like she's known them for years. She cares for them."[67]

Czech caseworkers refused to classify their clients on the basis of their material needs. In fact, those I interviewed expressed deep ambivalence about welfare targeting and means testing. Some of them feared that such an approach would restrict them from helping clients and leave a series of problems undetected. Others worried about the degrading and humiliating practices that accompanied such tests. Still others questioned the assistance logic underlying welfare targeting. They rejected this approach with universal arguments about the state's responsibility to protect all families. As one welfare worker put it, "The help we give is for all families and children. It must remain that way. It should not matter how much the parents make. This is really irrelevant."[68]

Moreover, most of the Czech welfare workers I interviewed were unwilling to rank-order their clients' needs. When I asked them to describe their clients' most pressing needs, they resisted. I was told that it was important not to create a hierarchy of needs. Instead, clients' needs had to be understood as comprehensive and interconnected. Welfare workers spoke quite passionately about the different problems facing their clients—social, psychological, interpersonal, and material problems that conspired to make their lives difficult. Welfare workers often reprimanded me when I asked them to categorize their clientele; they refused to speak about their clients in general. I was told that there was no "typical" client; they rejected any attempt to get them to generalize. "They are different, all individuals," one welfare worker explained to me in an interview. "I cannot say anything general about them."[69]

This is not to imply that Czech welfare workers had glorified views of their clients. Many of them complained about how difficult their work had become and how some clients had become unpleasant to work with. They recognized that some clients were more demanding, upset, angry, and fixated on money, but they usually gave a context for this behavior, and followed evaluative statements with explanations. It was almost as if they were ashamed to reveal that they held negative sentiments about their clients: one had to remember how unstable and vulnerable family life had become; one could not forget that Czech families faced new economic pressures and financial constraints. The caseworkers believed all of this left their clients feeling ashamed. "They should not feel that way," one explained. "We are nice. Really. We are here to care for them."⁷⁰

Of course, it is hard to imagine that Czech welfare offices are really run like big, happy families. In my interviews, I did get a glimpse of one way this construction broke down. There was a group of clients that Czech welfare workers refused to include in their happy families—the Roma, or "Gypsies." When they spoke of the Roma, welfare workers' tone changed. Suddenly, they were willing to generalize. They were quick to invoke a pathological imagery: The Roma were lazy. They lied. They were mean and angry. They were welfare cheats. They were undeserving. They had too many children they could not support. They were uncultured. And they were driven by money. One welfare worker's comments about her Romany clients encompassed all of these ideas:

> They [Romany clients] are impossible to deal with. All they care about is money. When it is one day late, they come storming into the office, with their whole family, so many children. Screaming and yelling. They do not read the rules or listen. They just flip out. I have their big families in this small office, with the kids all running around and making a mess. They pick up my things and break them. This is natural [for them]. It is chaotic and unmanageable.⁷¹

Comments like this indicate that Czech welfare workers' familial ideology may not translate smoothly into reality. Yet this does not negate the importance of the discourse itself. As in Hungary, Czech state actors adhered to an idealized vision of the family as a guardian of social stability and peace, but in the Czech Republic this vision was deployed to justify the state's continued support of the domicile. Socialist politicians appropriated it to call for an expansion of welfare benefits; liberal politicians used it to imagine a way out of the demographic crisis; and welfare workers formed it into an institutional mission. This differential use of familialism offers critical insights into its political malleability and implicit gendered agenda.

Welfare Reform with a Familial Face

This chapter has told a tale of two East European welfare states, a tale with a series of lessons. First, it points to important variations among the welfare regimes of the region. Although representatives from the IMF and the World Bank would like East Europeans to believe that welfare liberalism is the only model for reform, it clearly is not. To some extent, Hungary adheres to this liberal model of reform, producing a bifurcated system that tracks some recipients into a social insurance sphere and others into a social assistance sphere. Labor force participation and poverty are the key determinants of this tracking. By contrast, the Czech Republic adheres to a more social-democratic reform model, resulting in a tripartite welfare system comprising social insurance, social subsidy, and social assistance spheres. Eligibility is conferred through labor force participation, familial responsibility, and material need.

Second, the variation between these welfare systems is rooted in particular historical, political, and economic circumstances. In Hungary, reform began as a critique of state socialism and then became more global in nature; it started by targeting local policies and then moved to national provisions. In the Czech Republic, welfare reform began once the postsocialist transition was underway and thus was linked to domestic politics, wrapped up in the struggles among political parties and trade unions. Although preliminary, this analysis suggests that these divergent paths can be explained by the timing, the site, and the role of global actors in welfare reform. Clearly, these arguments need further elaboration. Through additional comparisons among East European cases, we can begin to theorize the forces underlying welfare reform and conceptualize how, within the same region, alternative welfare models are becoming hegemonic.

Such comparisons will also illuminate how different welfare models are rationalized and justified to the population. In the Hungarian and Czech contexts, I uncovered variation in these modes of legitimation. What made this variation particularly significant was that both Hungarian and Czech political actors rely on narratives of the family to package and sell their reform agendas. And while their visions of the family are strikingly similar, they are used for very different political ends. This is true both within and between these countries. Narratives of the ideal family tend to be associated with Christian conservatives and nationalist politicians. While these political groups certainly mobilize such imagery, socialist and liberal politicians also deploy familial discourses in their political struggles. Moreover, in the East European context, this use of familialism is often presumed to be an ideological tool to facilitate the state's abdication of social responsibilities. While this may be true in Hungary, familialism serves opposite political ends in the Czech Republic. In this way, familialism appears to be quite a malleable and flexible discourse. Far from determining the scope or direction of state action, it can be used in competing and even conflicting ways.

Finally, underlying all this variation was a striking commonality. In its different incarnations, East European familialism remains insensitive to the family as a gendered institution. It is premised on overly idealized and unrealistic conceptions of the family that ignore the ways in which families become sites of conflict, tension, and power struggles and obscure the fact that they comprise competing interests and complex divisions of labor. By lumping all family members together and reifying the family as itself an actor, East European familialism may end up exacerbating gender inequality and shifting new burdens onto women. Perhaps this is most obvious in Hungary: As politicians call on the "family" to take on more social obligations, women become increasingly overworked; as nationalists and welfare workers set out to fix failed families, women get blamed. Yet this is also true in the Czech Republic: Its welfare provisions do not treat all family members equally; they often end up supporting women only as caretakers and decommodifying their labor. These commonalities thus warn of the dangers of familial politics separated from gender politics—or of a familialism divorced from feminism.

10

"THEY SAY, 'OH GOD, I DON'T WANT TO LIVE LIKE *HER*!'"

The Marginalization of Mothering in German Post-Socialism[1]

ELIZABETH C. RUDD

Suburbs of apartment blocks are arrayed along East Berlin's subway line U5. U5 ends at Hönow, the outermost edge of Berlin and the site of one of the last housing estates built under state socialism. I rode the subway to Hönow in the summer of 1994, four years after German unification, to interview Mr. and Mrs. Acker about the effect of the postsocialist transformation on their work-family balance. It was hot and the streets were still and quiet. The apartment buildings lined the street like tan boxes with tiny, bare balconies stacked in neat, symmetrical piles. I interviewed the Ackers in their small livingroom crammed with a couch, low table, and large "Schrankwand," an all-in-one unit of bookshelves, knick-knack display cases, and cupboards common in East German apartments.

Combining work and family had gotten a lot harder for the Ackers, especially Mrs. Acker. In state socialist East Germany, Mrs. Acker's workplace had accommodated her family. She had taken a year of paid maternity leave after the birth of their second son. She had then requested and received several months of unpaid leave because her infant son was not strong enough for all-day childcare. When she returned to her job as a kindergarten teacher, her son was considered well enough to be placed in all-day infant care, but Mrs. Acker knew that often she would need to stay home with him because of his frequent sicknesses.

At that time, under East German laws, Mrs. Acker's workplace was obliged to allow her six weeks of paid leave annually to care for a sick child.[2] In consultation with her supervisors, she was hired as a floating temporary kindergarten teacher available to fill in when other teachers missed work. In this way, Mrs. Acker's absences would not disrupt a class of kindergartners, and she could retain her full-time job, while staying home with her son when he was sick. As Mrs. Acker was explaining this to me, Mr. Acker interjected:

> That was completely understandable, that you couldn't lose your job. That's one of the things lost with the unification.... [In East German times] if a child needed to be cared for, your job was secure.

Mr. Acker's comment implied that in post-socialist, unified Germany, caring for a child could jeopardize your job. In fact, in 1994, four years after unification, Mrs. Acker worked for the same employer. However, her full-time workweek had increased by a few hours, paid leave available to care for a sick child had dropped to 20 days (from 30) annually, and she had begun sending her son to school even when she suspected he would be better off at home.[3]

Mrs. Acker's shift in priorities resulted directly from changes in the state's role in the economy and associated changes in the state's dominant gender ideology following unification. As part of a socialist system, East Germany's economy was planned and directed by the state. The state guaranteed employment for everyone (with the exception of political dissidents). The gender ideology of the East German state promoted full employment of mothers. To achieve this, the state provided free infant care, childcare, and after-school programs and required socialist employers to help women combine work and family.

When West German political and state-administrative institutions were established in former East Germany after the economic and political unification in 1990, the state's role in the economy changed. The West German state guaranteed the conditions of economic activity but did not directly control the economy; it left economic actors considerably more freedom to pursue goals of production and profit rather than social goals. Further, the dominant gender ideology in West German social policy saw motherhood as incompatible with women's participation in the labor market on equal terms with men.

As a worker in East Germany, Mrs. Acker had been guaranteed job security. As a mother of two she had been allowed to work a few hours less than full time each week without loss of pay. She had received a paid day off each month for housework. After German unification, East German policies designed to help mothers combine work and family were abandoned. The collapse of the East German economy and emergence of a capitalist labor market led to high unemployment. Mrs. Acker tried to maintain her commitment to both work and mothering in post-socialist Germany, but the institutional changes pushed her toward protecting her job and away from mothering.

Post-socialist transformations in Central and Eastern Europe provide unique opportunities to observe social institutions in the making because state-socialist institutions were organizationally different from, yet functionally similar to, institutions in capitalist economies. A case in point was the arrangements for combining work and family. At a time when few married women worked outside the home, August Bebel's widely read and influential book, *Woman Under Socialism*, proclaimed women's participation in paid employment on terms equal with men as one of the most highly valued goals of socialism.[4] For a combination of ideological and expedient reasons, communist parties in the Soviet Union and Eastern Europe pursued some aspects of this goal.[5]

One result was legendarily high employment rates for women in state-socialist systems; in many states by 1980 more than 80 percent and in some places more than 90 percent of women of childbearing age held paid employment.[6] But how was this achieved? Did women stop having babies? Were children all magically inoculated against every flu and sickness, while elderly parents died quickly when still healthy? Did men take over women's caregiving and domestic work? Given women's high employment rate, how did state-socialist societies help women combine work and family? And what happened to this work-family solution as capitalist institutions emerged in post-socialist societies?

In this chapter I provide a brief description of the East German solution to combining work and family and the institutional changes that followed immediately upon German unification. I present the stories of three East German mothers, Mrs. Acker, Mrs. Jaeger, and Mrs. Roesler, which show how the institutional transformations played out in different ways in women's lives. I conclude with a discussion of how the interweaving of state, economy, and gender in these women's stories explains the marginalization of mothering in contemporary market economies.

The three cases discussed here are from the sample of 38 East German couples with children interviewed for my dissertation.[7] The method of data collection was fieldwork and in-depth interviews that I conducted in German. Interviews were transcribed verbatim by native speakers of German and analyzed by me for common themes and individual stories. Each of the mothers represents a different mode of accommodating typical patterns of risk and opportunity faced by East German women in the market economy.

These modes of accommodation arise out of the interplay of institutional contexts and the work-family strategies of the couple. "Work-family strategy" refers to a plan of action for implementing a desirable work-family balance. This concept is based on Arlie Hochschild's concept of "gender strategy" but is not analogous.[8] An individual's attempt to enact a gender ideology is a gender strategy, and paid employment and domestic work are critical resources for the enactment of masculinity and femininity, respectively.[9] Thus gender strategies are a basic element of work-family strategies. I use the concept of work-family strategy because I want to focus on changes that occurred within marriages in the balance of domestic work and paid employment.

Biographical narrative is useful for capturing connections between the post-socialist transition and family and gender in everyday life.[10] Post-socialist transformation dislodged work and family activities from East German institutions and began to weave them haphazardly and unevenly into the emerging West German-style capitalist institutions. In telling their stories, respondents articulated both economic and moral mappings of this transformation. They worked to figure out the post-socialist economic game—its rules, risks, and rewards—and simultaneously interpreted the game as encoding a particular hierarchy of social values.

This moral mapping of the emerging market economy identified changes in the social value of work and family experienced in the transformation. As I will illustrate with the stories of the Ackers, Jaegers, and Roeslers, respondents reinterpreted continuing family and gender strategies and/or fashioned new strategies as they positioned themselves within their ongoing economic and moral mappings of the emerging market economy. Public discussions, news of friends and family members, and the practical experiences of balancing work and family provided information for respondents' mappings. Likewise, economic and moral mappings of the emerging institutions shaped respondents' experiences of work and family and helped create a cultural context that marginalized mothering.

"Working Mothers": East Germany's "Simultaneous" Solution to Combining Work and Family

East Germany was founded as a sovereign state in what had been the Soviet zone of occupied Germany.[11] Throughout its existence (officially October 7, 1949 to October 3, 1990, the date of political unification with West Germany), the question of women's roles at work and in the family was of critical importance in the East German state's ideological and economic competition with capitalist West Germany. Socialists upheld women's equality as an important social goal and defined women's equality as women's full participation in paid employment. The East German state also desperately needed women's labor.[12]

East German policy on women developed in three broad historical phases.[13] Even before the East German state was founded, the Soviet Military Administration mandated the principle of equal pay for equal work, a measure that signaled commitment to women as workers.[14] Equal pay for equal work was part of the first policy phase (1946–1965), which emphasized protecting mothers and moving women into paid labor. In the second phase (1963–1972), women's education and skill levels were improved so they could take on better and more highly skilled jobs. The state set up special courses for women to learn skills needed for "leading positions" in workplaces. To facilitate women's employment, the state and enterprises began building childcare facilities for the provision of free infant care, childcare, and after-school programs.

By the 1970s most East German women were working full time and women's qualification and education levels were high.[15] Yet, as more women entered full-time paid employment, the birth rate dropped rapidly, indicating the difficulties of combining women's family roles with full-time paid employment. The third policy phase (1973–1989) aimed to ameliorate these problems.[16] Policies included allowing parents of three or more children paid sick leave to care for sick children; increasing the length of paid maternity leave; providing financial support for mothers enrolled at the university; giving mothers of three or more children and single mothers of two or more children a 40-hour workweek (instead of the normal $43^{3/4}$ hours) with full pay; and continuing to expand child care services.[17] A closer look at the third phase reveals an early concern with promoting a higher birth rate and a continuing commitment to women working full time, continuously over the life course like men. Starting in 1976, however, this commitment gave way somewhat to short periods of leave from work for women. Although part-time work was still viewed as undesirable and only allowed for women with exceptional caretaking burdens, the state lengthened paid maternity leave and expanded paid leave to care for sick children.[18]

Cultural images of women in East Germany reflected these policy changes. Coinciding with the state's goal of moving women into paid employment, during the 1950s and 1960s the ideal woman in popular East German magazines appeared "made for work from head to toe."[19] Men were called on to help at home and accept women in the workplace. Mirroring and promoting acceptance of women in paid employment, in later periods women's presence in industrial settings appeared normal, and women were portrayed as autonomous and self-directed. The everyday problems of combining work and family became a theme and the "socialist" nuclear family was idealized. Always present were images of the employed woman and mother.[20]

In the late 1980s, on the eve of state socialism's collapse and the unification of East and West Germany, the "simultaneous" solution to combining work and family, in which women combine motherhood with continuous, full-time employment over the life course, was well established in East Germany.[21] Most East German women worked full time but were also mothers. About 90 percent of women had at least one child and most children were born before the mother's twenty-sixth birthday.[22] Further, while many West German women left the labor force for extended periods in order to be mothers, in East Germany most women worked continuously over the life course, while taking short leaves for childbirth and infant care.[23] East German women themselves were strongly committed to their roles in *both* work and family life.[24]

State socialist policies undergirding women's "simultaneous" combining of work and family included pressure to hold a job, low wages, and political commitment to women's full employment as a measure of women's equality.

Free childcare was available for most children aged 0–5, and after-school programs were available for most children under age 11. Women aged 16 and older had access to reproductive technologies as part of universal health care, maternity leave was paid, and many mothers received a paid day off every month for "housework." Workplaces were required by law to help women combine full-time employment with motherhood.[25] The East German state proclaimed women's high employment rate one of its great achievements and evidence of socialism's superiority over capitalism.[26]

In East Germany, as in other state-socialist countries, policy facilitated women's labor force attachment, while simultaneously reinforcing women's traditional responsibilities for child care, family life, and domestic work. East German families generally relied on two incomes and coordinated two full-time jobs, yet women carried the responsibility for monitoring and assuring successful work-family balance.[27] With the collapse of state socialism, the conditions that had sustained this arrangement for combining work and family were rapidly transformed.

The most dramatic, immediate impact of unification upon former East Germany was economic collapse.[28] Within two years, almost half the jobs in the former East Germany were lost.[29] Simultaneously, East German state-socialist institutions crumbled, and a long process of building an institutional order according to models supplied by West Germany began. The East German state had planned and directed the economy; in contrast, a capitalist economy is predicated upon a separation of economic and state power. The West German state has a legitimate interest in regulating, monitoring, and even shaping economic activities, but much of the economy is privately owned. Post-socialism involved a massive privatization of the East German economy.

Privatization was not the result of a simple "withdrawal" of the state. Indeed, the role of the West German state in providing financial and administrative resources and the legal framework for every aspect of the reorganizing economy and polity made it an indispensable actor and critical force shaping the institutions emerging in post-socialist Germany. Nor, however, was this a redeployment or reform of the state. While the state per se did not reform, East Germans experienced a thorough reorganization of the relationship between state and economic institutions. The institutional transformation changed the practical and ideological resources available for solving the everyday problems of combining work and family.

The state-socialist commitment to full employment and to special measures for assisting *women's* full employment were abandoned. Reproductive work was further privatized. As noted above, the East German state had relied on women's private domestic and family work, but this labor had been recognized and supported by socialist policies such as subsidized childcare and by socialist enterprises through on-site childcare, the housework day, and shorter workweeks for mothers.

In contrast, privatizing firms and new, capitalist employers had little reason to help women combine work and family. These employers sought to avoid the costs of accommodating women's family roles by hiring men if possible. Male and female employees alike felt pressured by the threat of unemployment to "act as though you have no other loyalties, no other life."[30] Amid high and rising unemployment, women's chances for finding work were much worse than men's. In the first half of 1994 unemployment rates reached 10.4 percent for men and 21.3 percent for women.[31]

In a cruel irony, just as economic changes undermined job security in general and women's employment chances in particular, other changes increased the desirability of maximizing income. The East German mark had not been freely convertible and had to be exchanged on the black market in order to get the hard currency needed to buy coveted consumer goods produced in capitalist countries. Economic unification of East and West Germany converted East German incomes into West German currency. East Germans with disposable income now had access to the cornucopia of the capitalist world's consumer goods and services, including cars, household appliances, electronics, clothes, and foreign vacations.

The threat of unemployment and the volatility of prices made maximizing income a prudent response to an uncertain future. With the collapse of the state-socialist economy, the relative costs of consumer items and basic expenses reversed. While electronics and household appliances became much cheaper in relation to monthly income, the cost of basic expenses such as rent, food, and utilities began to rise. The "carrot" of consumer goods and services and the "stick" of rising basic expenses and high unemployment made people increasingly attentive to the goal of income maximization, although the attention was couched in attitudes varying from scornful to uninhibited embracing of this orientation.

The convergence of rising economic uncertainty for families in a context of increasing consumption-based stratification and discrimination against women in employment played out in a variety of ways in real people's lives. The three cases presented here illustrate three different modes used by women confronting typical patterns of risk and opportunity offered by the market economy in former East Germany. These modes are employment continuity, mobility, and exit. The women's stories show how the reorganization of the state and economy amplified conflicts between work and family, especially for women.

From "Working Mother" to Workers or Mothers

In the cases analyzed below, each woman's work-family strategy in post-socialist Germany was shaped by the intersection of institutionalized gender roles, employment opportunities, family income and consumption goals, and gender relations in her marriage. Each woman's circumstances posed challenges for combining work and family. As they sought to make sense of these challenges and fashion responses to them, the women became aware of the changing social value of mothering.

"Working" is not necessarily opposed to "mothering." Women themselves often view their paid employment as part of the contribution they make as mothers to their families.[32] In other words, working for pay can be a strategy for being a good mother. The women in my sample did, in fact, view earning money as a desirable way for them—as women, wives, and mothers—to contribute to their families. However, women distinguished between contributing income and "mothering."

Being a mother included spending time with children and doing things with the whole family. Mothering meant engaging in hands-on activities and being involved in children's everyday lives. Furthermore, respondents noted some things—such as caring for a small child with fever—that only mothers can do really well. Thus while contributing financially to the family was critical, being a mother required spending time with children and having the flexibility to respond to family and children's needs. In their moral mappings of the economic transformation, respondents identified a declining value for these hands-on, time-consuming activities of mothering.

Mrs. Acker: The Struggle to Maintain Employment Continuity

Above I related the extraordinary accommodations Mrs. Acker obtained from her workplace in East German times and the deterioration of her conditions for combining work and family after German unification. But what did these changes mean for Mrs. Acker and her family? While both Mr. and Mrs. Acker continued to work full time in the wake of socialism's collapse, the risks and opportunities offered by the emerging market economy changed their work-family strategy and led Mrs. Acker to question its viability.

At the time of the interview (four years after unification), Mr. and Mrs. Acker had been together for more than nine years and married for six. They had two sons, aged twelve and seven, at home. The older boy was from Mr. Acker's first marriage. Mrs. Acker had become the boy's primary parent almost simultaneously with becoming involved with Mr. Acker. In the period leading up to East Germany's demise, Mrs. Acker was employed as a kindergarten teacher. Mr. Acker, a machinist, had worked for the same employer continuously, except for his years of military service, since beginning his apprenticeship.

The Ackers were unusual in that neither of them had experienced unemployment after unification. Indeed, from this point of view, the Ackers were "winners" of the turn in German politics. Moreover, they felt their relative income and their material standard of living had notably improved; Mrs. Acker explained that they were much more likely to buy things they wanted:

> Well, the situation now is so—we both have work and together we earn good money, so we can afford to indulge in things and we can buy things and new things that aren't really necessary. Things, where before [unification] we would have said, oh that'll last a few more years, now we say—no, we want something new now!

However, high unemployment and economic restructuring changed the way they balanced work and family and infused their work-family conflicts with new anxieties. The demands of work came to dominate their family life even more than they had in socialist times, forcing them to shift the relative value of paid employment and mothering.

Mrs. Acker described how employment insecurity had affected her experience balancing work and family, leading her to shift her priorities toward protecting her job.

> And today [in contrast to before unification], you say to yourself, oh go ahead just one more day.... If he gets really sick, they'll call you at work, if he completely falls apart or something.

She emphasized that this was very different from her attitude in East German times:

> I wouldn't have done that before [unification]. If I'd noticed in the morning that my child wasn't feeling well, I would have marched off to the doctor straight away and thought that my child comes first.

When she could count on employment security and her workplace was compelled to accommodate her role as a mother, Mrs. Acker "thought that my child comes first," as a matter of course. In contrast, in a context of economic restructuring and high unemployment, she felt compelled to put her job first.

> But [after unification] if I miss work every month or every other month, now, well.... It doesn't mean I'll be fired right away, but it's already too much hearing that "What, not again?"

For Mrs. Acker the context of employment insecurity infused missing work occasionally to care for a sick child with destabilizing anxieties about losing her job. In the micro-level practices of everyday life, she changed her behavior and her priorities. Although she felt that it was not quite right, she shifted in favor of protecting her job and away from protecting her child's health.

In practice, Mrs. Acker bore the brunt of the amplified conflicts between work and family. Mr. Acker was not as involved with the children. He stated that when he got home from work he did not have the energy to engage with small children. He pointed out, "Not everyone is a trained kindergarten teacher," implying that he lacked both the will and the skill to be an involved parent.

In post-socialist Germany, Mrs. Acker's workweek increased and her employment security decreased, so that carrying both family life and her full-time job pushed her to the limits of her capacities. During the interviews she appeared near exhaustion. She confided that she indulged in fantasies of taking her younger son with her and "living by myself," leaving Mr. Acker alone with their older son. She had also reluctantly considered quitting her job but did not want to give up the family's new consumption opportunities or further undermine her precarious position in the job market.

The Ackers, like other respondents, registered these changes in their economic and moral mappings of the emerging market economy. Their economic mappings identified new opportunities such as consumer goods in the form of "something new now!" The primary risk was the palpable threat of unemployment. Their moral mappings identified a change in the relative ranking of the social values of work and mothering. As Mr. Acker emphasized, in East German times, "if a child needed to be cared for, your job was secure." In contrast, after unification caring for a child could lead to losing your job. While the Ackers downplayed the amplification of gender hierarchy encoded in these mappings, they shared dismay over the devaluation of mothering.

Mrs. Jaeger: The Dilemma of Employment Mobility

Mrs. Jaeger was even more a "winner" of German unification than Mrs. Acker. Mrs. Jaeger's experience in banking and her professional degree positioned her to succeed in the banking boom in post-socialist eastern Germany. The drop in the East German birth rate after unification threatened the viability of kindergartens and thus the security of Mrs. Acker's job as a kindergarten teacher.[33] In contrast, the rush to implement up-to-date, capitalist banking systems throughout former East Germany created jobs in banking. Yet Mrs. Jaeger's career success showed her that the occupational structure she confronted in the West German banking industry was degrading to her as a woman and a mother.

At the time of the interview, the Jaegers had been together for fourteen years and married for thirteen. They had three children, aged twelve, nine, and four. Mrs. Jaeger held a full-time job as a loan officer, while her husband was a skilled carpenter, employed as the custodian of a state library. The family lived in a large apartment on the library grounds. Mrs. Jaeger worked full time in a savings and loan; her job paid well, and, after unification, the family income allowed the Jaegers to acquire several new labor-saving devices.

In 1990, Mrs. Jaeger was at home with her third baby on the one and a half years of paid maternity leave she was eligible for under East German law. Her first disappointment with the labor market was that she was unable to return to the job she held before unification. While her job still existed and technically she was allowed to return to it, she had been out of the workplace during the first year and a half of restructuring from a socialist enterprise to a capitalist financial institution. When she returned to work, no accommodations were made to train her, and she was treated with disrespect. She explained:

> There, the bosses, who were left over from East German times, told me directly that they didn't value me at all, that as a woman I should figure out whether I want to work or have children.

While many East German workplaces had been compelled to accommodate women's parenting and homemaking roles in various ways, this experience signaled the indifference of the restructured savings and loan. Due to the institutional transformations described above as well as high unemployment, the managers of the savings and loan were free to avoid what they perceived as the extra costs of hiring a mother.

While Mrs. Jaeger was not actually fired, her employer made it difficult for her to remain on the job. She continued:

> ... in the two years I was home with my baby, to learn that all overnight ... everything that had happened in the two years, or rather the one and a half years after the unification that I'd been at home.

Because the workplace was so unpleasant and it was impossible to make up the lost year and a half under those conditions, she quit her job.

Next she was disappointed in her search for part-time work, but this was initially mitigated by the availability of unemployment benefits. Because Mrs. Jaeger was the mother of three children, including a baby under three, the Employment Office considered her desire for part-time work legitimate. Her previous employer could not offer her a part-time position, thus she received unemployment benefits (at a part-time rate) while she looked for a part-time position. A year of looking did not turn up any part-time positions in her field. She wanted to work, so she decided to apply for full-time jobs. She was offered the first one she applied for.

The attitude of her new bosses, whom she described as ambitious young men who had come from West Germany to leap over a few career steps, was much nicer.[34] They wanted to hire her and occasionally expressed awe at her ability to master the "double burden" of full-time work and mothering. Despite this positive attitude, she found the organization of work in her new job made handling the "double burden" much more difficult than it had been in East German times. She described the work routine as relentless pressure and the workplace as only valuing employees who wanted high-powered careers.

The pressure to produce in her new job meant that she put in overtime hours. Even when she did not stay late, she felt more tired at the end of the day than she had previously. She explained,

> Well, I'd say, that most of the day you get work shoved at you and you always get to the point where you can see that you just won't be able to complete

something, there's just not enough time and there's too much to have a good overview, so you can't really ration it out and know oh, I can take care of that in three days, but instead there comes a point where you just don't have a clear picture of what you have to do.

Despite her ability to keep up with the work, she felt her efforts were not recognized as they should have been because she did not want a high-powered career. She felt she was in constant danger of being pushed to work 12- to 14-hour days like the managers or simply being ignored. She explained:

> They don't see that as a woman you want to do a high-level job without being a total career woman. You're always on the edge and in danger of falling off one way or the other. If you do a job well, you're in danger of being pushed into a high-powered career path, where you don't want to go. And if you say that out loud, then they'll drop you like a hot potato.

The changes in Mrs. Jaeger's work life flowed from the institutional transformation that changed the relationship between the state and the economy. Because the state had controlled the economy under state socialism, banking had been less important than in capitalist economies. Reflecting its relatively low status and regular hours, banking in East Germany was highly feminized, about 90 percent of employees being women. Most mid-level management positions, such as branch manager or representative, were also filled by women in East Germany. In comparison, in West Germany, only about 60 percent of the banking workforce was female and most management positions were held by men. With the transition to capitalism, banking in former East Germany became an exciting, important sector and it was rapidly restructured according to West German models.[35]

One reason Mrs. Jaeger was able to meet the demands of her new workplace was that Mr. Jaeger was an involved and self-motivated father and homemaker. So that his wife could have more leisure time with the family, he had arranged his schedule so that he could be home when the kids got home from school. Together Mr. Jaeger and the kids did household tasks such as vacuuming or planning the evening meal, so that when Mrs. Jaeger arrived home she would be free to relax with her family. The Jaegers' approach to sharing both paid work and domestic work enabled Mrs. Jaeger to be a reliable full-time employee and gave her more time with her family. Nevertheless, she believed that she was still perceived as being less than fully committed to her job.

The Jaegers mapped the risks and opportunities of the emerging labor and consumer markets and engaged in a simultaneous moral mapping. They recognized the advantages of a two-income family, pointing out happily that after German unification they had purchased a washing machine and other labor-saving devices. Mrs. Jaeger felt there were many opportunities for women in banking because of its expansion. Yet the reorganization and division of work into low-status jobs and high-powered careers excluded a professional woman who wanted to spend time with her family. Mrs. Jaeger's moral mapping identified these changes as devaluing mothering.

Mrs. Roesler: The Meanings of Employment Exit

Although Mrs. Acker and Mrs. Jaeger found their work drawing them away from being mothers, employment allowed them to buy desirable consumer goods. In contrast, Mrs. Roesler decided that the income generated did not offset the costs of working. At the time of the interview, she was at home with her children, aged three and eight. She had been home for three years and worked full time for one of the four years since unification. Her three-year-old suffered from asthma, and she believed that during the winter the extra stress of being in kindergarten full time would be too hard on his health.[36]

Despite the fact that her husband's salary was very low and the family had significant debt, Mrs. Roesler decided—against her husband's wishes—to stay home at least for the winter to protect her son's health. In her view, the collapse of state socialism and the emergence of West German–style institutions had freed her as a mother but created significant tensions within her marriage. Her husband favored an income-maximizing work-family strategy, while she placed a higher value on mothering.

In East Germany, Mr. Roesler had earned about twice as much as his wife, and his extensive contacts with relatives in capitalist countries had allowed them to live above average. In post-socialist Germany, all East Germans had access to West German consumer markets, so that special relationships with people outside East Germany were no longer needed to obtain hard currency and goods from the West; Mr. Roesler's contacts were of no special worth. Furthermore, while his income as a skilled worker had placed him near the top of the scale in East Germany, it was low within the emerging income stratification based on West German standards.

In contrast, after unification typical jobs in Mrs. Roesler's field of medical laboratory technician paid more than what her husband earned. She explained:

> At first my husband didn't accept my decision to stay home this winter, because, he said, think of the income loss and think of the money, all the things we won't have and how low we'll fall again. . . . It's really important to him that I work again, because I can earn a lot in my field and we've had heated discussions about this.

Although the couple agreed that she could earn "decisively" more than he, a role reversal was not an option; both felt that Mr. Roesler could never stand the stress of staying home with the children. Mrs. Roesler emphasized her husband's lack of competence in domestic skills ranging from handling a child's sleeping problems to preparing lunch.

Despite the problems in her marriage, Mrs. Roesler felt that the West German institutional order provided her much more freedom as a mother. This feeling stemmed from her efforts to gain official permission to stay home with her first son during East German times because she felt he wasn't strong enough to survive the crèche, the facility for the care of 0–3-year-olds.[37] But her doctor refused to certify her child as "unfit for the crèche."

She remembered this angrily. Had she obtained the certification, she would have received 500 marks a month to stay home with her child. She commented that the "average income of a woman in East Germany was about 700–800 marks a month," concluding that she could have managed easily with 500 marks. Instead, she kept her job but missed so much work that her income sometimes fell as low as 200 or even 100 marks in any given month.[38] With this income it was impossible to make ends meet, so she received some money from the Youth Office ("*Jugendamt*") and from her parents.[39] After unification she felt freer and no longer at the mercy of authorities, as she explained:

> [In East German times] the doctors said if the child was fit for the crèche, that was the doctor's decision, not the mother's. . . . That's what I find really good now, that you can decide for yourself what to do with your kids.

In addition, Mrs. Roesler believed that she was materially better off than she had been in the socialist system. However, she emphasized that being surrounded by rapidly and visibly increasing consumption standards made it more difficult for her to live relatively modestly. She compared her situation at the time of the interview to her life as a single mother in East German times (before she met Mr. Roesler) and concluded that although she had actually *been* worse off before unification, she *felt* worse off after unification.

> And I was very badly off some of the time with Daniel [her first child] because I didn't have anyone to help make ends meet, I had to do everything alone. And when you had used up the paid leave for sick kids, well then it was over and you didn't get any more money and there was no magic solution. Your standard of living was not propped up by the state. I mean, things could get really bad. That's what I compare back then when I was alone with Daniel, *in theory I was actually worse off. But I didn't feel it as such. I experienced that differently then, because I didn't have the view of wealth and well-being that I have now. Now you feel that much more intensely.* (emphasis added)

I want to emphasize that Mrs. Roesler made the same decision—to prioritize caring for her child herself over earning income—before and after unification. However, she describes different dissatisfactions surrounding this choice in each context. In the East German context she felt angry about being at the mercy of authorities. In the context of the emerging market economy she felt materially deprived. Mrs. Roesler's recognition of her relative material deprivation within the emerging market economy was linked to her moral mapping, which identified consumerism as gaining in value and opposed to mothering.

Instead of acquiescing in her husband's monetary definition of family needs and her own intensified feelings of lagging behind widespread consumption standards, Mrs. Roesler grounded her rejection of consumerism in her commitment to mothering. She explained that the health of her child was more important than keeping up with rising material standards. Further, she felt that most people in former East Germany did not place the high value on mothering that she did. In her words:

> Especially now, most people are just completely focused on getting more money in any way they can and ... the children suffer from that in lots of families, because both parents work ten or twelve hours. But for me, I have to say, I didn't have a baby for that. ... I can do without a fancy vacation or whatever. ...

Mrs. Roesler's way of being a good mother by staying home even though "lots of people don't understand that" resulted in concrete, everyday experiences of having less than her peers. She explained that her family "lags behind" in "accomplishments" since unification. When I asked her what she meant, she explained:

> Well, that—it might sound crass, but the simple fact of what's in the refrigerator, shopping, what you buy, what you have for the weekend, what things you cook, what kinds of drinks you buy and whether and how often you go out to eat, whether you go to the movies, theater, or opera and such. ... And when I look around among my friends, they're better off, in fact—the things they do with their free time. It's as simple as how you live, what you drink, what you eat, what you wear. ...

This passage conveys the palpable, everyday experience of relative material deprivation. She experienced herself as lagging behind as she ate, drank, and dressed. However, because she embraced mothering and mapped mothering in opposition to the market values of money and consumerism, she also experienced herself as a good mother as she ate more cheaply and dressed more shabbily than her peers.

For Mrs. Roesler, the decision to have a child at all was in opposition to the material values she perceived as dominant in post-socialist Germany. She commented, "Well, the trend is, as I'm sure you've heard or read, that after the unification the birth rate in the East dropped by 80 percent."[40] In her view, women of her generation were not having children because "they think they'll lose their jobs and then not be able to enjoy their lives because of their children."

Mr. and Mrs. Roesler's market situations contradicted their gender identifications. The gender hierarchy encoded in the high value the market placed on income-maximization and unencumbered workers threatened to divide them from each other. Although Mrs. Roesler was better positioned to maximize income, she rejected this pursuit and found positive meaning in relative poverty, experiencing it as part of being a good mother. Although Mr. Roesler was willing to help more at home so that his wife could work for pay, his wife deemed this work-family strategy unworkable. Mr. Roesler failed according to the values of the emerging market economy because of his low salary. Yet he could not find positive meaning in the family's poverty.

Mrs. Roesler reflected her husband's opinion as much as the judging eyes of a nonspecific "generalized other" when she explained:

> At this time in the East, material values have become overly important. These things are a lot more important to lots of people than children—I mean, having a child is planned to fit in somewhere sometime, but—well, they see—the mothers, who have children and they see me and they see others. And they say, "Oh God, I don't want to live like her!"

Continuity, Mobility, Exit, and the Marginalization of Mothering

Mrs. Acker, Mrs. Jaeger, and Mrs. Roesler illustrate three different work-family strategies fashioned to accommodate the risks and opportunities of the postsocialist market economy: employment continuity, mobility, and exit. Taken together the cases illustrate how the emerging hierarchy of values linked to the transformation marginalized women's roles and identities as mothers.

For Mrs. Acker, high unemployment infused the practice of occasionally missing work to care for a sick child with destabilizing anxieties about possibly losing her job. While Mrs. Acker was pressured by fears of unemployment to "act as though" she were not a mother, Mrs. Jaeger was pressured to "act as though" by the prestige hierarchy at her workplace. In her transformed profession of banking, she identified high-powered careers and low-status jobs. Although her bosses explicitly acknowledged her status as a mother, the prestige hierarchy at work pressured her to "act as though" she were not a mother.[41]

Mrs. Acker and Mrs. Jaeger struggled to keep "worker" and "mother" together in their lives even as the transformed labor market and workplace exerted pressure to split the "worker" from the "mother." Mrs. Roesler, in contrast, rejected the simultaneous work-family strategy—at least for a while. While she defiantly proclaimed her commitment to mothering in opposition to pursuing higher levels of consumption, she was intensely aware of the emerging consumption-based lifestyles of her peers.

In different ways, each of these women was caught in the cultural dynamic initiated by the institutional transformation following the collapse of the East German state and the expansion of the West German state in its place. The West German state introduced a new relationship between the state and economic institutions. It brought social policies informed by a gender ideology opposed to working mothers. In the process, work and family activities were dislodged from state socialist institutions and linked to new patterns of risk and opportunity. The women comprehended changed risks and opportunities of work-family strategies through a process I call "economic mapping"—working to figure out the economic risks and rewards, as well as the rules in the emerging market economy.

Economic mapping was linked to a process I call "moral mapping," which identified changes in the social value of work and mothering encoded in the institutional transformation. As the prestige and opportunities associated with employment rose, a woman's role and identity as a mother became a liability in the labor market and in the workplace. Drawing on firsthand experiences with their own work-family strategies and secondhand information about the market economy, the women mapped a sharp decline in the societal value accorded to mothering.

Beyond Post-Socialism: The Marginalization of Mothering in Contemporary Market Economies

The pattern of risks and opportunities offered by the market economy shaped East German women's work-family strategies. The emerging market economy led to increasing costs of employment exit and amplification of work-family conflict in strategies of employment continuity. Being a mother became a liability for getting a job, keeping a job, and achieving recognition at work, while giving up income in favor of caring for children led to intensified feelings of material deprivation and social exclusion.

East German women had rich cultural resources to draw on in fashioning work-family strategies of employment continuity, mobility, and exit. Yet, as Ann Swidler writes, cultural models "root and thrive" or "wither and die" depending upon the "concrete situations in which these cultural models are enacted."[42] East German women's efforts to combine working and mothering ran into trouble in an institutional context that materially and symbolically opposed income-earning to mothering, placed a higher value on paid employment and made mothering a liability in the labor market.

The economic conditions engendering this cultural dynamic are familiar features of contemporary market economies: increasing social stratification reflected in consumption-based differentiation of lifestyles; continual pressure for economic privatization; workplace inflexibility in relation to employees' family responsibilities; and volatility in labor and consumer markets. Because these conditions characterize contemporary market societies, I believe East German women's experiences illustrate a more general cultural process linked to marketization: the reproduction of institutional practices and everyday life experiences that marginalize mothering.

11

REINSTATING THE FAMILY

Gender and the State-Formed Foundations
of China's Flexible Labor Force[1]

EILEEN M. OTIS

As a result of market reforms, China's major urban centers are dependent on the low-wage labor of migrants from the nation's countryside. One hundred million rural people have flocked to China's urban centers to find work in new and restructured industries;[2] forty percent of these are women.[3] China's tremendous economic growth, combined with the diminished state provision of urban services, has heightened consumer demand for a range of services that are now performed by female migrant laborers.[4] Such massive migration can potentially weaken family structures as wage labor brings rural women a measure of independence. Yet the service work into which women are channeled draws them into a suffocating arena of urban toil and fosters their subordination to urban customers and employers. Even though the state advances an ideology of gender equality, a complex of state agencies structures the unregulated labor market niche into which migrant women are funneled and shores up rural patriarchal family structures.

The state has made this flexible supply of low wage labor available to urban employers through amended residential policies that reinforce family structures. These policies confine migrants to unregulated labor markets and prevent them from settling in cities.[5] As a result, migrants are dependent on their rural families for long-term support, and families subsidize migrants' urban labor, allowing employers to minimize labor costs.[6] China's residential policies create an urban labor system that is highly responsive to fluctuations in industries such as service, manufacturing, and construction.[7] Hence, the exclusion of migrants from urban settlement produces a flexible, low-wage labor force that contributes to economic expansion and at the same time preserves the privileges of urbanites who enjoy legal inclusion.[8] Due to their positions in urban labor markets and within rural family structures, this set of institutional arrangements has specific effects on migrant women.

These effects are particularly apparent in the urban service industry, which is a major employer of female migrants and a central site of China's economic restructuring.[9] While there are a number of ethnographic studies of migrant women working in manufacturing, service industries have thus far been neglected.[10] Inexpensive services flourishing in the unregulated economy have replaced those multiple services that were contained within the Maoist era work unit and have in large part been enabled by the low-wage labor of rural migrant women.[11] Fluctuations in demand, an absence of labor protection, and a system of recruitment that restricts the work to young unmarried women, make migrant women extremely vulnerable in urban service work.

Such highly flexible labor markets are often viewed as a product of decreased state regulation, especially in contrast to the socialist system of labor allocation. However, China's flexible labor force has not been formed in the wake of the state's withdrawal from regulation of the economy. China's market reform economy departs from a neoliberal image of the market's invisible hand and illustrates the crucial role states play in structuring labor markets.[12] By analyzing the state's reliance on households to form labor markets, in this chapter I trace out the ways in which the spheres of state, society, and market are mutually constituted.[13] The state regulates labor movement through a complex of health, security, employment, and reproductive policies that restrict migrant urban settlement.[14] Meanwhile, rural family structures provide an economic buffer to support this flexible workforce. While migrants work in cities, their rural households are responsible for providing care for children, the elderly, and the infirm.[15] Migrants return to their rural households when there is no longer work for them in the cities. In turn, state policy implementation supports patriarchal village governance structures.

Scholars have pointed to the centrality of kin networks in shaping the terrain of China's reform-era economy.[16] There is, however, little recognition of the role of the state in supporting family structures and reproducing family ties within the economy. In her pathbreaking research on female migrant factory workers, Ching Kwan Lee argues that reform-era factories are insulated from direct state interference, which allows for a system of labor control informed by localistic kin networks.[17] However, by widening our optic from the localistic kin structures that organize hierarchies within the workplace to the institutional and ideological context for the formation of localistic, kin-based labor discipline, we can see how state policies shape particular work arrangements. In other words, work arrangements are embedded in a larger institutional complex created by state policies. While Lee suggests that the social organization of the labor market informs labor control, I argue that the state plays a central role in shaping the contours of contemporary urban labor markets.

This helps to explain what Lee finds paradoxical: that migrant women are able to return home to their villages at any time, yet they submit to a highly coercive labor regime. When we fully appreciate the role of the state, it becomes clear why women might submit to coercive work structures. First, rural family structures exclude women from long-term residence in their natal villages. Because their claim to land rests upon marriage, women's ties to the land do not constitute a straightforward alternative to urban labor. Second, state residential policies exempt migrant women from legal protections and rights in workplaces. Because women are caught between urban work structures that ensure their vulnerability and family structures that force their eventual exclusion, they submit to coercive work regimes. In other words, the coercive regime of labor control is not made possible *in spite of* the fact that migrant women can return home as Lee suggests,[18] but precisely *because* state policies form the basis for unregulated labor markets and reinforce patriarchal family structures.

By illuminating the points of articulation between the family and the economy enabled by a complex of state policies, we can understand the gendered structure of China's reform institutions.[19] Research on China's internal migration policies has not analyzed the underlying gendered structure of these policies.[20] The forms of exclusion created by residential policies create a class of female service workers deprived of "urban citizenship" who are positioned within a gendered space of liminality. This liminal space can be defined as a state of double exclusion: migrant women are neither full citizens of urban centers where they labor, nor can they claim full membership within their natal villages. Rural women have always experienced a degree of liminality, since they inevitably marry out of their own villages. As the old adage goes, they are "spilled water"—a temporary presence in their rural homes.[21] Even though male and female migrants are both excluded from urban citizenship, the rural marriage system excludes women from ongoing presence in their natal villages. Men settle in their natal villages, and they can continue to migrate once they are married.[22] The rural patrilocal marriage system dictates that women relocate to their husbands' village upon marriage and minimizes ties with their natal families.[23] Once women marry, they are prevented from further migration.[24] State policies regulating migration reinforce their exclusion in urban centers.

State residential policies have potentially contradictory effects, particularly as the experience of migration prompts women to reinterpret family structures. In part as a response to their urban marginality, migrant women who, for the first time, experience a measure of autonomy, hope to reconstruct their relationships to home as they feel a greater sense of loyalty to their natal families once in the city. Their wages allow them a degree of independence from their families but urban restrictions on permanent settlement, in conjunction with urban employers' reluctance to hire women once they reach their late twenties, pressure women to submit to domestic patriarchal marriage arrangements. Migrant women hope to prolong wage employment to defer and possibly avoid marriage so that they can maintain close ties with their natal families. As migrant women adjust to the urban center, the prospect of returning home only to be married into a husband's village—one in which gender hierarchies are perpetuated—is increasingly objectionable. At the same time that migration reinforces patriarchal family structure, it also creates the conditions for its disruption.

The remainder of this chapter analyzes the structural and cultural forces confronted by migrant women in the urban center and the ways women interpret and navigate this new urban terrain. First, I examine the residential policies that create the basis for migrants' structural exclusion, specifically, their restriction to the unregulated labor sector. Second, I explain how these structural exclusions legitimate migrants' cultural exclusion from the urban center. Together these forms of exclusion push women back to the countryside and pressure them to submit to the rural marriage system. I present migrant women's diverse responses to these conditions and suggest how their resistances could constitute a force for reshaping the marriage system.

Structuring Urban Exclusion

In 1958 the Chinese Communist Party implemented the household registration system (*hukou*) to stem urban population growth, eliminate unemployment, and minimize burdens on the welfare complex in the interest of urban industrialization.[25] Troubled by a massive influx of rural workers into urban centers in the years following the 1949 revolution, the government instituted *hukou* to freeze population movement by fixing individual place of lifetime residence to the place of birth and prohibiting spatial movement.[26] Exercise of the rights and entitlements of citizenship and access to welfare and food were available only within an individual's birthplace. *Hukou* divided residence into two broad categories, urban and agricultural, creating a two-tiered class system that guaranteed urban residents state-subsidized food, health care, education, housing, pensions, and other services through the urban work unit,[27] while denying these social benefits to rural workers, who constituted about three-quarters of China's population. Permitting only state-sanctioned population movement, the system fueled urban industrialization by guaranteeing the transfer of rural agricultural surplus to feed the urban proletariat and minimize urban unemployment.

In the reform era the state has adapted *hukou* regulations to create a temporary, flexible urban labor force. This adaptation is in part a response to the surplus of rural workers created by rural decollectivization. The reform-era redistribution of land once held by rural collectives to male-headed households has resulted in what is estimated to be a surplus of 200 million workers.[28] The state adapted the *hukou* laws to permit temporary employment of surplus workers and at the same time make available on the market an array of urban services, many of which had, in the past, only been provided by the work unit. At the same time, the market availability of food and living necessities that were, in the Maoist era, allocated through the urban work unit also made urban living possible for temporary workers. Popularly known as the "floating population" (*liudong renkou*), this reserve army of labor that employers can deploy or send home at will is made possible by the *hukou* system.

To enforce this flexibility, migrants are closely monitored by state institutions. In order to work in cities, the migrant must first obtain an identification card and a work permit. In addition, women must acquire a family planning certificate to ensure their adherence to the one-child-per-family policy. Once in the city, they must apply to the local public security bureau annually for a temporary residence permit, but only after passing an official health inspection; workers without such documentation can be sent back to their place of origin. The cost of these documents can for some workers exceed two months' salary, but for most represents between one-half and one month's salary. These fees are an important new source of revenue for urban state bureaus.[29] Only individuals who are gainfully employed can qualify for temporary residence, and police can legally check documentation and question migrants at any time. Dependents, children, and unemployed spouses are barred from living with employed spouses in the city.

As a result of their state-enforced "transience," rural women are relegated to the lowest paying, lowest prestige, sex-segregated work in the urban service sector.[30] Working in this sector affords no legal protections. The authorities can place unemployed migrants in a state detention center and eventually send them home. Hence, the urban residence permit continues to be a passport to relative privilege. Even as the urban welfare system evaporates, the residence permit system protects urban privilege by legitimating employment discrimination against migrants and barring their children's enrollment in urban schools.[31] Jobs in the primary sector of employment, such as international hotels, state-owned enterprises, foreign-invested firms, and white-collar work more generally are reserved exclusively for those who are permanent urban residents. These jobs are regulated by labor laws and offer access to a range of social benefits, like health and unemployment insurance, pensions, and housing subsidies. By permitting massive rural-to-urban migration and then limiting the legal rights and entitlements of migrants in urban centers, the state reproduces a two-tiered, urban-rural class system within the urban center. As a result, urban-rural class relations are constructed through what is becoming routine urban contact rather than isolation.

The *hukou* laws are the foundation for the cultural and institutional construction of migrant women in familial terms. For women, unregulated labor markets are restricted to those who are young and unmarried. Both state organs and popular media designate migrant women as "working little sisters" (*dagongmei*). This is a normative category as well as a descriptive one. It is a normative expectation among urban employers that migrant women will marry and the *hukou* system allows employers to dismiss them when they are of marriageable age and considered too old for frontline service work. Workplaces thus do not shoulder maternity leave and child care costs.[32] The designation "working little sisters" suggests that for migrant women, passage into adulthood cannot take place while working in the urban center. This term was taken up by the state-sponsored Women's Federation, which ran a support center for migrant women called the "Working Little Sister's Home" (*dagongmeizhijia*), perpetuating the paternalism embodied in the term and perhaps recognizing that migrant women might never establish their own homes in the city. A fictive home run by the state is the only legitimate one most migrant women can hope to claim in the city.

The temporary residence permit system creates opportunities for women to emerge from their rural contexts but places them within a liminal space in cities. To understand how they navigate the new urban terrain, between 1999 and 2000, I conducted semi-structured interviews in Mandarin with over sixty migrant women and talked informally with thirty more women in Kunming and Beijing. Kunming is the provincial capital of Yunnan province, in China's southwest interior, and Beijing is, of course, China's capital. The ages of migrant women in service were between fifteen and twenty-six, and most had been in the city between one and six years. They performed a variety of low-level, frontline service work such as serving food in restaurants, serving drinks and accompanying customers in karaoke bars, performing hair and facial work in salons, caring for children in private households, and selling office supplies. This chapter emphasizes similarities in the effects of *hukou* across regions.

Negotiating Rural Departure and Navigating the Urban Social Terrain

In the context of an enormous surplus of laborers in rural villages, young women are often the first to experience labor redundancy. Many feel utterly useless at home once they graduate from school, as nineteen-year-old Zhanglei[33] from a rural region near the northeastern city of Harbin explained:

> I didn't have anything to do. In the countryside, you're busy for a while during the harvest [or] a bit with planting. Other times, you just stay at home and watch TV. So I wanted to work. My parents didn't want me to go out and work but I didn't listen.

Certainly, their access to images of local and global urban centers mostly through television (an increasingly common household appliance in rural areas) compounds their desire to discover the city. Women expressed feeling an intolerable degree of boredom and restlessness at home, which is perhaps exacerbated by glamorous television images of cosmopolitan urban centers. It is not uncommon for rural women to drop out of school in order to seek work in the city; many feel that if they are not excelling in their education, then they are wasting household resources on school fees and books. This is what happened to twenty-one-year-old Hairei from rural Hebei: "I attended only one year of high school but I wasn't doing well in any classes . . . so I left to go to work. . . . There was nothing for me to do around the house." For such young women, a combination of limited expectations for schooling, a sense of dedication to assisting the family, as well as an eagerness to explore beyond the confines of their village and "see the world" (*jian shimian*) motivates their decision to seek work in the urban center.

Families rarely capitulate to their daughters' wishes to travel to urban centers. Parents are concerned about losing control over their daughters' activities and more generally fear the disintegration of the patriarchal family. Parents view a daughter's relocation to the city as a threat to both her physical safety and her virtue, as this twenty-year-old from rural Yunnan, Zhanggui, explained to me:

> [My parents] knew of a girl in the village who went to a local city to work, but a man tricked her and took her to Shanxi, where she was sold into marriage. She told her parents where she was, but Shanxi is too far away and they couldn't rescue her. Besides, she already has two children. She can't leave now—there's nowhere for her to go.

While most women eventually persuade their parents to allow them to migrate, approximately one-third of the women with whom I spoke said they found jobs in the city without parental permission, as in the case of eighteen-year-old Xiaoying from rural Hunan:

> I came to visit relatives in Beijing and I found a job. Then I told my parents I was already working here. My dad wasn't supportive. He [felt] the job puts me a level below what average people would do. But I couldn't return home because I had already taken the job.

As Xiaoying's quote indicates, labor migration presents rural women with opportunities to defy parental authority.

When they depart from the countryside, women imagine the city as a site of opportunities for personal transformation and upward mobility. But when they enter the urban center, they encounter harsh working conditions and a narrow sphere of mobility. Despite the new possibilities migration creates for circumventing parental authority, the residential system structures women's ongoing dependence on and eventual return to their rural families. Migrant women's ultimate return home is also underwritten by the demanding conditions of labor and reinforced by the feminized structure of service sector work.

As mentioned above, the residence permit system confines migrants to work that is unregulated, temporary, and low-paying. Within the unregulated sector, male and female migrants are channeled into different types of work: men most often enter construction work, while migrant women are hired into service sector and manufacturing jobs.[34] Employers select young, nubile, women for frontline service work. Once women approach their late twenties, employers replace them with fresh recruits from the ample pool of young migrant workers. Employers perceive women's primary status as future wives and mothers, which justifies paying low wages and offering only temporary, low-status work.[35] Women have little choice but to eventually return home for marriage.[36] For this reason migrants describe their work as a "spring rice bowl" (*qingchunfan*), a term that is particularly relevant for migrant women, whose youth and beauty are the basis of their employment. Together, young women's ongoing identification with the domestic sphere, their perceived tractability, and the predominance of male clientele lead to the feminization of service work.

So miserable are work conditions that migrant women can hardly imagine laboring in the city indefinitely. Labor laws are disregarded in the unregulated sector. It is not unusual for women to work between 15 and 18 hours a day and live in shabby dormitories or to sleep where they can inside the establishment. Liuling, a waitress in Beijing, summed up work conditions: "Our work environment is wretched." Workers' wages range from 150 yuan (about $19 U.S.) per month for live-in nannies to 800 yuan (about $100 U.S.) for skilled beauticians. Waitresses and hostesses make wages in the low to middle range of this scale.

In the unregulated service sector, employers systematically mandate women's obedience through monetary penalties. Most employers require workers to pay a deposit equivalent to one-quarter to a full month's salary before starting work, so that they will not depart without two weeks to one month's notice.[37] Workers' pay is often docked if they are late, take unscheduled leaves, or break equipment, including glasses and dishes. If workers are seen talking back to guests or displaying what the employer considers to be a bad attitude they can also be subjected to a monetary penalty. If workers fail to collect payment for a restaurant meal or other services rendered, employers deduct the amount from their pay checks, as nineteen-year-old Zhanglei explained:

> After the guest ordered his food he said it tasted bad. He didn't pay the bill. . . . He just insulted me, [saying] "I've been in Beijing so many years and I've never seen anything like this, you small child how can you act like this?". . . . We had to pay for the food ourselves. They took over forty yuan out of my salary.[38]

While monetary penalties can be severe, many women feel the worst part of the job is the anger they incur from employers in the course of adjusting to their new work regimens, as Xiaohe, a Beijing waitress from rural Anhui, explains:

> If we make a small mistake, [the boss] cusses you out.... He just scolds you. When that happens, I can't even eat—I sit on the terrace, miss home, and cry.

Urban customers are quick to lash out at migrant service workers, especially when staff have to enforce the rules of their workplace among urban customers. When service workers are the bearers of bad news—for example when they must inform a customer that a menu item is unavailable—urbanites can become irate. The depth of disrespect for migrant workers became clear to me when a local urban acquaintance visited my Kunming dormitory, which was staffed by migrant women who were responsible for checking all guests' identification cards. My acquaintance chaffed at this gatekeeping, her voice reverberating through the halls as she accused the migrant dorm worker requesting her identification card of ignorance and incompetence. On a number of occasions, I witnessed similar incidents, in which urbanites burst out in angry tirades against migrant workers.

The youth, gender, low education, and structural vulnerability of migrant women invites an unrelenting paternalism among customers.[39] In addition to workplace arrangements, restrictive state policies such as the *hukou* system can reinforce authority relations between customers and workers. Customers incessantly and impatiently order frontline workers about. Those subject to the most intimate forms of control and surveillance are nannies who live with the families they serve. Many young women (approximately one-fourth of the women I interviewed) begin their urban service careers as nannies. A seventeen-year-old from rural Anhui, Lihong, describes her first job as a nanny:

> [My employer] was finicky, and frugal. I just came to the city and I was used to eating a lot. She wasn't happy about that.... When I wanted to read a book, she would tell me that it takes too much electricity to keep the light on.

Living with their employers, nannies are constantly monitored, and their mobility and food consumption are subject to restriction.

Paternalism easily shades off into sexual harassment, which workers report encountering frequently. Xiaohe describes some of the inappropriate customer behavior she encounters:

> Usually after guests drink a lot they get fresh with us. There's a guest—he feels me, my hands and ... if it's excessive then this is unacceptable. Our work is really bitter.

Workers suffer from the close association of service work with prostitution, which reinforces the reputation of such work as low status and dishonorable.

By placing service work within the same unregulated sector as prostitution, *hukou* hinders its redefinition as an honorable occupation.

Migrants' intimate contact with demanding urban customers discourages any hope of urban upward mobility. They quickly realize that without an urban education and an urban residence permit, possibilities for gaining a permanent foothold in the city are minimal. Furthermore, migrant women spend most of their waking hours working, and they have few opportunities to find friendship or build a community of support in the city. Their families are their sole source of emotional and material support, and most women call or write home weekly. Their reliance on the family, together with the unregulated and demanding nature of service work, ensures that young women will return to their villages for marriage.

If structural exclusion bars migrant women from decent wages and work conditions, then cultural exclusion places the responsibility for their limited opportunities squarely on their own shoulders. The residence permit system fosters such cultural exclusion of migrants. Urbanites routinely refer to migrants as "outsiders" (*waidiren*) for whom they rarely conceal their disdain. I was repeatedly warned by urbanites that I should avoid contact with migrants because they are assumed to be a dangerous, criminal element. Urbanites view migrants as "the unsightly but indispensable presence in the heart of China's civility."[40] Because they can claim no permanent residence in the city, they are deeply suspect. As Xuling, who migrated to Beijing from Hunan, points out:

> [Urbanites] don't trust us because we don't have a permanent address here in the city. They think we will just steal from them and return to our homes in the countryside.

The temporary residence permit system that ensures their "transience" leads state agencies, the media, and urbanites to describe them as a "floating population," which suggests that they are aimless itinerants and conceals their fundamental role in sustaining the urban economy.

A government entreaty to enhance the quality (*suzhi*) of the population blames China's "backwardness" on the educational, reproductive, hygienic, and technological deficiencies of the rural population, further legitimating the cultural exclusion of rural migrants.[41] The theme circulates widely in the popular media and suffuses the popular imagination as an explanation for China's economic problems. This discourse shifts responsibility for education from society and state to the individual and is frequently deployed by urbanites as a charge against migrants. Urbanites blame migrants (rather than, for example, uneven state investment in rural and urban economies) for low levels of rural education and ultimately for China's underdevelopment.

Among migrant workers, the women employed in the service sector are most visible, making them also the most vulnerable to the appraising eye of the urbanite. While migrant workers in manufacturing encounter the disapproval of urbanites when they visit urban commercial districts on their days off, female service workers confront this disdain routinely in their jobs. Concern about "quality" legitimates public evaluation of their appearance and behavior. Hairei, a Beijing waitress, describes her feeling of belittlement: "People from the city look down on people from the countryside because they have city residence—[to them] we are hillbillies." Zhangyan speaks of her experience of urban discrimination: "Customers always have that disgusted kind of look because I am from the countryside; they think we are of a different class." Liuling, a twenty-four-year-old from rural Anhui, developed a critical stance: "We are outsiders [and] of no importance to them.... They've learned that by using us they can earn more money." Their sense of degradation is compounded by stereotypes that link service to prostitution. Such stereotypes indict these young women as transgressing proper moral boundaries due to the "public" nature of their work.[42] The *hukou* system and this government-sponsored discourse on quality (*suzhi*) shape urban disparagement of migrant workers.

Young women partially internalize this discourse on quality. They not only feel degraded because of their rural origins, they also feel ashamed of their relative lack of education. The educational level of most of the migrants I interviewed did not extend beyond middle school, and almost a third had only completed primary school. Those who drop out of school in order to make money in the urban center express profound regret over their decision, like nineteen-year-old Chenhong from rural Gansu, who dropped out during middle school:

> I took for granted [the opportunities for learning] when I was in school. I felt I had too little time on my hands. Now I regret [dropping out].

For migrants the decision to abandon education is irrevocable. Once a student is out of the educational system for a few years, there are few opportunities to re-enter; the urban *hukou* policies bar them from participating in urban educational systems. Zhanglei expressed regret that she left school to work in the city:

> I feel I have wasted my time here. I was supposed to take a test to get into high school, but I thought coming to the city was going to be fun. So here I am today. I am now nineteen and cannot re-enter school.

In addition to a deep sense of regret and embarrassment over their lack of education, workers also feel that their accents and dialects brand them as "hicks," which discourages them from speaking to urbanites. Numerous women shared Xiaohe's assessment, "No one knows where you are from when you don't talk, but when you open your mouth then they know you are a peasant."

Experiencing urbanites' biases on a routine basis wounds migrant women's sense of pride. Many eventually become indignant and quite critical of urban attitudes. Ultimately, most migrant women feel there is no proper place for them in the urban center. In the words of Liling, a Beijing waitress, "It's meaningless for me to stay in Beijing for 10–20 years because people treat you contemptuously." For most, their only hope for reclaiming pride, self-esteem, and dignity lies in returning to the countryside. Together cultural and structural exclusion push them back to their rural origins, but once home they face a marriage system that forces them to move out of their natal villages and settle in those of their husbands. The skills and forms of capital they acquire in the city inspire many to attempt to renegotiate the rural marriage system.

Learning to Talk Back

Of course migrant women do not passively accept their subordinate urban position; they use new forms of cultural capital and skills acquired in the urban center to claim inclusion. Most readily adopt urban styles and habits, purchasing contemporary fashions and makeup as well as adapting their speech and manner in an attempt to disguise their rural origins and counter urban stereotypes about rural people's alleged "low quality" (*suzhi di*). As Hongyang, a waitress from rural Zhejiang, put it, "If you wear makeup . . . people think you're a clean type." Many believe that the use of makeup communicates positive messages about class, hygiene, and vitality.

Women who had been in the city for over a year developed increased self-confidence and verbal agility to manage unruly customers. Interactions with customers and clients necessitated a quick tongue and wit, whether to sell goods, negotiate with customers over the price of their meal, or fend off the frequent sexual advances of male customers. For example, customers occasionally pressured food servers to give them "face" in front of their guests and clients by insisting that they drink and sing with them. Xiaobo, a twenty-one-year-old Kunming waitress originally from rural Sichuan, found ways to manipulate and manage guests:

> Well, if the guests want me to drink with them, I would decline . . . [and] drink tea instead, and make some flattering remarks. By doing this, I give them what they need—I put them up on a pedestal.

Migrants who perform saleswork artfully manipulate urban stereotypes of poor rural migrants. In order to persuade customers to purchase their wares, they often use their perceived deprivation as a sales tactic. Minxiao from rural Jiangsu, who had a job selling office supplies, used her plight in this way:

I make them sympathize with me, you know, a young country girl working so hard trying to sell supplies. I told them that back in my village my family eats porridge for every meal and that I often go hungry. That works pretty well.

Others found the nerve to talk back to guests, sometimes even publicly condemning their behavior. Lipei, a Beijing waitress from rural Hebei, describes how she deals with unruly guests:

If [a guest] complains about us, we won't give him face.... We'll tell him off (*shuo ta*) right to his face.... After all, we're all people. Why can he complain about me? He's not higher ranking than me. We're all equal. We should all be equal.

At least in the sphere of work, women surmount embarrassment over their accents and develop skills to manage relationships with a range of urbanites. Liuling from rural Anhui proudly announced:

Well, I've studied how to speak—I can speak now. In the past I couldn't speak. Now when I meet people I dare to speak whereas in the past I was too shy. I don't care about a person's status, if I meet a high status person I dare to speak with him.

Wenli, a beauty salon worker, spoke of her newfound courage: "At first I didn't know anything, but then after a while, you learn which type of people have what kind of defects and problems—you learn how to deal with conflicts." Women find a critical voice in the urban center, one they use in an attempt to fend off the worst offenses.

Just as women find a voice and learn to assert themselves in the urban center, they also develop a more assertive attitude within their rural families, as did Liuling from Anhui province: "I speak up more at home now. My family all say that I've changed since I've been to the city—they say that I have more courage (*dan da*)." Newfound confidence and verbal skills endow migrant women with the resources and ability to potentially renegotiate their place in the rural village.

Part of what allows women to find a voice within both their families and their work is the great pride they take in earning a wage. Wenli exclaimed, "The happiest day was the first that I arrived here, and walking out of school, stepping into the society, the wage that I made that very first month." Access to wages led women to redefine their relationship to their families. In the following sections I examine how migrant women reinterpret rural practices and their places within these practices. Their experience of independence in the urban center leads them to question and revise notions of gender-appropriate behavior, especially those relating to marriage and filiality.

Re-interpreting Rural Practices

> [In the countryside] the men make all the decisions,
> and the women have to follow. I don't think I want that.
> I feel that times have changed.
> —Xiaobo, a twenty-one-year-old from rural Sichuan

As migrant women adjust to the urban center, they reformulate their relationships to family in a number of ways. Their ability to earn a wage and their urban sophistication endow them with new resources and the will to attempt to renegotiate their role in the family. The forms of behavior and dress adopted so they might pass as urbanites in Beijing and Kunming also become markers of status in their rural villages. Women feel that after working in the city for an extended period, they have distinguished themselves from female friends who stayed at home and married. A young beauty salon attendant from rural Zhejiang describes how she has become a more complex individual:

> I've seen different aspects of society, I've developed more knowledge about the world. At home ... we never hear our parents speak about the things we see here. I have different views than my family now. In the past I never really thought much about anything. [Now that I'm in the city] everything is so complicated, you see more things, have more problems, and there are more contradictions.

Liuling claimed to have developed a set of sensibilities quite apart from women her age who remained in the village:

> I have very little in common with them.... The girls who stayed at home have been exposed little to the world outside. They only contact people that they've grown up with. It's different for me because I get to deal with all kinds of people.

Hongwen, a Karaoke bar escort from rural Jiangsu, adopted an urban view of rural people:

> Rural people tend to be inflexible. People who have worked in the city are smarter because they've seen more things, they know a little bit of everything. Ever since I came here, I've become less and less timid.

Migrants represented their urban experiences as a privileged source of knowledge which became a basis upon which they attempted to claim higher status in their rural homes.

The development of a voice in their rural homes was made possible by their sense of urban sophistication and their ability to contribute to the family income. As Viviana Zelizer has noted, money is not merely a neutral medium of exchange; it becomes imbued with diverse social meanings as it enters relationships within families and in other institutions.[43] For most migrant women, urban wage labor affords them their first opportunity to control money. Through their wages, they attempt to redefine their relations to home and family; money allows them to express their filial piety in novel ways and thereby redefine the concept.

Through the process of redefinition, migrant women attempt to strengthen ties to their own families by linking the notion of "filial" to their new independence as wage earners. In the past, filial piety has been defined as obedience to parents through a set of role obligations that were by and large not negotiable. The migrant women with whom I spoke, many of whom migrated despite their parents' objections, redefined filial piety to encompass their voluntary contributions to the family income. A recurring theme throughout my interviews is the voluntary nature of gift and money-giving, which demonstrates a solidified bond with migrants' natal families. Those who send home presents and money emphasize that their parents do not expect or require these offerings; women willingly and selectively shared their income.[44] For example, Liling, who is from Zhejiang and works in a Beijing beauty salon, told me, "[My parents] don't want my money. They just want me to be independent, to be able to feed my own stomach." This stands in contrast to studies of female factory workers in Taiwan, which shares China's patrilineal family system. There, daughters who were deployed by families as an economic resource were required to send money home as part of their duties to the family.[45]

Although migrant women are developing a more critical stance toward the gender practices and attitudes of the countryside, many feel a stronger bond with their natal families once away from home. Most expressed a deep longing to be among family and recounted with nostalgia the natural beauty and open space of their rural villages. Somewhat ironically, migration enhances the possibilities of strengthening lasting ties to their natal homes. Many young, migrant women solidify their bonds with their natal family through the "filial" act of sending money home, as exemplified by Xianghua's description of offerings made to her parents:

> I have been here for six months and already I've sent about ten packages home with friends.... Even though they don't need presents, I need to give them presents.... This is a way for me to show my love for them and piety. *My parents don't need presents but they are very happy to receive my piety.* (emphasis added)

Women establish a variety of arrangements with their families for handling remitted money. For some the money is a gift for their parents to use as they deem fit. For others the parents save or manage the money for their daughters to be used eventually for a dowry. Zhuhua, a migrant from a poor mining village in Yunnan, worked out a mutually beneficial arrangement with her family:

> I send money home for my parents to keep for me. They loan it out at an interest rate of 6 percent. I've already sent over 2,000 yuan (about $250 U.S.). My parents are using the interest for themselves; I keep the principal.

Migrant women felt they had enhanced their position in the household as a result of their regular remittances:

> My village was very poor and all the neighbors looked down on my family because we only had daughters. It was very hard on my father because he had little help with working the land and he's not very healthy. But then my sister and I went to the city and we sent back money so my parents no longer have to work the land. They just live off the money we send them. The neighbors no longer think it is bad to have daughters. They realize that daughters can contribute to the household.

Although this realization has clearly not altered the desire to have sons in rural China, judging from the rates of female infanticide,[46] it offers some young women the possibility of (re)negotiating their status and power in their natal household.

While providing remittances as a strategy for improving their status in the family is limited by the nature of the rural family structure in China and state policies reinforcing it, migrant women do take enormous pride in their ability to make significant contributions to their households. If it has no other effect, earning a wage enhances their self-image and sense of efficacy. A number of women commented that even though they do not send money home, they are proud of easing the burden they represent for the household by becoming independent wage earners. The sacrifices they make for their rural families tie them closer, at least emotionally, to the natal household. Many hope to someday start their own small business in their own village and thereby overcome the "backwardness" of the countryside that is so disparaged among urbanites. Others revalued their family's connection to the land and its role in sustaining urban China in response to urban bias. Liaoli, a twenty-two-year-old from rural Anhui who had been in the city for three years, announced defiantly:

> Rural people produce the rice that they [the urbanites] eat, and they look down on rural people. But what would they eat if it weren't for the peasants? I can always go home and work the land, but if they lost their jobs, they wouldn't have anything to eat.

Migrant women experience a sense of pride in urban dependence on rural food producers and value the land as a source of security unavailable to urbanites.

But after experiencing a degree of independence and observing the relative gender equality of the urban center, migrant women become critical of the marriage system that requires that they marry into a husband's village. Instead they hope to find an arrangement that will allow them to visit freely and maintain strong ties to their natal families, and they are reluctant to substitute obligations to a husband's family for their strongly felt loyalty to their natal families.

Marriage

> When I return home and see my friends who are married with children, I feel that their lives are so boring and restricted. But ... I must return home to get married. I can't work in the city all of my life.... When I go home [for visits], my parents introduce me to potential husbands. I've met six at this point. I don't like any of them. Their skin is too dark and they don't know how to dress.... If I marry a rural man, I must obey him but I want my freedom. I'm not willing to work for my husband, to wash his socks and do what he tells me. I like being independent.
> —Xiaorong, Beijing kabob restaurant waitress

The newfound disapproval for the countryside captured in this statement, together with reluctance to accept the inevitability of their return for marriage, captures the plight of China's migrant women who hope to continue to escape persisting gender hierarchies in rural villages. In rural settings, men's power and privilege is anchored in family and village governance structures. Particularly in the far periphery from which most migrants hail, patrilineal structures and their accompanying practices persist.[47] Even though women tend to marry into better off villages, for those from the rural hinterlands, even their hypergamous prospects are unsavory to them. The rural household responsibility system, the linchpin of China's market reform policy, has reinforced the traditional marriage system, which dictates that women settle in their husband's village.[48] It has done so by redistributing land to households that are defined by their male membership. Hence, reform-era policies have formally restored male household authority. Women have rights to land "on paper," but because they move to their husbands' villages upon marriage, they are forced to forfeit any claim to the land that their family cultivates and which is passed along to male members of the family. This perpetuates women's status as temporary inhabitants of their natal villages and as outsiders in their husband's village, while sons inherit family property. It also creates a gender hierarchy in which women are seriously devalued, as Hongyang from Zhejiang related to me:

> My mother told me that when I was first born, my father ignored me. He put me underneath the bed and didn't care for me even when I cried. Of course, he

wanted a boy—boys can carry down the family name. But with a girl, once you are married, you can't come back [to the family] any more.

The expectation that sons will care for parents in their old age due to their close proximity to their parents reinforces a gender hierarchy in which women are severely devalued.

In addition to marital structure and property rights, the implementation of the family planning policy also institutionalizes gender hierarchy. It does so by allowing rural families to have a second child only if the first is a girl. Sex discrimination is apparent in rural China's high rates of female infanticide.[49] While some speculate that this might enhance the value of women as marriage partners, it has led to their increased commodification, evidenced by the growth of black market trafficking in brides and sex industry workers.[50] The recently implemented election system, which allows villages to call assemblies at which male heads of household vote, rather than general assemblies at which all villagers are enfranchised, also reinforces gender hierarchies. As one migrant woman remarked, "Men make all the decisions in my parents' village; when there's a meeting or an election each household just sends the father." Due to the reform-era reconstitution of gender hierarchies, returning home to be married into a husband's village becomes an unattractive option.

As a result of the virtual inevitability of their return home, their spatial distance from family authority, and the opportunities they have had to witness the relative gender equality enjoyed by urban women, migrant women reevaluate rural marriage structures. Their removal from the immediate influence of family authority allows some to struggle for an increased degree of self-determination, and few are willing to submit to marriage outside of their village arranged by their parents. When evaluating the possibilities for marriage, migrant women tend to have four different responses. First, some want to pursue the slim possibility of marriage to an urban man. While most felt this would be a desirable marriage arrangement, the structure of the residential policies made it virtually impossible.

The *hukou* system discourages marriage to male urbanites since state policy requires that children of such urban-rural "mixed" marriages inherit the residence of the mother. Children without an urban residence permit are barred from access to urban education.[51] As this twenty-three-year-old nanny originally from rural Jiangsu explains:

> My boyfriend wanted to marry me but his parents objected because I was from the countryside. Any children we have will take on my rural residence. His parents wanted their future generations to have opportunities for education and work in the city. They looked down on me.

A second option discussed more frequently by migrant women was to defer marriage indefinitely or refuse to marry. Some women had resisted their parents' matchmaking efforts by repeatedly declining engagement to the rural men to whom they were formally introduced. One woman's parents introduced her to ten potential marriage partners, none of whom suited her. A daring few considered the possibility of never marrying. Bairong articulated her revised views on marriage in light of her urban wage-earning experience:

> But for me, when I get to that age, I don't feel that I have to get married. I feel that it is most important to have your own career. I've changed my perception towards life. Basically I want to live a little happier and more comfortably.

Hairei from rural Hebei also declared her desire to be independent: "A woman should take her fate into her own hands; she shouldn't rely on a man too much."

A third option migrant women mentioned was to select their own rural marriage partner in the city without parental intervention and eventually secure the approval of their parents after engagement. This was Liming's plan. She was a restaurant hostess originally from Hunan who had a boyfriend from what she believed to be a much better-off village in Jiangsu, where she hoped to move after they married.

When asked about marriage, women most frequently express an interest in returning home in order to negotiate a marriage within their natal villages.[52] While many are willing to return home, and a significant portion express a desire to invest their skills and labor in improving their own villages, few women are willing to relocate to a prospective husband's village. In moving to the city, women experience a new commitment to their natal household and hope to arrange their future so that they may maintain close ties with their own parents and family. Chenhong explained why working in Kunming and delaying marriage allowed her to enjoy a closer relationship to her natal family:

> When I get married I won't be able to go to my parents' house for spring festival. When you're married you have to stay with your husband's parents for spring festival. Now that I'm working I can go home and spend spring festival with my parents.

Many of the women I interviewed echoed Chenhong's remarks and hoped to continue to enjoy holidays and special occasions with their natal families. Few of the women I spoke to were willing to return home to be married out of their villages. As one woman remarked, "The most important thing is to take good care of my parents. I will find a boy that feels the same way. Otherwise, I won't marry him."

If such attitudes are representative of migrant women's sentiments, then their eventual negotiation of marriage might counteract some of the trends that are strengthening rural patriarchal control. Each of the four approaches to marriage that women discussed represents an attempt to claim a degree of self-determination where family and governance structures otherwise limit it. Each alternative represents a reinterpretation of rural women's marriage options and the role of the family in making decisions about the future. Their experience of the urban center and its relative gender equality,[53] along with their new wage-based independence, lend them a critical perspective on village gender hierarchies. As they begin to reinterpret such inequalities, they create a potentially enlarged sphere of influence to alter their future prospects.

Conclusion

China's economic reforms rely on state-coordinated articulations of family and market. Through its restructured residential policies, the state has made a large pool of temporary laborers available for low-wage work in urban centers. In order to curtail migrants' demands on urban employers and urban services, *hukou* policies exclude them from urban citizenship, force them into work in the unregulated sector, and ultimately reinforce ties to their rural families. Therefore, while migration and labor market participation can pose a potential threat to the coherence of rural family structures, the *hukou* system reconstitutes the rural family by pushing migrant women back to their rural villages. At the same time, policies regulating rural life—such as the household responsibility system, the family planning policy, and the village election system—reinforce gender hierarchies through reform-era governance structures, while women's access to land is compromised by the rural marriage system. Taken as a whole, these state policies leave migrant women few alternatives but to labor under harsh conditions in the hope that their contributions to family might bring them future relief from rural patriarchy. Together, migrant women's urban and rural liminality—their state of double exclusion—offers them few alternatives to secondary sector work. When the state's role in organizing labor markets embedded in family structures is taken into account, we can explain why migrant women submit to coercive work regimes.

But *hukou* policies have potentially contradictory consequences for rural families. While China's flexible labor markets rely on and reinforce rural family structures, they also provide rural women with some limited opportunities to renegotiate those structures. Even though many defy parental authority by traveling to the urban center for work, once in the city they invest their natal homes with greater sentimental and symbolic value. Due to the nostalgia they feel for their rural homes and the isolation they experience within urban centers, rural women often feel stronger bonds with their natal villages after migrating to the city. For many single rural women, movement to the city offers opportunities to consolidate ties to their natal villages by redefining filial piety through voluntary gifts and remittances. After working in the urban center migrant women are less willing to relocate to a husband's village after marriage.

Migration might allow women some limited leverage to make new arrangements for maintaining close ties to their natal families. Their reinterpretation of the marriage system registers their intent to renegotiate gender hierarchy. The material and cultural capital that they accumulate in the urban center offer them tools to engage in this renegotiation. In the interstices of urban and rural structures, they seek to maintain strong ties with their natal homes and circumvent a marriage tradition that forces them to sever ties with those homes.[54] While their predicament is structured by intersections of state, family, and market that lend a particular gender character to China's market reform institutions, perhaps these intersections will also prove to be the means by which they alter their long-term prospects.

12

MARKETS NOT STATES?

The Weakness of State Social Provision for Breadwinning Men in the United States

ANN SHOLA ORLOFF

Investigations of "maternalism," "parental policies," "male breadwinner regimes," and "gendered welfare regimes" have over the last decade reshaped thinking about welfare states, uncovering the substantial contribution that gender relations and family dynamics have made, and continue to make, to the shaping of systems of social provision and regulation.[1] And finally, after over a decade of feminist critique, some prominent scholars of the "power resources" and institutionalist approaches have followed the lead of gender researchers in their recent work, attending to family welfare provision, gender equality measures and women's political activities and orientations.[2] This work goes a long way toward rectifying the neglect of the experiences of citizens—mainly women—who do not fit the description of the "standard" and implicitly male worker of earlier welfare-state analysis.

But to the extent mainstream researchers have taken an interest in gender, it is framed as a question about women's difference from men, and their inability to be like male workers that is the problem: women, unlike men, need maternity and parental leave, and services in order to combine employment and childrearing (or caring for the aged and disabled).[3] Men's dependence on women's caregiving is invisible; nor is there any recognition of the inevitability of caregiving and dependence.[4] In other words, analysis is androcentric and men remain the unmarked and understudied gender category. Thus even as scholarship has filled in our understanding of women's social citizenship, we have come up against the limits of focusing on women alone (to say nothing of problems in defining the category of women), as has been the case throughout the field of gender studies. It is not possible to understand—or change—women's situations without also understanding and changing men's.[5] Women's caregiving and their labor market participation are (at least partly) related to men's; the gender inequalities in wages, employment opportunities, and social provision linked to the gender division of labor and household formation are thus (at least partly) conditioned on men's practices. Building on studies of women's "maternalist" political action, and of state regulation of and provision for women as mothers, broader examinations of the politics of gender and family are very welcome.

Men as family members or as gendered workers and political actors have not attracted so much attention, nor have there been many investigations of how state policies shape gender and family relations in ways relevant for men and for masculinities.[6] Of course, mainstream comparative research until recently has focused on men—because of analysts' interest in social provision for "typical" workers, but this research ignores men *as men*—as opposed to men as workers or citizens or needy persons. Although social theory lately has been preoccupied with deconstructing dominant categories such as whiteness, masculinity, heterosexuality, this preoccupation has not yet transformed studies of welfare states. These concerns motivate a turn toward understanding the sources—institutional, political, social, cultural—of men's practices in the context of both gender and familial relations. In addition, there are practical or policy-related interests in men's situations, especially as fathers, related, for example, to a purported "crisis of fatherhood," and its link to welfare policies in the United States, or, in Scandinavia, to men's take-up (or lack thereof) of newly expanded parental leave benefits, which have been designed to encourage men's participation.

In this chapter, I will do two things. First, I selectively review the gender-sensitive and mainstream literatures which help us to map the relatively unexplored terrain of men and social provision. The explicitly gendered analysis of scholars such as Jane Lewis, in her work on "male breadwinner regimes," is critical for understanding men's gendered positions.[7] Yet it focuses too tightly on the gendered assumptions about care and paid employment guiding policymakers, occluding other significant institutional features of policy regimes. Therefore, the comparative insights of the gender-blind literature can be useful in understanding the role of systems of social provision in constituting men's gendered positions, including as breadwinners, fathers, and husbands, for they highlight the institutional arrangements by which welfare (income and care) is provided, the rights claims citizens can make for state support for themselves or their households, and the ways in which welfare states contribute to stratification.[8] These accounts must be reconstructed to elucidate their gendered implications (for men or women), and this is the analytic strategy my collaborators and I have pursued.[9]

Then, second, I use this reconstructed analytic framework—gendered welfare regime analysis—to examine the gendered positioning of men in U.S. social provision, in comparative perspective.[10] The United States offers an interesting window on the ways in which regimes do and do not institutionalize male breadwinning, as in the last thirty years or so it has gone from being a strong breadwinner regime to one promoting employment for all, but via a quite different path than the Scandinavian regimes. Unlike the Scandinavian state-led transition to the dual-earner model, in the United States, it appears that markets have played a more significant role.[11]

Research on Gender and Welfare States: Implications for Men

Welfare regimes have now been extensively analyzed in gendered terms, though the substance of those terms differs.[12] Some analysts see modern welfare systems as "patriarchal," or at the least, unfavorable to women, because of the economic vulnerability of women-maintained households, the gender gap in poverty rates, and the fact that benefits targeted on women's need, such as child care or maternity leave, receive less favorable treatment than do needs related to the labor market, such as retirement. These features are particularly pronounced in the United States, where solo mothers have very high poverty rates and the lack of citizenship entitlements to paid leave, social assistance, or health insurance particularly disadvantages women, who are less likely to have access to private-sector income and services. But in these formulations, it is unclear whether women's disadvantage is merely a deeper version of the disadvantages faced by all—including men—in a residual system, or if it contrasts with men's advantages.

In another important strand of the gender-sensitive literature—that which identifies a "two-tier" gendered welfare state in the United States—men serve as a foil for demonstrating women's inequality, as when analysts ask if women's benefits and programs are as good as men's, or if men's and women's prescribed roles are the same.[13] In this view, the two tiers of social policy reflect and recreate gender stratification: one tier, "welfare," is targeted on the problems of families, serves mainly women, and is stingy and intrusive, and another, "social security," is targeted on the problems resulting from labor markets (retirement, for instance), serves (retired) wage-earning men, and offers more generous benefits and honorable treatment. (The fact that the wives of these men and other women are the majority of social security beneficiaries is less often remarked upon.) The "top" tier seems to be held as an ideal; the implicit criticism of the system is that women and/or people suffering from family "failures" are not treated as well as are men or those confronting labor market problems.[14]

Gender differentiation and its links to women's inequality have long claimed feminists' analytic attention, but there has been a greater appreciation lately of the potential for states to be "women-friendly," to use the term coined by Helga Hernes, if they help women to reconcile paid work and caregiving or to participate politically, for example.[15] Analysts tend to see woman-friendliness as progress toward material equality with men, access to employment, services, and personal autonomy. What would be a "man-friendly" state? Do we have one already? Is it one reproducing unequal gender relations, the gender division of labor and women's dependency on men, particularly as expressed in the male breadwinner-female carer family? Or would men fare better under a less gender-differentiated and more equal system? What, then, are men's interests?

Earlier feminist work explicitly assumed that all women had—and should recognize—common interests in changing current gender arrangements, and that their gender interests ought to be primary. It was also assumed that all men had some interest in sustaining "patriarchy." But the assumption that women or men constitute unitary classes, with common and deducible interests, has been utterly undermined in more recent feminist scholarship, although debates continue about the modes by which categories are constructed and the extent to which they might be resisted, transgressed, used strategically, or overcome.[16] However, even today, among the institutionalist and power resource approaches that dominate all forms of welfare regime analysis—both gendered and not—one often finds an implicitly utilitarian understanding of "women's interests" and an assumption that the Swedish social-democratic model represents the best approximation of "woman-friendliness," reflecting their Marxist theoretical heritage.[17] On this account, women's interests lie simply in entering the paid workforce, gaining some relief from unpaid caring labor performed in families through the provision of state services, and obtaining individual rather than derived entitlement to benefits.[18] More historicized analyses, however, are challenging this view; and I will return to this point below. Men's purported interests usually have been left unspecified, or linked to ahistorical concepts such as "patriarchy." Socialist-feminist analysts might have questioned the extent to which working-class men's class interests could subvert their interests *as men*, but "men's interests as men" were usually assumed to be contrary to women's emancipation *as women*.

Interestingly, the old socialist-feminist view also seems to be echoed in Bob Connell's recent and highly-regarded *Masculinities*, in which he argues that men's interests as men are to preserve the arrangements which produce a "patriarchal dividend"—higher wages, relief from unpleasant domestic work, and so on—for all men (albeit unevenly), even if they might profit from subverting other aspects of hegemonic masculinity.[19] An "exit politics" based on a radical critique of the existing gender order can be expected to be taken up by only a few, according to Connell, although he holds out hope for some men to ally with movements for women's emancipation on the basis of their interests as members of other sorts of groups, such as working-class or environmental organizations. In other parts of his work, Connell argues for historically-grounded analysis, but his pronouncements about men's interests in preserving the "patriarchal dividend" appear to apply to all advanced capitalist democracies.

Two exemplary historical analyses provide an interesting counterpoint to Connell. Studies of support for family reproduction in inter-war France and Britain by Susan Pedersen and Jane Jenson suggest that working-class men fought with employers, state bureaucrats, and feminists, among others to earn a wage sufficient for supporting a family, without need for employer or state-provided supplements or married women's wage-earning.[20] In other words, they wanted family wages and women out of the workforce. Yet these "interests," or better, political goals, did not extend to all men across classes. Employers—all men, and most supporters of dependent wives and children themselves—opposed paying breadwinner wages to workingmen because it would have cut into their profits, and, in France, because women were a significant part of the labor force in some industries. To put it too crudely, class trumped gender and family status. Meanwhile, state elites—again men and family "heads" themselves—maneuvered among trade union and employers' groups, religious bodies, and others in pursuit of reproductive goals, critical to them given the geopolitical context of the time. They were looking to bolster working-class families' capacities to bear and rear children, and depending on the context, were willing to consider political measures to provide family allowances (funded publicly or by employers) and to offer childcare services that would allow mothers' employment *or* to accede to unions' demands for higher wages and the exclusion of women from the labor force.

Thus, working-class men achieved their goals in Britain, but not in France, due to the differing capacities of key political actors and organizations. Britain developed a male breadwinner-supporting welfare state, while the French developed a set of "parental" policies which made possible women's combining paid work and care (initially, this was far from contemporary notions of "woman-friendliness," as it was coupled with women's legal subordination to their husbands and lack of the vote). It appears then, that at least some men—elites—sacrificed gender solidarity around the "patriarchal dividend" (represented in these cases by the family wage) on the altar of their class or geopolitical goals. Perhaps state support for men's breadwinning is a political achievement of working-class men, at a particular time and place, rather than a more universal gender interest?

While questions about men's possible interests may be useful for unearthing and challenging assumptions that too often remain implicit (and unmeasurable), I would argue that the whole apparatus of "interests" is quite problematic. Defining interests—or needs, subjects, identities, and subjectivities, or of accounting for the constitution of social groups and discerning their shifting and overlapping boundaries—has been at the center of contemporary debate in social theory and political analysis.[21] A particularly important feminist contribution critiques the assumption of an atomized individual as the subject in discussions of "objective" interests, or utilities; how, for example, could such a premise accommodate the activities and goals of mothers caring for, and sacrificing for, children? Are they victims of false consciousness? Knowing agents of an "ethic of care"? Even to ask such questions makes clear that simple assumptions about individuals' and groups' gendered and other goals, personal and political, will no longer do. All of this work cautions against assuming that we can "read off" or deduce politically-salient identities and interests from social structures; rather, these must be understood in specific historical, political, and discursive contexts. In short, it denies that we can specify "objective" or "strategic" interests for any groups. We ought to abandon the search in favor of a more contextual and historical approach to the construction of political goals, ideologies, groups, and identities.

These insights can be taken back to considerations of welfare or policy regimes, which are nationally varied, historically constructed constellations of policies and relationships across states, markets, families, and other institutions, in which we may discern logics of provision and regulation, more or less unitary, more or less complementary across policy arenas. Once particular sets of arrangements are institutionalized, political actors build up expectations and understandings, and make decisions and investments of time and resources that are not easy to revise or undo. In short, they develop interests in particular solutions to problems, given particular sets of institutions (whatever might be preferable in an ideal world). There has been a good deal of discussion, for instance, about the extent to which different regimes construct women as "workers or mothers," and an appreciation that under different circumstances, women may place their political bets on opening women's opportunities for wage-earning or on better protection for full-time caregivers. Moreover, this has changed over time, as, for example, when "maternalist" political forces have declined in strength. We should investigate similar issues with respect to men.[22] Are men approached mainly as family heads or breadwinners or simply as wage-earners? In other words, do regimes target men in their reproductive roles or in their capacities as workers? Or are the two kinds of roles linked in understandings of wage-earning as the very fulfillment of fatherly duties? How are these roles defined? How do class, racial, ethnic, sexual, and other differences among men articulate with these gendered statuses? And how does all this influence the political goals articulated by different groups of men? The identities, ideologies, goals and desires produced in part by existing regimes can be investigated utilizing the gendered welfare regime framework, giving us purchase on both the effects on gender relations of particular regimes and the points of tension likely to influence social politics in ongoing reforms of welfare states.

Gendered Welfare Regime Analysis

Feminist analysts' key contributions to the study of policy regimes has been to show that welfare states differentiate by gender and that family caregiving, mainly by women, is critical to societal welfare. And by pursuing these insights, they have uncovered significant variation in the political shaping of gender relations and of family and household forms. Men—if healthy and able-bodied—have always been expected to be gainfully employed. Until very recently, women were not subject to the requirement to be employed, but have always been expected to provide care; increasingly, care is expected in combination with employment as demands for commodification have extended to women (although with differing assumptions about full- versus part-time work and parental leave). Moreover, women have faced requirements related to sexual morality and domestic capabilities that have never been extended to men. Policymakers assumed that families were and should be in the breadwinner-caregiver model; the logic of the gender division of labor was near-universal in the industrialized capitalist West as welfare states formed and matured. Heterosexual, married couples were to be the foundation of households rearing children. In the contemporary period, we are witnessing changes in assumptions about families and the gender division of labor, and associated restructurings of social provision, making this a potentially fruitful time to investigate the effects for men.

Jane Lewis' concept of "male breadwinner" regimes, with countries manifesting strong, modified, or weak (tending to a dual-earner model) versions, has been quite useful in comparative investigations of the impact of welfare states on men, given that men's principal gender role in the West has been "breadwinner."[23] In Lewis' formulation, in strong male breadwinner regimes, men are privileged in access to jobs, enjoy advantages in tax treatment and welfare programs, and are paid family wages; women are excluded from paid work (or advantaged positions) and subordinated within a male-headed family; care is provided privately, in the family. What varies in this framework is the strength of the advantages given to male breadwinners, the extent to which women were excluded from paid work, and the extent to which the state absorbs some care functions from the family.[24] Thus, Lewis' analysis—and that of most feminist welfare regime researchers—centers on the gender division of labor, or gender differentiation, and the ways this has contributed to gender inequality.[25] Many studies show cross-national and historical differences in the patterns of women's paid and unpaid work, with associated differences in gender ideologies, particularly ideals of motherhood. While some countries' policies are designed to allow women to combine paid work and caregiving, others are designed to encourage women's domesticity and full-time caregiving.[26]

Welfare regime differences in constructing women as worker/carers, full-time mothers, and the like, are becoming well known.[27] However, there is little if any systematic cross-national investigation about how social provision affects patterns of men's paid and unpaid work. Indeed, the tendency to refer to regimes which support women's employment as "dual earner" obscures the possible variation in men's caregiving—are such regimes also "dual carer," or do men remain free of caregiving responsibilities while women add wage-earning to care work? Are there different cultural assumptions and ideologies about masculinities and fatherhood? This might be rectified within the framework of Lewis' concept by extending our research to incorporate men in the gender division of caregiving labor. Yet policy assumptions about the gender division of labor are not the only factor affecting men's practices. Lewis does note, as have other feminist analysts, the significance of public-private splits in caregiving; in this view, private provision, understood as *family* provision, undergirds the breadwinner regime.[28] But I contend that we need a broader understanding of countries' institutional arrangements, in which we combine feminist and mainstream understandings of the "public/private split": mainstream scholars have until recently focused on state/market differences as the key public/private divide, while feminists oppose the "private" family to the "public" world of markets and states. Thus, we need to look at the relative emphasis on states, markets, and families. It turns out that an emphasis on "private" sources of income and services—the market—can undermine the male breadwinner regime. Let me deal with these issues in turn.

A cursory look at the literature on welfare regimes indicates little cross-national variation in men's positions in the division of paid work and unpaid caregiving work; everywhere, they are paid workers, and are scarce among those providing unpaid care. But are men in fact everywhere breadwinners, that is, workers able to support caregiving wives? Do men receive special recognition as fathers or as husbands? And what form does this take? Some countries offer men the opportunity to take parental leave, that is, to participate in caregiving; others give married men or fathers cash benefits to supplement their wages to compensate for the financial burden of supporting a family. In the United States, access to parental leave is gender-neutral, but the leave is unpaid. Some countries have developed active labor market policies to ensure employment; this may be aimed explicitly at men, to bolster their capacities to be breadwinners, while elsewhere—Sweden is well known in this regard—policies are gender-neutral. The United States has traditionally offered little or no special help of any kind to fathers, although in the last few years we are seeing some very limited policy developments, mainly on the local level and often in connection with child support collection efforts, to help disadvantaged men to become "responsible" fathers, especially by enhancing their employability. But neither fathers nor any other Americans can claim the right to a job. Policies with respect to child support enforcement and paternity establishment also vary. In some countries, fathers not living with their children are not expected to contribute to their financial support (or to taking care of the children). Elsewhere, especially where public sources of support for children are more limited, as in the United States, (biological) fathers are increasingly expected to make financial contributions to their children's upbringing. Clearly, these are different ways of approaching men as fathers, and of institutionalizing cultural assumptions and ideals of fatherhood. Regimes also contribute to inequalities in the material resources available to different groups (based on gendered identities or position in the division of labor, but also on other social differences).

Class inequalities are consequential for capacities to support households; and we know from decades of research that while all capitalist countries feature some inequality, countries vary in the extent to which the state ameliorates market-generated inequalities. The United States is at the low end of the scale on this feature; thus, men of different classes have quite different levels of resources and capacities to support families. And there is as well variation cross-nationally, and among men within countries in access to jobs sustaining a breadwinner position. In Kathleen Gerson's study of family roles among a group of American men of different class and racial backgrounds, she found many men who were unwilling or unable to sustain breadwinning roles.[29] But while a small minority of the non-breadwinner men she interviewed for her study turned to an egalitarian division of paid and unpaid labor with their partners, the majority of these men turned to an "autonomous" role bereft of most family ties, leaving the work of caregiving (and the financial burden of childrearing) relegated to the mothers of their children. Students of U.S. racial inequality, among others, have become concerned of late about the dim prospects for poor and low-skilled fathers, disproportionately men of color, to contribute financially and otherwise to their children's support; these men are positioned quite differently from the men whose advantaged labor market positions give them capacities to be "responsible" fathers and valued partners—as these roles are currently defined.[30]

Regime analysis has stressed the significance of the institutional "division of labor" in the provision of income and services, among states, markets, and families, and of the extent to which social provision is organized in terms of citizenship rights, particularly social rights (as opposed to discretionary social assistance, or charity). These features bear on social inequality, the balance of power among political actors, and the extent of individuals' life choices; unremarked by regime analysts, but clearly significant for gender analysis, they also affect men's capacities to support households or to care for children. To the extent that access to income and services are rooted in private institutional spheres, they are vulnerable to erosion if individuals lose employment or if overall labor market conditions change.

Gøsta Esping-Andersen and others in the power resources tradition highlight decommodification, or the extent to which individuals' typical life situations are free from dependence on the labor market, resulting from well-developed social rights.[31] This, they contend, is at the core of the state's emancipatory potential—it counteracts the central capitalist process of commodification. However, they are thinking of the situation of workers (implicitly male) vis-à-vis the market, not about men in terms of their position in gender relations. The United States is a "liberal" regime with a strong role for markets and limited state provision; citizens must secure their living from the market—there is little decommodification.³² Still, benefits that offer a "back-up" to family wages, even if they simultaneously secure men's labor market participation (that is, are not particularly decommodifying), affect men's capacities to be breadwinners.

Interest in decommodification may obscure the fact that employment (commodification) itself may be problematic, yet, arguably, the commitment to full employment (activation) is the most significant aspect of the decommodifying social-democratic regimes.³³ After all, not all social groups have equal access to the jobs that allow personal independence and access to decommodifying benefits. Access to paid work (and to the services that facilitate employment for caregivers) are critical gender dimensions of welfare regime variability given the importance historically of women's exclusion from employment, and the linkage of citizenship rights to employment. But this is also of significance for men, for markets do not reliably produce employment for all men (any more than for women). To the extent that employment is the basis for access to citizenship rights and household formation, countries' variable commitment to full employment or active labor market policies is significant for both men and women.

Social rights to benefits and services are also significant vis-à-vis gender (and generational) relations within families. In earlier work, I focused on the ways in which welfare benefits, provision of services, and employment regulations affect the capacity to form and maintain an autonomous household, a dimension which indicates an individual's ability to survive and support their children without being forced to marry or enter into other family relationships.³⁴ This is clearly relevant to women, whose decisional autonomy has been compromised by familial economic dependencies. But I would argue that this dimension is also relevant for men. Decommodification varies cross-nationally, but men's capacities to form and maintain autonomous households vary less. However, the mode of gaining capacities for household formation and maintenance differs depending on the institutional mix of states, markets, and families in the provision of care and cash, and whether states offer social rights to employment or to the resources needed to sustain a household. In all Western states, the vast majority of men gain the capacity to head households through their market work; since their inception, most income-maintenance programs served as "back-ups" to the family wage system, allowing men to continue to support their families when they lose their wage-earning capacities temporarily (unemployment, temporary illness, or disability) or permanently (retirement, disability).³⁵

State policies also differ in how—and if at all—the capacity to form and maintain households is supported for subgroups of men and women defined in terms of "race," ethnicity, immigration status, class, sexuality, and so on. In the contemporary United States, while employment is promoted for everyone, employment is not guaranteed, and those who cannot work (at least in the formal labor market) are thereby denied the capacities to support an autonomous household. This has distinctly racial dimensions. Among the long-term unemployed and those suffering from lack of employment opportunities, there are a disproportionate number of people of color. Finally, the capacity to form an autonomous household implies more than individual independence—it also gets at whether women and men, gays and straights, are allowed to have as well as to support families, thus reflecting the character of regulations of sexuality, custody, reproduction, marriage, divorce, and household composition. We might call this the "right to a family."

In the remainder of this chapter, I explore how men have been treated over time in U.S. social policy, with attention to their roles as fathers. I am especially interested in the institutional sources of support for fathers—states, markets, families—as well as how men as fathers have been positioned vis-à-vis households' needs for cash and care.

Why the United States? The United States is only one of many states in which policies until recently were guided by gendered assumptions that men would be breadwinners and women full-time housewives and mothers. These assumptions were encoded in the legislation that established modern social provision in the United States. (in the 1910s–1940s), and remained robust until at least the 1960s, when reforms rendered most provisions formally gender-neutral (as was the case in other strong breadwinner regimes as well). Beginning in the 1960s and 1970s, anti-discrimination legislation and the mobilization of women of all races (and men of color) broke the hold of white men on "good jobs," and helped to promote an alternative to breadwinner ideology, though adherents of "traditional" gender ideology continue to press their cause politically. Yet while other breadwinner regimes (for example, Germany, the U.K.) have for the most part sustained men's breadwinning, the United States has moved toward a far weaker version of the model, both in everyday practices—dual-earner households are the majority of households with children, and in policy assumptions—men and women are expected to be workers. But workers have never gotten much help from the state to sustain households, especially through public employment guarantees.

The United States is cross-nationally unusual in the extent to which state social provision is limited to elderly, retired workers (both men and women) and very poor single parents, mainly women. The majority of the working-aged population—men, women, fathers, mothers, and their children—is simply left outside the umbrella of the welfare state, forced to rely on private sources of cash and care: markets and families. This gap in provision, which is arguably one of the most consequential features of the U.S. social policy regime for gender, class, and racial inequalities, has received far less attention from policymakers or policy analysts than welfare or social security.[36]

I contend that men's breadwinner status in the United States has been rooted more in the market than in state social provision than has been the case in other breadwinner regimes. Men's breadwinning and fatherhood have been less protected *politically* in the United States than elsewhere, and therefore was subject to erosion once economic conditions shifted (as they have across the West since the early 1970s).[37] Moreover, the capacity to "head" or support a household has been based principally on labor market status, and therefore stratified by class and race, as well as gender. Historically, economic conditions—especially relatively high wages—and the legal toleration of discrimination in favor of white men meant that many men were able to provide for their families relatively well, although others were left unable to support families because of labor market discrimination and/or poor wages. Coincident with the rise of women's labor market participation and the shift to gender-neutrality in employment law and social provision in the 1970s and 1980s, the labor market, unfettered by institutionalized labor regulations, shifted in ways unfavorable to many blue-collar men—men who in the decades immediately after World War II had been able to be breadwinners. Economically-disadvantaged men—disproportionately men of color and unskilled men—are sometimes left unable to be breadwinning husbands and to sustain households. Nor does the state provide positive incentives, such as paid parental leaves or family allowances paid to fathers, to induce men to take up fatherhood, in either egalitarian or more "traditional" modes.[38]

Men in U.S. Social Provision

In the United States, the market has predominated in sustaining men as breadwinners, with the partial exception of the New Deal era, when state provision assumed an unusually strong role (relative to earlier and later periods). To the extent that state social policies address men as fathers—which is quite limited—they are expected to contribute cash rather than care; but for the most part, the "privacy" of family life in the liberal regime means that men and women are left free—from state interference or support—to construct their households as they will, but only as they can afford. The lack of state support to workers in the United States points to policy characteristics highlighted by regime analysts: the strong emphasis historically on markets (employment) and families rather than states as sources of income and services, the underdevelopment of social rights and the lack of public commitment to full employment, a feature that may be linked to the liberalism of U.S. politics.[39] It is true that after the development of some key social insurance programs in the 1930s, the U.S. system of social provision, though less developed than European welfare states, nonetheless provided sufficient security for most men so that they could continue to head households if out of work temporarily or when retired. But the public safety net depends on citizens having (private) employment most of the time. Moreover, without citizenship-based benefits U.S. men (and women) depend on their employers, their families, or the market for income and most services; the U.S. system features low decommodification. Thus, most U.S. men's political and social identities are forged outside the welfare state; in terms of gaining capacities to head households—to be fathers, their status as employees of particular corporations, which are often the source of important benefits as well as income, is more significant than their status as worker-citizens.

Let me stress the theoretical point: the role of the state is consequential, but in the U.S. case, it is *the absence of state welfare benefits and services*, rather than their presence, that commands attention. However, for a minority of men, usually those who turn to black market or criminal activities when unable to find family-sustaining employment in the legitimate labor market, the state—though not in its guise as a provider of welfare—takes a more hands-on role, that of policeman, jailer or, less drastically, establisher of paternity and enforcer of child support obligations.

Gender Difference in Early U.S. Social Policy and Politics

The origins of modern welfare provision are to be found in the late nineteenth and early twentieth centuries, when, across most countries in the industrializing West, there emerged new forms of social protection for citizens against a range of different problems of income interruption and economic dependency—old age pensions or insurance, unemployment compensation, benefits for widowed mothers and the like. These replaced (only partially at first) the old systems of poor relief which had stood as the sole protection against utter destitution, but at the price of citizenship rights and social respectability. During this formative era, alliances of overwhelmingly male working-class movements and male intellectual, political, and reform elites advocated programs that would give public benefits to male breadwinners that they might continue to support their families financially even when they lost their jobs or wage-earning capacities. In addition, in a "maternalist" strand of welfare politics, reformers (mainly women) proposed state support to women in their roles as mothers as well as protective labor legislation for women workers and infant and maternal health programs.[40] Some also fought for the "endowment of motherhood" for all, conferring political recognition on mothering and providing an income which would free women from economic dependence on husbands. This general approach did not succeed, at least partly because of men's opposition.[41] The initial programs of social provision were deeply gendered, designed to fit and reinforce the dominant form of the gender division of labor, with men as breadwinners and women as primary caretakers and domestic workers (and sometimes as secondary wage earners). In no case were these programs intended to provide *alternatives* to the market for men or to marriage for women, although that was to some extent their unintended consequence, particularly as programs expanded in the post-World War II years.

Programs addressing the risks associated with family break-up, along with limited protection against work accidents, were the first forms of modern social provision in the American states. This was quite different from the pattern in Europe, where initial breakthroughs came in protections against labor market problems: work accidents and forced retirement.[42] Following a campaign by a number of women's voluntary groups, and despite the resistance of most of the forces of organized private charity, almost all states had enacted mothers' pension programs by the 1920s.[43] Mothers' pensions offered cash assistance to a relatively limited clientele of widowed, and in some cases divorced, deserted, or never married mothers with children at home. These programs were a back-up for the "failures" of the family wage system for women who lacked a breadwinning spouse, allowing some women and their children to survive without husbands (albeit in relatively deprived circumstances). Reformers preferred these as the solution to the destitution and break-up of widowed-mother families, rather than the expansion of childcare services which would have allowed these (and other) women to work for pay.[44] Protective labor legislation for women was also enacted at this time, justified in terms of protecting women's maternal capacities or as a second best alternative to universal worker protections, which could not pass judicial scrutiny at this time.[45] But while states might support women's caregiving in various ways, men's wage earning did not receive similar public support.

Employers, most politicians, and the national leadership of the American Federation of Labor were all committed to the ideas of voluntarism, which held that men should and could earn their living as individuals freely contracting with employers.[46] Unfettered labor markets were the province of full citizens—that is to say, men. In this view, only because women were "different" could they be protected. Many state-level labor federations and a number of working-class fraternal orders did support protections aimed at working men such as old age pensions, but without the support of political elites and the broader middle-class public, such programs were unsuccessful, in contrast to analogous programs in Europe and the Antipodes.[47] Thus, class differences among men marked the political struggles around programs that would have given state support to households headed by wage-earning men. The sole exception was state-level workmen's compensation legislation, passed in almost all states, which required employers to insure their workers against industrial accidents and sometimes established state regulatory boards. By the 1920s, a handful of states had enacted old age pension laws, but these were extremely limited—more elderly people got assistance through poor relief and veterans' pensions than they did from these early laws.[48] As in other industrializing and urbanizing countries, American states passed new laws in this period which stiffened regulation aimed at fathers who failed to provide for their children, applied especially to those whose families applied for relief, which we may recognize as an antecedent to the welfare reform-child support enforcement link seen in more recent times.[49] Breadwinning did not get much help from the state, but states would enforce it.

In sum, assumptions about breadwinning men and caregiving wives were widespread, and informed the programs and regulatory legislation that were established in the Progressive Era. However, material support to breadwinning men from the state was not part of the U.S. regime, which marks it as cross-nationally distinctive among other Western states. In Europe and Australasia, public pensions and health coverage were made available to workers (mainly men), even as disciplinary measures to deal with "family failures" were also enacted, so breadwinning was both regulated and supported.[50]

The Uneven Institutionalization of a Welfare State for (Male?) Workers

Progressive Era reformers entertained notions of public support to individual initiatives, but by the business-dominated 1920s, it was reliance on the market that was celebrated. Some private companies did establish very limited programs for their employees ("welfare capitalism"). The market was expected to provide for (male) workers, who were in turn expected to provide for their wives. It was only with the economic collapse of the Great Depression that faith in market solutions to welfare problems was shaken, making possible a new set of public initiatives in President Franklin Roosevelt's New Deal.[51] The Social Security Act, the "charter legislation" for the U.S. version of the welfare state, was passed in 1935. Again in contrast to the Progressive Era, concern focused on the plight of unemployed and forcibly retired wage-earners, understood as male breadwinners, and women's issues did not emerge on the political agenda.[52] Labor standards legislation was extended to men for the first time in the United States with passage of the Fair Labor Standards Act in 1938. A number of other initiatives—both public benefits and public employment—addressed the concerns of wage-earning men. Had they all survived the 1930s, the United States might have had a welfare state that guaranteed the position of breadwinning men in working age and retirement, as was the case, for example, in Scandinavia, where social-democratic initiatives laid the groundwork for active labor market policies, supplemented by social provision for the aged or others deemed unemployable.[53] But in the United States, public provision for working aged men, taking the form of innovative public employment schemes like the Works Progress Administration, were not continued past the economic crisis.[54] Instead, only provision for the unemployed and those considered unemployable—the elderly and single mothers (mostly but not only white)—continued past the war, while working men were again to rely on the market.

Roosevelt, Democratic politicians, the organized elderly (of both sexes), and unions backed social protection for the aged.[55] Popular groups preferred a noncontributory pension (that is, a form of social assistance). However, in the Social Security Act, policymaking elites, motivated largely by fiscal concerns, established actuarially strict contributory social insurance programs against the risks of income loss due to retirement and unemployment for wage earners—almost all, though not exclusively, men.[56] The contributory feature worked toward a system under which wage earners, at that time mainly men, would be advantaged vis-à-vis those outside the labor market, at that time mainly women. Congress included provisions excluding from old age insurance certain occupational groups dominated by people of color and women of all races.[57] Retired workers would claim benefits by working for a minimum number of years in a covered occupation and making contributions through a payroll tax evenly split between employers and employees (in contrast to most countries, there is no government contribution). Gendered labor market arrangements in the United States, as elsewhere, made it likely that men would be most able to claim retired-worker benefits in such a system, although eligibility was gender-neutral.[58] To deal with the elderly poor who were not covered by old age insurance, state-level old age pension programs were given federal financial backing. Elderly women were to be helped in this way—as would the many aged poor men who had not had time to build up contributions; Suzanne Mettler points out that this established a (gender) "divided citizenship."[59] (It was only in the 1950s that more people got benefits under old age insurance than through the state-level pensions.)

The fullest instance of support to households headed by breadwinning men and supporting stay-at-home wives came when the old age insurance program was fundamentally altered by the addition of dependents' and survivors' benefits in the 1939 Amendments to the Social Security Act. After these changes, these programs became the heart of state support to breadwinning men, but only when they could no longer work for wages. Interestingly, this policy shift stemmed in part from a different aspect of liberal ideology and practice: not wanting to build up substantial cash reserves under state control. Thus, extra benefits were coupled with a change to pay-as-you-go financing, resulting in financial windfalls to the early cohorts of Social Security recipients. But the policymakers drafting these amendments were informed by the logic of the male breadwinner; they assumed that male breadwinners should be able to support their spouses and, after their deaths, survivors, and thought in any event that women should be out of the labor force.[60] Survivors' and dependents' benefits were made available to all widows and spouses of covered wage earners, but these benefits could not be claimed in combination with a workers' retirement benefit; thus, employed women and single people in effect would subsidize couples receiving both dependents' and retirement benefits.[61]

In the old age provisions of Social Security, then, one sees the breadwinner-housewife logic at its most robust. This was coupled with what were to become substantial material supports that allowed elderly men to maintain their status as household heads even when they retired, rather than facing the less attractive options of the time: working until death or outright incapacity, or, becoming dependents in the homes of their children. (Non-contributory old age pensions, without gender differentiation, accomplished some of the same effects without reinforcing the gender division of labor; however, for reasons having little to do with gender and too complicated to discuss here, this form of provision was phased out by 1970.)[62]

Elderly retired workers, and all workers who knew they faced old age, were a critical constituency of New Deal social politics. But under the rubric of Social Security, direct support to *working-aged* families was limited to those without a male breadwinner (and only some of these). Mothers' pensions programs, run by states, were given federal funding and some oversight, and renamed Aid to Dependent Children.[63] Until 1961, the only two-parent families eligible for ADC were those in which one parent was incapacitated. Again, the assumption was that a healthy man should be able to support himself and his dependents, and should not need state assistance except in cases of temporary unemployment. While access to caregiving support was gender-neutral, it was also decidedly residual, reserved only to the poorest mothers without husbands to support them; caregiving and the support of families was a private matter and not the government's business. Many people of color were excluded from coverage by leaving administration to states; where women of color were a significant part of the labor force, as in most of the South, they could be denied assistance as "employable mothers."[64]

What of support to breadwinning men themselves? New supports to working-aged men were also developed by Roosevelt administration policymakers—especially notable were public employment measures and public works—but these were not given the permanent status of the Social Security provisions, and were treated as "temporary" relief, to be limited to the period of economic crisis.[65] Thus, the only permanent help to working-aged men came through unemployment insurance, financed through employer contributions, which was also legislated on the national level in the 1935 Social Security Act.[66]

With mobilization for World War II, unemployment dried up, but concerns about employment resurfaced after the war. Full employment initiatives were proposed in the 1940s, but these were defeated by a newly energized conservative coalition, as unions found their political capacities undermined, and only a watered down Employment Act was passed.[67] Moreover, with federal proposals for health insurance and other benefits stymied by a more conservative political climate, newly organized workers turned to collective bargaining to gain benefits from employers.[68] Workers in auto, steel, and other mass production industries gained coverage equal to or superior to those nationally guaranteed to workers in Europe, but of course, not all workers or citizens had access to these benefits. Other public policies also contributed to men's capacities to head households and get by on a single wage, but these were outside the "welfare state," as defined in political discourse. Obviously, the economic expansion and relatively high wages of the time were critical. But in addition, veterans' benefits, expanded widely with the G.I. Bill, which gave support to home ownership and education, and general support to suburbanization and inexpensive housing, helped to undergird the baby boom and "traditional"—meaning breadwinner/caregiver—families.[69] Thus, many breadwinning men in the United States understood their positions as sustained by *private* arrangements, or by virtue of their status as *veterans*, and *not* by the welfare state.

Programs of social provision in the United States, as initiated in the 1930s and institutionalized in the two following decades, were designed to fit and reinforce the gender division of labor as manifested in male breadwinner-female carer families, and the income security system was marked by a work/family dualism. As this structure of modern social provision was institutionalized at a time when the work and family patterns of men and women were far more distinctive than they are today, work-related programs have tended to serve men while almost all of the clients of family-related programs have been women. These policies further institutionalized the gender division of labor, and underlined distinctive gender identities: worker in the case of men, wife or mother in the case of women. Differentiation by gender and by social function (work and caregiving/domestic work) was the explicit aim of social policy. Inequality in the benefits available to men and women was its concomitant, whether the explicit aim of policy or not. Women—at least "good" ones—were exempted from the compulsion to participate in the labor market (as well as the opportunity to do so!) because of their caregiving work. But for men, there was no alternative to employment except under strict conditions of eligibility—in the short term, unemployment insurance, or when permanently retired, old age insurance (or pensions). The only route to honorable coverage for men was through wage earning, for women, through marriage to a wage earner. In short, commodification (directly for men, indirectly for women) was a critical element of the system. Again, there are significant contrasts to other countries, where men's position as breadwinners received more substantial state support—where welfare states were the source not only of old age and unemployment insurance, but also of health insurance and family allowances for workers' families.

(Failed) Initiatives to Help Breadwinners in the 1960s and 1970s

Private employment and associated benefits, backed up by Social Security, worked well for most Americans, yet significant portions of the population were left out of prosperity even as the coverage of occupations under Social Security became virtually universal by the 1960s. Responding to a diverse range of political forces, including the civil rights movement, President Lyndon Johnson in 1965 initiated the "War on Poverty," which encompassed a number of efforts to deal with those who did not enjoy the benefits of rising wages, and employment and social insurance programs—prominently, the black and Latino urban poor.[70] Many of these efforts targeted men as breadwinners.[71] Training programs and various public employment schemes were touted as ways to bring these groups into the mainstream, attacking both persistent poverty and racial segregation. Blacks were understood by many policymakers to be suffering from dysfunctional families, and bolstering the position of men as breadwinners and family "heads" was proposed as a cure.[72] Jill Quadagno documents, however, that as these programs challenged whites' prerogatives in favored employment, they ran into political opposition.[73] Most programs associated with the War on Poverty ultimately fizzled out, but one unambiguous achievement of this period was the transformation of old age insurance into a "retirement wage" through benefit increases and a significant decrease in aged poverty, particularly among retired wage-earning men.[74]

Responding partly to concerns, perhaps most famously voiced in the Moynihan Report, that AFDC encouraged marital break-ups and the "pathology" of female-headed households since it was made available principally to single parents—in other words, since it did not help families "headed" by men—President Richard Nixon authorized experiments with a Negative Income Tax (NIT) in the early 1970s.[75] But the NIT-type "Family Assistance Plan" (FAP), which would have helped many two-parent families and bolstered the position of poorer, especially minority, male workers was politically damaged because it was found to be associated with an increased probability of "family break-up" (that is, divorce). Probably more damaging was the opposition of Southern conservatives in Congress because of FAP's projected effect on local labor markets; it would have bolstered the position of wage workers, men and women, in the South and Southwest too much. Some Northern liberals joined them in opposition because it would have meant lower payments to members of their constituencies who relied on welfare (AFDC) payments.[76] Rather than the radical reform the FAP would have been, eligibility for "welfare" was expanded and take-up of benefits increased, temporarily as it turned out. AFDC continued, but more indicative of the changes to come in the 1980s and 1990s was the addition of work incentives and new federal efforts around child support collection.

There was no unified support—among men (or among elites)—for providing material public benefits to breadwinning men, even as conservative family ideologies, extolling men's paid work in support of stay-at-home motherhood and castigating child care as "communistic," found numerous and influential advocates. But liberal thinking on gender, favoring an end to sex discrimination, was also gaining adherents. Welfare state programs were made fully gender neutral in the 1960s and 1970s through legislation and court decisions, although the underlying gendered division between programs targeted on family and the labor market was unchanged.[77]

Policy developments reinforced patterns in which welfare was reserved to the elderly, (some of) the unemployed, and very needy single-mother families, while other citizens had to rely on the market. Except for food stamps—a success due to an unusual configuration of forces—failure was the fate of all initiatives that would have extended services or economic support to the working-aged population, whether male breadwinners (for example, training, public employment), women workers (for example, expanded child care), or both men and women (universal health insurance—we got Medicare and Medicaid instead).[78] Notably, this pattern of state intervention helped to solidify the racialization and (perhaps to a lesser extent) feminization of welfare, positioning (many) white men as "self-reliant" taxpayers and employees, rather than as worker-citizens or father-citizens.[79] This helped to set the stage for the 1980s politics of backlash, in which many citizens set themselves against "welfare," though not against the parts of the state, most notably social security, in which they had a stake.

In contrast to the welfare states of Europe, which in this period "squeezed out" the market through the expansion of public programs to near universal coverage, the vast majority of the working-aged U.S. population was not incorporated in the welfare state through public programs of benefits, training, or services.[80] Nor did caregiving work escape from the private sphere to which it had been relegated in the New Deal; although legislation to expand child care services was considered, it was defeated.[81] Instead, the United States limited public child care to economically needy or educationally disadvantaged children. Private services have since expanded, with tax incentives as encouragement. Here, too, there is a contrast with at least some European countries; in this era, Scandinavian social-democratic governments considerably expanded public child care services and also began to support fathers' caregiving activities, as with paid parental leaves.[82] Only Social Security (meaning contributory old age insurance and medical coverage) provided visibly public protection to almost all citizens, and it retained its political popularity, but it offered little political "cover" to other aspects of the U.S. welfare state.

Attacks on Welfare and Contemporary Welfare-State Restructuring

The turn from welfare-state expansionism and toward retrenchment got underway quietly under President Jimmy Carter, but President Ronald Reagan ostentatiously attacked social spending, fundamentally challenging the politics of welfare expansion and changing state fiscal calculations forever with his tax cuts. Cutbacks were held off in politically popular programs such as Social Security's old age coverage, but politically vulnerable programs such as AFDC were hit hard and the anti-state sentiments stirred up were useful in undercutting governmental fiscal capacities.[83] Reagan Republicans promoted an ideology of the unfettered, deregulated market, of tax cuts and self-reliance as the road to well-being, appealing to those who saw themselves as free of welfare "dependency." Deregulating labor markets exacerbated trends in which the economic position of less skilled men deteriorated, and women continued to join the labor force for longer periods of their lives as families now saw their standard of living as dependent on two earners. Conservatives and Republicans have favored deregulation even though it produces trends such as these, which undermined the breadwinner family so central to their thinking. A nascent authoritarian-paternalist strain among conservatives argued that those who received welfare—and the fathers of their children—did not face structural barriers but were "behaviorally dependent" and should be forced to behave properly.[84] Here one sees the seeds of policy initiatives to tighten child support enforcement and paternity establishment that have flourished in the contemporary period. Again, there is the familiar pattern of enforcing men's financial responsibilities while doing little to materially support breadwinner—or even simply wage earner—status; the level of moral exhortation (allegedly supported by social science research) about marriage, sexuality, and responsible fatherhood harkens back to the Progressive Era.[85]

Initiatives to expand coverage to working-aged men (and women) failed in the 1940s and 1970s, while in the 1980s, efforts to cut back on Social Security were stymied, but attacks on the already residual system of social provision for the working-aged poor had some success. Thus, the welfare state in the United States has a very distinctive form: coverage is concentrated on the elderly, while the majority of the working-aged population must depend on employment (or marriage to employed persons) with very little safety net. Much public attention focused on poverty among women, especially single mothers, yet there was an initially less visible erosion of the economic positions of many men, particularly men without college educations and poor men of color. Countless commentators note increasing income inequality over the 1980s and into the early 1990s, as well as the declining prospects of less skilled men, usually with little attention to gendered consequences.[86] Yet analysts such as William Julius Wilson and Kathleen Neckerman, foreshadowing the concerns of the "fragile families" wing of the fatherhood responsibility movement, linked the poor employment prospects of such men to their unsuitability as marriage partners.[87] If they couldn't be breadwinners—or at least economic providers—they were much less likely to marry. However, as would-be welfare reformers and the pro-marriage wing of the fatherhood responsibility movement soon began to point out, these men still fathered children, who were provided for by social assistance. While not exciting as much opprobrium as "welfare mothers," "deadbeat dads" who did not support their children have increasingly garnered concern.[88]

Without public protection for workers and trade unions, significant groups of men have been losing ground in terms of the quality of their employment (wages, access to privileged positions). In the "golden age," many U.S. breadwinners had their positions bolstered through *private* collective bargaining agreements, yet these were not guaranteed by the state. Once political and economic conditions changed, the unions were devastated, and market-based protections ("fringe benefits") for certain groups of formerly breadwinning men—particularly the less skilled—eroded considerably. At the same time, women's employment rates rose sharply with rising demand for women's labor, a well-developed gender-equity employment policy, the lack of support for women's unpaid care giving, the emergence of easily accessible divorce, and relatively cheap childcare.[89] Along the deteriorating conditions faced by some men, this has meant that a substantial number of women have been able to make inroads into "breadwinner" positions, or at the very least have gained the earnings capacities to support households.[90] This has occurred even as other women are increasingly impoverished, while the men who might once have been their husbands have been economically marginalized and, seemingly, have lost their potential as "marriageable" males (according to Wilson). Meanwhile, unemployment insurance is less and less effective in securing workers against the risks of unemployment, while unemployed women and men who cannot qualify for coverage under Unemployment Insurance (UI), or who have exhausted their benefits, must rely on other, income-tested sources of support: Food Stamps, locally-run general relief (available in only some cities), or Temporary Assistance to Needy Families (TANF) (if they have children).[91]

While the social politics spawned from the War on Poverty and its aftermath set the stage for the various backlashes of the Reagan era, this deterioration of men's position arguably also helped to elect Bill Clinton, even though his election relied disproportionately on the votes of women, especially unmarried ones, some of whom were also suffering the ill effects of Reagan-era increases in inequality and absolute declines in economic well-being. The problems of wage earners who couldn't "make work pay" was central to Clinton's political agenda, although policy initiatives to improve their situation were only unevenly successful.[92]

Among the working-aged population, it is only poor men who are being targeted as fathers and (potential) wage earners in need of government assistance via the welfare state, and only if their children's mothers have applied for social assistance. Welfare reform has featured new initiatives to impose fatherhood and economic providing on these men, sometimes accompanied by services.[93] But other strands of policy, working through the tax system, would assist low-wage fathers and mothers if they are employed. While the first set of policies highlights gendered roles—(welfare, single) mother, (absent, "deadbeat") father—the second targets low-wage-earning *parents*, effacing gender difference in an attempt to assist families.

Child support enforcement and paternity establishment, significant components of welfare reforms for the last three decades, work to enforce "breadwinner" or at least "income-sharer" roles on men (and women without custody of their children; it is gender-neutral in its targeting of non-custodial parents, although the majority of these are indeed men).[94] Provisions have again been strengthened in the 1996 Personal Responsibility and Work Opportunity Act which eliminated AFDC and established TANF.[95] Child support policy is understood as the public enforcement of a private, individual responsibility to support one's children. The state does not give benefits, but requires (not married) mothers and fathers to accept its services and cooperate with its efforts to establish and enforce child support obligations. Paternity establishment has also gained a higher profile as never-married mothers, even more than divorced mothers, are seen as responsible for many social problems.[96] Reducing the state's financial burden of supporting nonmarital children is one key motive for strengthening such policies, but clearly there is also a cultural component to the promotion of "responsible fatherhood" and marriage. Here is a clear example of the impact of liberalism—favoring private over public institutions—on gender relations. Given that public sources of support—family allowances, for instance—are all but ruled out, there are few options to increase funds going to single-parent families other than forcing or encouraging women to work for pay and men to contribute support.

There is no debate among policymakers about men's family roles; they should be employed, and they should provide for children they father. In both child support and paternity establishment, the state continues to assume the traditional gender division of labor and addresses men primarily as wage workers insofar as it requires them to pay child support yet does not require them to directly care for their child(ren). Nor does it require them to marry the mothers, although attempts to encourage marriage are being stepped up. In effect, paternity establishment policy attempts to "make men accountable" for their nonmarital heterosexual activity and enforcing child-support orders means that divorced fathers cannot evade their provider roles. These policies can be seen as processes of "disciplining fathers into breadwinning," although they have been only unevenly successful even in their own terms of getting non-custodial fathers to contribute financially to their children. Men's status as wage workers and family members are fused, such that a good father must be a good worker. And as welfare reform's impact on women has progressed, more attention has focused on how to make the men who father children receiving welfare into "responsible" fathers.

But there are differences in emphasis between different wings of the "fatherhood responsibility movement" as to what poor men need first: encouragement or mandates to become husbands if they are fathers (the so-called pro-marriage wing) or economic support to become "marriageable" (the "fragile families" approach).[97] For both groups, biological fatherhood brings financial responsibility, not any kind of *citizenship entitlement* to employment or benefits to assist in heading a household or contribute to raising children. But, perhaps, charity, faith-based services, or even local government bodies might assist some low-income fathers to assume responsibility. This trend has coalesced with broader cultural concerns about "fatherhood in crisis," reflected above all in the "decline of marriage," and the rise of divorce and nonmarital childbearing.

The "fragile families" wing of the fatherhood movement highlights the importance of providing economic means for men's "responsible" fathering and for marriage. This dovetails to some extent with the Democrats' strategy of "making work pay," which was to help low-income employed men as well as women, and allow both to be better parents and providers. In the influential version put forward by David Ellwood, Undersecretary of Health and Human Services in the Clinton administration, two-parent families would gain access to new benefits, including health insurance and expanded earned income credits; single mothers on welfare would lose their exemption from the requirement to be employed, but would get services to help them to work for pay.[98] This was an American version of an "individual model" of welfare, far more limited in coverage than the Scandinavian versions and with no explicit attention to caregiving, but similar in the expectation that all would work for pay and dual-earner families would be the norm. Clinton did not succeed in legislating many of the elements of this package; welfare reform was taken over by Republicans and made far more deterrent. But there were a few policy successes directed at low-income employed mothers and fathers by which their capacities to contribute to family support were somewhat enhanced: the increase in the minimum wage and the expansion of the Earned Income Tax Credit. Since the election of President George Bush, Democratic policy reformers have continued to stress the themes of "making work pay," but also now embrace initiatives that explicitly target poor fathers to help them to be involved with their children, to become and stay employed and out of prison, and possibly, to marry their children's mothers.[99]

The Republican vision emphasizes the importance of marriage per se, but has offered little to men who are not successful in the labor market. Republicans favor traditional gender roles but they have been unwilling to use substantial state resources to supplement men's wages or support mothering and caretaking work directly (as have Christian conservatives in, say, Germany). They hope to curtail women's autonomy by promoting a traditional moral agenda and restricting access to abortion and public services and benefits (in hopes that this will prevent women from having children out of wedlock or deciding to divorce). Men's providing will be supported materially through tax cuts only; this means that only men well-off enough to pay substantial taxes gain from these policies, although the Republican-led "cultural war," valorizing traditional masculine virtues, may also be appealing to other (working-class) men. The pro-marriage wing of the fatherhood responsibility movement includes Republican policy intellectuals affiliated with conservative think tanks, although there are also self-styled policy liberals who tout marriage.

While pro-marriage or responsible fatherhood initiatives, which have been considered as part of the welfare reauthorization legislation in 2002, have become politically charged and explicitly linked to visions of proper gender and sexual relations, a separate policy stream has been expanding, offering gender-neutral help to poor employed parents: parents who have earnings—the working poor, male or female—are eligible for a modest Earned Income Tax Credit (EITC), claimed through the tax system. The EITC, unlike other elements of the U.S. system of social provision, was expanded several times in the 1980s and 1990s, most significantly in Clinton's 1993 budget package, surpassing AFDC spending in 1992 and by 1996, doubling it.[100] The EITC provides targeted benefits for the working poor with children. So parenthood is important, but eligibility is gender-neutral; there is no special help for men as fathers, and assistance is tied to employment (indeed, the majority of the funds are going to single mothers, although low-wage fathers are being helped as well).[101]

This measure bolsters the incomes of those parents in the paid labor force, thus complementing recent policies that push (poor) mothers into paid work. However, it represents something of a departure vis-à-vis fathers, who had been basically excluded from state assistance under earlier policies. Changes in the labor market, notably the decline of jobs with "family-supporting" wages, have made it more difficult for people, including men, to rely on purely private sources of family support. Yet this help comes only to those fathers (and mothers) who are employed; in giving gender-neutral help to employed parents, U.S. policy here, too, links family roles to employment, for women and men.[102]

The emphasis, ideologically and materially, on private sources of welfare for both cash and care has been consequential for gender relations and men's positions. The strong emphasis on private responsibility for all but the aged means that men's identities—as fathers, citizens, workers—are not forged within the welfare state, but outside it, or even in opposition to it. Retirees are a partial exception here, but to some extent, gaining entitlement to social security is seen as parallel to market-based strategies for retirement investments and does not necessarily undermine this market orientation, which means the dominant identity for many men and some women is that of employee. This also implies that the key gender identity of family provider also depends on employment, and gets little backing from state programs. For low-wage employees, this may be beginning to change slightly with the expansion of the Earned Income Tax Credit, which supplements the earnings of low-income wage earners, both men and women, who are supporting children. But since this is administered through the tax system, rather than being a welfare benefit, the employment relation continues to be underlined.

Conclusion: Markets, Policy, and Gender

Today, as has been the case for most of the history of the United States, men must depend on markets (employment) for income and most benefits and services. They have little freedom *not* to engage in paid work; as we have long known, the U.S. welfare state does not promote decommodification (and increasingly, women are also subject to commodification). Moreover, class and racial stratification is reinforced in this system; one's status in the labor market largely determines the quality of one's health insurance, pension benefits, and so on. Indeed, compared with other countries' systems, men (and women) in the United States depend most on their situation as *employees* of specific corporations (or other employers) rather than on worker status per se, as linked to citizenship and contributions to public programs. Even the needy cannot get assistance unless they work ("workfare" in TANF or "real" work with earned income in EITC).

What about men's gender identities, and men's status as fathers? Parenthood receives scant support apart from what individuals can gain in the labor market, supplemented by tax credits for the poor, tax exemptions for the better off. Thus, men are treated principally as workers and employees, and get little bonus from being family "heads." Social security provides some advantages to "housewife-maintaining families" in that when wage earners retire, their wives will get coverage; yet given how many women now engage in paid employment at some point in their lives, this benefit will accrue to fewer and fewer people even if it is not phased out sometime in the future. To the extent that men have family households, they must earn the means to support them in the market; it is men's (on average) superior market positions that underwrite superiority in the family rather than direct state backing to breadwinners. Of course, it is important not to lose sight of *indirect* state benefits for household heads: the home mortgage interest deduction, for instance, the advantages of which accrue disproportionately to the affluent. (But again, crucially, this extends to employed women.)

It is also notable that, in comparative perspective, this system has proved relatively open to women. Those women who can succeed in the labor market gain the capacity to form households and support children, and increasing numbers do so, or at least contribute significant sums to family incomes. Most women cannot easily support a middle-class standard of living on their own earnings alone, but many men are in a similar position. Those excluded from favorable labor market positions—disproportionately but far from exclusively women—are the losers in this system. The openness of the labor market to women, under pressure from women's movements and state regulation, has had repercussions for gender relations in families and elsewhere, helping to undermine further the male breadwinner family.

The New Deal was something of an aberration in the history of the U.S. gendered welfare regime (as it was in other ways as well). For this is the only period in modern history in which the state offered substantial direct material support to men as breadwinners during their prime working years as well as in retirement. The lasting parts of the New Deal are those directed at citizens deemed not employable. During other significant periods of policy development, the Progressive Era as well as the 1960s and 1970s, the expectation that working-aged men would be employed and thus provide for their families without assistance from the welfare state has been sustained against suggested reforms which would have directed benefits or regulatory protection at men as breadwinners or workers.

Today, it may be that we are creating a limited departure from the policy legacy of treating men principally as workers or employees. To the extent that fathers are unable to sustain families on wages alone, they can be assisted through the EITC—as can mothers. Thus, the restructured labor market, with its expanding pool of low-wage work, in addition to its other social effects, may also be responsible for developing a policy the premise of which is that not all fathers can support families on their own with wages. It is also noteworthy that this policy is not limited to fathers. New lines of disadvantage now catch both men and women, while labor market participation remains the privileged form of entitlement in the United States. Without the kinds of state support for families such as child allowances available in other developed countries, U.S. fathers must depend on their capacities and luck in the labor market. Thus, one might well refer to a "crisis" in fatherhood for those men unable to contribute economically to their families' support—a part of an overall crisis of reproduction for marginalized groups of citizens and residents of one of the richest countries on earth.

NOTES

Notes to Introduction

1. For reviews of this literature, see Linda Gordon, "The New Feminist Scholarship on the Welfare State," in *Women, the State, and Welfare*, ed. Linda Gordon (Madison, WI: University of Wisconsin Press, 1990); Ann Orloff, "Gender in the Welfare State," *Annual Review of Sociology* 22 (1996): 16–80; Diane Sainsbury, *Gender, Equality, and Welfare States* (New York: Cambridge University Press, 1996); Lisa Brush, "Love, Toil, and Trouble: Motherhood and Feminist Politics," *Signs* (1996): 21; and Sonya Michel, "Maternalism and Beyond," paper presented at the Workshop on Maternalism, International Institute for Social History, Amsterdam, January 2002.

2. See Seth Koven and Sonya Michel, eds., *Mothers of a New World: Maternalist Politics and the Origins of Welfare States* (New York: Routledge, 1993); Gisela Bock and Pat Thane, eds., *Maternity and Gender Policies: Women and the Rise of European Welfare States* (London: Routledge, 1991); Linda Gordon, *Pitied but Not Entitled: Single Mothers and the History of Welfare* (Cambridge, MA: Harvard University Press, 1995); Susan Pedersen, *Family, Dependence and the Origins of Welfare States* (Cambridge: Harvard University Press, 1993).

3. See Robin Muncy, *Creating a Female Dominion in American Reform, 1890–1935* (New York: Oxford University Press, 1991); Regina Kunzel, *Fallen Women, Problem Girls: Unmarried Mothers and the Professionalization of Social Work* (New Haven: Yale University Press, 1993); Theda Skocpol, *Protecting Soldiers and Mothers* (Cambridge: Harvard University Press, 1992).

4. See Koven and Michel, *Mothers of a New World*; Gwendolyn Mink, *The Wages of Motherhood* (Ithaca, NY: Cornell University Press, 1995).

5. Koven and Michel, *Mothers of a New World*, 5.

6. See Eileen Boris, "The Power of Motherhood: Black and White Women Redefine the Political," in *Mothers of a New World*, ed. Koven and Michel; Bock and Thane, *Maternity and Gender Policies*; Gordon, *Pitied but Not Entitled*; Mink, *Wages of Motherhood*; Pedersen, *Family, Dependence and the Origins of Welfare States*.

7. Ann Orloff, "Farewell to Maternalism: Welfare Reform, Ending Entitlement for Poor Mothers, and Expanding the Claims of Poor Employed Parents," forthcoming in *Signs*.

8. See Lata Mani, *Contentious Traditions: The Debate on Sati in Colonial India* (Berkeley: University of California Press, 1998).

9. See Katherine Verdery, "From Parent-State to Family Patriarchs: Gender and Nation in Contemporary Eastern Europe," *East European Politics and Societies* 8 (1994): 225–55; Susan Gal and Gail Kligman, *The Politics of Gender after Socialism* (Princeton, NJ: Princeton University Press, 2000); and Lynne Haney, "Familial Welfare: Building the Hungarian Welfare Society, 1948–1968," *Social Politics* 7 (2000): 101–22.

10. See Sonya Rose, *Which People's War? National Identity and Citizenship in Wartime Britain, 1939–1945* (forthcoming, Oxford University Press).

11. For examples of contemporary forms of familialism, see Ching Kwan Lee, *Gender and the South China Miracle: Two Worlds of Factory Women* (Berkeley: University of California Press 1998); and Christina Gilmartin et al., eds., *Engendering China: Women, Culture, and the State* (Cambridge: Harvard University Press, 1994).

12. Julia Adams, "The Familial State: Elite Family Practices and State-Making in the Early Modern Netherlands," *Theory and Society* 23 (1994): 505–39; and Adams, "Culture in Rational-Choice Theories of State Formation," in *State/Culture: State Formation after the Cultural Turn*, ed. George Steinmetz (Ithaca, NY: Cornell University Press, 1999).

13. See George Steinmetz, "Introduction: Culture and the State," in Steinmetz, *State/Culture*.

14. In this sense, our use of familialism resembles Lynn Hunt's analysis of the familial narratives underlying the French Revolution, *The Family Romance of the French Revolution* (Berkeley: University of California Press, 1992). It also echoes social anthropologists' theories regarding reproduction as politics; see Faye Ginzburg and Rayna Rapp, eds., *Conceiving the New World Order: The Global Politics of Reproduction* (Berkeley: University of California Press, 1995); and Ginzburg and Rapp, "The Politics of Reproduction," *Annual Review of Anthropology* (1991): 311–43.

15. See, inter alia, Timothy Mitchell, *Colonizing Egypt* (Cambridge: Cambridge University Press, 1988); Mani, *Contentious Traditions;* Partha Chatterjee, *The Nation and Its Fragments*: *Colonial and Postcolonial Histories* (Princeton: Princeton University Press, 1993).

16. See, inter alia, Julia Clancy-Smith and Frances Gouda, eds., *Domesticating Empire: Race, Gender and Family Life in French and Dutch Colonialism* (Charlottesville: University Press of Virginia, 1998); Lisa Pollard, *Nurturing the Nation: The Family Politics of Colonizing and Liberating Egypt* (forthcoming, University of California Press).

17. For widow remarriage in India, see Mani, *Contentious Traditions;* Chatterjee, *The Nation and Its Fragments;* and Tanika Sazkar, "The Hindu Wife and the Hindu Nation," *Studies in History* 8 (1992): 213–35. For child marriage in India, see Antoinette Burton, "From Child Bride to 'Hindoo Lady': Rukhmabai and the Debate on Sexual Responsibility in Imperial Britain," *American Historical Review* 103 (1998): 1119–46. For clitoridectomy, see Ronald Hyam, *Empire and Sexuality: The British Experience* (Manchester, U.K., and New York: Manchester University Press, 1980); and Susan Pedersen, "National Bodies, Unspeakable Acts: The Sexual Politics of Colonial Policy-Making," *Journal of Modern History* 63, no. 4 (1991): 647–80.

18. Mrinalini Sinha, *Colonial Masculinity: The 'Manly Englishman' and the 'Effeminate Bengali' in the Late Nineteenth Century* (Manchester, U.K., and New York: Manchester University Press, 1995).

19. See Sazkar, "Hindu Wife," Chatterjee, "Colonialism, Nationalism and the Colonized Woman," and Chatterjee, "A Religion of Urban Domesticity: Sri Ramakrishna and the Calcutta Middle Class," in *Subaltern Studies VII: Writings on South Asian History and Society*, ed. Partha Chatterjee and Gyanedra Pandey (Delhi, India: Oxford University Press, 1992), 40–68.

20. Pederson, "National Bodies," Pollard, *Nurturing the Nation*.

21. Ann Stoler has argued that colonies were laboratories for defining behavior for the metropole; see Fredrick Cooper and Ann Laura Stoler, eds., *Tensions of Empire*: *Colonial Cultures in a Bourgeois World* (Berkeley: University of California Press, 1997).

22. Martha Lampland, "Family Portraits: Gendered Images of Nation in Nineteenth-Century Hungary," *East European Politics and Societies* 8 (1994): 287–316; Gail Kligman,

The Politics of Duplicity (Berkeley: University of California Press, 1998); and Verdery, "From Parent-State to Family Patriarchs."

23. Verdery, "From Parent-State to Family Patriarchs," 230.

24. Joanna Goven, "Gender Politics in Hungary: Autonomy and Antifeminism," in *Gender and the Politics of Postcommunism*, ed. Nanette Funk and Magda Mueller (New York: Routledge, 1993).

25. Ibid.; see also Lynne Haney, *Inventing the Needy: Gender and the Politics of Welfare in Hungary* (Berkeley: University of California Press, 2002).

26. Gal and Kligman, *Politics of Gender after Socialism*, 68.

27. Goven, "Gender Politics in Hungary: Autonomy and Antifeminism."

28. Verdery, "From Parent-State to Family Patriarchs."

29. Gal and Kligman, *Politics of Gender after Socialism*, 70.

30. For more on these shifts, see Barbara Einhorn, *Cinderella Goes to Market* (London: Verso, 1993); Nanette Funk and Magda Mueller, eds., *Gender and the Politics of Postcommunism* (New York: Routledge, 1993); and Susan Gal and Gail Kligman, eds., *Reproducing Gender: Politics, Publics, and Everyday Life after Socialism* (Princeton, NJ: Princeton University Press, 2000).

31. Zionism, as conceived by its early architects, combined a rejection of the Enlightenment visions of the body politic that had failed to give European Jews equality with reifications of Enlightenment ideals.

Notes to Chapter 2

1. Public Records Office (hereafter PRO), Great Britain, Foreign Office (hereafter, FO) 141/522/9085, April 10, 1919. This file contains reports for the Foreign Office regarding European and American coverage of the 1919 demonstrations.

2. PRO/FO 141/751/8941. May 11, 1919. Dispatch no. 216 from Consul General Sir Milne Cheetham (1869–1938) to British Foreign Secretary Lord Curzon (1859–1925).

3. Juan R.I. Cole, *Colonialism and Revolution in the Middle East: Social and Cultural Origins of Egypt's 'Urabi Movement* (Princeton, NJ: Princeton University Press, 1993).

4. Ronald Robinson and John Gallagher, with Alice Denny, *Africa and the Victorians: The Official Mind of Imperialism* (London: Macmillan, 1981).

5. Cited in Alfred Milner, *Britain's Work in Egypt, By an Englishman in the Egyptian Service* (London: T. Edinburgh and A. Constable, 1892), 3.

6. PRO/FO 141/168. Dispatch from Dufferin to Granville, November 18, 1882.

7. PRO/FO 141/168. Dispatch from Dufferin to Granville, January 26, 1883.

8. PRO/FO 633/84. "Situation in Egypt. Lord Cromer's Account," n/d.

9. Edward Dicey, "Our Route to India" in *The Nineteenth Century* 1 (1877): 660–84.

10. Alfred Milner, *England in Egypt* (London: E. Arnold, 1909), 21–23.

11. Clara Boyle, *Boyle of Cairo, A Diplomat's Adventure in the Middle East* (London: Titus and Sons, 1965), 38.

12. Ibid., 36–37.

13. Dicey, "Our Route to India," 674.

14. Egyptian Ministry of Education, *Programmes de l'enseignement primaire et de l'enseignement secondaire appovés par arrete ministeriel 849 en date du 16 September 1901* (Boulaq, Egypt: Matba'at al-Ahiliyya, 1901).

15. Parliamentary Papers, *Report on His Majesty's Agent and Consul-General on the Finances, Administration and Condition of Egypt and the Sudan* (London: Harrison and Sons, 1905), 571.

16. Egyptian Ministry of Education, *Program al-durus: al-madaris al-ibtida'iyya* (al-daraja al-ula) (Boulaq, Egypt: Matba'at al-Ahiliyya, 1885).

17. Egyptian Ministry of Education, *Programmes*.

18. *Parliamentary Papers, Report on His Majesty's Agent and Consul-General on the Finances, Administration and Condition of Egypt and the Sudan*, 1916.

19. Egyptian National Archives, 'Abdiin Collection, Box 230, 1922.

20. See Lisa Pollard, *Nurturing the Nation: The Family Politics of Colonizing and Liberating Egypt 1805–1922* (forthcoming, University of California Press); Mona L. Russell, *Creating the New Woman; Consumerism, Education and National Identity in Egypt, 1863–1922* (Ph.D. diss., Georgetown University, 1997); Omnia Shakry, "Schooled Mothers and Structured Play: Child Rearing in Turn-of-the-Century Egypt," in *Remaking Women: Feminism and Modernity in the Middle East*, ed. Lila Abu-Lughod (Princeton, NJ: Princeton University Press, 1998), 126–70.

21. Sayyid Afandi Mohammad Ahad, *Kitab al-tahliya wal-targhib fil tarbiyya wal-tahdhib* (Cairo: Matba'at al-Amiriyya, 1911).

22. Egyptian Ministry of Education, *al-Tahaja wal-mut'alia* (Boulaq, Egypt: Matba'at al-Amiriyya, 1911).

23. Hasan 'Abd al-Aziz, *Durus al-akhlaq* (Cairo: Ministry of Public Instruction, 1913), 6.

24. Hasan 'Abd al-Aziz, *Durus al-akhlaq al maqadara 'ala tulab al sana al-ula* (Cairo: Ministry of Public Instruction, 1913), 40.

25. Ami Ayalon, *The Press in the Arab Middle East* (Oxford: Oxford University Press, 1995) and Cole, *Colonialism and Revolution*.

26. *al-Hilal*, September 8, 1900.

27. *al-Ustadh*, August 3 and November 29, 1892.

28. *al-Manar*, 1901: 6.

29. *al-Muqtataf*, January 1, 1895.

30. Ibid.

31. Ibid.

32. See Beth Baron, *The Women's Awakening in Egypt: Culture, Society and the Press* (New Haven: Yale University Press, 1994); Russell, *Creating the New Woman*; and Marilyn Booth, "'May Her Likes Be Multiplied': Famous Women, Biography and Gendered Prescription in Egypt, 1892-1935," *Signs* 22, no. 4 (1997): 827–90.

33. *Jaridat al-Fatah*, 4 (893): 166.

34. See Russell, *Creating the New Woman*, and Booth, "May Her Likes Be Multiplied."

35. Deeb, *Party Politics in Egypt*, 53.

36. Ibid., 64; and Abd al-Rahman al-Rafa`i, *Thawrat 1919* (Cairo: Dar al-Ma`arif, 1967), 68–69.

37. *Discours Politiques, Prononcé par Ahmed Loutfi al-Sayyid* (Cairo: Impremerie al-Garidah, 1909), 5–6.

38. Ahmed Lutfi al-Sayyid Pasha, *Safahat matwiyya min tarikh al-haraka al-istiqlaliyya fi Misr* (Cairo, 1946), 20–22.

39. *Oeuvres du Congrès National Egyptien, Tenu a Bruxelles le 22, 23, 24 Septembre, 1910* (Bruges, Belgium: St. Catherine's Press, 1910).

40. PRO/FO 141/748/8822 March 23, 1919.

41. PRO/FO 848/12 March 23, 1919.

42. PRO/FO 848/12 January 1920.

43. *al-Lata'if al-Musawwara* (Illustrated Niceties), August 20, 1920.

44. Ibid. August 2, 1920.

45. Ibid. August 27, 1919.
46. Ibid. January 2, 1920.
47. Ibid. July 19, 1920.
48. Ibid. April 28, 1919.
49. The poem was also carried in *al-Ahram, al-Sufur*, and other journals. Another of Hafith al-Ibrahim's poems, "To Children," was also commonly circulated in the Revolutionary press.
50. See, for example, *al-Sufur,* May 8 and May 15, 1919.
51. Margot Badran, *Feminists, Islam and Nation: Gender and the Making of Modern Egypt* (Princeton, NJ: Princeton University Press, 1995).
52. *al-Ahram,* July 5, 1919.
53. *al-Lata'if al-Musawwara,* June 9, 1919.
54. This image of the "nation" or constitutional government was rare at the time of the Revolution. It had previously appeared in the press in 1906, when Mustafa Kamil was represented petitioning the French government for Egypt's freedom. The French government is represented in the same sort of Greco-Roman costume. Again upon the occasion of Kamil's funeral, Egypt is depicted in similar attire. See *Sajil al-hilal al-musawwar, 1892–1992* (Cairo: Dar al-Hilal, 1992), vol. 1, 80 and 454–55.
55. Partha Chatterjee, *The Nation and Its Fragments: Colonial and Postcolonial Histories* (Princeton, NJ: Princeton University Press, 1993); Ann Stoler and Frederick Cooper, eds., *Tensions of Empire: Colonial Cultures in a Bourgeois World* (Berkeley: University of California Press, 1997); Lata Mani, *Contentious Traditions: The Debate on Sati in Colonial India* (Berkeley: University of California Press, 1998).
56. Seth Koven and Sonya Michel, eds., *Mothers of a New World: Maternalist Politics and the Origins of Welfare States* (New York: Routledge, 1993).
57. Mohammed Fadel, *Nasser 56* (Cairo: 1996).

Notes to Chapter 3

1. Nancy Armstrong and Leonard Tennenhouse make a similar argument for U.S. colonists in *The Imaginary Puritan: Literature, Intellectual Labor, and the Origins of Personal Life* (Berkeley, CA: University of California Press, 1992).
2. Donna Haraway, *Primate Visions: Gender, Race, and Nature in the World of Modern Science* (New York: Routledge, 1989); Ann Stoler, "Rethinking Colonial Categories: European Communities and the Boundaries of Rule," *Comparative Studies in Society and History* 13, no. 1 (1989): 134–61; Stoler, "Making Empire Respectable: The Politics of Race and Sexual Morality in 20th Century Colonial Cultures," *American Ethnologist* 16, no. 4 (1989): 634–60; "Stoler, Carnal Knowledge and Imperial Power: Gender, Race, and Morality in Colonial Asia," in *Gender at the Crossroads of Knowledge: Feminist Anthropology in the Postmodern Era,* ed. Micaela di Leonard (Berkeley: University of California, 1991), 51–101; and Ann Stoler and Frederick Cooper, eds., *Tensions of Empire: Colonial Cultures in a Bourgeois World* (Berkeley: University of California Press, 1997); Gaytri Chakravorty Spivak, "Can the Subaltern Speak," in *Marxism and the Interpretation of Cultures,* ed. Cary Nelson and Lawrence Grossberg (Urbana: University of Illinois Press, 1988): 271-316. Spivak, "Cultural Talks in the Hot Peace: Revisiting the 'Global Village,'" in *Cosmopolitics,* ed. Pheng Cheah and Bruce Robbins (Minneapolis: University of Minnesota Press, 1998); Spivak, "Cultural Studies Questionnaire," *Travesia* 3, nos. 1–2 (1994): 286; and Spivak, *Outside in the Teaching Machine* (New York: Routledge, 1993).

3. Kenneth Ballhatchet argues that the first "lock hospital" was in India, and its initial purpose was prevention of contagion from leprosy; see *Race, Sex, and Class under the Raj: Imperial Attitudes and Policies and their Critics, 1793–1905* (London: Weidenfeld and Nicolson, 1980).

4. Gail Hershatter, *Dangerous Pleasures: Prostitution and Modernity in Twentieth-Century Shanghai* (Berkeley: University of California Press, 1997), 6–7.

5. For work on prostitution as labor, see Christine Stansell, *City of Women: Sex and Class in New York, 1789–1860* (New York: Knopf, 1986); Judith Walkowitz, *Prostitution and Victorian Society: Women, Class, and the State* (New York: Cambridge University Press, 1980); Luise White, *Comforts of Home: Prostitution in Colonial Nairobi* (Chicago: University of Chicago Press, 1990); Hyam, *Sex and the British Empire*. For scholarship on prostitution as symbol, transgression, and site of disease, see Alain Corbin, "Commercial Sexuality in Nineteenth Century France: A System of Images and Regulations," *Representations* 14 (spring): 209–18; Alan Brandt, *No Magic Bullet: A Social History of Venereal Disease in the United States Since 1880* Expanded ed. (New York: Oxford University Press, 1987); Ruth Rosen, *The Lost Sisterhood: Prostitution in America, 1900–1918* (Baltimore: Johns Hopkins, 1982); Kathleen Barry, *Female Sexual Slavery* (New York: New York University Press, 1979); Hershatter, *Dangerous Pleasures*.

6. For prostitution and social organization, see e.g., Peggy Pascoe, *Relations of Rescue*; Guy, Walkowitz, Stansell, Rosen in *The Lost Sisterhood*, 12.

7. Cynthia Enloe, *Bananas, Beaches, and Bases: Making Feminist Sense of International Politics* (Berkeley: University of California Press, 1990).

8. Kenneth Ballhatchet, *Race, Sex, and Class under the Raj: Imperial Attitudes and Policies and their Critics, 1793–1905* (London: Weidenfeld and Nicolson, 1980); see also David Arnold, *Colonizing the Body: State Medicine and Epidemic Disease in Nineteenth-Century India* (Berkeley: University of California Press, 1993); Vron Ware, *Beyond the Pale: White Women, Racism, and History* (New York: Verso, 1992); Philippa Levine, "Venereal Disease, Prostitution, and the Politics of Empire: The Case of British India," *Journal of the History of Sexuality* 4, no. 4 (1994): 579–602.

9. Frederick Whiting, "The Social Hygiene Movement," Rockefeller Archive Center, Rockefeller Family Archives, Record Group 2, Rockefeller Boards. Series 3, Subseries 2, Box 6, File 40, 1916.

10. Arnold, *Colonizing the Body*, 84.

11. Stoler makes this point as well in "Carnal Knowledge."

12. Cited in Ballhatchet, *Race, Sex and Class under the Raj*, 14.

13. Levine, "Venereal Disease, Prostitution, and the Politics of Empre," 586–87; Elizabeth Van Heyningen, "The Social Evil in the Cape Colony 1868-1902: Prostitution and the Contagious Diseases Acts," *Journal of Southern African Studies* 10, no. 2 (1984): 170–97.

14. Ballhatchet, *Race, Sex and Class under the Raj*, 40–67; 144–59. Arnold, *Colonizing the Body*, 83–87.

15. See, e.g., Nancy Armstrong, *Desire and Domestic Fiction*

16. Levine, "Venereal Disease, Prostitution, and the Politics of Empre," 586–87.

17. James Frances Warren, "Prostitution and the Politics of Venereal Disease: Singapore, 1870-98," *Journal of Southeast Asian Studies* 21, no. 2 (1990): 360–83; Lenore Manderson, "Colonial Desires: Sexuality, Race, and Gender in British Malaya," *Journal of the History of Sexuality* 7, no. 3 (1997): 372–88; Stephanie Beswick and Jay Spaulding, "Sex, Bondage, and the Market: The Emergence of Prostitution in Northern Sudan, 1750-1950," *Journal of the History of Sexuality* 5, no. 4 (1995): 512–34.

18. Mary Murnane and Kay Daniels, "Prostitutes as 'Purveyors of Disease': Venereal Disease Legislation in Tasmania, 1868-1945," *Hecate* 5 (1979): 5-21.

19. See Carol Summers, "Intimate Colonialism: The Imperial Production of Reproduction in Uganda, 1907-1925" *Signs* 16, no. 4 (1991): 787-807. Megan Vaughan, *Curing Their Ills: Colonial Power and African Illness* (Stanford, CA: Stanford University Press, 1991), 132-37, and Diana Jeater, *Marriage, Perversion, and Power: The Construction of Moral Discourse in Southern Rhodesia, 1894-1930* (Oxford: Clarendon Press, 1993).

20. Elizabeth Van Heyningen, "The Social Evil in the Cape Colony 1868-1902," 173.

21. Sueann Caulfield, "The Birth of Mangue: Race, Nation, and the Politics of Prostitution in Rio de Janeiro, 1850-1942," in *Sex and Sexuality in Latin America*, ed. Daniel Balderston and Donna Guy, (New York: New York University Press, 1997). Regulation was introduced in Cuba in 1873. Ligia Vigo, "Gendered and Racialized Discourses on Prostitution in Havana (1873-1926): A Nation-Building Project," unpublished paper; David McCreery, "This Life of Misery and Shame: Female Prostitution in Guatemala City, 1880-1920," *Journal of Latin American Studies* 18 (November 1986): 333-53; Sheldon Garon, "The Oldest Debate? Prostitution and the State in Imperial Japan," *American Historical Review* 98, no. 3 (1993): 710-32; Laurie Bernstein, *Sonia's Daughters: Prostitutes and their Regulation in Imperial Russia* (Berkeley: University of California Press, 1995).

22. Van Heyningen, "The Social Evil in the Cape Colony 1868-1902," 177.

23. Manderson, "Colonial Desires," 378. Manderson makes this point more broadly in her *Sickness and the State*. Similarly, Nancy Hunt looks at questions of maternal health in relation to the reproduction of a colonial labor force in the Belgian Congo in "Le Bebé en Brousse" in Stoler et al., *Tensions of Empire*.

24. Ratnabali Chatterjee, "The Indian Prostitute as a Colonial Subject: Bengal 1864-1883," *Canadian Women's Studies/Les Cahiers de la Femme* 13, no. 1 (1992): 51-55; Egal Feldman, "Prostitution, the Alien Woman and the Progressive Imagination, 1910-1915" *American Quarterly* 19 (1967): 195.

25. Warren, "Prostitution and the Politics of Venereal Disease."

26. See Eileen Findlay's excellent discussion of the uses of Puerto Rico in "Love in the Tropics: Marriage, Divorce, and the Construction of Benevolent Colonialism in Puerto Rico, 1898-1910," Gilbert Joseph, Catherine LeGrand, and Ricardo Salvatore, *Close Encounters of Empire: Writing the Cultural History of U.S. Latin American Relations* (Durham, NC: Duke University Press, 1998).

27. The sources for this account are legion. For a discussion of the *Maine* and its historiography, see Louise Perez, "The Meaning of the *Maine*: Causation and the Historiography of the Spanish-American War," *Pacific Historical Review* 58, no. 3 (1989): 293-322; for a particularly influential account of U.S. imperialism as a tale of innocents abroad, see George F. Kennan, *American Diplomacy, 1900-1950* (Chicago: University of Chicago Press, 1951); for an early and trenchant critique of the notion of American innocence see William Appleman Williams, *The Tragedy of American Diplomacy* (New York: Dell, 1960); for another, see Charles Vevier, "American Continentalism: An Idea of Expansion, 1845-1910," *American Historical Review* 65 (1960): 323-35 and Walter LaFeber, *The New Empire: An Interpretation of American Expansion, 1860-1898* (Ithaca, NY: Cornell, 1963); among the more influential responses (insisting on the imperialism as accident thesis) was James A. Field, Jr., "American Imperialism: The Worst Chapter in Almost Any Book," *American Historical Review* 83 (1978): 645. A feminist-revisionist account may be found in Kristin

Hoganson, *Fighting for American Manhood: How Gender Politics Provoked the Spanish-American and Philippine-American War* (New Haven: Yale University Press, 2000).

28. Oscar Compomanes, "1898 and the Nature of the New Empire," *Radical History Review* 73 (1998): 1.

29. Amy Kaplan, "Left Alone with America," in Kaplan and Donald Pease, *Cultures of United States Imperialism*.

30. Compomanes, "1898 and the Nature of the New Empire," 1–14.

31. This is actually only partially true even of the mainland United States; there were quite a number of short-lived municipal ordinances between 1870 and 1910, including in St. Louis, Detroit, Minneapolis, Buffalo, Philadelphia, Cincinnati, San Francisco, and Douglas, AZ. For the U.S. regulation campaign, see Burnham, 890-92; Pivar, 50-77; Rosen, 9. Historians have consistently underestimated the number of municipal ordinances that were enacted between 1870 and 1910; Brandt, for example, mentions only St. Louis (p. 35). For Buffalo, Philadelphia, and Cincinnati, see Ludwig Weiss, "The Prostitution Problem in Its Relation to Law and Medicine," *JAMA* 47, no. 25 (December 22, 1906): 2074.

32. Brandt, *No Magic Bullet*, 35.

33. Herman Goodman, "The Antivenereal Disease Campaign In Panama," *Journal of Social Hygiene* 9 (1923): 160-67; D. J. Pivar, "The Military, Prostitution, and Colonial Peoples: India and the Philippines, 1885-1917," *Journal of Sexuality Research* 17, no. 3 (1981): 256-69; A. J. Orenstein, "Sanitary Inspection of the Canal Zone," *Public Health Papers and Reports* 28 (1913): 65-76; Excerpt from a report of the Health Department of the Panama Canal Zone *Social Hygiene* 5, no. 2 (1919): 259-64.

34. Howard Zinn, *The Twentieth Century: A People's History* (New York: Harper, 1998), 139.

35. Goodman, "The Antivenereal Disease Campaign in Panama," 160-67; Pivar, "The Military, Prostitution, and Colonial Peoples: India and the Philippines, 1885-1917," 256-69; Orenstein, "Sanitary Inspection of the Canal Zone," 65-76; Excerpt from a report of the Health Department of the Panama Canal Zone, 259-64.

36. "Military Government of Santo Domingo, Executive Order No. 96," printed in the *Gaceta Oficial* 33: 2859, NA, RG 350, Bureau of Insular Affairs, War Department.

37. Charles Jenkinson, "Vera Cruz: What American Occupation Has Meant to a Mexican Community," *The Survey* 33 (1914): 138.

38. "A Warning Cry for Our Troops on the Border," *Literary Digest* 53 (1916): 254.

39. Hugh Hampton Young, *Hugh Young: A Surgeon's Autobiography* (New York: Harcourt, 1940), 301.

40. Jenkinson, "Vera Cruz: What American Occupation Has Meant to a Mexican Community," 138.

41. Vigo, "Gendered and Racialized Discourses," 3.

42. *Investigation of Panama Canal Matters, Hearings Before the Committee on Inter-Oceanic Canals of the U.S. Senate*, vol. one, 928-81. My thanks to Julie Greene for this cite.

43. Goodman, "The Antivenereal Disease Campaign in Panama," 162.

44. Luis Dery, "Prostitution in Colonial Manila," *Philippine Studies* 39 (1991): 475-89.

45. Ian Tyrell, *Women's World/Women's Empire: The Women's Christian Temperance Union in International Perspective, 1880–1930* (Chapel Hill: University of North Carolina Press, 1991), 191-217.

46. M. J. Exner, "Prostitution in its Relation to the Army on the Mexican Border," *Social Hygiene* 3, no. 2 (April 1917): 220.

47. Walkowitz, *Prostitution and Victorian Society*.
48. Quoted in Enloe, *Bananas, Beaches, and Bases*, 83.
49. Tyrell, *Women's World/Women's Empire*, 195.
50. Van Heyningen, "The Social Evil in the Cape Colony, 1868-1902," 177.
51. Ibid., 197-212; Whiting, "The Social Hygiene Movement," 1.
52. Quote, NWCTU, *Annual Report*, 1897, p. 107, cited in Tyrell, 206. The question of Somerset's support for regulation was the major issue of the WWCTU convention of October, 1897, resulting in protest and resignations of WCTU leaders in the British colonies and elsewhere, including Australia, India, New Zealand, South Africa, Canada, France, Denmark, and Sweden. In January 1989, as Willard's impending death threatened to exacerbate this fracture in the ranks of the WCTU, Lady Henry Somerset recanted. Tyrell tells this story, 202-209.
53. Antoinette Burton, "The White Woman's Burden: British Feminists and 'The Indian Woman,' 1865-1915," in *Western Women and Imperialism: Complicity and Resistance*, ed. Nupur Chaudhuri and Margaret Strobel (Bloomington: Indiana University Press, 1992), 137-57. Quote, 145.
54. Warren, "Prostitution and the Politics of Venereal Disease"; Garon, "The World's Oldest Debate."
55. Manderson, "Colonial Desires." See also her *Sickness and the State: Sexuality, Race and Gender in British Malaysia, 1870-1940* (New York: Cambridge University Press, 1996).
56. Ballhatchet, *Race, Sex and Class under the Raj*; Ratnabali Chatterjee, "The Indian Prostitute as a Colonial Subject: Bengal 1864-1883."
57. F. B. Smith, "The Contagious Diseases Acts Reconsidered," *Bulletin of the History of Medicine* 3 (1990): 197-215.
58. Walkowitz, *Prostitutes and Victorian Society*, introduction.
59. Karen Offen, "Depopulation, Nationalism, and Feminism in Fin-de-Siècle France," *American Historical Review* 89 (June 1984):648-76; Alisa Klaus, "Depopulation and Race Suicide: Maternalism and Pronatalist Ideologies in France and the United States," in *Mothers of a New World: Maternalist Politics and the Origins of Welfare States*, ed. Seth Koven and Sonya Michel (New York: Routledge, 1993), 188-212.
60. Prince A. Morrow, "The Control of Syphilis and Venereal Diseases," *Boston Medical and Surgical Journal* (February 7, 1907): 170 (paper read before the Boston Library and the Suffolk District Medical Society, Dec. 19, 1906); Morrow, "Venereal Diseases and Their Relation to Infant Mortality and Race Deterioration," *New York Medical Journal* (1911): 1317.
61. *The Shield*, 1897. Cited in Burton, "The White Woman's Burden," 142.
62. José Flores Ramos, "Virgins, Whores, and Martyrs: Prostitution in the Colony, 1898-1917," in Felix Matos Rodrigues and Linda Delgado, eds. *Puerto Rican Women's History: New Perspectives* (Armonk, NY: M.E. Sharpe, 1998), 83-104.
63. James Dietz, *Economic History of Puerto Rico: Institutional Change and Capitalist Development* (Princeton, NJ: Princeton University Press, 1986), 21-25; José Luis González, *El País de Quatro Pisos*, 35-37; Adalberto López, ed., *The Puerto Ricans: Their History, Culture, and Society* (Cambridge, MA: Schenkman Publishing Company, 1980), 475-90.
64. Muñoz Marín in *La Democracia*, 1893; quoted in Eileen Findlay, "Decency and Democracy: The Politics of Prostitution in Ponce, Puerto Rico, 1890-1900," *Feminist Studies* 23, no. 3 (1997): 471-99; 476.
65. A. Hyatt Verrill, *Porto Rico: Past and Present and San Domingo of Today* (New York: Dodd, Mead and Co., 1926 [c. 1914]), 139-40.

66. Sylvester Baxter, "Porto Rico Under the Stars and Stripes: A Quarter Century of Progress," *The American Review of Reviews* 67 (1923): 504; Arthur Warner, "Progress (and Poverty) in Porto Rico," *Nation* 117, no. 3032 (1923): 159.

67. Victor Clark, et al., *Puerto Rico and Its Problems* (New York: Brookings Institute, 1930) summarizes the death rate figures from the annual governor's reports. From 1900 to 1930, the death rate remained relatively constant, between 22 and 25 per thousand.

68. Ramos, "Virgins, Whores, and Martyrs."

69. Howard Kern, *Special Report of the Attorney General of Porto Rico to the Governor of Porto Rico Concerning the Suppression of Vice and Prostitution in Connection with the Mobilization of the National Army at Camp Las Casas, February 1, 1919* (San Juan: Bureau of Supplies, Printing, and Transportation, 1919).

70. Findlay, "Love in the Tropics."

71. *Union Signal*, 3 May, 1917, 3 (Microfilm edition, Roll 26).

72. Unsigned article, "WCTU Joins Hands with Police Department in Fight Against Vice," *Union Signal* (August 29, 1918): 7 (Microfilm edition, Roll 27); for representations as "girls," see, e.g., "Report on Arecibo Hospital" and "Awakening in Porto Rico."

73. Warwick Anderson, "Where is the Postcolonial History of Medicine?" *Bulletin of the History of Medicine* 72 (1998): 522-30. My thanks to Nyan Shah for clarifying the quarantine point for me; see his *Contagious Divides: Epidemics and Race in San Francisco's Chinatown* (Berkeley: University of California Press, 2001).

Notes to Chapter 4

1. Jacques Le Rider, *Modernity and the Crises of Identity: Culture and Society in Fin-de-Siècle Vienna,* trans. Rosemary Morris (New York: Continuum, 1993).

2. Steven M. Cohen and Paula E. Hyman, eds, *The Jewish Family: Myths and Reality* (New York: Holmes & Meier, 1986); and Sabine Hödl and Martha Keil, eds., *Die jüdische Familie in Geschichte und Gegenwart* (Berlin: Philo Verlagsgesellschaft mbH, 1999).

3. Michael A. Meyer, *The Origins of the Modern Jew: Jewish Identity and European Culture in Germany, 1749–1824* (Detroit: Wayne State University Press, 1967), 8.

4. Michael A. Meyer, *Jewish Identity in the Modern World* (Seattle: University of Washington Press, 1990), 6.

5. Chae Ran Freeze, *Jewish Marriage and Divorce in Imperial Russia* (Hanover, NH: Brandeis University Press, 2002), 11–12.

6. Mitchell B. Hart, *Social Science and the Politics of Modern Jewish Identity* (Stanford: Stanford University Press, 2000), 75.

7. The Zionist use of the term "assimilation" is thoroughly analyzed in Michael Stanislawski, *Zionism and the Fin de Siècle: Cosmopolitanism and Nationalism from Nordau to Jabotinsky* (Berkeley: University of California Press, 2001), 6-15. According to Stanislawski, it was used polemically to assert their belief that the Jews had no future in Europe.

8. Ritchie Robertson, "Reinventing the Jews: From Moses Mendelssohn to Theodor Herzl," in Ritchie Robertson and Edward Timms, eds. *Theodor Herzl and the Origins of Zionism: Austrian Studies VIII* (Edinburgh: Edinburgh University Press, 1997), 3-9.

9. Hugo Bergmann [Schmuel Hugo Bergman], *Tagebücher und Briefe,* ed. Miriam Sambursky, 2 vols. (Königstein, 1985): vol. I; 12; cited in Robertson, "From Moses Mendelssohn to Theodor Herzl," 7. For more on Bergmann, see Hillel J. Kieval, *The Making of Czech Jewry: National Conflict and Jewish Society in Bohemia, 1870–1918* (New York: Oxford University Press, 1988); and Adolf Gaisbauer, *Davidstern und Doppeladler:*

Zionismus und jüdischer Nationalismus in Österreich, 1882–1918 (Vienna: Böhlau Verlag, 1988).

10. David Biale, "Zionism as an Erotic Revolution," in Howard Eilberg-Schwartz, ed., *People of the Body: Jews and Judaism from an Embodied Perspective* (Albany: State University of New York Press, 1992), 283-307; Deborah Bernstein, ed., *Pioneers and Homemakers: Jewish Women in Pre-State Israel* (Albany: State University of New York Press, 1992); Rachel Elboim-Dror, "Gender in Utopianism: The Zionist Case," *History Workshop Journal*, 37 (1994): 99-116; Matti Bunzl, "Theodor Herzl's Zionism as Gendered Discourse," in *Austrian Studies* VIII, ed. Robertson and Timms, 74-86; Angelika Montel, "Women and Zionist Journalism: 'Frauen in der *Welt* der Männer,'" trans. Ritchie Robertson, in *Austrian Studies* VIII, ed. Robertson and Timms, 87-95; Margailit Shilo, "The Double or Multiple Image of the New Hebrew Woman," *Nashim: A Journal of Jewish Women's Studies & Gender Issues* 1 (Winter, 1998): 73-94; Claudia Prestel, "Zionist Rhetoric and Women's Equality (1897-1933): Myth and Reality," in *San Jose Studies*, 20/3 (1994): 4-28; and Billie Melman, "Re-Generation: Nation and the Construction of Gender in Peace and War—Palestinian Jews, 1900-1918" in *Borderlines: Genders and Identities in War and Peace, 1870–1930*, ed. Billie Melman (New York: Routledge, 1998): 121-40.

11. Biale, "Zionism as an Erotic Revolution," 283-84.

12. Michael Berkowitz, "Transcending 'Tzimmes and Sweetness': Recovering the History of Zionist Women in Central and Western Europe, 1897-1933," in *Active Voices: Women in Jewish Culture*, ed. Maurice Sacks (Urbana and Chicago: University of Illinois Press, 1995), 41; Michael Berkowitz, *Zionist Culture and West European Jewry before the First World War* (Cambridge: Cambridge University Press, 1993).

13. Otto Weininger, *Geschlecht und Charakter* (Munich, 1980). See also LeRider, *Modernity and Crises of Identity*, esp. chap. 9.

14. Klaus Hödl, *Als Bettler in die Leopoldstadt: Galizische Juden auf dem Weg nach Wien* (Vienna: Böhlau Verlag, 1994), 207-32.

15. Ibid., 208-209.

16. Charlotte Baum, Paula Hyman, and Sonya Michel, *The Jewish Woman in America* (New York: Dial Press, 1976).

17. George Mosse, *Nationalism and Sexuality: Middle Class Morality and Sexual Norms in Modern Europe* (Madison: University of Wisconsin Press, 1985), 1-2.

18. Ibid., 97.

19. Pieter M. Judson, "The Gendered Politics of German Nationalism in Austria," in *Austrian Women in the Nineteenth and Twentieth Century: Cross-Disciplinary Perspectives*, ed. David F. Good, Margarete Grandner and Mary Jo Maynes (Providence: Berghahn Books, 1996), 3, 13-14.

20. Shilo, "New Hebrew Woman," 74.

21. Biale, *Eros and the Jews: From Biblical Israel to Contemporary America* (New York: Basic Books, 1992), 178-79.

22. George L. Mosse, introduction to *Degeneration* (New York: Howard Fertig, 1968), xxiv; and Max Nordau, *Paradoxe* (Leipzig: Verlag von B. Elischer, 1886), 44-50, 93-96, 136, 230, 246-51. In these pages Nordau presented a very negative image of women in general. He asserted, for example, that all women were basically the same, that the woman was not a personality, but a kind (46). So-called original women could be explained either as a disease, or as a spiritual reversal of gender, a person with a woman's body and a man's character, viewpoints, and tendencies (47). He also said that the woman had no true ambition, was an enemy of progress (49) and a spiritual

robot (50). He said that there was only one form of female success, and that was to please men (93). Women were far more emotional than men (136) and had a more strongly developed sexual center (246).

23. Max Nordau, *Die Conventionellen Lügen der Kulturmenschheit* (Leipzig: B. Elischer Nachfolger, 1883), 262–63; part of this is cited in Stanislawski, *Zionism and the Fin de Siècle*, 27–8.

24. Stanislawski, *Zionism and the Fin de Siècle*, 28–30.

25. Max Nordau, *Das Recht, zu Lieben: Ein Schauspiel in vier Aufzugen* (Berlin, 1893); and *Doktor Kohn: Bürgerliches Trauerspiel aus der Gegenwart* (Berlin: Ernst Hoffman, 1902).

26. Stanislawski, *Zionism and the Fin de Siècle*, 92, citing Max Nordau, "Muskeljudentum," in Nordau, *Zionistische Schriften* (Cologne: Jüdischer Verlag, 1909), 379–81. Zionists used the terms ghetto Jew or mentality and *galut* Jew or mentality interchangeably.

27. See Alex Bein, *Theodor Herzl: A Biography of the Founder of Modern Zionism*, trans. Maurice Samuel (New York: Atheneum, 1970), 62–65; Ernst Pawel, *The Labyrinth of Exile: A Life of Theodor Herzl* (London: Collins Harvill, 1990), 121–29; Peter Loewenberg, "Theodor Herzl: Nationalism and Politics," in *Decoding the Past: The Psychohistorical Approach* (Berkeley and Los Angeles: University of California Press, 1985), 104–12; and Stanislawski, *Zionism and the Fin de Siècle*, 4–5.

28. Theodor Herzl, "Women and Zionism," *Zionist Writings*, 159–64.

29. *Complete Diaries of Theodor Herzl*, trans. Harry Zohn, ed. Raphael Patai, 5 vols. (New York and London: Herzl Press and Thom Yoseloff, 1960), vol. 3, 1044.

30. Theodor Herzl, *The Jewish State* (New York: Dover, 1988), 128.

31. Theodor Herzl, "The New Ghetto," in *Theodor Herzl: A Portrait for this Age*, ed. Ludwig Lewisohn (Cleveland and New York: World Publishing Company, 1955), 157.

32. Herzl, "The New Ghetto," 165.

33. Robert Wistrich, "Theodor Herzl: Zionist Icon, Myth Maker and Social Utopian," in *The Shaping of Israeli Identity: Myth, Memory and Trauma*, ed. Robert Wistrich and David Ohana (London: Frank Cass, 1995), 14.

34. Arthur Hertzberg, *The Zionist Idea: A Historical Analysis and Reader* (New York: Atheneum, 1959), 49.

35. Theodor Herzl, *Altneuland, Old-New Land*, trans. Paula Arnold (Haifa: Haifa Publishing Company, 1960), 55.

36. Ibid., 57.
37. Ibid., 59, 66.
38. Ibid., 60.
39. Ibid., 75–76, 91.
40. Ibid., 174.
41. Ibid., 81–85.

42. Priska Gmür, "'It Is Not up to Us Women to Solve Great Problems': The Duty Of the Zionist Woman in the Context of the First Ten Congresses," in *The First Zionist Congress in 1897—Causes, Significance, Topicality*, trans. Wayne van Dalsum and Vivian Kramer, ed. Heiko Haumann (Basel: Karger, 1997), 292.

43. Ibid., 292–93.

44. Stenographisches Protokoll der Verhandlungen des II. Zionisten-Congresses gehalten zu Basel vom 28. bis 31 August 1898 (Vienna, 1898), 239.

45. Gmür, "It Is Not Up to Us Women," 293–94.

46. "Zur zionistischen Frauenbewegung," *Die Welt* 4 (1900): 7–8.

47. "Frauenbewegung," 7. Glueckel of Hameln was actually literate and she did not dictate, but wrote, her memoirs. See *The Memoirs of Glueckel of Hameln*, trans. Marvin Lowenthal (New York: Schocken, 1977).

48. "Frauenbewegung," 8.

49. York-Steiner also addressed the *Wiener zionistische Frauenverein* in 1899 and 1900, and the *Erste zionistische Frauenverein* in 1909; see Heinrich York-Steiner, *Der Talmudbauer. Unterwegs. Erzählungen von H. York Steiner* (Berlin: Jüdischer Verlag, 1904).

50. York-Steiner, *Talmudbauer*, 175.

51. "Zur zionistischen Frauenbewegung," 7–8.

52. Bein, *Theodor Herzl*, 372–73.

53. Pawel, *Labyrinth*, 452.

54. Berthold Feiwel, "Die jüdische Familie, Die jüdische Frau," *Die Welt* 5/17 (April 26, 1901): 1–3.

55. Robert Wistrich, *The Jews of Vienna in the Age of Franz Joseph* (New York: Oxford University Press, 1989), 638–40.

56. Martin Buber, "Das Zion der jüdischen Frau," *Die Welt* 5/17 (April 26, 1901): 3–5.

57. Ibid.

58. Elena Lappin, "Die zionistische Jugendbewegung als Familienersatz?" in Hödl and Keil, eds., *Die jüdische Familie*, 161–91.

Notes to Chapter 5

1. Portions of this essay appeared in Laura Lovett, "Land Reclamation as Family Reclamation: The Family Ideal in George Maxwell's Reclamation and Resettlement Campaigns, 1897–1933," *Social Politics* 7 (2000): 80–100.

2. Joya Misra and Frances Akins, "The Welfare State and Women: Structure, Agency, and Diversity," *Social Politics* 5 (1998): 259–85, 264.

3. Eileen Boris and Peter Bardaglio, "The Transformation of Patriarchy: The Historic Role of the State," in *Families, Politics, and Public Policy*, ed. Irene Diamond (New York: Longman, 1983): 70–93; 80–81, 85.

4. The term is Mimi Abramovitz's, in *Regulating the Lives of Women* (Boston: South End Press, 1988).

5. Linda Gordon, *Pitied But Not Entitled* (Cambridge, MA: Harvard University Press, 1994): 55; Seth Koven and Sonya Michel, eds., *Mothers of a New World* (New York: Routledge, 1993).

6. Theda Skocpol, *Protecting Mothers and Soldiers* (Cambridge, MA: Harvard University Press, 1992); Sonya Michel, "The Limits of Maternalism: Policies Toward American Wage-Earning Mothers during the Progressive Era," in *Mothers of a New World*, ed. Koven and Michel, 277–320.

7. Mark Reisner, *Cadillac Desert: The American West and Its Disappearing Water* (New York: Penguin Books, 1986), 111.

8. G. Esping-Andersen, *The Three Worlds of Welfare Capitalism* (Cambridge, U.K.: Polity Press, 1990), 37.

9. Jane Lewis, "Gender and the Development of Welfare Regimes," *Journal of European Social Policy* 2 (1992): 159–73; Lewis, "Gender and Welfare Regimes: Further Thoughts," *Social Politics* 4 (1997): 160–77; Ann Shola Orloff, "Gender and the Social Rights of Citizenship: The Comparative Analysis of Gender Relations and Welfare States," *American Sociological Review* 58 (1993): 303–28, 317.

10. Andrew Hudanick, Jr., "George Hebard Maxwell: Reclamation's Militant Evangelist," *Journal of the West* 14 (1975): 108-19; Donald J. Pisani, "Reclamation and Social Engineering in the Progressive Era," *Agricultural History* 57 (1983): 46-63; Pisani, "George Maxwell, the Railroads, and American Land Policy, 1899-1904," *Pacific Historical Review*, 63 (1994): 179; Robert Autobee, "Every Child a Garden: George H. Maxwell and the American Homecroft Society," *Prologue* 28 (1996): 195-206.

11. Historians Katherine Jellison and Mary Neth demonstrate that a model of the rural family similar to that proposed by Maxwell was in fact widespread throughout the rural Midwest in the early twentieth century. Katherine Jellison, *Entitled to Power: Farm Women and Technology, 1913-1963* (Chapel Hill: University of North Carolina Press, 1993); Mary Neth, *Preserving the Family Farm: Women, Community, and the Foundations of Agribusiness in the Midwest, 1900-1940* (Baltimore: Johns Hopkins University Press, 1995).

12. William Lilley III and Lewis L. Gould, "The Western Irrigation Movement, 1878-1902: A Reappraisal," *The American West: A Reorientation*, Gene M. Gressley (Cheyenne, WY: University of Wyoming Publications, 1966), vol. 32: 57-77; Donald Pisani, *From Family Farm to Agribusiness: the Irrigation Crusade in California and the West, 1850-1931.* (Berkeley: University of California Press, 1984); Pisani, *To Reclaim a Divided West: Water, Law, and Public Policy, 1848-1902* (Albuquerque: University of New Mexico Press, 1992); Stanley Roland Davison, *The Leadership of the Reclamation Movement, 1875-1902* (New York: Arno Press, 1979).

13. Pisani, *Reclaim a Divided West.*

14. Autobee, "Every Child," 196.

15. Lilley and Gould, "The Western Irrigation Movement."

16. George Maxwell, "National Irrigation," *National Irrigation* 6 (1901): 99.

17. Ibid., 129.

18. Theodore Roosevelt, "First Annual Message," December 3, 1901. *The Works of Theodore Roosevelt* (National Edition). (New York, NY: Charles Scribner's Sons, 1926), vol. 17, 122-23.

19. Reisner, *Cadillac Desert*, 81. Elsewhere I argue that Roosevelt's Conservation and Country Life Commissions used a similar family ideal to support rural families and communities. See Laura L. Lovett, "Conceiving the Future: Nostalgic Modernism, the Family and Reproduction in the United States, 1890-1930," Ph.D. diss., University of California, Berkeley, 1998.

20. Gifford Pinchot, *Breaking New Ground* (New York: Harcourt, Brace, 1947), 188.

21. Maxwell was influenced by Roosevelt's policies and linked his Homecroft movement to conservation and forestry. George Maxwell, "Forestry and Homecrofts," *Maxwell's Talisman* (July 1906): 13.

22. Theodore Roosevelt, "The Man Who Works With His Hands," U.S. Department of Agriculture Circular. (Washington: Government Printing Office, 1907); rpt. in *The Works of Theodore Roosevelt*, National Edition (New York: Charles Scribner's Sons, 1926), vol. 16: 133.

23. Theodore Roosevelt, "Rural Life," *The Outlook* 95 (1910): 919-22.

24. George Maxwell, "A Problem for the Statesman," *The Homemaker* (1903): 138-40, 138.

25. George H. Maxwell, "Peace or War," manuscript, no date. George H. Maxwell Papers, Arizona Department of Library, Archives and Public Records, Archives Division, Phoenix, AZ, 15.

26. Maxwell, "National Irrigation."

27. Lowry Nelson, *The Mormon Village: A Pattern and Technique of Land Settlement* (Provo: University of Utah Press, 1952); and Raymond Witte, *Twenty-Five Years of Crusading: A History of the National Catholic Rural Life Conference* (Des Moines, IA: National Catholic Rural Life Conference, 1948).

28. Paul Conkin, *Tomorrow a New World: The New Deal Community Program*. (Ithaca, NY: Cornell University Press, 1959).

29. George Maxwell, *The First Book of the Homecrofters* (Watertown, MA: National Homecroft Association, 1906).

30. Carol A. Christensen, *The American Garden City and New Towns Movement* (1978; rpt. Ann Arbor, MI: UMI Research Press, 1986), 29–35.

31. Ibid., 35–40.

32. Mel Scott, *American City Planning Since 1890* (Berkeley: University of California Press, 1969), 80.

33. Both Ruth Maxwell and her brother, Donald Hebard Maxwell, attended MIT from 1904 to 1908. They followed the trajectory of their father's ideas to some extent, with Ruth studying architecture and Donald, sanitary engineering. MIT Class of 1908, Records of the Secretary 1909–1913, AC329, Massachusetts Institute of Technology Archives, Cambridge, MA.

34. Maxwell, *First Book*.

35. George Maxwell, "Educational Inspiration at Watertown, The "Back to the Land Movement," no date. George H. Maxwell Papers, Series 9–Miscellaneous. Arizona Department of Library, Archives and Public Records, Archives Division, Phoenix, AZ.

36. E. T. Hartman, "The Homecroft Guild: A New Sociological Experiment at Watertown," *Maxwell's Talisman* (July 1906): 10; rpt. from the *Boston Evening Transcript*, June 16, 1906.

37. Elizabeth S. Hill, "The School Garden Movement," *Maxwell's Talisman* (October 1905); Elizabeth S. Hill, "Nature Study and Gardening," *Maxwell's Talisman* (April 1906): 11.

38. George Maxwell, "The Homecroft Weavers of Watertown," *Maxwell's Talisman* (July 1906).

39. Susan Strasser, *Satisfaction Guaranteed: The Making of the American Mass Market* (New York: Pantheon, 1989).

40. Martha Banta, *Taylored Lives: Narrative Productions in the Ages of Taylor, Veblen, and Ford*. (Chicago: University of Chicago Press, 1993).

41. Beverly Seaton, "Making the Best of Circumstances": The American Woman's Back Yard Garden" in *Making the American Home: Middle-Class Women and Domestic Material Culture, 1840–1940*, ed. Marilyn Ferris Motz and Pat Browne (Bowling Green, OH: Bowling Green State University Popular Press, 1988), 90–104.

42. See Skocpol, *Protecting Mothers*, for more on Civil War soldiers' pensions.

43. Benjamin Horace Hibbard, *History of the Public Land Policies* (New York: Macmillan, 1924), 133; Jerry O'Callaghan, "The War Veteran and the Public Lands," in *The Public Lands*, ed. Vernon Carstensen (Madison: University of Wisconsin Press, 1963), 109–20; David Shi, *The Simple Life: Plain Living and High Thinking in American Culture* (New York: Oxford University Press, 1985), 222–26; Conkin, *Tomorrow*.

44. George Maxwell, "Soldier's Adjusted Compensation," *Maxwell's Talisman* 16 (June 1920).

45. Ibid.

46. Pisani, "Reclamation and Social Engineering."

47. Lawrence B. Lee, "The Little Landers of San Ysidro," *Journal of San Diego History* 21 no. 36, (1975); Henry S. Anderson, "The Little Landers' Land Colonies: A Unique Agricultural Experiment in California," *Agricultural History* 5 (1931): 145-49.

48. William Smythe, "The Little Landers of Los Angeles" (Los Angeles: House of the Little Landers, 1913).

49. Elwood Mead, *Helping Men Own Farms* (New York: Macmillan, 1920). Mead was explicit in his desire to see what he called "white families" become land owners and farmers in order to give them an advantage over the Japanese and "Hindoo" farmers in the Central Valley, whom Mead saw as threatening.

50. Daniel Rodgers, *Atlantic Crossings: Social Politics in a Progressive Age* (Cambridge, MA: Harvard University Press, 1998).

51. Mead, *Helping Men*.

52. Conkin, *Tomorrow*, 53.

53. David Danbom, *The Resisted Revolution: Urban America and the Industrialization of Agriculture, 1900-1930* (Ames, IA: Iowa State University Press, 1979).

54. Neth, *Preserving*, 214-15.

55. Jellison, *Entitled*; Neth, *Preserving*..

56. Abramovitz, *Regulating*.

57. Jellison, *Entitled*; Neth, *Preserving*..

58. Autobee, "Every Child"; Conkin, *Tomorrow*.

Notes to Chapter 6

I wish to thank Stuart Macintyre for his extremely useful comments on earlier drafts of this chapter, and Jane Carey for her magnificent research assistance. I am also indebted to Sonya Michel for her continued support of my work and to Lynne Hancy and Lisa Pollard for their incisive suggestions and comments.

1. Jack Lang—NSW Parliamentary Debates Session, 1929, Legislative Assembly, December 6, 1929, 2140.

2. Marilyn Lake, *Getting Equal: The History of Australian Feminism* (Sydney: Allen and Unwin, 1999), 52.

3. NSW Parliamentary Debates, Sessions 1925-1926, Legislative Council and Legislative Assembly, 1926, 2783.

4. Ibid.

5. Ibid., 2785.

6. Joy Damousi, *The Labor of Loss: Mourning, Memory and Wartime Bereavement in Australia* (Cambridge: Cambridge University Press, 1999), 69.

7. Bede Nairn, *The 'Big Fella': Jack Lang and the Australian Labour Party 1891-1949* (Melbourne: Melbourne University Press, 1986), 157.

8. Cora V. Baldock and Bettina Cass, eds., *Women, Social Welfare and the State* (Sydney: Allen and Unwin, 1983), 66-75.

9. Ellen Ross, "Good and Bad Mothers: Lady Philanthropists and London Housewives before World War I," in *Gendered Domains: Rethinking Public and Private in Women's History*, ed. Dorothy O. Helly and Susan M. Reverby (Ithaca, NY: Cornell University Press, 1992), 200.

10. Tamara K. Hareven, "The History of the Family and the Complexity of Social Change," in *American Historical Review* 96, no. 1 (1991): 111.

11. Leonore Davidoff, Megan Doolittle, Janet Fink and Katherine Holden, *The Family Story: Blood, Contract and Intimacy: 1830-1960* (London: Longman, 1999), 244-65.

12. *Sydney Morning Herald*, 29 May 1925.
13. Judith Allen, *Sex and Secrets: Crimes Involving Australian Women since 1880* (Melbourne: Oxford University Press, 1990), 130-56.
14. See Kereen Reiger, *The Disenchantment of the Home: Modernizing the Australian Family, 1880-1940* (Melbourne: Oxford University Press, 1985).
15. Stephen Garton, *Out of Luck: Poor Australians and Social Welfare* (Sydney: Allen and Unwin, 1990), 118-19.
16. Ibid., 120-21.
17. Evidence of Jean Daley, Transcript of the Select Committee on Widows' Pensions and Child Endowment, 1936, MS 9779, Box 1290 (a) State Library of Victoria, 294.
18. Ibid., 123.
19. NSW Parliamentary Debates, 1923, quoted in Aisla Burns et al., *Children and Families in Australia: Contemporary Issues,* (Sydney: Allen and Unwin, 1985), 44.
20. NSW Parliamentary Debates, Sessions 1925-1926, 2783.
21. Ibid., 2786-87.
22. Ibid., 2786.
23. Ibid., 2906.
24. Desma Jean Guthrie, "Widows and Welfare in Victoria in the 1920s and 1930s," M.A. thesis, University of Melbourne, 1984, 67.
25. Ibid., 84. The national average was 79.6 percent in 1921; 82.8 percent in 1933.
26. Ibid., 21.
27. NSW Parliamentary Debates, Sessions 1925-1926, 2909.
28. Susan Pedersen, *Family, Dependence, and the Origins of the Welfare State, Britain. and France 1914-1945* (Cambridge: Cambridge University Press, 1993), 139.
29. Ibid., 175.
30. Alison Holland, "Wives and Mothers Like Ourselves? Exploring White Women's intervention in the Politics of Race, 1920s-1940s," *Australian Historical Studies*, no. 117, (2001): 292-310.
31. Ibid.
32. NSW Parliamentary Debates Session 1929, Legislative Assembly, 6 December 1929, 2143.
33. Ibid., 2147.
34. NSW Parliamentary Debates, Session 1929, Legislative Assembly, 5 December 1929, 2108.
35. Ibid., 2111.
36. Ibid., 2115.
37. Ibid., 2142.
38. Ibid., 2110.
39. Ibid., 2110.
40. Victorian Parliamentary Debates, 2nd session 1937, 791.
41. "Progress Report of the Select Committee on Widows' Pensions and Child Endowment," Minutes of Evidence, Votes and Proceedings of the Legislative Assembly, Session 1936, Victorian Parliamentary Debates, 4.
42. Victorian Parliamentary Debates, 2nd session 1937, 791.
43. Evidence of John Henry, Secretary of the Children's Welfare Department and Inspector of Reformatory Schools, Transcript of the Select Committee on Widows' Pensions and Child Endowment, 1936, op. cit., 3.
44. Ibid., 16.

45. Ibid., 284.
46. Ibid., 303.
47. Silvan S. Tomkins, *Affect, Imagery, Consciousness: Volume III—The Negative Affects: Anger and Fear* (New York: Springer, 1991), 34.
48. Patricia Grimshaw and Graham Willett, "Women's History and Family History: An Exploration of Colonial Family Structure," in *Australian Women: Feminist Perspectives*, ed. Norma Grieve and Patricia Grimshaw (Melbourne: Oxford University Press, 1981/1983), 135.
49. Tamara K. Hareven, "History of the Family," 115.
50. File no. 42548, Date of Application, April 17, 1929, in Citizens Welfare Service of Victoria, Papers, University of Melbourne. All references to the files of the COS which follow, are in this collection.
51. Secretary COS to Superintendent, Dental Hospital, April 20, 1929, Ibid.
52. File no. 42532, Date of Application, April 13, 1929, Attached report on applicant, April 4, 1929.
53. File no. 31151, Date of Application, October 5, 1921.
54. Ibid., Secretary COS to the Rev. John Landelle, October 2, 1921.
55. Ibid.
56. File no. 32690, Date of Application May 20, 1924, Attached letter, June 2, 1924, COS to Dental Hospital.
57. File no. 32690, Date of Application, May 20, 1924.
58. File no. 32705, Date of Application June 10, 1924.
59. File no. 31242, Date of Application, November 25, 1921, Attached Report on application.
60. File no. 425332, Date of Application, April 13, 1929.
61. File no. 42743, Date of Application, May 14, 1929.
62. File no. 31263, Date of Application, December 5, 1921, Attached Report, December 16, 1921.
63. Ibid., Attached letter, December 17, 1921.
64. File no. 31639, Date of Application, June 28, 1922.
65. File no. 32635, Date of Application, April 23, 1924.
66. 30/8/1937, Case of Mrs. Ellen Greenfall, Item 1/10, Minutes, 1937–1940.
67. File no. 42556, Date of Application, April 17, 1929, Box 36.
68. File no. 43345, Date of Application, July 19, 1929.
69. Ibid., August 12, 1928.
70. Ibid., December 4, 1929.
71. Ibid., July 17, 1929.
72. Hareven, "History of the Family," 122.
73. John Kingsmill, *Australia Street: A Boy's-Eye View of the 1920s and 1930s* (Sydney: Hale and Iremonger, 1991), 14.
74. Ibid., 31.
75. File no. 43168, Date of Application, June 29, 1929.
76. Ibid.
77. File no. 43243, Date of Application, May 29, 1936.
78. File no. 31199, Date of Application, November 2, 1921.
79. File no. 43243, Date of Application, May 29, 1936.
80. File no. 32698, Date of Application, June 4, 1924.
81. File no. 32712, Date of Application, June 11, 1924.
82. File no. 32798, Date of Application, July 14, 1924.

83. File no. 42556, Date of Application, April 17, 1929.
84. File no. 42743, Date of Application, May 14, 1929.
85. File no. 43253, Date of Application, July 11, 1929.
86. File no. 55996, Date of Application, February 5, 1937.
87. File no. 55996, Date January 29, 1937.
88. File no. 42548, Date of Application, April 17, 1929.
89. Tomkins, *Affect, Imagery, Consciousness,* 136.
90. Ibid., 136.
91. Victorian Parliamentary Debates, 1937, 796.
92. File no. 32795, Date of Application, July 11, 1924.
93. Ibid.
94. J.E. Bain to the Editor, *Sun,* July 9, 1924.
95. Secretary to COS, July 14, 1924, to Editor of the *Sun,* July 14, 1924.
96. File no. 43626, Date of Application July 12, 1929.
97. The cases which were considered increased. In 1937, there were 1,986 cases considered, as opposed to 1902 in 1934, 1936 in 1935, and 1979 in 1936.
98. Evidence of Ann Moylan, Inspector, Children's Welfare Department, Transcript of the Select Committee on Widows' Pensions and Child Endowment, op. cit., 71.
99. Janine Bush, "Moral Missionary to Professional Social Worker—Victoria, 1920-39," in *Citizenship, Woman and Social Justice: International Historical Perspectives,* ed. Joy Damousi and Katherine Ellinghaus (Melbourne: University of Melbourne, 1999), 265.
100. Ibid., 264.
101. Ibid., 265.
102. *Argus,* February 6, 1935, 16.
103. Ibid., November 26, 1934, 13.
104. Quoted in Bush, "Moral Missionary, 272.
105. Ibid.
106. Elsie A. Baker, Letter to the Editor, Melbourne *Herald,* March 10, 1932, in Box 11, Australian Association of Social Workers, Papers, University of Melbourne Archives.
107. Robyn Muncy, *Creating a Female Dominion in American Reform, 1890–1935,* (New York: Oxford University Press, 1991), xiv; 66-67.
108. Evidence of Ann Moylan, 74.
109. Phil Cashen, "The Truant as Delinquent: The Psychological Perspective, South Australia, 1920-1940," *Journal of Australian Studies* 16 (May 1985): 71-83.
110. M.V. Gutteridge, "The Mental Hygiene of Childhood," *Medical Journal of Australia* 24 (January 1931): 107.
111. Ibid., 108.
112. Molly Ladd-Taylor and Lauri Umansky, eds., *"Bad" Mothers: The Politics of Blame in Twentieth-Century America,* (New York: New York University Press, 1998), 105, 11.
113. Item 1/10, Minutes, 1937–1940, entry July 18, 1938.
114. Item 1/10, Minutes, 1937–1940, entry, November 7, 1938.
115. Ibid.
116. Ibid., entry, December 5, 1938.
117. Ibid., entry, March 27, 1939.
118. Ibid., entry, September 25, 1939.
119. Ibid., entry, February 26, 1940.
120. Ibid., entry, August 26, 1940; September 9, 1940.

121. See Nikolas Rose, "Assembling the Modern Self," in *Rewriting the Self: Histories from the Renaissance to the Present*, ed. Roy Porter (London: Routledge, 1997), 224–48.

Notes to Chapter 7

1. Salvador Allende, *La realidad médico-social chilena (síntesis)* (Santiago: n.p., 1939). On the popular front era see Paul Drake, *Socialism and Populism in Chile, 1932–1952* (Urbana: University of Illinois Press, 1978); Tomás Moulian, "Violencia, gradualismo y reformas en el desarrollo político chileno," in *Estudios sobre el sistema de partidos en Chile*, ed. Adolfo Aldunate, Angel Flisfisch, and Tomás Moulian (Santiago: FLACSO, 1985); María Angélica Illanes, *"En el nombre del pueblo, del estado y de la ciencia (. . .)": Historia social de la salud pública, Chile 1880–1973* (Santiago: Colectivo de Atención Primaria, 1993); Thomas Miller Klubock, *Contested Communities: Class, Gender, and Politics in Chile's El Teniente Copper Mine, 1904–1951* (Durham: Duke University Press, 1998).

Following Moulian, I use the term "popular fronts" and the adjective "popular front" to designate the various governing coalitions of the 1939–1948 period that were made up of sectors of the center and left, and eventually sectors of the right. I use the terms "socialist" (which I do not capitalize) and "leftist" to refer to members of both the Socialist and Communist parties. I use "Socialist" (with a capital "S") to denote members of the Socialist Party.

2. Allende, *La realidad médico-social*, 3, 196.

3. Ibid., passim. On health and national security see Illanes, *"En el nombre."*

4. Between 1930 and 1950, the illegitimacy rate dropped from 32 to 25 percent. *Estadística Chilena* 18, no. 12 (Dec. 1945): 542; ibid. 23, no. 12 (Dec. 1950): 601; Chile Dirección General de Estadística, *Anuario estadístico año 1939: Demografía y asistencia social* (Santiago: n.p., 1941), 18; *Anuario estadístico año 1940: Demografía y asistencia social* (Santiago: n.p., 1942), 19; *Anuario estadístico año 1945: Demografía y asistencia social* (Santiago: n.p., 1948), 14; *Anuario estadístico año 1950: Demografía y asistencia social* (Santiago: n.p., 1954), 15. Furthermore, many participants in family reform efforts perceived a change. See, for instance, *Servicio Social* 23, no. 3 (May-Aug. 1949): 38; Blanca Urbina Moya, "Proyecciones del servicio social en la industria 'Fábricas Textiles Caupolicán-Chiguayante' S.A." (Memoria, Escuela de Servicio Social, Concepción, 1948), 108. Unless otherwise noted, all periodicals were published in Santiago.

5. On the weakness of the Chilean oligarchy see Tomás Moulian and Isabel Torres Dujisin, *Discusiones entre honorables: Las candidaturas presidenciales de la derecha 1938–1946* (Santiago: FLACSO, n.d.), 21–39.

6. Karin Alejandra Rosemblatt, *Gendered Compromises: Political Cultures and the State in Chile, 1920–1950* (Chapel Hill: University of North Carolina Press, 2000), esp. 6–9.

7. On "Chileanization" see Pedro Aguirre Cerda in *Unidad gráfica: Organo oficial del comité gráfico del frente popular* 1, no. 1 (9 Oct. 1938), and *Acción Social* 10, no. 81 (Sept. 1939): 1, 4.

8. The term "repertoire of rule" comes from Philip Corrigan and Derek Sayer, *The Great Arch: English State Formation as Cultural Revolution* (New York: Blackwell, 1985).

9. On the role of lawyers see James Morris, *Elites, Intellectuals, and Consensus: A Study of the Social Question and the Industrial Relations System in Chile* (Ithaca, NY: Cornell University Press, 1966). On public health physicians, see Illanes, *"En el nombre."*

10. For an attempt to create more horizontal ties between medical personnel and clients see, for instance, Carlos Salomón Rex, "Organización y funcionamiento de una Unidad Sanitaria," *Revista chilena de higiene y medicina preventiva* 8, no. 3 (Sept. 1946): 148–88. Examples of professionals who justified their actions in terms of the national

good can be found in Olga Cárcamo Lastra, "El servicio social en la Manufactura de Metales 'MADEMSA'" (Memoria, Escuela de Servicio Social, Ministerio de Educación Pública, Santiago, 1945), 17; *Boletín de la Sociedad Chilena de Obstetricia y Ginecología* 3, no. 3 (1938): 184.

11. For Socialist and Communist publications that used "scientific" discourse see *El Socialista* (Concepción), second fortnight (1938): 4; *Frente Popular* (1936): 10; *El Siglo* (Mulchén), (1936): 6; *La Palabra* (Valdivia), 1 (1936): 3.

12. *Boletín Médico-Social de la Caja de Seguro Obligatorio,* nos. 117-19 (1944): 347; Allende, *La realidad médico social.* See also *Vida Sana* (Temuco) 1, no. 1 (1938): 1.

13. Divorce was (and is) illegal, and politicians did little to pass divorce legislation. See *El Chiflón* 1, no. 4 (1942): 6; *La Crítica,* 1 (1942): 8.

14. Chile, *Código Civil* (Santiago: Dirección General de Prisiones, 1944), libro III. Children could be legitimated if the parents subsequently married, but this was not a simple procedure.

15. *Boletín Médico-Social de la Caja de Seguro Obligatorio,* nos. 117-19 (July-Sept. 1944): 349. On reforms of the Civil Code that made filiation easier to prove see René Rioseco Tapia, "Situación de los hijos ilegítimos y de la madre soltera ante la sociedad y la ley" (Memoria, Facultad de Ciencias Jurídicas y Sociales, Universidad de Chile, 1938).

16. Graciela Alvarez Pacheco, "El servicio social ante el problema de la madre soltera" (Memoria, Escuela de Servicio Social, Ministerio de Educación Pública, 1944), 145-46; Eliana Aqueveque Castro, "Experiencias obtenidas en práctica en la Caja de Habitación de Concepción" (Memoria, Escuela de Servicio Social, Universidad de Chile, Concepción, 1949), 28 *Pampa* (1949): 7.

17. Manuel Pimentel Orellana, "La medicina preventiva en sus aspectos económico y social" (Memoria, Facultad de Ciencias Jurídicas y Sociales, Universidad de Chile, 1948). On family allowances see Allende, *Realidad médico-social,* 32-36; *Boletín del Ministerio de Salubridad, Previsión y Asistencia Social* (1939): 39-43.

18. *Boletín del Ministerio de Salubridad, Previsión, y Asistencia Social* (1939): 39-55. On the Asociación see *Tribuna Social* (1946): 13-15; Raquel Yanulaque Garrido, "La Asociación Nacional de Dueñas de Casa," (Memoria, Escuela de Servicio Social, Universidad de Chile, Santiago, 1950).

19. On the benefits provided by the social security system see Flora Meneses Zúñiga, "La ley 4054 de seguro obligatorio de enfermedad, vejez e invalidez" (Memoria, Facultad de Ciencias Jurídicas y Sociales, Universidad de Chile, 1936); Inés Santana et al., "Algunos problemas sociales" (Santiago: n.p., 1943); Raquel Weitzman Fliman, "La Caja de Seguro Obligatorio" (Memoria, Facultad de Ciencias Jurídicas y Sociales, Universidad de Chile, 1947); Isabel Norambuena Lagarde, "El servicio social en la Caja de Seguro Obligatorio" (Memoria, Escuela de Servicio Social, Junta de Beneficencia, 1943). For publications that explained who did or did not have the right to benefits see *Revista del Trabajo* 5, no. 8 (1935): 75; *Vida Sana* (Valparaíso) 2, no. 9 (1943): 8; ibid. 2, no. 10 (1943): 8; ibid. 2, nos. 11-12 (1943): 8.

20. Delia Arriagada Campos, "Acción del servicio social en la Gota de Leche 'Almirante Villarroel' de Talcahuano" (Memoria, Escuela de Servicio Social, Ministerio de Educación Pública, Concepción, 1947), 11. See also *Pampa* 10 (1949): 7. This issue is explored in Klubock, *Contested Communities.*

21. *Vida Sana* (Valparaíso) 2, no. 9 (1943): 6.

22. On the evils of male sociability see *Servicio Social* 9, no. 4 (1935): 306. I explore this in greater depth in "Domesticating Men: State Building and Class Compromise in Popular-Front Chile," in *Hidden Histories of Gender and the State in Latin America,* ed.

Elizabeth Dore and Maxine Molyneux (Durham: Duke University Press, 2000), 262–90.

23. *La Crítica,* (1942): 3; *Vida Sana* (Valparaíso) 2, no. 10 (1943): 3.

24. *Vida Sana* (Valparaíso) 2, no. 10 (1943): 3 and 3, nos. 28–29 (1944): 1. See also *Vida Sana* (Valparaíso) 2, no. 9 (1943): 3.

25. *Vida Sana* (Valparaíso) 2, no. 10 (1943): 3.

26. *Vida Sana* (Temuco), second period, 1, no. 6 (1941): 3.

27. *Vida Sana* (Valparaíso) 2, no. 9 (1943): 5. Lucia Ponce Ponce, "Desaveniencias conyugales en el hogar del obrero municipal" (Memoria, Escuela de Servicio Social, Ministerio de Educación Pública, Santiago, 1945), 11–16, 61.

28. Rina Schiappacasse Ferretti, "El problema económico de la madre soltera estudiado en el Centro de Defensa del Niño" (Memoria, Escuela de Servicio Social, Ministerio de Educación Pública, Concepción, 1946), 57–58. See also Anna Mac Auliffe, "El trabajo de las visitadoras sociales en la Caja de Seguro Obligatorio," *Boletín Médico-Social de la Caja de Seguro Obligatorio,* no. 140 (1946): 199.

29. *Vida Sana* (Valparaíso) 2, no. 9 (1943): 3; *Aurora de Chile* 4, no. 14 (1949): 14–15.

30. *La Crítica,* 6 May 1942, 7, and 26 Oct. 1939, 10; *La Palabra Socialista* (Valdivia), 15 July 1939, 4. See also the Socialist newspaper *Liberación* (Tomé), 16 Sept. 1939, 2.

31. *El Progreso* (Curicó), 25 Nov. 1944, 2. On prohibition see Cámara de Diputados, sesiones ordinarias, t. 3, (1938): 3421–22.

32. Allende, *La realidad médico social,* 118; *Liberación* (Tomé), 16 Sept. 1939, 2; *El Progreso* (Curicó), 25 Nov. 1944, 2; *Claridad,* 23 Dec. 1937, 1; *La Crítica,* 14 Sept. 1942, 2.

33. Nora Ortega Fuentes, "Acción de la lucha antivenérea en Concepción" (Memoria, Escuela de Servicio Social, Ministerio de Educación Pública, Concepción, 1947), 58. See also *Alianza Democrática,* 11 Oct. 1946, 4. On the Departamento see Chile, Dirección de Información y Cultura, "Recopilación de las disposiciones y legales y reglamentarias sobre los servicios que integran la Dirección General de Información y Cultura" (Santiago: n.p., 1943).

34. *¿Qué hubo?* (1 Aug. 1939): 30; *Acción Social,* no. 84 (1939): 3–4; ibid., no. 81 (1939): 4; *CTCh,* second fortnight (1939): 10; *Acción Social,* no. 109 (1942): 2–10. On the Hogar Pedro Aguirre Cerda see *La voz de Conchalí,* second fortnight May 1947, 5; *El Centinela,* 4 March 1944, n.p. On the Centro Valparaíso, see *Vida Sana* (Valparaíso) 1, no. 8 (1942): 1, 4–6.

35. *Acción Social,* no. 84 (1939): 3–4; *La Crítica,* 17 (1939): 3; ibid., 28 Oct. 1939, 2; ibid., 26 Oct. 1939, 1; *Servicio Social* 19, nos. 2–3 (1945): 31.

36. Gudelia Seguel Morales, "Madre soltera" (Memoria, Escuela de Servicio Social, Ministerio de Educación Pública, Temuco, 1946), 50. The term "future mothers" is used for example in *Servicio Social* 11, no. 3 (1937): 160; *La Crítica,* 2 (1939): 6.

37. Urbina Moya, "Proyecciones del servicio social," 60–65; Ponce Ponce, "Desaveniencias conyugales," 64–69.

38. On the Asociación see *Tribuna Social* 1, no. 3 (1946): 13–15; *Servicio Social* 21, nos. 1–3 (1947): 70–72; Yanulaque Garrido, "La Asociación de Dueñas de Casa."

39. Urbina Moya, "Proyecciones del servicio social," 107–8, 112–13.

40. On consumer organizing and the Asociación see Rosemblatt, *Gendered Compromises,* chapter 3.

41. *Vida Sana* (Temuco) 1, no. 1 (1938): 2; *Vida Sana* (Valparaíso) 1, no. 3 (1942): 4, 6; ibid. 1, no. 4 (1942): 5; *La Crítica,* 2 Nov. 1939, 6; *Servicio Social* 20, no. 1 (1946): 46;

Helga Peralta, "La atención materno-infantil en la Caja de Seguro Obligatorio" (Memoria, Escuela de Servicio Social, Universidad de Chile, Santiago, 1951), 53; *Servicio Social* 11, no. 3 (1937): 166.

42. The quotation is reported in Margarita Pinto Ureta, "Estudio de las condiciones de vida de 100 familias atendidas en la Sociedad Gotas de Leche de Valparaíso" (Memoria, Escuela de Servicio Social, Valparaíso, 1951), 86–87. *Vida Sana* (Valparaíso) 1, no. 3 (1942): 6.

43. Arriagada Campos, "Acción del servicio social," 12. Allende, *Realidad médico-social,* 75.

44. Arriagada Campos, "Acción del servicio social," 30–33; Seguel Morales, "Madre soltera," 42–43, 59; Allende, *Realidad médico-social,* 103; *Servicio Social* 12, no. 4 (1938): 180–81; *Boletín del Ministerio de Salubridad, Previsión y Asistencia Social* (1939): 39–52.

45. For cases where social workers found employment for women as laundresses or domestic workers see María Vallejos González, "Organización de la oficina de servicio social en la sección arriendos del Comisariato Departmental de Talcahuano" (Memoria, Escuela de Servicio Social, Universidad de Chile, Concepción, 1951), 24–29; *Servicio Social* 12, no. 4 (Oct. 1938): 184–85. For cases where a social worker helped women obtain benefits from the fathers of their children see *Servicio Social* 12, no. 4 (1938): 183–84.

46. On the diverse formulations of family wage rhetoric see Rosemblatt, *Gendered Compromises,* chapter 2.

47. *Revista del Trabajo* 4 (1941): 13–14; ibid., 5 (1948): 44.

48. This point of view is expressed in Rosa Navarro Torres "El aborto como problema social" (Memoria, Escuela de Servicio Social, Ministerio de Educación Pública, Concepción, 1944), 42.

49. In reality, only a very small proportion of women workers took maternity leaves. *Revista del Trabajo* (1944): 35–36; *Revista del Trabajo* 4 (1941): 12.

50. For an early debate on the effects of protective legislation see *Revista del Trabajo* 2, no. 7 (1931): 49–51; ibid. 3, no. 1 (1933): 45; ibid. 3, no. 10 (1933): 68–76.

51. *Revista del Trabajo* 4 (1941): 12; Glasfira Orrego Navarro, "Estudio de los problemas económico-sociales presentados por 50 madres obreras y 50 madres dueñas de casa Centro San Eugenio CSO" (Memoria, Escuelo de Servicio Social, Junta de Beneficencia, Santiago, 1941), n.p.; *Boletín Médico-Social de la Caja de Seguro Obligatorio* 4, nos. 44–45 (1939): 18; *Servicio Social* 23, no. 3 (1949): 38.

52. *Servicio Social* 14, no. 1 (1940): 25. Cf. Peralta, "La atención materno-infantil," 77–78.

53. Allende, *Realidad médico-social,* 78–79; *Boletín-Social Médico de la Caja de Seguro Obligatorio* 4, nos. 44–45 (1939): 23 had a similar analysis. Cf. *Servicio Social* 14, no. 1 (1940): 27–28.

54. Norambuena Lagarde, "El servicio social en la Caja de Seguro Obligatorio," 24, 26. See also Alvarez Pacheco, "El servicio social ante el problema de la madre soltera," 72; Orrego Navarro, "Estudio de los problemas económico-sociales," passim.; *Vida Sana* (Valparaíso) 3, nos. 42–43 (1945): 3.

55. Quotations from Orrego Navarro, "Estudio de los problemas económico-sociales," 45; Norambuena Lagarde, "El servicio social en la Caja de Seguro Obligatorio," 26. See also Schiappacasse, "El problema económico de la madre soltera," 30–31; *Aurora de Chile,* 7 Oct. 1939, 17. Cf. Inés Santana et al., "Algunos problemas sociales," 10.

56. *Boletín de la Sociedad Chilena de Obstetricia y Ginecología* 3, no. 3 (1938): 200–5; *Servicio Social* 30, no. 2 (1956): 14; *Boletín Médico-Social de la Caja de Seguro Obligatorio* 4, nos. 44–45 (1939): 21. Cf. *Servicio Social* 14, no. 1 (1940): 29.

57. Alvarez Pacheco, "El servicio social ante el problema de la madre soltera," 107; *Boletín Médico-Social de la Caja de Seguro Obligatorio* 4, nos. 44–45 (1938): 12, 16; *Servicio Social* 14, no. 1 (1940): 9; ibid. 12, no. 4 (1938): 174.

58. A 1943 survey of 2,061 industrial and commercial establishments employing 35,074 women and girls found that 22.5 percent of employees were married with children; 7.7 percent were married without children; 7.6 percent were single with children; and 62.2 percent were single without children. *Revista del Trabajo* (1944): 35–36.

59. *Servicio Social* 12, no. 4 (1938): 172; Orrego Navarro, "Estudio de los problemas económico-sociales," 19; Urbina Moya, "Proyecciones del servicio social," 88–90.

60. *Servicio Social* 12, no. 4 (1938): 188; Arriagada Campos, 108; Urbina Moya, "Proyecciones del servicio social," 85, 108; *Servicio Social* 30, no. 2 (1956): 9–12.

61. Urbina Moya, "Proyecciones del servicio social," 88–90, 108; *Servicio Social* 23, no. 3 (1949): 41–43.

62. Haydee Charney Venegas, "Sindicatos textiles y sus relaciones con el Servicio Social" (Memoria, Escuela de Servicio Social, Ministerio de Educación Pública, Concepción, 1947), 76–95.

Notes to Chapter 8

1. Cynthia Brantley, Oral Interviews, Kenya Cashew nut Factory, Kilifi, Kenya. 1974.

2. Cynthia Brantley, Oral Interviews on Aging, Ribe, Kenya. 1980.

3. Center for Human Nutrition, London School of Hygiene and Tropical Medicine, University of London, Nyasaland Nutrition Survey Papers (CHN/NNS): 1940 Draft Report: "Report of a Nutrition Survey in Nyasaland." Carbon Copy, Box 5.

4. Malawi National Archives, Zomba, Malawi. MNA/Q; MNA/NCK (Nkotakota District). NDU Report on the First Two Years. (First NDU Report). Keppel-Compton, "Interim Report on the Work of the Nutrition Unit, Kota Kota District, Nyasaland, for the period 1st April 1940 to 31st December, 1941." 10 March 1942; NDU Report (Second NDU Report), 10 April 1943.

5. See Cynthia Brantley, *Feeding Families: African Realities and British Ideals of Nutrition and Development in Early Colonial Africa* (Portsmouth, NH: Heineman, 2002).

6. See the special issue, "Revising the Puzzle of Matriliny in South-Central Africa" of *Critique of Anthropology*, 17, no. 2 (1997).

7. CHN:NNS: Evidence and Reports. Boxes 1–5.

8. This included the three Nutrition Survey villages and 107 others.

9. Read was studying anthropology under Bronislaw Malinowski. BLPES/READ: Evidence and Reports.

10. Average population density in Africa was 10.55 per square mile; in Nyasaland it was 42.55.

11. The exception was the Southern Highlands, where tobacco and tea were grown on settler estates, mostly using immigrant Lomwe laborers.

12. *Report of the Committee to Enquire into Emigrant Labour*, 1935 (Zomba, Nyasaland: Government Printer, 1936).

13. Ibid.

14. Cynthia Brantley. "Through Ngoni Eyes: Margaret Read's Matrilineal Interpretations from Nyasaland." *Critique of Anthropology* 17, no. 2 (2000): 147–70.

15. Margaret Read, "Migrant Labour in Africa and Its Effects on Tribal Life." *International Labour Review* 45, no. 1 (1942): 605-31.

16. British Library of Political and Economic Sciences at the London School of Economics, London (BLPES). Margaret Read Papers, BLPES/READ 1/36: "Human Ecology and Social Behavior MS Draft."

17. Center for Human Nutrition, London School of Hygiene and Tropical Medicine, University of London, Nyasaland Nutrition Survey Papers (CHN/NNS): Margaret Read, "Notebook re: Survey Villages." (56 pp), Box 1.

18. BLPES/READ: 1/24 (Notebooks, Biwi [Namleta]; [Jere]; Kasamba [Liwewe].); 1/27: Preliminary Sociological Notes on Jere Village, Biwi [Namleta] Village, and Kasamba [Liwewe] Village; 1/36: Human Ecology.

19. Ibid.

20. Read, "Migrant Labour," 629.

21. MRC/PLATT 2167.

22. M. G. Marwick, "The Kinship Basis of Cewa Social Structure,' *South African Journal of Science*, 48 (1952): 261.

23. MNA/NCK: M2/17/16 Reports and Correspondence of the Nutrition Development Unit.

24. R. W. Kettlewell, *Agricultural Change in Nyasaland: 1945-1960*. Palo Alto, CA: Stanford University Food Research Institute, 1965. See also, Martin Chanock, "Agricultural Change and Continuity in Malawi," in *The Roots of Rural Poverty in Central and Southern Africa*, ed. Robin Palmer and Neil Parsons (Berkeley: University of California Press, 1977), 396-409.

25. Jean Davison, "Tenacious Women: Clinging to *Banja* Household Production in the Face of Changing Gender Relations in Malawi," *Journal of Southern African Studies*, 19:3 (1993), 417.

26. BLPES/READ: 1/24, 1/27, 1/36. Read, "Migrant Labour."

27. Village data is drawn from the London School of Hygiene and Tropical Medicine, CHN/NNS: The Nyasaland Nutrition Survey, Boxes 1-5; the Malawi National Archives, MNA/NCK Evidence and Documents; and the London School of Economics BLPES/READ, 1/24; 1/27; 1/36.

28. Data about these villages is drawn from the London School of Hygiene and Tropical Medicine, CHN/NNS: The Nyasaland Nutrition Survey, Boxes 1-5; the Malawi National Archives, MNA/NCK Evidence and Documents; and the London School of Economics BLPES/READ, 1/24; 1/27; 1/36.

29. CHN/NNS 1940 Draft Report:Table of Contents and Introductory Material.

30. Another hamlet (Chikaza) had earlier attached itself literally and philosophically to Chikaungu hamlet.

31. The mission station was ten miles away at Chitembwe.

32. The Survey measurements showed that individuals in this village, more than in the other two, had higher intake of calories for energy spent producing their food. CHN/NNS: Chapter 10: Energy Value of Food Intake in Relation to Requirements. I wish to thank E.A. Alpers, UCLA, for the hunger metaphor.

33. The [Anglican] Universities' Mission to Central Africa.

34. Liwewe's sister's son, also named Liwewe, had become the village headman upon the senior Liwewe's death, according to matrilineal practice, but his weak personality diminished his real authority.

35. BLPES/READ 1/36 Human Ecology.

36. BLPES/READ 1/27 "Sociological-Kasamba [Liwewe]"

37. Cynthia Brantley, Oral Interviews, Liwewe Village, August, 1992.

38. "When women were left for long periods without a husband to keep house for, they became careless cooks and made no efforts to maintain their household and children on the level which their husbands expected." Margaret Read, "Migrant Labour in Africa and Its Effects on Tribal Life." *International Labour Review* 45, 1 (1942): 627.

39. Margaret Read, "Migrant Labour in Africa and Its Effects on Tribal Life." *International Labour Review* 45, no. 1 (1942): 624.

40. Ibid.

Notes to Chapter 9

1. See Robert Deacon, *Global Social Policy* (London: Sage, 1997); Jan Adam, "Social Contract" in *Economic Reforms and Welfare Systems in the USSR, Poland and Hungary*, ed. Jan Adam (New York: St. Martin's, 1991); John Dixon and David Macarov, eds., *Social Welfare in Socialist Countries* (London: Routledge, 1992); and U. Gotting, "Destruction, Adjustment, and Innovations: Social Policy Transformation in Eastern and Central Europe," *Journal of European Social Policy* 4 (1994).

2. See G. Cornia, "Income Distribution, Poverty, and Welfare in Transitional Economies: A Comparison between Eastern Europe and China," UNICEF Occasional Papers, Economic Policy Series 44 (1994); and Guy Standing and Daniel Vaughn-Whitehead, eds. *Minimum Wages in Central and Eastern Europe: From Protection to Destitution* (Budapest: Central European University Press, 1995).

3. See Guy Standing, "Social Protection in Central and Eastern Europe: A Tale of Slipping Anchors and Lost Safety Nets," in *Welfare States in Transition: National Adaptations to the Global Economy*, ed. Gøsta Esping-Andersen (London: Sage, 1994); Michael Förster and István Tóth, *Szegénység és Egyenlőtlenségek Magyarországon és a Többi Visegrádi Országokban (*Poverty and Inequality in Hungary and Other Visegrad Countries) (Budapest: TARKI, 1998); and UNICEF, *Central and Eastern Europe: Transition Public Policy and Social Conditions* (Florence, Italy: UNICEF Child Development Centre, 1997).

4. See Elizabeth Rudd's chapter in this volume. Also see Barbara Einhorn, *Cinderella Goes to Market* (London: Verso, 1993); Maxine Molyneux, "Women's Rights and the International Context in the Post-Communist States," *Millennium: Journal of International Studies* 23 (1993): 1–27; Éva Fodor, "The Political Woman: Women in Politics in Hungary," in *Women in the Politics of Postcommunist Eastern Europe*, ed. Marilyn Rueschemeyer (New York: M.E. Sharpe, 1994); and Júlia Szalai, "From Informal Labor to Paid Occupations: Marketization from Below of Hungarian Women's Work," in *Reproducing Gender*, ed. Susan Gal and Gail Kligman. (Princeton: Princeton University Press, 2000).

5. Robert Deacon, "Social Policy, Social Justice, and Citizenship in Eastern Europe," in *Social Policy, Social Justice, and Citizenship in Eastern Europe*, ed. Robert Deacon (Aldershot, England: Avebury, 1992).

6. Gøsta Esping-Andersen, *The Three Worlds of Welfare Capitalism*. (Cambridge, U.K.: Polity, 1990).

7. See Mitchell Orenstein, "Transitional Social Policy in the Czech Republic and Poland," *Czech Sociological Review* 2 (1995): 179–96.

8. See Peter Gedeon, "Hungary: Social Policy in Transition," *East European Politics and Societies* 9 (1995): 433–58.

9. For an overview of the role of the family in regime analysis, see the special forum on the topic in *Social Politics* (1997) 4:2.

10. The data used in this chapter are somewhat unbalanced. My analysis of the Hungarian state is part of a much larger study I completed on the development of welfare from the inception of state socialism to the mid-1990s. For this analysis, see Lynne Haney, *Inventing the Needy: Gender and the Politics of Welfare in Hungary* (Berkeley: University of California Press, 2002). My data on the Czech case are far more limited. In fall 1999 and spring 2002, I reviewed policy documents, interviewed welfare workers, and observed welfare offices in Prague. Yet I was unable to have extensive contact with Czech welfare clients. Because of the limitations of my data, this analysis remains suggestive and its conclusions provisional.

11. Embedded in these trends is yet another paradox: Although Hungary went further in welfare targeting, its expenditures increased more dramatically than those of the Czech Republic. In 1990 Hungary devoted 22 percent of its GDP to social spending; by 1995, this percentage increased to 29 percent. This contrasts to the Czech Republic, which devoted 19 percent of its GDP to social spending in 1990 and 21 percent in 1995. Moreover, the Czech Republic has done a better job of avoiding large-scale deprivation. The Czech Republic has the lowest poverty rate in the region: In 1995, 7 percent of Czechs lived below the poverty line, as compared to 17 percent of Hungarians. And while an additional 13 percent of Czechs are in danger of falling into poverty, 21 percent of Hungarians occupy such vulnerable economic positions. Drawing all of these indicators together, Czech sociologist Petr Mateju calculated what percentage of the population had "lost" or "won" in the last decade. His findings are striking: In Hungary, 63.1 percent of the population were "losers," while 11.9 percent were "winners." In the Czech Republic, 36.1 percent were "losers" and 28.6 percent "winners." For more on these redistributive trends, see Petr Mateju, "Winners and Losers in the Post-Socialist Transition: The Czech Republic in Comparative Perspective," *Innovation* 9 (1996): 371–90; Lynne Haney, "A Tale of Two Welfare States: Social Policy Reform in Hungary and the Czech Republic," forthcoming in *Gender and Health in Transition*, ed. Peggy Watson (Cambridge: Cambridge University Press); and Förster and Tóth, *Szegénység és Egyenlőtlenségek* (Poverty and Inequality).

12. See Haney, *Inventing the Needy*.

13. For a more complete discussion of the politics of welfare reform in Hungary, see Lynne Haney, "Global Discourses of Need: Pathologizing and Mythologizing Welfare in Hungary," in *Global Ethnography*, ed. Michael Burawoy et al. (Berkeley: University of California Press, 2000); and Haney, *Inventing the Needy*.

14. See Iván Szelényi and Róbert Manchin, "Social Policy Under State Socialism: Market Redistribution and Social Inequalities in East European Socialist Societies," in *Stagnation and Renewal in Social Policy*, ed. Gøsta Esping-Andersen (New York: M.E. Sharpe, 1987); and Elemer Hankiss, "Kinek az Érdeke?" ("In Whose Interest?") *Heti Világgazdaság*, November 27, 1982.

15. For more on these welfare practices, see Haney, *Inventing the Needy*.

16. For an extensive discussion of the role of these agencies in Hungarian welfare reforms see Deacon, *Global Social Policy*; Gedeon, "Hungary"; Haney, "Global Discourses of Need."

17. Zsuzsa Ferge, "A Magyar Segélyezési Rendszer Reformja II," *Esély* 1 (1996): 25–42.

18. For more on the IMF and World Bank agendas for parental leave programs, see Joanna Goven, "New Parliament, Old Discourse: The Parental Leave Debate in Hungary," in Gal and Kligman, *Reproducing Gender*.

19. A few analysts have questioned the utility of the "liberal" label in the Hungarian context. For example, see O. Lelkes, "A Great Leap Towards Liberalism?: The Hungarian Welfare State," *International Journal of Social Welfare* 9 (2000): 92–102.

20. For more on the distinction between "social" and "societal" welfare in the East European context, see Zsuzsa Ferge, *A Society in the Making* (New York: M.E. Sharpe, 1979).

21. The Czechoslovak state did supplement this support with up to two years of unpaid leave. See Czechoslovak Ministry of Social Affairs, "Czechoslovakia," in *Social Welfare in Socialist Countries*, ed. John Dixon and David Macarov (London: Routledge, 1992).

22. Moreover, when international agencies showed up in the Czech Republic or Slovakia, they tended to be groups like the ILO, the European Union's PHARE program, and UNICEF. As many scholars have argued, these groups are much less doctrinaire and more open to local initiatives than agencies like the IMF and World Bank. See Deacon, *Global Social Policy*.

23. They may also help to predict what will happen to the Czech system in the future. In the last few years, the Czech government has been subjected to far more international pressure—not only from the IMF and World Bank, but also from its West European neighbors, as the Czech Republic prepares to enter the EU. It remains to be seen how the Czech welfare system will respond to such pressure.

24. For more on this voucher system, see Jiri Vecernik and Petr Mateju, *Ten Years of Rebuilding Capitalism: Czech Society after 1989* (Prague: Academia Press, 1999); and M. Tucek and V. Harmadyova, "Structural Changes and Social Mobility 1988–1995 in the Czech and Slovak Republics" in *Czech Sociological Review* 6 (1998): 99–114.

25. This drop was related to the large number of Czechs who sold their company shares in the late 1990s. For more on this, see Vecernik and Mateju, *Ten Years of Rebuilding Capitalism*.

26. See Martin Mácha, "Social Protection in the Czech Republic" (Prague: Center for Research on Social Transformation, 1998).

27. See Petr Mares and Ivo Mozny, "Poverty in the Czech Republic: Transformation or Transition?" (Prague: Center for Research on Social Transformation, 1996).

28. Mácha, "Social Protection in the Czech Republic."

29. Orenstein, "Transitional Social Policy."

30. Ibid., 189.

31. Jan Hartl, "Social Policy: An Issue for Today and the Future" in *Czech Sociological Review* 2 (1995): 209–19.

32. For more on these views, see Iván Szelényi, Szonja Szelényi, and Winifred Poster, "Postcommunist Political Culture in Hungary, *American Sociological Review* 61 (1996): 466–77.

33. Gil Eyal, Iván Szelényi, and Eleanor Townsley, *Making Capitalism Without Capitalists: The New Ruling Elites in Eastern Europe* (New York: Verso, 1998).

34. For example, see Faye Ginsburg and Rayna Rapp, *Conceiving the New World Order: The Global Politics of Reproduction* (Berkeley: University of California Press, 1995).

35. Susan Gal and Gail Kligman, *The Politics of Gender After Socialism* (Princeton: Princeton University Press, 2000).

36. See Martha Lampland, "Family Portraits: Gendered Images of the Nation in Nineteenth-Century Hungary," *East European Politics and Societies* 8 (1994): 287–316; Katherine Verdery, "From Parent-State to Family Patriarchs: Gender and Nation in Contemporary Eastern Europe," *East European Politics and Societies* 8 (1994): 225–55;

and Lynne Haney, "Familial Welfare: Building the Hungarian Welfare Society, 1948–1968," *Social Politics* 7 (2000): 101–22.

37. György Konrád, *Antipolitics* (New York: Henry Holt, 1984).

38. For more information on these parliamentary debates, see Haney, *Inventing the Needy*, chap. 5. Parliamentary records can also be reviewed on the internet at http://www.kerszov.hu/kzlcim/kzl.

39. Haney, *Inventing the Needy*, 185–87. See also Goven, "New Parliament, Old Discourse."

40. Haney, *Inventing the Needy*, chap. 5.

41. Ibid., chaps. 3–4.

42. This narrow focus was also a result of the organization of Hungarian welfare agencies. These were large, collective spaces that left little room for privacy. Caseworkers resembled assembly-line workers: cases were broken down into small pieces and given to different workers for processing. Most of their work occurred in an office setting; caseworkers rarely ventured out into their clients' communities. Home visits were no longer required for most cases. When required, home visits were contracted out to part-time employees who operated like piece-rate workers.

43. Haney, *Inventing the Needy*, 213.

44. Ibid., 214.

45. Author's interview #080211:23.

46. It would be far too simplistic to blame welfare workers for this focus. Some caseworkers seemed genuinely unaware of the severity of clients' other problems. These women left meetings with severely abused or depressed clients without an awareness of their turmoil. Other caseworkers seemed overwhelmed by the enormity of the issues confronting clients. Their insistence on maintaining boundaries was a survival strategy; they did not feel equipped to address the depth of their clients' troubles.

47. If such intervention failed to fix these families, there was state institutionalization. Contemporary welfare offices institutionalize roughly 2 percent of all Hungarian children. Moreover, 87 percent of these children were taken to state orphanages because their families were said to be materially deprived. For a detailed account of this institutionalization process, see Haney, *Inventing the Needy*.

48. Ibid., 185–90.

49. Goven, "New Parliament, Old Discourse," 296.

50. Ibid., 297.

51. Vaclav Havel, "The Power of the Powerless," in The *Power of the Powerless*, ed. Vaclav Havel et al. (London: Hutchinson, 1985).

52. Marie Cermáková, "Women and the Family—The Czech Version of Development and Chances for Improvement," in *Family, Women, and Employment in Central-Eastern Europe*, ed. Barbara Lobodzinska (London: Greenwood Press, 1995).

53. Hartl, "Social Policy," 216.

54. Czech Parliamentary Record, February 23, 1993. Act 84.

55. Quoted in Orenstein, "Transitional Social Policy," 185.

56. Czech Parliamentary Record, May 26, 1995. Act 117.

57. Ibid., Act 118.

58. For more on the Social Democrats' discourse of reform, see Czech Parliamentary Record, 1996 Acts 1360137 and 1997 Act 242.

59. Rebecca Nash, "A Familial Bureaucracy for Fewer Babies: Why Prague Welfare Accountants and Benefit Recipients Aren't Talking about Demographic Crisis," unpublished manuscript.

60. Ibid., 4
61. Radio Prague, March 27, 1998.
62. Part of this was related to the overall organization of the welfare system. Czech welfare workers did far more than distribute poor relief to materially needy clients; they also administered parental entitlements, provided legal advice, and treated psychological problems. To carry out these diverse tasks, Czech welfare workers received administrative, legal, and psychological training. Given all they were responsible for, welfare workers divided up their caseloads geographically. Caseworkers were assigned to particular neighborhoods rather than specific aspects of cases. Home visits were not contracted out to temporary workers—caseworkers did these visits themselves.
63. Their closeness to the surrounding community was enhanced by the length of time they had been in their jobs. Most welfare workers had worked in this sphere for at least a decade; 50 percent of those I interviewed had worked in it for over 15 years. Welfare workers expressed how fortunate they felt to have maintained these jobs over the years—since state-sector positions were more secure and came with more social benefits than other types of work to which these women had access.
64. Author's Interview #0602, November 29, 1999.
65. Author's Interview #0622, March 4, 2002.
66. Author's Interview #0609, December 5, 1999
67. Author's Interview #0620, February 8, 2002.
68. Author's Interview #0612, December 10, 1999.
69. Author's Interview #0603, November 29, 1999.
70. Author's Interview #0613, December 19, 1999.
71. Author's Interview #0614, December 19, 1999.

Notes to Chapter 10

1. This chapter is based on dissertation research supported by grants from the Social Science Research Council, the National Science Foundation, the Fulbright Foundation, the Institute of International Studies, the Center for German and European Studies, and the Center for Working Families at the University of California, Berkeley, and my parents, Tom and Anna Rudd. I thank my sister, Rebecca Rudd, for her sharp editing and Rebecca Upton, Janet Dunn, and Eileen Otis for many useful discussions of this piece. An earlier version of this paper was presented at the conference "Work and Family: Expanding the Horizons" held March 3–4, 2000, in San Francisco. Direct inquiries to Elizabeth C. Rudd at erudd@mich.edu or Center for the Ethnography of Everyday Life–ISR, 426 Thompson St., PO Box 1248, University of Michigan, Ann Arbor, MI 48106–1248
2. In the period shortly before German unification, East German regulations allowed paid leave to care for sick children of four weeks annually for single mothers of one child. Six weeks were allowed for all mothers of two children, eight weeks for mothers of three and so on up to thirteen weeks. In exceptional situations the father or the grandmother could take this leave. Pay was at a rate of between 70 and 90 percent of the leave-taker's net average earnings. In unified Germany after 1992 regulations were actually more generous in some ways. Parents were allowed ten days of paid leave to care for a sick child annually for each child up to age twelve. For married couples this meant that in a family with two children under twelve, each parent would be eligible for 20 days (that is, 4 weeks) per year to care for a sick child. The parents could not give each other their leave. A single parent was eligible for 20 days of such leave

per child per year. These details are reported in Heike Trappe, "Selbständigkeit–Pragmatismus–Unterordnung" Ph.D. dissertation (Freie Universität Berlin, 1994), 32.

3. According to respondents, kindergarten teachers in East Germany just before unification had a 40-hour workweek consisting of 34 "contact hours" per week and six hours for preparation time that could be worked at home or at the workplace. Teachers who were mothers of two or more young children had a shorter workweek of 31 contact hours and six "preparation" hours. After unification, standard workweeks changed in accord with industry-wide collective bargaining agreements. According to Mrs. Acker, the hours of the kindergarten teachers were set at 40 per week. This increased the workweek for mothers like Mrs. Acker, who had enjoyed shorter hours and the monthly paid day off known as the "housework day." West German kindergarten teachers at that time had a full-time workweek of 38.5 hours.

4. Bebel's book *Die Frau und der Sozialismus* was first published in 1883 and then revised after the 1884 publication of Friedrich Engels' *The Origin of the Family, Private Property, and the State*. According to Lewis Coser's introduction to the Schocken Books 1971 paperback edition (translated from the 33rd German edition!), the book had gone through 50 editions and been published in at least 15 different languages by the time of Bebel's death in 1913.

5. For accounts of the similarities across the region see Jacqueline Heinen, "Inequalities at Work: The Gender Division of Labour in the Soviet Union and Eastern Europe, *Studies in Political Economy* 33 (1990): 39–61; Hilda Scott, "Eastern European Women in Theory and Practice," *Women's Studies International Quarterly* 1 (1978): 180–99; and Katherine Verdery, "From Parent-State to Family Patriarchs: Gender and Nation in Contemporary Eastern Europe," *East European Politics and Societies*, 8, no. 2 (1994): 225–55. For Hungary, see Eva Fodor, "Smiling Women and Fighting Men: the Gender of the Communist Subject in State Socialist Hungary," *Gender & Society* 16, no. 2 (2002): 240–63; and Lynne A. Haney, *Inventing the Needy: Gender and the Politics of Welfare in Hungary* (Berkeley: University of California Press, 2002). For Germany, see Elizabeth D. Heineman, *What Difference Does a Husband Make? Women and Marital Status in Nazi and Postwar Germany* (Berkeley: University of California Press, 1999) and "Single Motherhood and Maternal Employment in Divided Germany: Ideology, Policy, and Social Pressures in the 1950s," *Journal of Women's History* 12, no. 3 (2000): 146–72; Virginia Penrose, "Vierzig Jahre SED-Frauenpolitik: Ziele, Strategien und Ergebnisse," *Frauenforschung* 4 (1990): 60–77; and Susanne Diemer, *Patriarchalismus in der DDR: Strukturelle, kulturelle und subjektive Dimensionen der Geschlechterpolarisierung* (Opladen: Leske & Budrich, 1994). For the Soviet Union, see Gail Lapidus, *Women in Soviet Society: Equality, Development, and Social Change* (Berkeley: University of California Press, 1978). For Czechoslovakia, see Hilda Scott, *Women and Socialism: Experiences from Eastern Europe* (London: Alison and Busby, 1976).

6. Source: International Labour Office, "Economically Active Population Estimates and Projections, 1950–2025," 1986, Table 2. Work rates for Swedish women were in the mid-70 percent range and American women's rates were well below 70 percent at this time.

7. Elizabeth C. Rudd, "Coping with Capitalism: Gender and the Transformation of Work-Family Conflicts in Former East Germany," Ph.D. diss., University of California, Berkeley, 1999.

8. "Strategy" refers to a plan of action developed in a particular situation

constructed on the basis of both thoughts and feelings about the situation. Arlie Hochschild defines gender strategy as a "complex of thought, feeling, and action" drawing on cultural notions of manhood and womanhood. See Hochschild with Anne Machung, *The Second Shift* (New York: Avon Books, 1989): 192. The concept of "strategy of action" is developed by Ann Swidler in her article "Culture in Action: symbols and strategies," *American Sociological Review* 51 (1986): 273–86. In my view, "strategies" must be understood as both present and/or future oriented and as implemented with varying degrees of success or lack thereof.

9. Julie Brines, "Economic Dependency, Gender, and the Division of Labor at Home." *American Journal of Sociology* 100, no. 3 (1994): 652–88; Hochschild and Machung, *Second Shift*; Candace West and Don H. Zimmerman, "Doing Gender," *Gender & Society* 1, 2 (1987): 125–51.

10. Prue Chamberlayne, Joanna Bornat, and Tom Wengraf, "Introduction: the biographical turn," in *The Turn to Biographical Methods in Social Science: Comparative Issues and Examples,* ed. Chamberlayne, Bornat, and Wengraf (London and New York: Routledge, 2000), 1–30.

11. After World War II, Germany was divided into zones by the occupying powers (France, Great Britain, the United States of America, and the Soviet Union). The French, British, and American zones joined together to become the Federal Republic of Germany, also known as West Germany.

12. See Ingrid Arbeitlang's Diplomarbeit "Frauen- und Familienpolitik in der DDR: Eine Analyse der Gleichberechtigungsmaßnahmen in den 70er und 80er Jahren," written in the Department of Political Science at the Free University of Berlin (1991); Susanne Diemer, *Patriarchalismus in der DDR*; Heineman, *What Difference does a Husband Make?*, chapter 7, and "Single Motherhood and Maternal Employment in Divided Germany;" Penrose, "Vierzig Jahre SED-Frauenpolitik."

13. Penrose, "Vierzig Jahre SED-Frauenpolitik," develops this periodization.

14. In contrast, West German policy focused on women as wives and mothers. See Heineman, *What Difference Does a Husband Make?*, chapter 7.

15. See Gisela Helwig, *Frau und Familie: Bundesrepublik Deutschland–DDR* (Köln: Verlag Wissenschaft und Politik Berend von Nottbeck, 1987); Sybille Meyer and Eva Schulze, *Familie im Umbruch: Zur Lage der Familien in der ehemaligen DDR, Studie im Auftrag des Bundesministeriums für Familie und Senioren, Schriftenreihe Band 7* (Stuttgart-Berlin-Köln: Kohlhammer, 1992): 23–35; and Gunnar Winkler, ed. *Frauenreport '90* Im Auftrag der Beauftragten des Ministerrates für die Gleichstellung von Frauen und Männer Dr. Marina Beyer. (Berlin: Verlag die Wirtschaft GmbH, 1990).

16. Penrose, "Vierzig Jahre SED-Frauenpolitik."

17. Helwig, *Frau und Familie*; Penrose, "Vierzig Jahre SED-Frauenpolitik."

18. Trappe, "Selbständigkeit–Pragmatismus–Unterordnung."

19. This phrase is used by Ina Merkel in her study of changing images of women in East German popular magazines. See Merkel, "Leitbilder und Lebensweisen von Frauen in der DDR," in *Sozialgeschichte der DDR,* ed. Hartmut Kaelble, Jürgen Kocka, and Hartmut Zwahr (Stuttgart: Klett Cotta, 1994), 359–82. "Von Kopf bis Fuß auf Arbeit eingestellt" (made for work from head to toe) refers to a song Marlene Dietrich sang: "Von Kopf bis Fuß auf Liebe eingestellt" (made for love from head to toe).

20. Merkel, "Leitbilder und Lebensweisen von Frauen in der DDR."

21. Trappe, "Selbständigkeit–Pragmatismus–Unterordnung" and Heike Trappe "Work and Family in Women's Lives in the German Democratic Republic," *Work and Occupations* 23, no. 4 (1996): 354–77.

22. Winkler, Frauenreport '90, 27; Meyer and Schulze, *Familie im Umbruch*, 16.

23. Trappe, "Work and Family in Women's Lives in the German Democratic Republic," and Meyer and Schulze, *Familie im Umbruch*, 23-35.

24. Jutta Gysi and Dagmar Meyer, "Leitbild: berufstätige Mutter—DDR –Frauen in Familie, Partnerschaft und Ehe," in *Frauen in Deutschland: 1945–1992* ed. Gisela Helwig and Hildegard Maria Nickel (Berlin: Akademie Verlag, 1993); Meyer and Schulze, *Familie im Umbruch*, 48-52; Irene Dölling, "Culture and Gender," in *The Quality of Life in the German Democratic Republic: Changes and Developments in a State Socialist Society* ed. Marilyn Rueschemeyer and Christiane Lemke (Armonk, NY, and London: M.E. Sharpe, Inc., 1989), 43-44.

25. Helwig, *Frau und Familie*, 146-47, 150-51; Sabine Berghahn and Andrea Fritzsche, *Frauenrecht in Ost und West Deutschland - Bilanz -Ausblick*, (Berlin: Frauenbuch bei Basisdruck Verlagsgesellschaft, 1991), 39-43, 50-51.

26. Ute Gerhard, "Die staatlich institutionalisierte 'Lösung' der Frauenfrage. Zur Geschichte der Geschlechterverhältnisse in der DDR," in *Sozialgeschichte der DDR*, ed. Hartmut Kaelble, Jürgen Kocka, and Hartmut Zwahr, 383.

27. Consensus on this point is represented by: Arbeitlang, "Frauen- und Familienpolitik in der DDR," Diemer, *Patriarchalismus*; Dölling, "Culture and Gender"; Gysi and Meyer, "Leitbild: berufstätige Mutter—DDR–Frauen in Familie, Partnerschaft und Ehe"; Christel Lane, "Women in Socialist Society with Special Reference to the German Democratic Republic," *Sociology* 17, no. 4 (1983): 489-505; Meyer and Schulze, *Familie im Umbruch*.

28. This collapse actually started before unification with the currency union of July 1990 which caused East German enterprises to lose both domestic and foreign markets.

29. Gerhard Bosch and Matthias Knuth, "The Labor Market in East Germany," *Cambridge Journal of Economics* 17, no. 3 (1993): 295-308; Gregory B. Wilpert, "Collapsing Lives: Unemployment, Political Consciousness, and Civil Society in East Germany," Ph.D. diss., Brandeis University (1993), 38-43.

30. Rosabeth Moss Kanter, *Work and Family in the United States: A Critical Review and Agenda for Research and Policy*. Social Science Frontiers: Occasional Publications Reviewing New Fields for Social Science Development (New York: Russell Sage Foundation, 1977), 15

31. *Employment Observatory: East Germany*, no. 1 (1992) and no. 15 (1995).

32. See Anita Garey, *Weaving Work and Motherhood* (Philadelphia: Temple University Press, 1999); and Evelyn Nakano Glenn, "Social Constructions of Mothering: A Thematic Overview," in *Mothering: Ideology, Experience, and Agency*, ed. Glenn, Grace Chang, and Linda Rennie Forcey (New York: Routledge, 1994), 16.

33. In "Demographic Shocks After Communism: Eastern Germany, 1989-1993," *Population and Development Review* 20, no. 1 (1994): 137-52, Nicholas Eberstadt reports that East Germany's total number of live births was 60 percent less in the first five months of 1993 than in the same period in 1989. The annualized crude birth rate dropped from 13.3 per thousand for January-May 1989 to 5.1 per thousand in 1993. Eberstadt, concludes this "drop in fertility is unprecedented for an industrialized society during peacetime," 138.

34. Mrs. Jaeger referred to the phenomenon of ambitious West German managers coming to East Germany where there was the chance to earn hardship pay and advance more quickly than otherwise possible because of the rush to establish West German-style business organizations in the eastern part of Germany.

35. Hildegard Maria Nickel reports research on gender and restructuring in the banking sector in former East Germany in "Mitgestalterinnen des Sozialismus—Frauenarbeit in der DDR," in *Frauen in Deutschland*, ed. Helwig and Nickel, 251–54. According to Mrs. Jaeger, the need to rely on the existing East German workforce in banking meant that the West German banks which rushed to fill the eastern banking void had been forced to hire women in positions which had been exclusively filled by men in West Germany.

36. Kindergarten in East Germany was attended all day by most children aged three to six. In 1994, most three-to-six-year-old children in former East Germany were still attending all-day kindergarten.

37. Although Mrs. Roesler did not emphasize this, in East German times, having a job was a requirement—it was considered your social duty to be engaged in "social production." A person without a job was suspected of gaining income illegally. Married women had more freedom in this respect because they could claim to be supported by their husbands, which was considered legitimate even though less desirable than holding a job.

38. As a single mother of one child, at that time she was eligible for four weeks of paid leave to care for a sick child. See Arbeitlang, "Frauen- und Familienpolitik in der DDR."

39. Most discussions of women in East Germany assume that basic living standards were guaranteed through the fact that most women worked most of their working-age lives, however, cases such as Mrs. Roesler's show that in fact some women did fall back on social welfare measures due to their care-taking roles. As far as I know this aspect of the East German social welfare apparatus has not been studied.

40. Actually the decline was smaller, but still extreme. See n. 33 above.

41. The phrase "act as though" comes from Rosabeth Moss Kanter, *Work and Family in the United States: A Critical Review and Agenda for Research and Policy* (New York: Russell Sage Foundation, 1977), 15.

42. Swidler, "Culture in Action," 280

Notes to Chapter 11

1. The research conducted for this paper was supported by a 1999–2000 University of California Pacific Rim Research Fellowship and by a Grant from the University of California, Davis, Women's Consortium. I am grateful to the following individuals for offering feedback on different versions of this paper: Nicole Biggart, Fred Block, Lynne Haney, Estee Neuwirth, Lisa Pollard, Elizabeth Rudd, Preston Rudy, Bindi Shah, G. William Skinner, Eva Skuratowicz, Vicki Smith, and Li Zhang. I am deeply indebted to the migrant women who took time to talk with me, invited me into their dormitories, and befriended me. This paper was presented at the American Sociological Association meetings, 2000. A version of this paper won the 2002 Cheryl Miller Award for outstanding contributions to the field of women and work, from SWS (Sociologists for Women in Society).

2. Jutta Hebel and Gunter Schucher, "Recent Changes in the Chinese Labour System and New Approaches to Labour Market Policies," in *Floating Population and Migration in China: The Impact of Economic Reforms*, ed. Thomas Scharping (Hamburg: Verbund Stiftung Deutsches Ubersee-Institut, 1997) 119–48.

3. Dorothy J. Solinger, *Contesting Citizenship in Urban China: Peasant Migrants, the State, and the Logic of the Market* (Berkeley: University of California Press, 1999).

4. Deborah S. Davis, "Introduction: A Revolution in Consumption," in *The Consumer Revolution in Urban China*, ed. Deborah S. Davis (Berkeley: University of California Press, 2000).

5. Solinger, *Contesting Citizenship*.

6. Michael Burawoy makes a similar argument in the case of South African Apartheid laws: "The enforcement of pass laws externalizes the supplies of unemployed labor and the processes of labor-force renewal to areas where those not gainfully employed are legally permitted to reside. . . ."; see Burawoy, "The Functions and Reproduction of Migrant Labor: Comparative Material from Southern Africa and the United States," *American Journal of Sociology* 81, no. 5 (1976): 1060.

7. This type of flexibility is what Smith terms "restrictive." It creates a vulnerable and insecure workforce by transferring the costs of market instability to workers. This contrasts with an "enabling" approach to flexibility, which emphasizes greater worker involvement and increased investment in worker training. See Vicki Smith, "Institutionalizing Flexibility in a Service Firm: Multiple Contingencies and Hidden Hierarchies," *Work and Occupations* (August 1994): 284–308.

8. For analyses of immigration and structures of citizenship see Dorothy J. Solinger, "Citizenship Issues in China's Internal Migration: Comparisons with Germany and Japan," *Political Science Quarterly* 114, no. 3 (1999): 435–78; Dorothy T. Solingen, *Contesting Citizenship in Urban China*.

9. Xiushi Yang finds that in Zhejiang more migrant women are employed in service than in manufacturing.; see Yang, "Interconnections among Gender, Work, and Migration: Evidence form Zhejiang Province," in *Re-drawing Boundaries: Work Households, and Gender in China*. (Berkeley: University of California Press, 2000), 209. See also Solinger, *Contesting Citizenship in Urban China: Peasant Migrants, the State, and the Logic of the Market*; Cindy Fan, "Migration, Gender, and the Labor Market" (paper presented at the Immigration in Contemporary China Conference, University of California, Los Angeles, 1998).

10. Studies of China's migrant women employed in manufacturing include, Anita Chan, *China's Workers under Assault: The Exploitation of Labor in a Globalizing Economy* (Armonk, NY: M.E. Sharpe, 2001); Anita Chan, "The Culture of Survival: Lives of Migrant Workers through the Prism of Private Letters," in *Popular China: Unofficial Culture in a Globalizing Society*, ed. Perry Link, Richard P. Madsen, and Paul G. Pickowicz (New York: Rowman and Littlefield, 2002), 163–88; Ching Kwan Lee, *Gender and the South China Miracle: Two Worlds of Factory Women* (Berkeley: University of California Press, 1998); Pun Ngai, "Becoming *Dagongmei* (Working Girls): The Politics of Identity and Difference in Reform China," *The China Journal* 42 (1999): 2–18; Feng Xu, *Women Migrant Workers in China's Economic Reform* (New York: St. Martin's Press, 2000).

11. As the basis for organizing the Maoist-era urban cradle-to-grave system of welfare, the work unit provided housing, food, education, and medical care for workers at their location of work; see Andrew Walder, *Communist Neo-traditionalism: Work and Authority in Chinese Industry* (Berkeley: University of California Press, 1986).

12. Fred Block, "The Roles of the State in the Economy," in *The Handbook of Economic Sociology*, ed. Neil Smelser and Richard Swedberg (Princeton: Princeton University Press, 1994), 691–710; Sean O'Riain, "States and Markets in an Era of Globalization," *Annual Review of Sociology* 26 (2000): 187–213; Karl Polanyi, *The Great Transformation* (Boston: Beacon Press, 1957). For an analysis of the state's increased

regulatory role since economic reform in China, see Vivienne Shue, *The Reach of the State: Sketches of the Chinese Body Politic* (Stanford, CA: Stanford University Press, 1988).

13. For analyses of the embeddedness of markets in familial and cultural structures in East Asia, see Nicole Woolsey Biggart, "Explaining Asian Economic Organization: Toward a Weberian Institutional Perspective," *Theory and Society* 20 (1991): 199–232; Gary G. Hamilton and Biggart, "Market, Culture, and Authority: A Comparative Analysis of Management and Organization in the Far East," *American Journal of Sociology* 15 (1988): S52.

14. Of course the state is not a homogeneous institutional form but rather comprised of diverse agencies with differentiated structures; see Lynne Haney, "Homeboys, Babies, Men in Suits—The State and the Reproduction of Male Dominance," *American Sociological Review* 61, no. 5 (1996): 759–78.

15. Ellen R. Judd, *Gender and Power in Rural North China* (Stanford: Stanford University Press, 1994).

16. Lee, *Gender and the South China Miracle*; Josephine Smart and Alan Smart, "Obligation and Control—Employment of Kin in Capitalist Labour Management in China," *Critique of Anthropology* 13, no. 1 (1993): 7–31.

17. Ching Kwan Lee, "Engendering the Worlds of Labor: Women Workers, Labor Markets, and Production Politics in the South China Economic Miracle," *American Sociological Review* 60 (1995): 378–97.

18. Ibid., 380.

19. For a discussion of the gendered assumptions built into organizational structures see Joan Acker, "Hierarchies, Bodies, and Jobs: A Theory of Gendered Organizations," *Gender and Society*, 4 (1990): 159–79.

20. Kam Wing Chan, *Cities with Invisible Walls: Reinterpreting Urbanization in Post-1949 China* (Hong Kong: Oxford University Press, 1994); Tiejun Cheng and Mark Selden, "The Origins and Social Consequences of China's Hukou System," *China Quarterly* 139 (1994): 644–68; Solinger, *Contesting Citizenship*.

21. Margery Wolf, *Revolution Postponed: Women in Contemporary China* (Stanford, CA: Stanford University Press, 1985). In China's rural periphery, whence a majority of migrant women originate, gender hierarchies are maintained, in part, by an enduring patrilineal tradition—one that has declined in salience in regions closer to urban centers. See G. William Skinner, Mark Henderson, and Yuan Jianhua, "China's fertility transition through regional space—Using GIS and Census Data for a Spatial Analysis of Historical Demography," *Social Science History* 24, no. 3 (2000): 613–52.

22. Yang, "Interconnections among Gender, Work, and Migration," 206–7.

23. In some regions patrilocal marriage within the village became a more acceptable practice during the Maoist era, especially among poor villages. Maoist-era collectivization leveled inequalities within the village, and exacerbated inter-village socio-economic hierarchies. As a result prospective brides were unwilling to marry into villages at the bottom of the hierarchy. Marriage partnerships within such villages became increasingly endogamous. Scholars predict that market reforms will curtail intra-village marriages. See, for example, William Lavely, "Marriage and Mobility under Rural Collectivism," in *Marriage and Inequality in Chinese Society*, ed. Rubie S. Watson and Patricia Buckley Ebrey (Berkeley: University of California Press, 1991), 286–312; Mark Selden, "Family Strategies and Structures in Rural North China," *Chinese Families in the Post-Mao Era*, ed. Deborah Davis, Stevan Harrell, and Joint Committee on Chinese Studies (U.S.) (Berkeley: University of California Press, 1993),

139-64. The present research suggests that in the context of the *hukou* system, migrant women could become a force for increased intra-village marriage.

24. Occasionally women migrate along with their spouse, but this is exceptional.

25. Kam Wing Chan, *Cities with Invisible Walls*; Cheng and Selden, "Origins and Social Consequences"; Solinger, *Contesting Citizenship*; and Li Zhang, *Strangers in the City: Reconfigurations of Space, Power, and Social Networks within China's Floating Population* (Stanford: Stanford University Press, 2001).

26. Only state-organized migration was permitted; see Walder, *Communist Neo-traditionalism*.

27. Ibid.

28. Zhang, *Strangers in the City*.

29. Solinger, *Contesting Citizenship*.

30. Ibid.

31. Some primary sector firms are allowed to hire rural workers as casual laborers for jobs that urban workers are unwilling to perform.

32. Xu, *Women Migrant Workers*.

33. All names used in this chapter are pseudonyms.

34. Work in manufacturing tends to be concentrated in the Southeast Coastal special economic zones while all urban centers employ service workers. See Lee, *Gender and the South China Miracle*.

35. Xu, *Women Migrant Workers*.

36. Older women might be hired to perform backstage cleaning, dishwashing, etc. They might also be hired to work as nannies in private households, but this was somewhat unusual as employers preferred younger workers who were perceived to be more docile and tractable.

37. Where uniforms are worn, women are expected to offer deposits for them as well. If the uniforms are damaged, the deposit is forfeited.

38. Zhanglei's salary was 300 yuan per month.

39. see Linda Fuller and Vicki Smith, "Consumers' Reports—Management by Customers in a Changing Economy," *Work, Employment and Society* 5, no. 1 (1991): 1–16; Arlie Russell Hochschild, *The Managed Heart: Commercialization of Human Feeling* (Berkeley: University of California Press, 1983); Robin Leidner, *Fast Food, Fast Talk* (Berkeley: University of California Press, 1993).

40. Ann Anagnost, *National Past-times: Narrative, Representation, and Power in Modern China: Body, Commodity, Text* (Durham, NC: Duke University Press, 1997), 136. Comparing the *hukou* system to ethnicity-based citizenship laws in the nations of Japan and Germany, Solinger suggests that in China restrictions on internal migration reinforce what can be viewed as an ethnic divide between those from urban and rural areas. In China, she argues, " . . . the response to outsiders . . . starts from highly exclusionary, culturally-superior, ethnocentrically-informed stances," Solingen, *Citizenship Issues in China's Internal Migration: Comparisons with Germany and Japan*, 457.

41. Ann Anagnost, *National Past-times: Narrative, Representation, and Power in Modern China*, 120–21. The incitement to enhance the quality of the population was prompted in part by a State Council report placing responsibility for China's "backwardness" on the inadequate quality of the rural population. The government promotes the one child per family population policy through such appeals.

42. For discussions of this assumed association see Lee, *Gender and the South China Miracle*.

43. Viviana A. Zelizer, *The Social Meaning of Money: Pin Money, Paychecks, Poor Relief, and Other Currencies* (Princeton, NJ: Princeton University Press, 1997).

44. For a similar finding for migrant factory workers see Xu, *Women Migrant Workers*.

45. Lydia Kung, *Factory Women in Taiwan* (New York: Columbia University Press, 1994); Janet Salaff, "Women, the Family, and the State: Hong Kong, Taiwan, and Singapore: Newly Industrialized Countries in Asia," in *Women, Employment, and the Family in the International Division of Labor*, ed. Sharon Stichter and Jane L. Parpart (Philadelphia: Temple University Press: 1990), 98–136. Comparing Taiwan's patrilineal family system to Indonesia's bilateral system, Wolf asserts that the latter system offers rural factory women more room to negotiate autonomy from the family. She argues that kinship structures play a central role in shaping the experiences and consequences of wage work for women. See Diane L. Wolf, *Factory Daughters: Gender, Household Dynamics, and Rural Industrialization in Java* (Berkeley: University of California Press, 1992). However, Xu astutely points out that family systems "acquire specific meanings as a result of political, economic and sociocultural change." *Women Migrant Workers*, 139. China's socialist revolution weakened the patrilineal extended kinship system and mandated women's involvement in agricultural production. Women's work contributions were tracked through a system of work points (even if work points were ultimately allocated to the male family head). As we shall see in a later section of this chapter, reforms have strengthened but not entirely restored village patriarchy.

46. Susan Greenhalgh and Jiali Li, "Engendering Reproductive Policy and Practice in Peasant China: For a Feminist Demography of Reproduction," *Signs* 20, no. 31 (1995): 601–41.

47. Skinner, Henderson, and Jianhua, "China's fertility."

48. Researchers suggest that decollectivization will reinforce the traditional practice of extra-village patrilocal marriage; see n. 23 above.

49. Susan Greenhalgh, "The Evolution of the One-Child Policy in Shaanxi, 1979-88," *China Quarterly* 122 (1990): 191–229.

50. Ren Xin, *Economic Reform and Domestic Trafficking of Women and Children in China* (Berkeley: University of California Press, 2001); P. Zhuang, "On the Social Phenomenon of Trafficking in Women in China," *Chinese Education and Society* 26, no. 3 (1993): 33–50.

51. Families without urban residence have the option of paying a special tuition rate for access to urban schools. This rate is far beyond the amount of money most families are able to afford.

52. Few spoke of the possibility of uxorilocal marriage, that is, arranging for a prospective husband to relocate within the bride's residence. When I asked my informants about uxorilocal marriage, they treated this as entire untenable option. Hence, when my informants spoke of marriage within their own villages, they referred to virilocal marriage, that is, moving into the home of their husband's family.

53. Although migrant women experienced gender inequality at work, they were also exposed to urban marriage arrangements that allowed women and men to reside independently of parents. Urban women are not prevented from visiting their natal families regularly and often offer them substantial support.

54. As the present chapter is based on research conducted in the urban center, I am not able to assess the success of women who expressed an intention to alter village practices. Understanding how migrant women actually negotiate family structures will be a critical part of the future research agenda.

Notes to Chapter 12

1. See Seth Koven and Sonya Michel, *Mothers of a New World: Maternalist Politics and the Origins of the Welfare States* (London: Routledge, 1993); Theda Skocpol, *Protecting Soldiers and Mothers* (Cambridge: Harvard University Press, 1992); Susan Pedersen, *Family, Dependence and the Origins of the Welfare State: Britain and France, 1914–1945* (New York: Cambridge University Press, 1993); Jane Lewis, "Gender and the Development of Welfare Regimes," *Journal of European Social Policy* 2 (1992): 159–73; Diane Sainsbury, *Gender, Equality and Welfare States* (Cambridge: Cambridge University Press, 1996); and Julia O'Connor, Ann Shola Orloff, and Sheila Shaver, *States, Markets, Families: Gender, Liberalism and Social Policy in Australia, Canada, Great Britain and the United States* (New York: Cambridge University Press, 1999).

2. See Gøsta Esping-Andersen, *Social Foundations of Postindustrial Economies* (New York: Oxford University Press, 1999); Walter Korpi, "Faces of Inequality: Gender, Class and Patterns of Inequalities in Different Types of Welfare States," *Social Politics* 7 (2000): 127–91; Evelyne Huber and John Stephens, *Development and Crisis of the Welfare State: Parties and Policies in Global Markets* (Chicago: University of Chicago Press, 2001); and Paul Pierson, ed., *The New Politics of the Welfare State* (New York: Oxford University Press, 2001). Indeed, work on gender and the welfare state has become something of a growth industry. For examples of these reviews, see Ann Shola Orloff, "Gender and the Welfare State," *Annual Review of Sociology* 22 (1996): 51–70; Julia O'Connor, "From Women in the Welfare State to Gendering Welfare Regimes," *Current Sociology* 44 (1996): 1–124; and Lynne Haney, "Engendering the Welfare State," *Comparative Studies in Society and History* 40 (1998): 748–67. There are a host of comparative studies of provision for solo mothers or for older women, of the organization of caring work, and of state support to women's labor force participation through the provision of public services such as child care, along with cross-national research on poverty among households headed by women and gender poverty gaps. For example, see Sainsbury, *Gender, Equality and Welfare States*; Barbara Hobson, "No Exit, No Voice: Women's Economic Dependency and the Welfare State," *Acta Sociologica* 33 (1990): 235–50; Jane Lewis, "Gender and Welfare Regimes: Further Thoughts," *Social Politics* 4 (1997): 160–77; Gertrude Schaffner Goldberg and Eleanor Kremen, *The Feminization of Poverty: Only in America?* (New York: Praeger, 1990); Mary Daly and Jane Lewis, "The Concept of Social Care and the Analysis of Contemporary Welfare States," *British Journal of Sociology* 51 (June 2000): 281–98; Mary Daly, *The Gender Division of Welfare: The Impact of the British and German Welfare States* (Cambridge, U.K. and New York: Cambridge University Press, 2000); Simon Duncan and Rosalind Edwards, *Lone Mothers, Paid Work and Gendered Moral Rationalities* (New York: St. Martin's Press, 1999); Irwin Garfinkel and Sara McLanahan, *Single Mothers and Their Children: A New American Dilemma* (Washington, DC: Urban Institute, 1986); Karen Christopher, "Welfare State Regimes and Mothers' Poverty," *Social Politics* 9 (2002): 60–86; Janet Gornick, Marcia Meyers, and Katherin Ross, "Supporting the Employment of Mothers: Policy Variation Across Fourteen Welfare States," *Journal of European Social Policy* 7 (1997): 45–70; and Jay Ginn, Debra Street, and Sara Arber, *Women, Work, and Pensions: International Issues and Prospects* (Buckingham, U.K.: Open University Press, 2001). Historians and historically-inclined social scientists have investigating the gendered origins of welfare states at the end of the nineteenth and beginning of the twentieth century, highlighting the key role of women reformers making political claims for social rights on the basis of their role as mothers—what today's scholars call "maternalism," and the significance

of early social provision for mothers and their children. Among many fine recent works, see Koven and Michel, *Mothers of a New World;* Linda Gordon, *Pitied but Not Entitled: Single Mothers and the History of Welfare* (New York: Free Press, 1994); Skocpol, *Protecting Soldiers and Mothers*; Gisela Bock and Pat Thane, ed., *Maternity and Gender Politics: Women and the Rise of the European Welfare States, 1880s–1950s* (New York: Routledge, 1991); Joanne L. Goodwin, *Gender and the Politics of Welfare Reform: Mothers' Pensions in Chicago, 1911–1929* (Chicago: University of Chicago Press, 1997); and Gwendolyn Mink, *Wages of Motherhood: Inequality in the Welfare State, 1917–1942* (Ithaca, NY: Cornell University Press, 1995).

3. The tendency to focus on women and difference is sometimes found in feminist scholarship as well, although here we are more likely to find the observation that the enduring inequalities in families, polities, and labor markets associated with women's disproportionate responsibility for caregiving and domestic labor cannot be overcome without some change in men's behavior and the structure of work—as well as the more common (and mainstream) plea for greater state support of care services and income assistance.

4. See Bettina Cass, "Citizenship, Work, and Welfare: The Dilemma for Australian Women," *Social Politics* 1 (1994): 106–24; Anthony McMahon, "Male Readings of Feminist Theory: The Psychologization of Sexual Politics in the Masculinity Literature," *Theory and Society* 22 (1993): 675–95; Martha Fineman, *The Neutered Mother, the Sexual Family, and Other Twentieth Century Tragedies* (New York: Routledge, 1995); and Eva Kittay, "Human Dependency and Rawlsian Equality," in *Feminists Rethink the Self,* ed. Diana Tietjens Meyers (Boulder, CO: Westview, 1997).

5. See Nancy Fraser, *Justice Interrruptus* (New York: Verso, 1997).

6. Notable exceptions include Jane Jenson, "Gender and Reproduction: Or, Babies and the State," *Studies in Political Economy* 20 (1986): 9–45; R.W. Connell, *Masculinities* (Berkeley: University of California Press, 1995); Pedersen, *Family, Dependence and the Origins of the Welfare State*; Arnlaug Leira, "Caring as Social Right: Cash for Child Care and Daddy Leave," *Social Politics* 5 (1998): 362–78; Barbara Hobson, ed., *Making Men into Fathers* (New York: Cambridge University Press, 2002). For a suggestive analysis of men's familial roles in pre-modern states, see Julia Adams, "The Familial State: Elite Family Practices and State-Making in the Early Modern Netherlands," *Theory and Society* 23 (1994): 505–39.

7. See Lewis, "Gender and the Development of Welfare Regimes," and "Gender and Welfare Regimes." See also Sainsbury, *Gender, Equality and Welfare States.*

8. For example, see Gøsta Esping-Andersen, *The Three Worlds of Welfare Capitalism* (Cambridge, U.K.: Polity Press, 1990) and *Social Foundations of Postindustrial Economies*; Walter Korpi and Joakim Palme, "The Paradox of Redistribution and Strategies of Equality: Welfare State Institutions, Inequality, and Poverty in the Western Countries," *American Sociological Review* 63 (1998): 661–87; and Pierson, *The New Politics of the Welfare State.*

9. See Ann Shola Orloff, "Gender and the Social Rights of Citizenship: The Comparative Analysis of Gender Relations and Welfare States," *American Sociological Review* 58 (1993): 303–28; and O'Connor, Orloff, and Shaver, *States, Markets, Families.*

10. Note, however, that I examine only one set of state policies important for the constitution of gender—the system of social provision, including programs of social insurance and assistance, in the context of the overall welfare regime (including the absence of public provision as well as private benefits). Family law has been a key site for examining the regulation of gender, families and sexuality, including fatherhood

(e.g., the Defense of Marriage Act of 1996). See Fineman, *The Neutered Mother, the Sexual Family, and Other Twentieth Century Tragedies*; and Nancy Cott, *Public Vows: A History of Marriage and the Nation* (Cambridge: Harvard University Press, 2001). However, for reasons of space, I will examine this arena only insofar as it has become involved in the state's social welfare functions. Indeed, one might argue that the focus on large-scale social provision offers a new angle of vision on how masculinities and fatherhood are constructed for parts of the population that for the most part escape the regulatory apparatus of the courts.

11. Richard Freeman, "The Feminization of Work in the USA: A New Era for (Man)kind?" in *Gender and the Labour Market*, ed. Siv Gustafsson and Daniele Meulders (New York: St. Martin's, 2000); and Esping-Andersen, *Social Foundations*.

12. The term "welfare regime" emerged in the context of the comparative literature on systems of social provision, in which it has been common to refer to "welfare states," taking the term popularized in post-WWII Europe and applying it more broadly as a kind of shorthand for all Western systems of social provision, even while at least occasionally exploring the merits and historic specificity of the term. See Esping-Andersen, *Three Worlds*, chap. 1 and *Social Foundations*, 33–35; and Pierson, *New Politics*. The term "welfare regime" is meant to connote a broader set of institutions than is captured by the term "welfare state." Going beyond welfare *states*, this concept pushes us to examine the interplay between public and private institutions, including families, while continuing to recognize the constitutive importance of states for social relations, and the ways in which the character of state programs shape gendered and other identities, political goals, inequalities. See O'Connor, Orloff, and Shaver, *States, Markets, Families*. If one thinks of "welfare" most broadly as encompassing income, services, and care, then the welfare regime may be defined as "the combined, interdependent way in which welfare is produced and allocated between state, market, and family." Esping-Andersen, *Social Foundations*, 34–35.

13. See Diana Pearce, "Toil and Trouble: Women Workers and Unemployment Compensation," in *Women and Poverty*, ed. Barbara Gelpi et al. (Chicago: University of Chicago Press, 1986); and Barbara Nelson, "The Origins of the Two-Channel Welfare State: Workmen's Compensation and Mothers' Aid," in *Women, the State and Welfare*, ed. Linda Gordon (Madison: University of Wisconsin Press, 1990).

14. Feminist work on the cross-national and historical variation in policies makes it clear that not all systems can be characterized as "two-tier" like the United States. Moreover, even in the United States, women are found among recipients of both "top" and "bottom"-tier benefits. See Sainsbury, *Gender, Equality and Welfare States*; Ann Shola Orloff, "Gender in Early U.S. Social Policy," *Journal of Policy History* 3 (1991): 249–81; and O'Connor, Orloff, and Shaver, *States, Markets, Families*. Sonya Michel argues that the United States has a three-tier system: provision for workers, for their dependents, and for those relying on public assistance. See "The Benefits of Race and Gender: Democracy and Equity in America's Public/Private Welfare State," paper presented at the Social Science History Association, Chicago, 2001. And one could even add a fourth tier—the programs, locally and unevenly provided, for the categories of people who do not even qualify for public assistance (most childless and non-disabled adults, for example).

15. Helga Hernes, *Welfare State and Woman Power* (Oslo: Norwegian University Press, 1987). The fact that some analysts use the term "gender-friendly" when discussing provisions relevant for women's well-being indicates just how far we still need to go in weaning people from the idea that "gender equals women."

16. See Denise Riley, *"Am I that name?": Feminism and the Category of "Women" in History* (Minneapolis: University of Minnesota, 1988); Patricia Hill Collins, *Black Feminist Thought* (Boston: Unwin, Hyman, 1990); Judith Butler, *Gender Trouble* (New York: Routledge, 1990); Linda Zerilli, "Doing without Knowing: Feminism's Politics of the Ordinary," *Political Theory* 26 (1998): 435-58; and Linda Nicholson and Steven Seidman, eds., *Social Postmodernism: Beyond Identity Politics* (New York: Cambridge University Press, 1995). Differences based on racial, national, or ethnic identities have often precluded solidarity among women from different groups. Women of particular racial or ethnic groups or classes have promoted policies that best served their own group's interests, for example, in creating supervisory and administrative positions for educated women within welfare bureaucracies or in promoting birth rates among favored racial, religious, or ethnic groups. See Bock and Thane, *Maternity and Gender Politics*; Claudia Koonz, *Mothers in the Fatherland: Women, the Family, and Nazi Germany* (New York: St. Martin's Press, 1987); Gordon, *Pitied but Not Entitled*; Koven and Michel, *Mothers of a New World*; and Marilyn Lake, "Mission Impossible: How Men Gave Birth to the Australian Nation—Nationalism, Gender and other Seminal Acts," *Gender and History* 4 (1992): 305-22. While it has been more typical for gender-sensitive analyses to focus on the inequities between men and women in the sharing of caring and domestic work, the question of how caring work is shared increasingly focuses on issues of race/ethnicity/nationality—for example, Glenn points to the role of women of color in taking some of the burden of caring labor from white women's shoulders, while "letting men off the hook." See Evelyn Nakano Glenn, "From Servitude to Service Work: Historical Continuities in the Racial Division of Paid Reproductive Labor," *Signs* 18 (1992): 1-43. Blumstein and Schwartz reported that the most common way for the dual-earner upper-middle class couples they interviewed to cope with housework and other domestic work was to hire someone else to do it. See Phillip Blumstein and Pepper Schwartz, *American Couples: Money, Work, Sex* (New York: William Morrow, 1983).

17. In a refreshing departure from the Swedophilia of many commentators on gender and welfare, Lewis notes some of the problems associated with the dual breadwinner (social-democratic) model, thus differing with mainstream views about what social welfare arrangements best promote women's interests. See Lewis, "Gender and Welfare Regimes"; and Jane Lewis and Gertrude Astrom, "Equality, Difference, and State Welfare: Labor Market and Family Policies in Sweden," *Feminist Studies* 18 (1992): 59-87. She is wary of assuming, as do Esping-Andersen and many other authors, that modern welfare regimes have an "emancipatory effect . . . particularly in respect of the opportunities they present for paid employment" of women, even as she is critical of the assumption embodied in many systems of social provision that women are full-time caregivers. Her solution? "We have to consider their [women's] right not to engage in paid work (decommodification) and by extension their right to do unpaid work, and *also* their right to do paid work and by extension their right not to engage in unpaid work." It is an interesting intellectual exercise to consider how all this applies to men—particularly the right "not to care." Many analysts are being pushed to consider ways to ensure that men do some of the work of care. See Kevin Olson, "Recognizing Gender, Redistributing Labor: A Capabilities Approach," *Social Politics* (forthcoming).

18. The content of "women-friendliness" differs little from that developed by scholars who had believed that women's ultimate gender interests could reliably be deduced from a structural analysis of gender. For example, echoing classic Marxist

distinctions between "subjective" and "objective" (class) interests, Molyneux distinguished two types of gender interests—practical and strategic. Practical gender interests are derived inductively from women's positioning within existing gender relations and if realized would improve (some) women's material situation but would not necessarily fundamentally challenge the gender order. See Molyneux "Mobilization without Emancipation? Women's Interests, the State and Revolution in Nicaragua," *Feminist Studies* 11 (1985): 232. But Molyneux, like many others, was also committed to the idea that unity can be built among women—even in the face of differences—on the basis of their "strategic gender interests," deduced from feminist analyses "of women's subordination and from the formulation of an alternative, more satisfactory set of arrangements to those which exist," often linked to the welfare state in provisions such as adequate child care. See also Denise Kandiyoti, "Bargaining with Patriarchy," in *The Social Construction of Gender*, ed. Judith Lorber and Susan Farrell (Thousand Oaks, CA: Sage, 1991); and Deborah Rhode, *Speaking of Sex: The Denial of Gender Inequality* (Cambridge: Harvard University Press, 1997). Are the more satisfactory arrangements for women necessarily less satisfactory for men? This is not addressed. But neither can this type of analysis cope with the historically specific and constructed character of groups and their goals.

19. Connell, *Masculinities*.

20. See Pedersen, *Family, Dependence and the Origins of the Welfare State*; and Jenson, "Gender and Reproduction."

21. Among many others, see Michèle Barrett and Anne Phillips, eds., *Destabilizing Theory: Contemporary Feminist Debates* (Stanford, CA: Stanford University Press, 1992); Butler, *Gender Trouble*; Judith Butler and Joan W. Scott, eds., *Feminists Theorize the Political* (New York: Routledge, 1992); Nicholas B. Dirks, Geoff Eley, and Sherry B. Ortner, eds., *Culture/Power/History: A Reader in Contemporary Social Theory* (Princeton, NJ: Princeton University Press, 1994); Nancy Fraser, *Unruly Practices: Power, Discourse, and Gender in Contemporary Social Theory* (Minneapolis: University of Minnesota Press, 1989) and *Justice Interrruptus*; Nicholson and Seidman, *Social Postmodernism*; and Linda Zerilli, "Feminism's Flight from the Ordinary," in *Vocations of Political Theory*, ed. Jason Frank and John Tamborino (Minneapolis: University of Minnesota Press, 2000).

22. This can and should be extended to consider other sorts of identities and associated goals—Europeans, heterosexuals, whites, citizens, and so on—and how these are articulated with particular masculine identities

23. Lewis, "Gender and the Development of Welfare Regimes."

24. Lewis was more concerned with gendered assumptions—the *logic* of policy—than with outcomes, such as the level of poverty among single mothers, but she concedes that as one looks at a greater range of male breadwinner regimes, differences among countries in outcomes become clear, even if the logic of supporting male breadwinner-female housewife families is the same. See Lewis, "Gender and Welfare Regimes," 169. Knijn notes that breadwinner models have also varied in terms of the extent of support given to women as caregivers with independent entitlements versus as wives with only derived benefits; for example, in the Netherlands, support to breadwinners was accompanied by support to solo mothers engaged in full-time caregiving. Trudie Knijn, "Fish without Bikes: Revision of the Dutch Welfare State and its Consequences for the (In)Dependence of Single Mothers," *Social Politics* 1 (1994): 83–105.

25. I have argued elsewhere that these elements should be conceptualized as parts of welfare state stratification, thereby making linkages between mainstream analyses

such as Esping-Andersen's and the feminist approach; we should be insisting on the need to explore gender along with class and other forms of inequality. See Orloff, "Gender and the Social Rights of Citizenship."

26. France and the Scandinavian countries (and the Eastern European states before 1989) stand out as examples of regimes that put substantial resources into public policies—public child care and elder care, parental leaves—that ease combining paid work and motherhood. See Jenson, "Gender and Reproduction"; Arnlaug Leira, *Welfare States and Working Mothers* (Cambridge University Press, 1992); Anette Borchorst, "The Scandinavian Welfare States—Patriarchal, Gender Neutral or Woman-Friendly?" *International Journal of Contemporary Sociology* 31 (1994): 1–23. In contrast, Britain, Holland, and Germany have directed resources toward allowing women to devote their time to domesticity either through direct payments to women or additional supports to male wage-earners. See Knijn, "Fish without Bikes"; Ilona Ostner, "Lone Mothers in Germany Before and After Unification," in *Lone Mothers in European Welfare Regimes: Shifting Policy Logics*, ed. Jane Lewis (Philadelphia: Jessica Kingsley Publishers, 1997); and Lewis, "Gender and the Development of Welfare Regimes." The "Latin Rim" countries have policies based on the assumption that families will "do it themselves," poorly developed services and a concomitant trade-off between paid work and childrearing. See Chiara Saraceno, "The Ambivalent Familism of the Italian Welfare State," *Social Politics* 1 (1994): 60–82. The U.S. and Canada, while among the countries supporting women's domesticity as recently as the 1960s, have in the last couple of decades moved towards supporting women's employment through market mechanisms. See O'Connor, Orloff, and Shaver, *States, Markets, Families*.

27. See Barbara Hobson, "Solo Mothers, Social Policy Regimes, and the Logics of Gender," in *Gendering Welfare States*, ed. Diane Sainsbury (London: Sage, 1994).

28. See Mary Ruggie, *The State and Working Women* (Princeton, NJ: Princeton University Press, 1994).

29. Kathleen Gerson, *No Man's Land* (New York: Basic Books, 1995).

30. For example, see Ronald Mincy, "What About Black Fathers?" *The American Prospect* 13 (2002): 8; and Anna Gavanas, *Masculinizing Fatherhood: Sexuality, Marriage and Race in the U.S. Fatherhood Responsibility Movement*, Ph.D. diss., Stockholm University, 2001. Moreover, men differ in their patterns of fathering children, with African-Americans more likely to report having children by a number of women.

31. Esping-Andersen, *Three Worlds*.

32. The United States is seen by most analysts as a liberal policy regime, where liberalism in social policy is taken to imply a preference for private rather than state provision, and a reluctance to interfere politically with the functioning of the market—market capitalism constrains the role of the state vis-à-vis economy and society. See Karl Polanyi, *The Great Transformation: The Political and Economic Origins of Our Time* (Boston: Bescon Press, 1957). A commitment to precluding substantial public provision of services and income and limiting the extent of income redistribution does set limits on policymaking. Still, there have been recurring debates among adherents of liberalism over the extent to which state intervention is necessary to undergird responsible individual initiatives, mitigate against market and family "failures," and ensure a "level playing field" by guaranteeing certain rules of the game and social minima. These pit "classical" or "neo-liberals" against "social" or "new" liberals. See O'Connor, Orloff, and Shaver, *States, Markets, Families*, chap. 2; and Ann Shola Orloff, *The Politics of Pensions: A Comparative Analysis of Britain, Canada, and the United States,*

1880–1940 (Madison: University of Wisconsin Press, 1993), chap. 5. In American usage, "liberalism" usually refers to "social liberals"—those who are willing to use the state, at least to some degree, to guarantee social minima and regulate markets. Liberalism has also been associated with a range of different gender ideologies, from support for the traditional gender division of labor and the male breadwinner family to gender egalitarianism.

33. Esping-Andersen now pays far more attention to this issue, see Esping-Andersen, *Social Foundations of Postindustrial Economies*.

34. Orloff, "Gender and the Social Rights of Citizenship." There are at least three possible sources for this capacity: caregivers' cash benefits, a citizen's wage, or paid work. For anyone with children, elderly relatives, or others dependent on care, support services are necessary to entering employment (these may be provided by wives, mothers, daughters, sisters, or other relations—even male ones—the state or the market).

35. Until recently, however, women did not have equal access to such programs, principally because they were not in full-time employment, although in some cases because program rules discriminated against women explicitly (e.g., by not offering the same spousal benefits to men and to women workers).

36. Thus, a presumed "crisis of fatherhood" is linked by some analysts to targeted cash assistance ("welfare") programs that allow women to support themselves without men, but not to the overall shape of the U.S. policy regimes. To the extent it is more framed as a problem of the entire society, it is construed as largely cultural or moral. See David Blankenhorn, *Fatherless America: Confronting Our Most Urgent Social Problem* (New York: Basic Books, 1995).

37. Esping-Andersen, *Social Foundations of Postindustrial Economies*.

38. See Livia Olah, Eva Bernhardt, and Frances Goldscheider, "Coresidential Paternal Roles in Industrialized Countries: Sweden, Hungary and the United States," in *Making Men into Fathers*, ed. Barbara Hobson (New York: Cambridge University Press, 2002); and Irene Wennemo, *Sharing the Costs of Children: Studies on the Development of Family Support in the OECD Countries* (Stockholm: Swedish Institute of Social Research Dissertation Series, No. 25, 1994).

39. See Esping-Andersen, *Three Worlds* and *Social Foundations*; Margaret Weir, *The Politics of Jobs* (Princeton, NJ: Princeton University Press, 1992); Orloff, *Politics of Pensions*; and O'Connor, Orloff, and Shaver, *States, Markets, Families*.

40. Koven and Michel, *Mothers of a New World*.

41. See Lake, "Mission Impossible"; and Pedersen, *Family, Dependence and the Origins of the Welfare State*.

42. See Peter Flora and Jens Alber, "Modernization, Democratization and the Development of Welfare States in Western Europe," in *The Development of Welfare States in Europe and America*, ed. P. Flora and A. Heidenheimer (New Brunswick, NJ: Transaction Press, 1981); Skocpol, *Protecting Soldiers and Mothers*; and Orloff, *The Politics of Pensions*.

43. Orloff, *The Politics of Pensions*.

44. See Sonya Michel, *Children's Interests/Mothers' Rights: The Shaping of America's Child Care Policy* (New Haven: Yale University Press, 1999).

45. See Susan Lehrer, *Origins of Protective Labor Legislation for Women, 1905–1925* (Albany, NY: State University of New York Press, 1987); and Ulla Wikander, Alice Kessler-Harris, and Jane Lewis, eds., *Protecting Women: Labor Legislation in Europe, the United States, and Australia, 1880–1920* (Urbana: University of Illinois Press, 1995).

46. See Orloff, *The Politics of Pensions*, chap. 4.

47. Ibid, chaps. 5, 7.

48. Some analysts have seen these early policy developments as the beginning of the "two-tier" welfare state, arguing that workers' compensation established a superior (in terms of benefits and treatment), "male" stream of welfare and mothers' pensions an inferior "female" stream. See Nelson, "The Origins of the Two-Channel Welfare State." I contend elsewhere that these programs reflected gender differentiation, but that they did not yet institutionalize gender inequality. See Orloff, "Gender in Early U.S. Social Policy." Programs established during the New Deal did more to contribute through policy to gender differentiation and gender inequality.

49. Michael Willrich, "Home Slackers: Men, the State and Welfare in Modern America," *Journal of American History* 87 (2000): 460–89.

50. In the Australian case described by Castles, a "wage earners' welfare state" accomplished this through protectionist economic policy and public wage regulation which gave men higher wages than women, supplemented by pensions. Francis Castles, "The Wage Earners' Welfare State Revisited: Refurbishing the Established Model of Australian Social Protection, 1983-1993," *Australian Journal of Social Issues* 29 (1994): 120–45. See also Sheila Shaver, "Gender, Class and the Welfare State: The Case of Income Security in Australia," *Feminist Review* 32 (1989): 90–110.

51. Orloff, *Politics of Pensions*, chap. 9.

52. Barbara Hobson, "Feminist Strategies and Gendered Discourses in Welfare States: Married Women's Right to Work in the United States and Sweden," in Koven and Michel, *Mothers of a New World.*

53. Margaret Weir and Theda Skocpol, "State Structures and the Possibilities for 'Keynesian' Responses to the Great Depression in Sweden, Britain, and the United States," in *Bringing the State Back In*, ed. Peter Evans, Dietrich Rueschemeyer, and Theda Skocpol (New York: Cambridge University Press, 1985).

54. See Edwin Amenta, *Bold Relief: Institutional Politics and the Making of Modern American Public Social Provision, 1929–1950* (Princeton, NJ: Princeton University Press, 1998).

55. See Edwin Amenta, Bruce Carruthers and Yvonne Zylan, "A Hero for the Aged: The Townsend Movement, the Political Mediation Model and United States Old-Age Policy, 1934–1950," *American Journal of Sociology* 98 (1992): 308–39.

56. Orloff, *The Politics of Pensions*, chap. 9.

57. See Robert Lieberman, *Shifting the Color Line: Race and the American Welfare State* (Cambridge: Harvard University Press, 1998).

58. In contrast, when Britain established a similar contributory system in the mid-1940s, there was one key difference—through the the "married woman's option," women could opt for paying reduced taxes and give up their right to independent benefits. It is now phased out, on the assumption that they would get spousal benefits based on their husbands' contributions.

59. See Suzanne Mettler, *Dividing Citizens: Gender and Federalism in New Deal Public Policy* (Ithaca, NY: Cornell University Press, 1998).

60. See Alice Kessler-Harris, "Designing Women and Old Fools: The Construction of the Social Security Amendments of 1939," in *U.S. History as Women's History: New Feminist Essays,* ed. Linda K. Kerber, Alice Kessler-Harris and Kathryn K. Sklar (Chapel Hill: University of North Carolina Press, 1995). Had the originators attached a "dependents' bonus" to the benefit of the retired wage earner's income, this would have been consistent. But for various reasons, this was not done, as it was in Britain and Australia, for example. Thus, spousal benefits, though derived from wage-earners' records of contributions, were and are paid directly to wives. Paradoxically, this may

give them greater legitimacy and political support in the current period, as well as creating a rather dramatic "independence effect" for the older widowed women who are enabled to live on their own, without having to depend on sons or sons-in-law for their support.

61. See Edward McCaffery, *Taxing Women* (Chicago: University of Chicago Press, 1997); and Madonna Harrington Meyer, "Making Claims as Workers or Wives: The Distribution of Social Security Benefits," *American Sociological Review* 61 (1996): 449–65.

62. Jill Quadagno, *The Transformation of Old-Age Security* (Chicago: University of Chicago Press, 1988).

63. It may be worth noting that ADC was made explicitly gender-neutral—fathers or any other caretaker of children could claim it, which sets these benefits for sole parents apart from those available in other countries (e.g., Canada and Australia), where they went to women only. However, almost all U.S. claimants have been women.

64. Lieberman, *Shifting the Color Line*; and Mettler, *Dividing Citizens*.

65. See Margaret Weir, "The Federal Government and Unemployment: The Frustration of Policy Innovation from the New Deal to the Great Society," in *The Politics of Social Policy in the United States*, ed. Margaret Weir, Ann Shola Orloff, and Theda Skocpol (Princeton, NJ: Princeton University Press 1988); and Amenta, *Bold Relief*.

66. Weir, *The Politics of Jobs*.

67. Ibid.; and Nelson Lichtenstein, "From Corporatism to Collective Bargaining: Organized Labor and the Eclipse of Social Democracy in the Postwar Era," in *The Rise and Fall of the New Deal Order, 1930–1980*, ed. Steve Fraser and Gary Gerstle (Princeton, NJ: Princeton University Press, 1989).

68. Beth Stevens, "Blurring the Boundaries: How the Federal Government Has Influenced Welfare Benefits in the Private Sector," in Weir, Orloff, and Skocpol, *Politics of Social Policy*.

69. See Theda Skocpol, "Delivering for Young Families: The Resonance of the GI Bill," *The American Prospect*, 28 (1996); and Dolores Hayden, *Redesigning the American Dream: The Future of Housing, Work and Family Life* (New York: Norton, 1984).

70. See Weir, "The Federal Government and Unemployment," in Weir, Orloff, and Skocpol, *Politics of Social Policy*.

71. Jill Quadagno, *The Color of Welfare: How Racism Undermined the War on Poverty* (New York: Oxford University Press, 1994).

72. Michael Brown, *Race, Money and the American Welfare State* (Ithaca, NY: Cornell University Press, 1999).

73. Quadagno, *Color of Welfare*.

74. John Myles, "Postwar Capitalism and the Extension of Social Security into a Retirement Wage," in Weir, Orloff, and Skocpol, *Politics of Social Policy*.

75. See Quadagno, *Color of Welfare*.

76. Ibid; and Christopher Howard, *The Hidden Welfare State: Tax Expenditures and Social Policy in the United States* (Princeton, NJ: Princeton University Press, 1997), 65–69.

77. For example, until 1977, dependents' and survivors' benefits were available without question to female spouses, but for male spouses to qualify, financial dependence had to be proven. In the wake of a successfully-argued gender discrimination lawsuit (brought by a man who was denied a dependent's benefit), this double standard gave way to gender-neutrality in spousal benefits. See Richard Burkhauser and Karen Holden, eds., *A Challenge to Social Security: The Changing Roles of Women and Men in*

American Society (New York: Academic Press, 1982). Similarly, benefits for surviving children were made gender-neutral in the 1970s.

78. Kenneth Finegold, "Agriculture and the Politics of U.S. Social Provision: Social Insurance and Food Stamps," in Weir, Orloff, and Skocpol, *Politics of Social Policy*.

79. See Quadagno, *Color of Welfare*; and Brown, *Race, Money and the American Welfare State*.

80. Esping-Andersen, *Three Worlds*.

81. Michel, *Children's Interests/Mothers' Rights*, chap. 7.

82. See Linda Haas, *Equal Parenthood and Social Policy: A Study of Parental Leave in Sweden* (Albany: State University of New York, 1992); and Leira, *Welfare States and Working Mothers* and "Caring as Social Right."

83. See Paul Pierson, *Dismantling the Welfare State?: Reagan, Thatcher, and the Politics of Retrenchment* (New York: Cambridge University Press, 1994); and John Palmer and Isabel Sawhill, eds., *The Reagan Record* (Cambridge, MA: Ballinger, 1984).

84. See Working Seminar on Family and American Welfare Policy, *A Community of Self-Reliance: The New Consensus on Family and Welfare* (Washington, DC: American Enterprise Institute, 1987); for commentary, see Weir, Orloff and Skocpol, *Politics of Social Policy*.

85. See Alice O'Connor, *Poverty Knowledge: Social Science, Social Policy, and the Poor in Twentieth-century U.S. History* (Princeton, NJ: Princeton University Press, 2001).

86. See Esping-Andersen, *Social Foundations*; Katherine McFate, "Trampolines, Safety Nets or Free Fall? Labor Market Policies and Social Assistance in the 1990s," in *Poverty, Inequality and the Future of Social Policy: Western States in the New World Order*, ed. McFate, Roger Lawson, and William J. Wilson (New York: Russell Sage, 1995).

87. William J. Wilson, *The Truly Disadvantaged: The Inner City, the Underclass, and Public Policy* (Chicago: University of Chicago Press, 1987) and *When Work Disappears: The World of the New Urban Poor* (New York: Knopf, 1997); and Kathryn Neckerman, Robert Aponte, and William Julius Wilson, "Family Structure, Black Unemployment, and American Social Policy," in *Politics of Social Policy*, ed.Weir, Orloff, and Skocpol. For more on Fragile Families, see Gavanas, *Masculinizing Fatherhood*.

88. See Garfinkel and McLanahan, *Single Mothers and Their Children*; and Irwin Garfinkel, Sara McLanahan, and Daniel Meyer, *Fathers under Fire: The Revolution in Child Support Enforcement* (New York: Russell Sage, 1998).

89. See Daphne Spain and Suzanne Bianchi, *Balancing Act: Motherhood, Marriage and Employment among American Women* (New York: Russell Sage, 1996); and Esping-Andersen, *Social Foundations*, 166.

90. Freeman, "The Feminization of Work in the USA."

91. Long-term unemployed childless men and women (or parents who are not living with their children) have nothing but Food Stamps; arguably, they receive the worst treatment under the U.S. social policy regime. Food stamps were the only federal program available to any poor person who met the criteria of a very low income and limited assets. However, recent changes in Food Stamps in association with welfare reform have increased work requirements so that they are unavailable for people out of work for more than a short time.

92. David Ellwood, "Welfare Reform as I Knew It: When Bad Things Happen to Good Policies," *The American Prospect* 26 (1996): 22–29.

93. See Jason DeParle, "Welfare Overhaul Initiatives Focus on Fathers," *New York Times* electronic edition, September 3, 1998. On the political linkage between work requirements for women on welfare and enhanced child support enforcement target-

ting fathers, see Kathleen Casey and Susan Carroll, "Women in the 104th Congress and Welfare Reform Legislation," in *Reinventing the Welfare State? Feminist Theory and Comparative Analyses of the U.S. and Europe*, ed. Nancy Hirschmann and Ulrike Liebert (New Brunswick, NJ: Rutgers University Press, 2001).

94. Garfinkel, McLanahan, and Meyer, *Fathers under Fire*.

95. Gwendolyn Mink, *Welfare's End* (Ithaca, NY: Cornell University Press, 1998).

96. See Blankenhorn, *Fatherless America*.

97. See Gavanas, *Masculinizing Fatherhood*; and Mincy, "What About Black Fathers?"

98. David Ellwood, *Poor Support: Poverty in the American Family* (New York: Basic Books, 1988) and "Welfare Reform as I Knew It."

99. See Jodie Levin-Epstein et al., "Spending Too Much, Accomplishing Too Little: An Analysis of the family Formation Provisions of H.R. 4737 and Recommendations for Change" (Washington, DC: Center for Law and Social Policy, 2002).

100. See Myles and Pierson, "Friedman's Revenge."

101. See Ann Shola Orloff, "Ending the Entitlements of Poor Single Mothers: Changing Social Policies, Women's Employment and Caregiving," in Hirschmann and Liebert, *Women and Welfare*.

102. Most Western countries recognize the burdens of childrearing for all families but have typically addressed this burden through family allowances. See Jonathan Bradshaw, John Ditch, Hilary Holmes, and Peter Whiteford, "A Comparative Study of Child Support in Fifteen Countries," *Journal of European Social Policy* 3 (1993): 255–71; and Wennemo, *Sharing the Costs of Children*. However, especially in the English-speaking countries, there has been an increase in the use of tax credits to help such families. See O'Connor, Orloff, and Shaver, *States, Markets, Families*; and Myles and Pierson, "Friedman's Revenge."

CONTRIBUTORS

Cynthia Brantley is Professor of History at the University of California, Davis. Her work on Africa began in Nigeria, and subsequent research took her to Kenya, where she studied African resistance and produced *The Giriama and Colonial Resistance in Kenya, 1800–1920* (1981). Her recent book, *Feeding Families: African Realities and British Ideas of Nutrition and Development in Early Colonial Africa* (2002) analyzes colonial nutrition research in Kenya, Malawi, and Gambia from 1925 to the 1950s. Her current research in Tanzania addresses a potential nutrition development crisis as women have fewer resources available to feed their families.

Laura Briggs is Assistant Professor of History at the University of Arizona.

Joy Damousi is Associate Professor in the Department of History at the University of Melbourne. She has published widely in the fields of Australian labor history, women's and feminist history, and gender and war. Her latest publication is *Living with the Aftermath: Trauma and Nostalgia in Post-War Australia* (2001).

Lynne Haney is Assistant Professor of Sociology and Associate Director of the Center for the Study of Gender and Sexuality at New York University. She has published and conducted research on gender and the state in both the United States and Eastern Europe. She is the author of *Inventing the Needy: Gender and the Politics of Welfare in Hungary* (2002) and one of the authors of *Global Ethnography: Forces, Connections, and Imaginations in a Postmodern World* (2000).

Laura Lovett is an adjunct professor in the Gender Studies Program at Dartmouth University.

Ann Shola Orloff is Professor of Sociology at Northwestern University. She has published widely in the fields of gender, political sociology, and feminist theory. Her latest book, co-authored with Julia O'Connor and Sheila Shaver, is *States, Markets, and Families: Gender, Liberalism, and Social Policy in Australia, Canada, Great Britain, and the United States* (1999).

Eileen M. Otis is a Ph.D. candidate in the Department of Sociology at the University of California, Davis.

Lisa Pollard is Assistant Professor of Middle Eastern History at the University of North Carolina, Wilmington. She has published on gender and state-building in nineteenth- and early-twentieth-century Egypt. Her book on familial relations in Egypt under British colonial occupation will appear in 2004.

Alison Rose is an independent scholar based in Cambridge, Massachusetts.

Karin Alejandra Rosemblatt is Associate Professor of History and Director for the Program on Latin America and the Caribbean at Syracuse University. She recently co-edited *Race and Nation in Modern Latin America*.

Elizabeth C. Rudd is a post-doctoral research fellow at the Institute for Social Research at the University of Michigan. She works within the Center for the Ethnography of Everyday Life, an Alfred P. Sloan Center for Working Families. She is writing a book on work-family conflicts in German post-socialism.

INDEX

Adams, Julia, vii, 5
African Lakes Company, 142
Aid to Families with Dependent Children (AFDC), 233, 235, 236, 239
Allende, Salvador, 119, 120, 124, 135
   La realidad médico-social chilena, 119, 120, 135
Australian Federation of Voters, 99
Australian Labor Party (ALP), 99, 101, 106
   Women's Central Committee, 106
Australian Nationalist-Country Party, 104–5

Bebel, August, 181
Birth rate
   In Czech Republic, 174
   In Germany, 183
Bokros Reforms, 164, 170
British Administration
   In Egypt
      Anglo-Egyptian rule, 18
      Lord Cromer, 20, 25
      Lord Gladstone, 19
      Occupation of 1882, 8, 17, 19
      Policy, 19, 20
      Protectorate State, 17
   In Nyasaland
      Administration 1930s and 1940s, 10, 140, 142
      Diet and nutrition, 140–43
      Economic policies, 141, 143, 144, 147, 148
      Occupation, 142
      Views of African families/family policy, 141, 143, 145, 146, 149, 155
British Welfare State, 221
Buber, Martin, 64, 77–79
   "Zion of the Jewish Woman," 78

Cerda, Aguirre, 119, 122, 124
Charity Organization Society
   In Australia, 100, 108. 109. 112, 113, 117
Chilean Popular Fronts Governments, 12, 119, 121–25
   Female-directed reforms, 131–37
   Feminine section of General Work Inspection, 135
   La Crítica, 130, 131
   Male-directed reforms, 127–31
   National-popular state, 121
   Vida Sana, 127, 128
   Welfare Agencies, 123–26

Chewa, 146–48, 150, 151
Chonyi, 139, 140, 155
Child support
   Enforcement of, 229, 237, 238, 239
Charter, 77, 165
Children's Welfare Department
   In Australia, 100, 115, 116
Clitoridectomy, 6
Colonial medicine
   In Africa, 47
Connell, Robert, 220
Consumption, 185, 186, 187, 188, 191, 192, 193, 195
Contagious Diseases Acts, 41–43, 46, 52–58, 62, 63
   In Africa, 46, 47
   In India, 44, 45
   In Puerto Rico, 9, 41, 46, 52–58
Czech Social Democratic Party, 167, 172, 173, 174

Departmento de defensa de la raza y aprovechameinto de las horas libres, 130
Dutch Reform Church in Africa, 150

Earned Income Tax Credit (EITC), 240, 241, 242, 243
Economic reform
   In China, 196, 197, 215, 216
   In Czech Republic, 166
   In Germany, 184, 185
Education
   In Egypt
      Adab and *tarbiyya,* 22, 23, 27
      Educational system, 21–23
      Home economics/*tadbir al-manzil,* 25–28
      Textbooks, 22, 23
Effendiyya, 17, 18, 21, 24, 28, 30, 34
Ellwood, David, 240
Esping-Andersen, Gosta, 160, 161, 225
Eyal, Gil, 168, 169

Fatherhood
  Benefits for, 218, 224, 241
  Crisis of, 218, 237, 239, 243
  Ideologies of, 223, 239, 240
  Social policies for, 218, 222, 227, 228, 238, 242
  In Egypt
    Freedom Orphanage, 34–36
    Hafiz Bey Ibrahim poem, 35
Fatherhood Rights Movement, 237, 239, 240
Feiwel, Berthold, 77, 78
  Democratic-Zionist Faction, 77
  Judische Volksstimme, 77
French Welfare State, 220, 221

Gal, Susan, 169
Germany
  Re-unification, 179, 180, 184
Gerson, Kathleen, 225
GI Bill, 233
Goven, Joanna, 172

Ha'am, Ahad, 65
Havel, Vaclav, 173
Hernes, Helga, 219
Herzel, Theodore, 10, 64, 65, 67, 70–74, 76–78
  Altneuland (1902), 71, 72, 76
  Der Judenstaat (1896), 71, 72
  The New Ghetto (1894), 71, 74
Hochschild, Arlie, 181
Horn, Gyula, 172

India
  1857, 22
  British soldiers in, 43, 44
  Burmese concubines in, 45
  Child marriage, 3, 6
  Sati, 3, 6
International Monetary Fund (IMF), 163, 165, 176

Jenson, Jane, 220

Housewives' Association
  In Chile, 126, 132

Kellner, Leon, 64, 75, 76
Kenya, 139
Khedives
  Isma`il, 20, 23, 24, 29, 30
  Mohammad `Ali, 17
  Tawfiq, 19, 20

Klaus, Vaclav, 167, 168, 173
Kligman, Gail, 169
Konrád, György, 170, 173

Labor Market
  Emergence of Capitalist in Germany, 180, 182, 184, 188, 190, 195
  Female participation in, 197, 199, 228, 237, 238, 242
  Reforms in China, 196, 197
  Rise of low-wage in China, 196, 197, 203, 215
  Sex-segregation of, 200, 202, 217
Lang, Jack, 101
Lewis, Jane, 218, 223, 224

MacKinnon, Catherine, 237
Male Breadwinner
  Logic of, 227, 229, 231, 232, 235, 239
  Regimes, 217, 218, 220, 221, 223, 224, 228, 234, 242
Marx, Karl, 67
Maternalism, vii, 1–4, 86, 140, 161, 162, 217, 218, 229
Maternity benefits
  In Czech Republic, 165, 166, 167, 168
  In Germany, 179, 183, 184, 188
  In Hungary, 160, 161, 168
  In United States, 217, 219
Maxwell, George, 68–89
  Homecroft Ideal Movement, 90–97
  Talisman, 90
Mead, Elwood, 95–97
  Delhi and Durham, 95–96
Mettler, Suzanne, 232
Michel, Sonya, vii, 2, 140
Migration
  Effect on Kinship in China, 197, 198, 209, 210, 216
  Effect on Marriage System in China, 212, 213, 214
  Household Registration System (hukou), 196, 198, 199, 200, 201, 203, 205, 206, 212, 213, 215
  Rural to Urban in China, 197, 199, 202
Missions and missionaries
  In Africa, 142
Monynihan Report, 235
Mothers' Pensions (see also Widows' Pensions), 230, 233

Nash, Rebecca, 174
Nationalist Movements
  In Egypt, 17, 19, 21, 22, 34, 36

Press, 24–28, 30, 34–37
Revolution of, 1919 18, 27–36
`Urabi, Ahmed, 19
Zaghlul, Sa'ad, 27, 34
New Deal, 228, 231, 233, 236, 242
New Hebrew Man, 67, 69, 72, 79
Nordau, Max, 64, 65, 69, 78
  The Conventional Lies of Our Civilization (1883), 70
  Doktor Kohn (1902), 69, 70
  Jewry of Muscles, 69, 70
  The Right to Love (1893), 69, 70
Nyasaland
  19th-century occupation of, 142
  British administration, 1930s and 1940s, 10, 140, 142
  British economic policies in, 141, 143, 144, 147, 148
  British role in diet and nutrition, 140–43
  British views of families, family policy, 141, 143, 145, 146, 149, 155
  Machona, 149, 151, 152
  Margaret Mead's work on, 146–49, 151, 154
  Nutrition Survey, 138–39, 141, 146, 149, 150

Obligatory Insurance Fund
  In Chile, 123, 126, 130

Palestine, 9, 72, 73
  Creation of the State of Israel in, 64
  Jewish Pioneers in, 81
  Yishuv, 81
Patrimonialism, 4, 5, 7, 140, 148
Pedersen, Susan, 220
Personal Responsibility and Work Opportunity Reconciliation Act of 1996, 2, 14, 239
Poverty, 160, 162, 163, 170, 172, 175, 218, 238
Price subsidies, 160, 163, 166, 184
Progressive Era
  Family policy in
    Producer family and producer-family ethics, 86, 87, 96
  Land Irrigation Programs during
    National Irrigation Association and *The National Homemaker*, 87, 90
    National Irrigation Policy Resolution of 1901, 88
    Wright Act of 1887, 87
  Land Programs during
    Back-to-the-Land Movement, 90, 91

Country Life Movement, 95
Homestead Act, 93, 94
Social policy in, 231, 237, 242
Urban Movement during
  City Beautiful Movement, 91
  Parks and Playgrounds Movement, 91
Prostitution
  In China, 204, 205, 213
  In India, 44, 45, 47
  In Puerto Rico, 58–61
  U.S. regulation of, 42, 50, 51–53, 58
Puerto Rico
  Abolition of slavery in, 59
  Government after 1801, 59
  Government after 1895, 59
  Liberal Abolutionist Movement, 59, 60
  Monarchists in, 59
  Ponce, 58, 59

Race
  Inequality, 226, 227, 228, 242
  Welfare State, 225, 236,
Reproductive Policy
  In China, 200, 211, 213, 215
Roma, 160, 162, 176

Scandinavian Welfare States, 219, 224, 231, 236, 240
Social Security Act of 1935, 231, 232, 233, 237
  1939 Amendments, 232
Smythe, William, 95–97
  Irrigation age, 95
  "Little Lands Colonies," 95
Swidler, Ann, 195
Sydney Feminist Club, 99
  1925 Preseident Millicent Preston Stanley, 99, 101, 103
Szelényi, Iván, 168, 169
SZETA, 162, 165

Temporary Assistance for Needy Families (TANF), 238, 239, 242
Townsley, Eleanor, 168, 169

Unemployment
  In China, 201
  In Czech Republic, 166, 170
  In Germany, 180, 185, 187, 194
  In Hungary, 160, 163
  In United States
United States of America
  Battleship Maine, 48, 58
  Occupation of Cuba and Philippines, 48

United States of America (*cont.*)
  Occupation of Puerto Rico, 59, 60
  Participation of Berlin Conference, 49
  President Theodore Roosevelt, 48

Vienna, Austria, 9, 64, 71, 72, 75, 78, 80
  Die Neue Freie Press, 64
  Zionist Women's Association of, 70, 75, 76
Vodika, Jindrich, 173

War on Poverty, 234, 235, 238
Welfare offices
  In Czech Republic, 174, 175, 176
  In Hungary, 162, 170, 171, 172
Welfare regimes
  African, 140
  Corporatist, 160
  Feminist analyses of, 218, 219, 222
  Liberal, 1, 2, 11, 85, 99, 102, 136 161, 163, 164, 176, 225
  Social Democratic, 3, 160, 163, 176, 220, 226, 236
Widows' pensions
  In Australia, 99, 100

Widows' Pensions Bill
  In Australia, 102, 105, 106
Wilson, William Julius, 237, 238
Women's Christian Temperance Union, 52–58, 61, 62
  The Union Signal, 55, 56
Women's employment
  Part-time work in Germany, 183, 189
  Under Capitalism in Germany, 185, 186, 192
  Under State Socialism in Germany, 181, 182, 183
"Work-family Strategy," 181, 191, 194, 195
World Bank, 163, 165, 166, 176

Yao, 153, 154
York-Steiner, Heinrich, 64, 76, 77

Zelizer, Viviana, 210
Zionism
  Platforms, 10, 64–66
    Cultural, 65, 77–80
    Political, 65, 69–77
    Second Congress, 74

HQ 515 .F345 2003

Families of a new world